CONTEMPORARY APPROACHES TO CONDITIONING AND LEARNING

THE EXPERIMENTAL PSYCHOLOGY SERIES

Arthur W. Melton · Consulting Editor

MELTON AND MARTIN · *Coding Processes in Human Memory, 1972*

McGUIGAN AND LUMSDEN · *Contemporary Approaches to Conditioning and Learning, 1973*

ANDERSON AND BOWER · *Human Associative Memory, 1973*

CONTEMPORARY APPROACHES TO CONDITIONING AND LEARNING

EDITED BY F. J. McGUIGAN

HOLLINS COLLEGE, VIRGINIA

and

D. BARRY LUMSDEN

NORTH CAROLINA STATE UNIVERSITY AT RALEIGH

 V. H. WINSTON & SONS

1973   Washington, D.C.

DISTRIBUTED BY THE HALSTED PRESS DIVISION OF

JOHN WILEY & SONS

New York   Toronto   London   Sydney

BF
319
M2

V. H. Winston & Sons, Inc., Publishers
1511 K St. N.W., Washington, D.C. 20005

Distributed solely by Halsted Press Division, John Wiley & Sons, Inc., New York.

Library of Congress Cataloging in Publication Data:

McGuigan, Frank J.
    Contemporary approaches to conditioning and learning.

    (The experimental psychology series)
    Includes bibliographies.
    1. Conditioned response. 2. Learning, Psychology of.
I. Lumsden, D. Barry. II. Title. III. Series.
BF319.M2   153.1′5   73-4663
ISBN 0-470-58428-9

CONTENTS

v

LIST OF CONTRIBUTORS

Numbers in parentheses indicate the pages on which the authors' contributions begin.

B. K. Cole, Queens College. (151)

W. K. Estes, Rockefeller University. (265)

W. Horsley Gantt, V. A. Hospital, Perry Point, Maryland, and Johns Hopkins University Medical School. (111)

Joseph Germana, Virginia Polytechnic Institute and State University. (245)

David A. Grant, University of Wisconsin-Madison, Wisconsin. (49)

James C. Johnston, University of Pennsylvania. (69)

Gregory A. Kimble, University of Colorado. (1)

J. Lang, Queens College. (151)

R. Mankoff, Queens College. (151)

F. J. McGuigan, Hollins College, Virginia. (173)

David Premack, University of California at Santa Barbara. (287)

Robert A. Rescorla, Yale University. (127)

Eli Saltz, Wayne State University. (21)

W. N. Schoenfeld, Queens College. (151)

Martin E. P. Seligman, University of Pennsylvania. (69)

Delos D. Wickens, The Ohio State University. (213)

PREFACE

The immediate stimulus for this book was the increasing dissatisfaction being expressed about our laws of conditioning and learning. This discontent has been manifested in a variety of ways, ranging from empirically established limitations in the generality of our laws, to inconsistent theoretical interpretations of basic phenomena. The works presented here constitute an effort to confront the problem by assessing the status of the field of learning and conditioning with the hope of nudging us toward an advanced level of theoretical organization. These articles will be of major interest to researchers, teachers, and graduate students in the psychology of learning and conditioning, education, behavior theory, cognition, and to psychophysiologists and linguistically oriented scholars concerned with learning processes.

While none of the authors seriously question the basic phenomena of conditioning and learning, they do express considerable skepticism about a number of our traditional, and often cherished, beliefs. For example, one author holds that "there never *has* been a learning theory". Several others indicate that new data are forcing us to drastically revise our diagrams for representing both classical and instrumental conditioning. Problems concerning the conditioning of cognitive processes create a major issue that runs throughout the volume, viz., whether or not cognitive models of learning can adequately solve some of the glaring shortcomings of existing models. Of considerable contemporary importance is the demonstration that some bodily systems are not susceptible to conditioning, in spite of previous conclusions to the contrary. A final example is how the priority concept of "contingency" undergoes critical, even scathing, empirical examination.

On the other hand, new data are presented that considerably strengthen some of our classical principles, clearly indicating that progress does not require abandonment of all that went on before. This evidence comes from an impressive array of sources—not only from traditional animal designs, but also from extensions into psychobiology and language behavior, to mention but a few. One may thus happily conclude that much *is* right in the field—it is merely that new problems often demand new solutions.

To meet the challenges, the authors offer a number of exciting and novel perspectives. As one reads these articles, it soon becomes apparent that the field of learning and conditioning is thriving; the dissatisfactions cited above are occurring because of courageous attempts of researchers and theoreticians to extend our basic principles, derived primarily from the study of lower organisms, to higher order processes. The consequences for the foreseeable future may well be a higher level, more general set of principles that encompass the phenomena represented by our traditional conditioning paradigms *and* such complex processes as memory, internal information processing, cognition, and linguistic behavior at both the overt and covert levels.

F. J. McGuigan

March, 1973

CONTEMPORARY APPROACHES TO CONDITIONING AND LEARNING

1
SCIENTIFIC PSYCHOLOGY IN TRANSITION

Gregory A Kimble
University of Colorado

It is clear that scientific psychology is in a period of fundamental change. Concepts (e.g., image) once beyond the pale are now important. Procedures once considered inferior (e.g., personal report) are now highly regarded. Problems for research (e.g., hypnosis) once carefully avoided are now the object of experimental attention by some of our most distinguished investigators. And processes once viewed with great suspicion (e.g., cognition) now dominate the scene. All of these are symptoms of a very general shift in orientation in psychology. They reflect an alteration of perspective that includes a great deal more than just the field of learning. Partly for this very reason, it seems appropriate in a volume like this to sketch this changing scene in broad strokes as a background for discussion by others who will fill in the details that depict the situation in the study of learning more exactly.

Another reason for discussing such materials here is that these changes in outlook have been gradual and insidious. Unless one takes the perspective provided by at least a few decades of history, the direction and extent of this transition are hard to appreciate. For that reason, what I want to do in this chapter is go back to the point in time when methodological guidelines last seemed firm and clear—the period just before and just after World War II. I shall describe the dominant themes that were widely accepted in that period. I shall review the types of criticism that accumulated against those themes. Finally I shall attempt a few guesses as to where scientific psychology, particularly the psychology of learning, is headed.

THE DOMINATING THEMES

No doubt different people would see the dominant themes of this earlier period in different terms, but I suspect that most of us would recognize the following description as containing certain essential points.

Environmentalism

The first and probably most obvious characteristic of the psychology of the 1940s and early 1950s was that it was in a strongly environmentalistic mood. This made learning the topic of central importance to the field. As a result, many of the most significant theoretical developments of the time were in the field of learning. Moreover, these same theorists and their colleagues also put forth the metatheoretical statements that had the greatest impact.

Operationism

Almost without exception, these statements advanced operationism and advocated the intervening variable approach to theory construction. The operational point of view was urged upon psychology by many different authors writing in a period covering the decades from 1910 to 1950. The important names are Bechterev, Bergmann, Bridgman, Carnap, Feigl, Hempel, Kantor, Koch, Pratt, Spence, Stevens, Tolman, and Watson. All of these men took a position that insisted upon an essential physicalism in science, according to which scientific statements are meaningful only if they are ultimately reducible to observations that can be made directly upon the physical world by any properly equipped observer. Put another way, statements of science were taken to be meaningful only if they could be described in a "thing level" language whose vocabulary contained only terms that referred to simple observables (objects and properties of objects) and to relationships. Essential to this way of thinking was a sharp distinction between what is directly observable and what is not.

Today this point of view seems obvious and even somewhat simpleminded. As recently as 1943, however, Hull felt compelled to devote considerable portions of the first two chapters of *Principles of Behavior* to a discussion of the point. He went to great pains to distinguish between the factual and explanatory aspects of science, between the physical and the metaphysical, between empirical and logical science, and between factually verifiable and unverifiable constructs. Even in 1943 it was frequently important to raise questions about the empirical bases of psychological concepts. Too often analysis revealed such bases to be totally lacking. One effect of such lacks was to surround certain topics with a web of operational suspicion that effectively prevented their study. I regarded this consequence as an unfortunate error and will have more to say about it later.

Intervening variables. Most psychologists found it impossible to live with the very strictest operationistic approach. The exclusive use of "thing level" terms omits almost everything that one wants to talk about in the field of psychology. Habit, motive, inhibition, memory, stimulus equivalence, and perception would be excluded, for these are not observables. The use of intervening variables provided an objective way of reintroducing such concepts through the strategy of relating them to antecedent operations of measurement in the first place and to subsequent attributes of behavior in the second. In the most influential paper to advocate this strategy, Tolman (1938) showed that it was possible to endow with scientific meaning such unlikely candidates for objectivity as *sign-gestalt-expectation*. In this paper Tolman also suggested a point emphasized later by several other writers. Intervening variables had an important role to play in what was coming to be accepted as the primary mission of psychology, the theoretical organization of empirical laws into a system that would relate behavior to determining antecedent conditions. To illustrate this role, suppose that a learning theorist is interested in four response measures (probability of occurrence, latency, resistance to extinction, and magnitude) and that he wishes to relate them to six independent variables (such things as amount and delay of reinforcement, stimulus intensity, and so on). Without the use of intervening variables it would take 24 separate laws to describe the relationships involved, six functions to relate each of the four response measures to individual independent variables. With the aid of an intervening variable like $S^H R$, the number of requisite laws reduces to 10, six defining $S^H R$ as a function of the independent variables, and four more depicting the response measures as functions of the intervening variable. Such simplification is a much sought after feature of scientific theory and constituted what seems to be a powerful argument supporting the intervening variable approach.

The Search for General Laws

The central position occupied by empirical laws in the psychology of learning placed heavy premium upon the development of adequate methods for their determination. This procedure sometimes was seen as a two-stage process which involved the isolation of variables in the first stage and the discovery of laws in the second. The first stage required only a two-group investigation to demonstrate that a given independent variable actually exercises control over a dependent variable of interest. The second stage required the parametric manipulation of this variable in order to determine its functional control over one or more response measures. At Yale and Iowa during this period, doctoral dissertations frequently consisted of the description of such parametric studies. The studies of Williams (1938) on number of reinforcements, Perin (1942) on hours of food deprivation, Kimble and Reynolds (Kimble, 1967, pp. 279–287) on the interstimulus interval function, and Grice (1948) on delay of reinforcement are representative.

It was assumed in this program of research that the laws obtained possessed wide generality, that individual and species difference could be ignored, that differences among organ systems were of no consequence, and that the laws of behavior applied with equal validity to whole organisms and to parts of them. Thus we find Hull (1943) developing his principle of afferent neural action on the basis of data obtained from the optic nerve of the horseshoe crab and then applying the principle to conditioning in intact mammalian organisms. The truly remarkable aspect of the situation was that in those days the incredible presumptuousness of such theorizing went almost completely unnoticed.

The same assumption of generality was inherent in the empirical work mentioned above. These studies possessed certain characteristic attributes: they typically contained large numbers of subjects per cell, and they were run under sophisticated conditions of physical and statistical control. With the development of analysis of variance, they were analyzed by this technique. Once more it is to be noted that both the procedures and the analysis were devised on an assumption of grand generality in which it was appropriate for individual differences to be eliminated and submerged. Such differences seemed commonly regarded as an unfortunate nuisance that could be excluded from consideration by relegating them to the appropriate error term.

Theory Construction and the Deductive Method

In the traditional way of thinking, these general laws provided the raw materials out of which an explanatory theory was to be developed. The methodology through which such theories were to operate was most carefully developed by Hull. Hull's characteristic style was to take the established laws just described as empirical hypotheses to use in the deduction of miscellaneous corollaries. Hence the name of the theoretical method—"hypothetico-deductive"—although "empirico-deductive" would be more accurate. Experimental tests of these corollaries then would provide the essential evidence for or against the theory. Representative samples of the use of this method were Hull's explanation for the selection of short routes to goals rather than long ones, shifts in performance levels with changes in amounts of reinforcement, the gradual divergence of acquisition functions of subjects learning under different levels of motivation, the asymmetry of generalization gradients where the underlying dimension is one of intensity, the fact of spontaneous recovery, and the ogival shape of acquisition functions where the index of learning is a probability measure. At the same time, other theorists were deriving their own empirical consequences from their own theoretical assumptions. Tolman predicted, and his students (e.g., Tolman & Honzik, 1930) offered demonstrations of, latent learning and place learning. Guthrie and Horton (1946) obtained evidence for learning in which the exact details of responses could be predicted from previous performance as Guthrie's theory required. In all of these efforts the overall strategy was the same, and all that differed was the degree of formality with which the deductive procedures were applied.

As was inevitable, tests of these deductions often failed. This happened oftener, of course, when the deductions were from an opposed theoretical position than when they were from the investigator's own; but even in the latter case, negative results insisted upon appearing now and then. In the face of data inconsistent with one's theory; two systematic possibilities always exist: alter the theory, or give it up completely. Most theorists begin with the first alternative. Taking examples from the work of Hull and Spence, these are some important theoretical changes that occurred in response to the persuasion of evidence. The underlying form of the generalization gradient, first taken to be an inverted U, became the familiar double-winged gradient. The amount of reinforcement, originally considered to have its effect upon habit strength, became a performance variable. The original treatment of extinction in terms of reactive and conditioned inhibition was supplemented by consideration of the influence first of generalization decrement and, later on, of set

Analysis. Indirectly considerations of the type just covered point to another attribute of traditional psychological theory. It was highly analytical in its approach. The learning theorists, for example, typically proposed a theoretical decomposition of the products of learning into two sets of factors. One set was a relatively permanent residual left in the organism as a result of practice. Some concept referring to learning (e.g., habit strength) was the most important example. The second was a set of relatively temporary consequences of motivational conditions, effortfulness of practice; and chance inhibitory fluctuations. The items in each of these categories depended upon a number of contributing independent variables.

In the final analysis the ultimate elements in the classical theories of learning were stimuli and responses. Following unspoken scientific philosophy adopted from Titchener and Watson who, in turn, took it from the British Empiricists, it was generally assumed that scientific psychology would be a kind of mental chemistry. The atoms of this system seemed obviously to be stimuli and/or responses. As everyone knows, Tolman tended to give stimuli greater importance than responses; and Skinner appeared to do the opposite. But none of the major theoretical figures seemed seriously to question the appropriateness of the original analysis. Such molecular analysis of behavior into tiny units eventually produced theories that were overly unwieldy and awkwardly cumbersome. This, no doubt, contributed to the eventual abandonment of the classical theories of learning. Such giving up may, however, have ignored a fact that we will still have to face: that the complexity developed in these theories might actually reflect an important aspect of an adequate theory—that the determination of even the simplest behavior is so complex that no simple theory can do it justice.

The Problem of Complexity

This leads us finally to the last major theme I wish to develop in describing traditional learning theory. Expressing it in the form of a question: If things are as complicated in the psychology of simple behavior as they appear to be, how shall we handle still more complicated forms of acquired behavior? From what has been said earlier, it may not be surprising to learn that the modal reaction was to refuse to deal with such behavior exactly for the reason of its complexity. Discovering the basic laws seemed the matter of first importance. Three other means of coping with the question can be noted, however. One was simply to treat complex behavior in the same terms as others treated conditioned responses. Using this approach, Kimble (1949) developed a theory of motor learning; Miller and Dollard (1941) presented accounts of certain aspects of social behavior and personality development (Dollard & Miller, 1950); Spence (1958) and his students dealt with the problem of the effect of anxiety on learning, and throughout the British Commonwealth there was a surge of activity that related everything from instinctive behavior to psychotherapy to conditioning theory in essentially unmodified form.

A version of this strategy that will figure in later portions of this chapter occurred in the field of verbal learning. The associations formed in mastering a serial or paired-associate list were treated as if they were conditioned connections. Forgetting was handled as if it were exactly analogous to the experimental extinction of such associations. Variables of demonstrated importance for conditioning, such as the distribution of practice, were manipulated within the context of the rote learning experiment. And there was a search for analogies to such conditioning phenomena as spontaneous recovery in the same experimental situation.

A second tactic was to treat certain variables as boundary conditions or as moderator variables exercising control over the function of others (e.g., Perin, 1942). This approach never took on the importance it might have, however, for a technical reason. An essential concept, that of statistical interaction, was not widely understood in psychology until after World War II, and by that time the era we are discussing now was nearly over.

The third means of coping with behavioral complexity was through the assumption (borrowed from William James and also from Watson) that complex behavior was linearly organized. The concept of mediation and, more specifically, the r_G-s_G mechanism were widely seen as potential ways out of the problem of complexity. This mechanism and a set of derivative concepts (mediated generalization, pure stimulus act) figured prominently in efforts to deal with topics that ranged from reasoning through symptom placement in neurosis to the behavior of the lynch mob.

CRITICISM

In quick summary, the dominant themes I have identified in traditional psychological theory are the following: *First,* the nature-nurture pendulum was far to the environmental end of its swing, a fact that made the topic of learning central to psychology. *Second,* operationism and the intervening variable approach to theory construction dominated the accepted philosophy of science in psychology. *Third,* the typical experimental strategy involved a search for general laws of behavior in which parametric studies on large samples and later elegant statistical analysis were employed. In this search the just-mentioned assumption of generality was central. Individual differences as well as differences among species, organ systems, and the details of experimental situations were typically neglected. *Fourth,* the general approach to psychological theorizing was strongly analytic. Theories of learning were constructed from basic laws involving stimulus and response elements which were put into relationships to one another that would allow the deduction of behavioral consequences. *Fifth,* complex behavior was most often handled either by ignoring the complexity or by treating it in terms of linearly organized chains of behavior.

In the field of learning, the psychologist whose work fit these specifications best was Hull, although Tolman ran him a close second overall and bested him in the area of methodological sophistication. Guthrie was recognized as belonging in the same tradition but was never taken seriously because of a chronic deficiency in the area of experimental work. Skinner seemed in another systematic world because of his penchant for becoming preoccupied with the performance of individual animals and the details of behavior under a disorderly collection of schedules. It is probably no accident that Guthrie's ideas and the methods of Skinner began to catch on only when the established approach typified in the work of Hull was coming under heavy methodological fire.

Although the Hullian type of theory dominated the era, criticism, if not effective, was at least persistent. The basis for this criticism seems now to have arisen from a vague intuitive objection to the operationistic approach and to the emphasis on analysis, both of which created the suspicion that something was being overlooked—something like relevance to everyday life or the nervous system. For operationism implies an S-R black box psychology at the most basic level. Such a psychology has no need for such fanciful conceptual adornments as human experience or neurophysiology. All that is essential is an account of antecedent conditions and a set of proven statements of how these antecedents control subsequent behavior. The account of behavior resulting from analysis was offensive to some individuals then, as now, because it seemed to rob behavior, particularly human behavior, of its organization, warmth, unique richness, freedom, and dignity. Miller, Galanter, and Pribram (1960) no doubt caught the mood of a common reaction precisely when they referred to the traditional approach as "nickel-in-the-slot Behaviorism." But the expression of personal disapproval is not apt to have much influence in matters of this type. Something more substantial is necessary. As it turned out, more telling criticisms of the basic themes mentioned in summary above had been accumulating. We turn to some of them next.

Environmentalism

The appeal of the environmentalistic emphasis had resulted in part from a lack of opposition: (*a*) Physiological psychology which might have exercised an important moderating influence had nothing much to say except in connection with the sensory processes and perception. It was essentially mute when confronted with questions related to motivation, learning, and other topics of interest to more psychologists. (*b*) In the meantime, attacks on the so-called instinct doctrine had been so successful that it was near heresy for a psychologist in the 1930s to suggest that behavior had *any* innate determination.

All of this has, of course, changed now: (*a*) The discovery of the limbic system and the reticular formation has brought arousal, attention, motivation, and reward well within the realm of physiological psychology. (*b*) As regards the innate determination of behavior, evidence from a variety of sources has forced psychology finally to face the facts not only that nonenvironmental processes are important, but also that the comfortable nature-nurture dichotomy is suspect. In particular the distinction between learning and maturation has lost its sharpness as a result of the work of the ethologists, Piaget, Harlow, and several developmental psychologists. To take just one example, the facts of imprinting are difficult to consider in a psychology that insists that a bit of acquired behavior must either be learned or be innately arranged to appear at a certain age. Instead, imprinted responses (and a variety of other reactions) seem to follow a regular pattern: the response is natively formed but depends for its eliciting stimulus upon experience.

There is reason to believe that this shift to a stronger nativist influence in psychology is just beginning. Some of the reasons for suspecting this will be mentioned in passing later. In the meantime, other attacks on the traditional theoretical psychology of learning need to be considered.

Operationism

As was mentioned above, the traditional operationistic position begins with the assumption of a fairly clear distinction between what is observable and what is not. As it turns out, this distinction is harder to maintain than formulators of the 1930s and 1940s suggest. Consider, for example, the following quotation from Spector (1966):

> Imagine a person who has been raised indoors where care has been taken never to expose him to air currents (because of some rare skin disease, for example). When he is first taken outdoors he may have to be told that the (for him) strange sensations he feels over the surface of his body are (or, are caused by) the wind blowing against him. (Similarly, for the noises he hears in the trees, etc.) He may, for a time, be forced to *infer* from these sensations to the presence of something else—the wind—on the basis of the physics he has learned during his confinement. For this person, "Wind" would not be an observation term. It would not occur in any singular, nonanalytic sentence which *he* could quickly decide whether to accept or reject. But eventually, it will become one. . . . A term which was once *not* an observation term for him and will have *become* one. He will have learned to observe the wind.
>
> But if this is correct, it would seem that the line between what is observed and what is not (and thus must be inferred) depends on how much the observer in question knows (or the amount of "training" he has), and will also vary in time for a given observer. Thus, we could not draw a *general* distinction between two types of terms—observational and non-observational.

Accumulated commentary of this type shows that the essential operational presupposition of traditional theoretical psychology has been the object of fundamental criticism.

The same thing holds for the closely related intervening variable approach. Several authors have pointed out that operational definitions tend to limit the meanings of concepts too strictly. Others, of whom Skinner may have been the first, showed that the simplification they provide is totally illusory when it comes to the prediction of individual behavior. The information one needs to make such a prediction is just as particular in a theory with intervening variables as it is with no theory at all. All of these issues are epistemological, however, and I do not feel competent to go into details. On the other hand this will not prevent my taking a position on the general issue in the final section of this chapter.

The General Laws of Behavior

There is more to say about traditional experimental strategy and the laws it allegedly produces. The first thing is that these laws are distressingly particular as to the context in which they apply. For example, almost every undergraduate who has had psychology believes in the immutable quality of the interstimulus interval function, which shows classical conditioning to be best at intervals of about 0.5 seconds. We now know, however, that these values are somewhat undependable in any context, and that outside rather particular experimental arrangements, there is reason to treat the function with suspicion. In support of this suspicion I merely list these points: (a) Parametric studies of eyelid conditioning run under similar circumstances have yielded optimal intervals ranging all the way from 0.25 seconds to 1.0 seconds. (b) The optimal interval may be much shorter than this (as in the case of the conditioned reaction of the nictitating membrane of the albino rabbit) or much longer (as is probably the case with most glandular responses). Beyond this, the work of Garcia, Revusky (e.g., Revusky & Garcia, 1970), and others shows that some conditioned associations can be formed with interstimulus intervals that are measured in hours, times that differ by an important order of magnitude from those usually considered in discussing this problem. (c) As with many other functions, results obtained with the manipulation of this variable within subjects are markedly different from those obtained in between-subject experiments (Kimble, Leonard, & Perlmuter, 1968). (d) There is some reason to believe that the function may differ from species to species, but variations in experimental method make it impossible to be certain. (e) In human subjects, instructions and schedule of reinforcement seem to have an effect upon the function (Kimble, 1971). From such evidence, it is gradually becoming clear that serious problems exist with respect to many of the parametrically established functional relationships. This calls into question one of the most basic strategies of traditional experimental psychology.

A similar but usually less important point can be made with respect to the contribution that experiments with large numbers of subjects have made to our science. It is beginning to be obvious that almost any variable you can think of will probably have some effect upon behavior, and that a statistically dependable influence can be demonstrated by piling up a sufficient number of data. A relatively unimportant consequence of this is the deadly quality of what is accepted for publication by many of our most prestigious journals. There are two more serious objections to studies with large Ns, however. One is related to problems associated with parametric studies just considered. This objection is that the combining of data from many individuals may produce an average function that does not describe the performance of a single subject contributing to it. This objection was advanced some time ago by psychologists sympathetic to the Skinnerian approach.

The other objection has been directed at our experimental procedures more recently. It is that the use of very large samples of subjects is nearly guaranteed to produce an apparent effect of an experimental manipulation, whether or not a real influence exists. To illustrate, suppose someone has a theory that aggressive sexuality is related to phases of the moon. As a test of the theory, he keeps track of rapes reported when the moon is full and when the moon is new. And to meet standard canons of scientific respectability, he does this for 100 communities and a dozen years. There is a virtual certainty that some statistically reliable result would occur. Neither experience nor intuition provides me with a means of predicting whether more rapes would occur when the sky is bright or when it is dim, but that, of course, is why we have two-tailed statistical tests. Although this example is too obvious to be impressive, Meehl (1967) has shown that the same logic applies in more subtle cases and that as N increases, the probability of obtaining results that confirm a theory approaches 0.5. The point is that, just as we should not depend too heavily on parametric studies which sample many values of the independent variable, neither should we put too much faith in a belief that there is safety in large numbers of subjects.

Individual differences. Finally, in this general vein it is important to say a word about the fact of individual differences and how they have been dealt with in traditional psychological theory. Particularly in experimental psychology, it is clear that the accepted concept of lawfulness and the orthodox experimental strategy have been directed toward the minimization of individual differences. Hull (1943) did include an exponent (i) that seems to refer to individual variation in rate of learning in his equation for habit growth ($S^H R = M\text{-}Me^{-iN}$). But Tolman (1938) may have expressed general opinion more accurately in his treatment of individual differences in terms of four variables: Heredity, Age, Temperament, and Endocrine conditions. One suspects that the obvious acronym was no accident.

Cronbach has recognized this feature as characteristic of most experimental psychology and has contrasted it with a different point of view. To present the contrast we can do no better than quote from him. Describing the two traditions, he says that if you are a standard experimental psychologist,

You turn to animals of a cheap and short-lived species, so that you can use subjects with controlled heredity and controlled experience. You select human subjects from a narrow subculture. You decorticate your subject by cutting neurons or by giving him an environment so meaningless that his unique responses disappear. You increase the number of cases to obtain stable averages, or you reduce N to 1, as Skinner does. But whatever your device, your goal in the experimental tradition is to get those embarrassing differential variables out of sight.

The correlational psychologist is in love with just those variables an experimenter left home to forget. He regards individual and group variations as important effects of biological and social causes. All organisms adapt to their environments, but not equally well. His question is: What present characteristics of the organism determine its mode and degree of adaptation [Cronbach, 1957, p. 674]?

Theory Construction

Here, as was the case in connection with the environmentalistic approach of the period being discussed, I believe that I can be brief. Everyone recognizes that the classical theories of learning were too loosely developed to deal in proper detail with everything they proposed to cover. This led, beginning in the 1950s, to a proliferation of miniature theories designed to handle the particulars in limited areas. More of this later.

In this section I wish merely to note that the analysis of behavior into stimulus and response elements and the attempts to reduce certain forms of behavior to these ultimate terms has now encountered certain difficulties. One of the most elegant applications of S-R analysis was Underwood's (see McGovern, 1964) amplification of interference theory to deal with transfer and forgetting in terms of competing and noncompeting highly specific associations. Almost before that beautiful theory was published, it was already in trouble. It became clear, for example, that subjects sometimes treated lists rather than just associations as units, that free recall followed some nonspecific plans that led to clustering, that people don't necessarily accept the nominal stimulus as the functional one, that responses may be segregated and organized prior to the development of associations, that some aspects of memory require us to consider the individual's criterion for producing a response, and so on. Most of these facts raise difficult problems for traditional S-R theory.

In the meantime, parallel considerations were posing hard questions for the process often taken as basic in such analytic theorizing—classical conditioning. Spence (Spence, Homzie, & Rutledge, 1964) took the first step and introduced considerations of set into the explanation of extinction. Kimble (1967, pp. 642–659) followed with more general discussions of the contributions of attitudinal and cognitive factors to classical conditioning. Grice (1972) interpreted the process in terms that others used to explain decision making. All of these developments put a great strain on the loins of a theory that ultimately relied on conventional S and R elements. It seems clear that the time has come to reconsider the usefulness of the analysis in which these terms are basic.

The Problem of Complexity

This last point leads directly to the problems associated with the treatment of highly complicated behavior. In this connection I have just one point to emphasize. It is that I find the arguments of the psycholinguists in this area quite convincing. Their thesis, of course, is that the very most important kind of complex behavior, language, could in no way derive its organization from a process of linear chaining, and that it is necessary to consider concepts like plan, deep structure, image, and exit rule in order to understand the pattern of verbal utterances. These concepts are all quite foreign to classical behaviorism. In order to make these critics a little ashamed of their characteristic tone of voice, perhaps I should mention once more that William James (to whom they no doubt react positively) developed the concept of linearly organized chains of behavior long before any of their favorite Behaviorist targets. But however directed, the criticism is still sound, and I believe it applies to traditional accounts of other instances of planned voluntary behavior.

FUTURE PROSPECTS

In this discussion so far, I have tried to do two things: to characterize an era in the history of psychology by the description of dominant themes, and then to describe the most important criticisms of these themes. As a kind of interim summary, let me remind you of the themes by reviewing the criticisms. *First,* developments in physiological psychology, ethology, and behavioral genetics show that biological variables of many sorts have important messages for the psychology of learning. The extreme environmentalist position is not tenable. *Second,* the operationistic tradition requires at the outset a reasonably clear-cut distinction between what is factually given and what is not, but it is easy to show that this distinction is fuzzier than it seems at first. *Third,* the experimental methods prompted by the traditional concept of lawfulness produced "nonlaws" that are undersirably specific, frequently trivial, and sometimes artifactual. Moreover, the facts of individual and other differences have now forced themselves upon us in a way that demands that they be considered in this context. *Fourth,* empirical tests of the classical theories have shown them to be quite incapable of explaining everything they were supposed to. As a result, a large collection of less ambitious theories currently dominates the scene. *Fifth,* the move to a treatment of nontrivial complex behavior with the aid of traditional theories has been less than successful. Specifically, the complete reliance upon a model that allows only for linear organization of responses, even when these responses are connected by mediational S-R links, no longer seems a promising approach.

With this as background, it is time now to turn to the question of where all this is leading. Obviously changes are called for, but what will they be like? On the way to attempting a partial answer, I would like to make a few observations on the basic question of how progress comes about in science. One useful view of this matter is described very neatly in a metaphor developed by the philosopher Stephen Toulmin (1967), although I am sure that he sees his statement, not as a metaphor, but as a serious hypothesis regarding the science of science. Toulmin argues that changes in science come about as a result of mechanisms that are identical to those involved in organic evolution. The essence of what he has to say is captured in the following quotation.

> At this point we can make explicit the intellectual model toward which this discussion has been leading us. For, in the course of expounding all these considerations, we have fallen again and again—quite naturally—into the vocabulary of organic evolution. Science develops (we have said) as the outcome of a double process: at each stage, a pool of competing intellectual variants is in circulation, and in each generation a selection process is going on, by which certain of these variants are accepted and incorporated into the science concerned, to be passed on to the next generation of workers as integral elements of the tradition. . . .
>
> "Scientific method" depends on only two fundamental maxims—freedom of conjecture, and severity of criticism. For, if the fundamental mission of scientific thought in any human generation is to adapt itself better to the demands of the existing intellectual situation, these will be precisely the two cardinal virtues of science. Freedom of conjecture enlarges the available pool of variants: severity of criticism enhances the degree of selective pressure. Just as, in the organic world, adequate adaptation can be achieved only given a sufficient rate of mutation and a sufficient selective pressure, so within the context of an evolutionary theory of scientific change, the double formula, "Conjectures and Refutations" makes perfect sense [p. 465–466].

To the two maxims made explicit in this quotation, it will be useful to add two more to complete the parallel to the science of evolution. One of these requires little more than mention: just as in biology, scientific evolution proceeds more slowly than it might because of the conservatism and resistance to change of established forms. The scientific establishment, represented by journal editors and the members of federal research review panels, shows a very strong tendency to maintain the theoretical status quo. In the face of this predatory influence, evolving theoretical species are insistently threatened with extinction. In Toulmin's terms, this influence tends to limit the pool of variants—to frustrate conjecture and so to inhibit evolutionary change.

The second point is that it is important to recognize the continuity that exists in the development of science. This is tantamount to emphasizing a principle of inheritance corresponding to evolutionary continuity. In these terms what I have been doing so far in this discussion has been describing a dominant species of scientific thought and pointing to the selective pressures bearing on it. What remains is the task of attempting to predict the attributes of an evolving systematic strain. To this end I shall deal once more with the basic ideas underlying the classical theories (omitting the environmental emphasis which seems to require no further comment), trying this time to say what seems likely to continue to exist and what seems on its way to going extinct.

Operationism

The intuitively based nonsense from which operationism serves to protect us continues to be urged upon us sometimes by people who ought to know better. For this reason I suspect that those of us who are interested in the development of a scientific psychology had better stick to our operational guns. This is not equivalent, however, to advocating the careful maintenance of an insensitivity to important problems or to insisting that an objective psychology must display the sterility of which it has often been accused. In fact, experimental work published in the last few years provides a convincing demonstration that we can begin to deal with such concepts as image, organization, plan, cognition, strategy, intention, and volition. However vaguely, these terms point to important aspects of behavior. It is time, I think, to accept the responsibility for dealing with them. What I cannot accept is the seemingly common conclusion that even to mention such matters is antioperational, some sort of epistemo-logical leprosy, unclean and possibly contagious. In actuality every one of these mentalistic sounding concepts has been the object of recent study by some fairly hard-headed psychologists who seem to have lost none of their scientific appendages. In every case it has been a straightforward matter to provide the concept with operational meaning either by reference to the subject's behavior, usually verbal behavior, or by introducing the concept as an inference based upon an objective description of experimental conditions.

Incidentally, so far as the importance of dealing with such concepts is concerned, I have noted with amusement the struggles of some psychologists to circumvent the problem by switching from human subjects to lower animals—as if the processes would go away if the subjects cannot tell you about them in verbal terms. I suspect, in actuality, that the processes are still there but that their study is made more difficult when one turns to organisms that contribute nothing in the form of a verbal report.

What all of this adds up to seems to be that the objective operational stance assumed by the classical theorists remains the only promising position from which to continue the development of a scientific psychology. At the same time, it has become clear that the approach needs to be liberalized and extended to cover a variety of processes that the psychology of the older era regarded as unnecessary. They now turn out to be necessary. The mentalistic sound of many of them is no obstacle to their operational treatment, however. What is involved is an utterly straightforward extension of the classical position of Tolman, Spence, and others who developed and advanced the intervening variable approach. Naturally, this does not solve the philosophical problem referred to above, but I am inclined to leave such problems to the philosophers.

The Search for Laws

The problems raised earlier about method seem to be more difficult to dismiss. The chief of these is that the laws we discover are so limited in their applicability. For this reason I now think that the amount of work that went into many of the classical parametric studies was greater than their generality warranted. At the present time it appears that a more fruitful strategy is to emphasize the problem of generalizability and to study the effects of our variables in many different contexts, sacrificing large N's and large numbers of points on the anticipated function if this is necessary. In this way we should get a better grasp on the extent to which the effects of these variables are similar with various situations, species, responses, age groups, instructional sets, motivational levels, schedules of reinforcement, and so on.

In this connection I believe that it is important to come right out and say that the standardization of method once advocated by some of our most influential psychologists must be rejected. The trouble with standardized methods is that what we learn with them stands a very strong chance of being limited to them, an almost totally counterproductive consequence. Although this point has not been dwelt upon and possibly not even recognized by psychologists in certain areas, the implied change in experimental strategy is already under way. In the field of verbal learning, for example, there is now a storm of activity that once seemed impossible in that apparently sterile field. It appears to me, at least, that this began at the exact moment that investigators recognized the possibilities inherent in approaches other than those provided by the memory drum and the serial anticipation method. Free recall and its various derivatives (modified free recall, modified modified free recall), cued recall, and the study of recognition memory are the most conspicuous results of this emancipation from the tyranny of standard methodology. They are also the focus of the research excitement mentioned above.

Individual differences. As Cronbach (1957) noted, a concern for the influence of individual differences upon performance has not been a part of the tradition of conventional experimental psychology, whose preoccupation has been with general laws. The study of individual differences has been the interest of a totally separate scientific subdiscipline in psychology. Recent years have seen the beginning of the dissolution of this sharp separation. Just in the field of classical conditioning, such variables as anxiety, social desirability, and suggestibility have been shown to be important. In my opinion this type of work needs to be extended, and extended in a direction of which the correlational theorists might or might not approve. What needs to be considered is the possibility that individual differences as they have usually been treated are only part of a much larger cluster of variables. What I have in mind here is the fact that a given personal variation is almost always taken by the correlational theorist to be a relatively permanent attribute of an individual (see the earlier Cronbach quotation). It is clear on various counts, however, that more temporary individual variations make important contributions to the learning process. The trait-state dichotomy proposed by Spielberger (1966) in connection with anxiety makes the essential point. Moreover, the powerful effects of instructions on conditioning show that the same individual may perform quite differently in even this simple situation, depending upon such momentary circumstances. It seems certain to me that self-instruction can have equally impressive effects. If this is so, the psychologist interested in learning once more is going to be forced into dealing with some intervening variables that would have seemed very peculiar to conventional experimental psychologists—the "demand character-istics" of experiments, the subjects' interpretations of the experimental procedures, and their attitudes toward those procedures. Peculiar or not, however, it has sometimes been found that these variables can account for two-thirds of the variance (Kimble, 1967, pp. 655–656) in a simple conditioning experiment. And variables that potent cannot be ignored forever.

It will also be important to depart from a complete reliance upon the standard correlational approach and to ask about the causes of individual differences. In the search for such causes, two types of investigation seem to have a great deal to offer. The first is the study of behavioral genetics, which is rapidly demonstrating a hereditary contribution to such important aspects of behavior as alcoholism, introversion, and cognitive style. The second is the study of early experience, which takes on an added significance in a psychology that concerns itself with behavioral variability as well as with modal trends. Fortunately, work in these areas is already going on and will continue without any special urging from general commentators on the current scene.

Theory Construction

I would hazard a guess that the methodological freedom described earlier in this paper is leading to a greater theoretical freedom. Hints of this are coming from many sources. Whether we feel comfortable with it or not, it seems to me that a part of what is happening is a return to theorizing that is somewhat general in scope. The several generations of computer-inspired flow-chart diagrams that bring together certain phenomena of perception, information processing, learning, memory, and retrieval limn in the outline of one characteristic style of the new theorizing. Although the ensuing comments may contain a large element of wishful thinking on my part, it seems to me that other trends are also becoming clear.

The deductive method. There is not much to say here. The prediction of con-sequences from theoretical assumptions has always provided the excitement in sci-entific work, and this shows no signs of important change. At the same time it is clear, however, that a shift to smaller experiments and greater diversity puts a new importance on the inductive side of the field, at least for the time being.

Analysis. Despite the objections of a vocal minority, analysis must continue if we are even to discuss our subject matter. As I heard Gustav Bergmann put it a long time ago, "A nonanalyzing science is an inarticulate science." What will emerge from the analysis now seems likely to be quite different in some respects from the stimulus and response elements in terms of which most of us are used to thinking. Among other things, this will put the problem of dealing with complex behavior in quite another light.

The Problem of Complexity

Let me begin with an example: as was mentioned earlier, the treatment of rote verbal learning (a complex form of behavior) in terms of specific S-R connections now appears to be of limited usefulness. People collect and organize materials in various ways that serve to minimize the role of specific associations For this reason, predictions about forgetting based on simple interference theory have gone wrong in many recent studies. At the same time, however, evidence is beginning to accumulate that the principles of interference may apply to clusters of materials. Thus B. R. Ekstrand and B. J. Underwood (personal communication) both have unpublished data to suggest that when paired associate lists are constructed in ways that lead the individual to form clusters of related words (e.g., names of animals), these clusters may be interfered with by learning interpolated materials involving other clusters. In this case, a theory developed for simple materials contributes to the understanding of more complex behavior.

Simultaneously an opposite thing has also been happening: ideas developed to handle complex behavior have been brought to bear on simple behavior. Referring back again to an example mentioned earlier, psychologists interested in language and influenced by the ideas of computing science have argued (with reason I think) that verbal behavior involves an overall program and cannot be understood in terms of the linear stringing together of phonemic elements. This program includes a plan for the completion of an utterance as well as for the verbal response itself. Now Liu (1968), among others, has shown that the same is true even of the simple responses involved in a reaction time experiment.

What all of this means is that the concepts identified in the analysis of simple learning are proving useful in treatments of complex behavior and *vice versa*. At the same time, of course, research and theorizing proceed and, as they do, behavioral categories are redefined, new causal conditions take on importance, and new explanatory concepts emerge. The list of such changes is long, and although I am tempted to ramble on about the ones I believe to be most significant (image, stages in the progress of learning, retrieval cue, biofeedback, the nature of memory storage, specific encoding, stimulus-response sympathies in conditioning, the hierarchical organization of habits, and environmental control of drives and emotions, just to name what comes to mind first), I must leave that to others who are contributing to this volume.

CONCLUSION

Having come to the end of this description of certain features of the changing picture in the theoretical psychology of learning, the points I would like to emphasize and leave the reader with are these:

1. It seems to me that there is an evolutionary rather than revolutionary relationship between learning theories of an older era and those that dominate

the current scene. I find it impossible to accept the common proposition that progress requires the abandonment of earlier insights.

2. New developments in biological psychology are putting the field of learning into a new perspective. Knowledge obtained in studies of the reticular formation, of the limbic system, and in behavioral genetics no longer allows the cavalier disregard of these topics. They have too much to suggest about underlying mechanisms and influences.

3. The characteristic of the older psychology that must be retained is its insistence upon an objective approach to behavior. I have no personal objection to calling this approach an operational behaviorism, but I do not wish to insist upon this terminological point, because that might interfere with the acceptance of a more important one. This traditional approach must be (and fortunately is being) liberalized and extended to the treatment of aspects of behavior that were once excluded.

4. Because of this liberalization, psychology is in a position now to investigate problems that were once considered illegitimate on methodological grounds. These include important aspects of personal experience, unusual psychological states and causes that until recently seemed beyond us.

5. If anything should be abandoned for the time being, it is the experimental strategy that allowed me in my doctoral dissertation (Kimble, 1947) to investigate eyelid conditioning at six intervals between 0.10 and 0.40 seconds with substantial numbers of subjects at each point. We need to worry more about the magnitude of effects and the generality of our laws.

6. The study of individual and other differences as they influence behavior deserves close attention as a part of this effort to determine the generality of our knowledge. This last point takes us back to the first. The aim of scientific psychology remains that of attempting to develop a generalized understanding of behavior. The transition I have been describing is a change in method rather than of ultimate objectives.

REFERENCES

Cronbach, L. J. The two disciplines of scientific psychology. *American Journal of Psychology*, 1957, **12**, 671–684.

Dollard, J., & Miller, N. E. *Personality and psychotherapy*. New York: McGraw-Hill, 1950.

Grice, G. R. The relation of secondary reinforcement to delayed reward in visual discrimination learning. *Journal of Experimental Psychology*, 1948, **38**, 1–16.

Grice, G. R. Conditioning and a decision theory of response evocation. In G. H. Bower & J. T. Spence (Eds.), *The psychology of learning and motivation: Advances in research and theory, VI*. New York: Academic Press, 1972.

Guthrie, E. R., & Horton, G. P. *Cats in a puzzle box*. New York: Holt, Rinehart & Winston, 1946.

Hull, C. L. *Principles of behavior*. New York: Appleton-Century-Crofts, 1943.

Kimble, G. A. Conditioning as a junction of the time between conditioned and unconditioned stimuli. *Journal of Experimental Psychology*, 1947, **37**, 1–15.

Kimble, G. A. An experimental test of a two-factor theory of inhibition. *Journal of Experimental Psychology*, 1949, **39**, 15–23.

Kimble, G. A. *Foundations of conditioning and learning.* New York: Appleton-Century-Crofts, 1967.

Kimble, G. A. Cognitive inhibition in classical conditioning. In H. H. Kendler & J. T. Spence (Eds.), *Essays in neobehaviorism: A memorial volume to Kenneth W. Spence.* New York: Appleton-Century-Crofts, 1971.

Kimble, G. A., Leonard, T. B., & Perlmuter, L. C. Effects of interstimulus interval and discrimination learning in eyelid conditioning using between and within-*Ss* designs. *Journal of Experimental Psychology,* 1968, 77, 652–660.

Liu, I. Effects of repetition on voluntary responses: From voluntary to involuntary. *Journal of Experimental Psychology,* 1968, 76, 398–406.

McGovern, J. B. Extinction of associations in four transfer paradigms. *Psychological Monographs,* 1964, 78 (Whole No. 593).

Meehl, P. E. Theory testing in psychology and physics: A methodological paradox. *Philosophy of Science,* 1967, 34, 103–115.

Miller, G. A., Galanter, E., & Pribram, K. H. *Plans and the structure of behavior.* New York: Holt, Rinehart & Winston, 1960.

Miller, N. E., & Dollard, J. *Social learning and imitation.* New Haven: Yale University Press, 1941.

Perin, C. T. Behavior potentiality as a joint function of the amount of training and degree of hunger at the time of extinction. *Journal of Experimental Psychology,* 1942, 30, 93–113.

Revusky, S. H., & Garcia, J. Learned associations over long delays. In G. H. Bower & J. T. Spence (Eds.), *The psychology of learning and motivation: Advances in research and theory, IV.* New York: Academic Press, 1970.

Spector, M. Theory and observation (I). *British Journal of the Philosophy of Science,* 1966, 17, 1–20.

Spence, K. W. A theory of emotionally based drive (D) and its relation to performance in simple learning situations. *American Psychologist,* 1958, 13, 131–141.

Spence, K. W., Homzie, M. J., & Rutledge, E. F. Extinction of human eyelid CR as a function of the discriminability of the change from acquisition to entinction. *Journal of Experimental Psychology,* 1964, 67, 545–552.

Spielberger, C. D. *Anxiety and behavior.* New York: Academic Press, 1966.

Tolman, E. C. The determiners of behavior at a choice point. *Psychological Review,* 1938, 45, 1–41.

Tolman, E. C., & Honzik, C. H. Introduction and removal of reward and maze performance in rats. *University of California Publications in Psychology,* 1930, 4, 257–275.

Toulmin, S. E. The evolutionary development of natural science. *American Scientist,* 1967, 55, 456–471.

Williams, S. B. Resistance to extinction as a function of the number of reinforcements. *Journal of Experimental Psychology,* 1938, 23, 506–522.

2
HIGHER MENTAL PROCESSES AS THE BASES FOR THE LAWS OF CONDITIONING

Eli Saltz
Wayne State University

The primary concern of this chapter will be to invert an old game: Instead of attempting to use the notions of instrumental learning and classical conditioning to provide new insights concerning "higher mental processes," the present paper will attempt to use some of the recent advances in the areas of human verbal learning and memory to provide new insights concerning instrumental learning and classical conditioning.

In the service of this enterprise, the paper is organized in the following manner. First we shall consider the general issue of using laws in one area of learning as a basis of prediction in a different area. Then we shall examine some of the general directions taken by recent theoretical developments in verbal learning. And finally, we shall examine the implications of these theoretical developments for our understanding of instrumental learning and conditioning.

THE CONCEPT OF A UNIFIED THEORY
OF LEARNING

Is there a single set of laws that govern all forms of learning? Over the years, a number of psychologists have assumed that such a set does, indeed, exist. This assumption has taken several different concrete forms. Guthrie (1930), for example, assumed that there is one basic law of learning, and that all forms of learning from classical conditioning to verbal learning and the acquisition of neuroses are instances of the operation of this law. Writers like Hull (1943) and Spence (1956), on the other hand, declared for a much more sophisticated form of this assumption. They assumed that instrumental and classical conditioning are the simplest forms of learning, and under the greatest experimental control;

therefore, the laws of conditioning (and particularly classical conditioning) should provide a good first approximation of the laws to be found in other types of learning. Hull (1935) himself, of course, pioneered in the attempt to use the laws of classical conditioning as a basis for explaining some of the phenomena of verbal learning. In this same tradition, Underwood (1948) has proposed that the laws describing the experimental extinction and spontaneous recovery of conditioned responses may be used as the bases of a theory that accounts for the phenomena of proactive and retroactive inhibition in verbal learning. In his chapter in the present book, Dr. D. D. Wickens accepts the Underwood position and describes a set of ingenious experiments designed to examine the generality of the position.

In short, most of the proponents of the position that there is a single set of laws for all forms of learning have assumed that conditioning is the best place to start looking for this set of laws. However, if we take a broader view of the entire issue, we shall see that this is not a logical necessity.

Let us attempt to state the concept of a unified theory for all types of learning in a very general manner. Assume that there is an underlying set of laws, A, B, C, D, E, . . . , which is in some sense basic to all other sets of laws concerning learning (viz., basic in the sense that it is capable of generating all the other sets of laws). At this point in scientific history we know relatively little about this set of underlying laws. However, we do have some empirical laws that describe restricted ranges of phenomena in various subareas of learning such as classical conditioning, instrumental learning, verbal learning, and so forth. We may refer to these empirical laws as "surface laws." Figure 1 presents a schematic representation of the relationship between the set of underlying laws and the various sets of surface laws. Presumably, at some future date we shall discover the underlying laws and a set of functions (illustrated as $f, f', \ldots$) which will permit us to generate each of the various sets of surface laws.

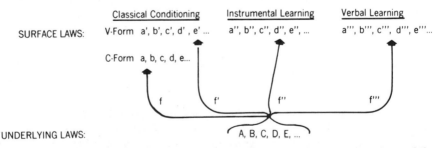

FIG. 1. Representation of the relationship between the laws underlying all learning, and the surface (empirically determined) laws known in each of several areas of learning.

From this point of view, there is no a priori reason to assume that any of the sets of surface laws is more basic than any other. Perhaps if classical conditioning were *simpler,* in some sense, than the other forms of learning (as Spence, 1956, claimed), this would be sufficient justification to consider it more basic. But is it simpler? The present writer believes that it would be difficult to defend such simplicity at this stage of our knowledge. Some of the reasons for such doubts are detailed elsewhere (Saltz, 1971). In brief, however, it can be stated that classical conditioning is an extremely complex set of phenomena which display a number of effects that are peculiar to the specific methodological constraints of the conditioning technique and which are, therefore, difficult to evaluate in terms of their generality for other forms of learning. One of the most intriguing aspects of this complexity is the suggestion from the work of Spence and Taylor (1951), Grant (1972), and others (see particularly Cerekwicki, Grant, & Porter, 1968) that there may be two types of classical conditioning, referred to as C-form and V-form conditioning. *Further, the same surface laws do not appear to be applicable to these two forms.* Which should we accept as the basic set of conditioning laws, those of the C-form or those of the V-form?

Since the existence of two forms of classical conditioning presents some interesting problems for the position that the laws of conditioning are basic to those of other types of learning, let us examine these two forms in somewhat greater detail. Using human subjects in eyelid conditioning, Spence and Taylor (1951) originally distinguished between the C- and V-form on the basis of the type of conditioned response emitted by the subjects. The V-form response resembled a voluntary eye blink, and therefore Spence and Taylor discarded subjects who gave this type of response. Apparently, they considered the subjects who emitted C-form responses to be "really" conditioned. More recently, Grant (1972) has presented data which suggests that V-form conditioners are no less "really" conditioned than are C-form, and that the V-form is not a self-instructed voluntary closure of the eye.

Examination of the literature shows that in many ways the laws of V- and C-form conditioning differ in detail, not in basic laws. For example, both V- and C-form learning curves increase as a function of number of CS-UCS pairings; also, increased UCS intensity produces greater probability of conditioned response in both forms. Thus, while V-form conditioning is usually more rapid than C-form, for the most part both display similar relationships with many other variables. The Cerekwicki et al. (1968) study is a striking exception to this generality. This study involved conditioned discrimination between sets of stimuli. For some subjects, the positive stimulus (always followed by a puff of air to the eye as the UCS) was any one of four words from a specific category such as animals (e.g., the words *bear, tiger,* etc.); the negative stimulus (never followed by a puff of air to the eye) was any one of four words from a different category (e.g., flower names). Under these conditions, the V-form subjects displayed differential conditioning, emitting the conditioned blinking response much more frequently to the positive stimulus than to the negative. The C-form subjects, on the other hand, showed virtually no differential conditioning. On the other hand, when only one single word was always used as the positive stimulus and a different single word as the negative stimulus, both C-form and V-form subjects showed differential conditioning.

In short, C-form conditioning is adequate when the subject needs only to respond to a discrete positive or negative stimulus. However, C-form conditioning is relatively poor when an adequate CR is dependent on the subject's processing the conditioned stimulus to abstract some form of *verbal meaning* from it. On the other hand, the processing of verbal meaning is no deterrent to V-form conditioning.

One possible explanation for the difference between C-form and V-form conditioning in their sensitivity to verbal meaning is that these two forms are mediated at different levels of brain function. The C-form, for example, may bypass the left hemisphere, while the V-form may involve left-hemisphere mediation. If this were indeed the case, then C-form conditioning would certainly be simpler than V-form, at least in the sense of being mediated at more primitive levels of brain function. From this point of view, one might argue that C-form conditioning is a likely source of "basic" laws. Note also that one of the advantages that Spence saw for conditioning as a source of basic laws was that it was relatively uncontaminated by language mediation.

On the other hand, if our objective is to discover a set of laws that will predict *human verbal learning,* the lack of sensitivity to meaning could make the laws of C-form conditioning the *last* place we would look, despite any presumed simplicity that might characterize these laws.

Turning back to Figure 1, we have seen that it is relatively arbitrary, at the present stage of our knowledge, whether we consider the laws of conditioning as basic and attempt to use these to predict verbal learning, or whether we consider the laws of verbal learning as basic and use these to predict the phenomena of conditioning. In general, we can expect the pressure of movement, across the area in Figure 1, to be such that theoreticians will consider as basic those areas which are relatively well developed empirically. The laws from such well-developed areas will then be used to predict to those areas which are less developed. Since our early knowledge of conditioning advanced much more rapidly than knowledge in other areas of learning, it was not surprising when early theoreticians thought of conditioning as somehow basic to other forms of learning.

In the past few years, tremendous advances have occurred in the areas of human learning and memory (and, indeed, in the entire area of "higher mental processes"). These advances have been both in empirical knowledge and in conceptualizations concerning the structures and functions basic to such psychological processes. Therefore, it should not now be surprising to find that at least some of the present-day theoreticians are looking to these advances in human learning and memory as a source of basic laws which may be applicable to instrumental learning and classical conditioning. The present chapter represents one such attempt. The chapter by Dr. W. K. Estes, in this book, represents another such attempt. There is nothing very mysterious about the development of this type of zeitgeist.

DEVELOPMENT OF TRENDS IN THEORIES
OF LEARNING

In one sense, at least, the position can be taken that, before some of the more recent developments in verbal learning, there never has been a *theory* of learning. There have been, of course, a number of important and ingenious theories which have attempted to account for the phenomena of instrumental learning and classical conditioning. However, the position can be defended that, with the possible exception of Pavlov's formulations, these have been theories of *performance,* rather than of learning. On what bases are these statements made? To understand this, it is first necessary to take a brief look at the history of conceptualizations in the learning area.

Is a Single Construct Sufficient to
Account for Behavior?

As I read the history of conceptualizations in the learning area, early theorists attempted to predict behavior on the basis of a small number of global concepts; increases in our knowledge concerning the relevant phenomena led to the postulation of greater numbers of theoretical constructs which were more finely differentiated from one another. Let us consider the classical trinity of Guthrie, Tolman, and Hull from this point of view.

For Guthrie (1930, 1935), learning consisted of the association between a stimulus and a response. This S-R association was the single theoretical construct formally recognized in the system. It accounted for both learning and extinction. How does it account for learning? If a stimulus and a response occur contiguously, Guthrie assumes that an association develops between them (e.g., if, in the presence of a *light* you turn *right,* the *light-right* S-R association is formed). Once an S-R association is formed, subsequent appearance of the identical stimulus should lead to the organism's performing the associated response. Interestingly enough, the identical mechanism is assumed to account for the *extinction* of a previously learned response: If a *new* response occurs in the presence of the stimulus, *this* response now becomes associated to the stimulus, and this leads to extinction of any previous associates to the stimulus (e.g., in the presence of the *light* you are forced to turn *left*; a *light-left* association is now formed, and this automatically extinguishes the previous *light-right* association).

Yet we know that performance will be influenced by a number of variables such as fatigue, level of motivation, and amount of previous reinforcement for making a given response. How does Guthrie deal with such variables in his single-factor theory? He considers all these variables to be aspects of the S-R association. Let us consider fatigue as an example. Fatigue alters the *internal* stimulus conditions of an organism. Therefore, if learning originally occurred in a nonfatigued state but the *external* stimulus (e.g., that *light*) is later presented when the organism is tired, the entire stimulus complex (internal plus external stimuli) is now very different from that which obtained during original learning—the R may not be elicited by this new S. Later, if the stimulus is presented again when the organism is no longer tired, the internal and external stimuli should again approximate those of original learning, and the response may occur again. Other variables are handled in a similar manner.

One of Tolman's (1932) most important contributions was to break down the single, global variable postulated by Guthrie, and to describe performance as a function of a number of interesting factors. Basic to this was Tolman's distinction between learning and performance. For example, an organism might learn from experience that if he turned left he would reach a circular room. Yet he might never again turn left because there was nothing in it for him (e.g., no food, drink, sex, or other form of reinforcement). From this point of view, reinforcement is a variable which is distinct from learning, but can interact with learning to produce a given performance.

From the standpoint of the breakdown of Guthrie's global performance variable, the crucial contribution made by Hull (1943) was to specify the relationship between learning and performance variables in greater detail than earlier theorists. For Hull, learning was conceptualized as an association between a stimulus and response; the strength of this association (symbolized as H) was determined by the number of times S and R were paired, followed by a reinforcement. In addition to the learning variable, H, Hull postulated a series of performance variables that interacted with H. These included: level of motivation (D); magnitude of reinforcement the organism received as a consequence of performing the response to be learned (K); and inhibition (I), a fatigue-like factor that accrued as a function of making the response being learned.

Hull proposed that these variables interacted in the following general manner to determine performance.

Performance $= (H \times D \times K) - I$

This formulation indicates that if there is no learning (viz., if $H = 0$), there will be no performance of the relevant response, since the statement in the parentheses will reduce to zero. The same thing will happen, of course, if either D or K reduces to zero. As the values of these variables increase over zero, the probability of response also increases. Fatigue (I) subtracts from $H \times D \times K$; therefore, the fatigued organism is less likely to respond.

Note that Hull, like Tolman before him, was primarily concerned with stating the relationship between a single learning variable and a complex set of performance variables (H, K, and I). Historically, as we move from Guthrie to Tolman to Hull, the expansion occurs in number and specificity of *performance* variables. Learning refers to a *single variable* for each of these theorists. For Guthrie and Hull this single variable is an S-R association. For Tolman, it is an S_1-S_2 association (e.g., in classical conditioning this association represents the organism's expectation that the conditioned stimulus, S_1, will be followed by the unconditioned stimulus, S_2; or, in maze learning, this association refers to the organism's expectation that turning left at a particular choice point, S_1, in the maze will lead to a blind alley, S_2).

Is it possible to have a theory of learning based upon a single learning variable? To answer this question, we must first state what we mean by a theory. If one set of laws, Set A, is capable of predicting a second set of laws, Set B, we call Set A the theory that "explains" Set B. From this standpoint, a theory of learning requires a *set* of learning variables whose interaction constitutes a *set* of laws which we can use to predict behavior. Instead, we find that the classical theorists had one learning variable and (in the case of Hull and Tolman, at least) a *set* of performance variables, and it was the interaction between these that was used to obtain a set of laws for the prediction of behavior. These were theories of performance rather than theories of learning. In this connection it is interesting to note that the word "learning" did not appear in the titles of the major works published by Tolman and by Hull (viz., "Purposive Behavior" and "Principles of Behavior" respectively).

Probably the first systematic attempt to postulate a learning variable in addition to the associative variable occurs in the work of E. J. Gibson (1940). She suggested the construct of *stimulus differentiation* as a learned factor. If we have experience with a stimulus, Gibson's notion suggested, the stimulus becomes less likely to become confused with similar stimuli, and this decrease in confusability (which she called *stimulus differentiation*) should facilitate later acquisition of associations to the stimulus.

The present writer has discussed the history of the stimulus differentiation construct elsewhere (Saltz, 1971). It is sufficient, in this book, merely to point out that Gibson's notion was greeted with great resistance from a number of prominent psychologists who considered the postulation of two different learning variables (the association plus stimulus differentiation) as unparsimonious. A number of studies were conducted which attempted to demonstrate that the differentiation effects reported by Gibson and her coworkers were actually mediated by associative processes, and that only the association need be considered as a learning construct after all. In the end it must be concluded that the evidence strongly supported Gibson's general position; a stimulus differentiation factor which is independent of associational strength appears defensible.

A Multifactor Position on Learning

In this section I shall present an outline of a multifactor theory of learning as I have developed it in the verbal learning area (Saltz, 1971). In the subsequent sections I shall attempt to show that this formulation may be of use in the areas of instrumental learning and classical conditioning.

The writer has proposed, in effect, that there is a "molecule" of learning—a complex system of factors, each of which is independently manipulable, but all of which must coexist and interact if learning is to exist.

But first, in what type of medium does this molecule exist? We assume that people must, in some manner, represent the stimuli which they encounter, and also their own responses to these stimuli. A longstanding problem in the psychology of higher mental processes is: How can we, as psychologists, represent the medium in which people perform these representational feats? I have assumed (Saltz, 1971, p. 33) that the molecule exists in a *cognitive space,* and have defined this notion of cognitive space as the "*set of dimensions* on which a person can react to the stimuli (both internal and external) of his environment." This is, in effect, an *n* dimensional space in which any actual event can be represented as the intersection of a number of relevant dimensions. As an example of such a representation, let us assume that we encounter a person whom we know to be a *father.* This person is the intersection of dimensions such as height (he is 5 feet 2 inches tall), weight (he weighs 235 pounds), eye color, etc., plus certain evaluative dimensions such as goodness (fathers are good, not bad), honesty, etc. In short, this father is represented as a *point in cognitive space.* (More properly, he is a *region* in the space, because he may fluctuate in weight, within limits, as well as in sagacity, honesty, etc. Thus, he may be represented by any of a number of points which are relatively close to one another in the space.)

From this point of view, what happens to the notion of the *association?* If Representation 1 (i.e., the intersection of dimensions that define Representation 1) elicits Representation 2, we say that these two representations are associated. It can be seen from this definition that the notion of *stimulus* differs from the notion of *response* only in function; they do not differ in terms of their characteristics as elements in the space. Thus, there is no reason why a given *light* (Representation 1) could not become associated to a given *buzzer sound* (Representation 2), though operationally it might become difficult to determine whether or not such an association had been formed since, typically, neither light nor buzzer occurs on dimensions that involve overt muscular or glandular responses. Note that if we could determine that such an association has been formed, we might be tempted to yield to old ways of thinking which we have borrowed from Pavlov, Guthrie, Hull, and others, and we might say that we were dealing with a stimulus-stimulus association! The reader has not, of course, been tricked, and he recognizes, in the example of the *light-buzzer* association, the well-studied issue of sensory preconditioning (e.g., Coppock, 1958). Ingenious operational techniques have been developed which indicate that such associations *can* be formed.

Given that the cognitive space is the medium in which the molecule of learning is assumed to exist, what are the elements that have been postulated as constituting this molecule? The writer (Saltz, 1971) has proposed four elements for such a molecule: (a) the association, (b) stimulus differentiation, (c) response differentiation, and (d) the boundary strength of the molecule. These four elements will be explained in the succeeding paragraphs.

The association. As here conceptualized, the association is not between a stimulus and a response, nor between two stimuli, but between two points in the cognitive space. Recent research in the verbal learning area has suggested that, for people at least (the case of the rat is less clear), the association forms on the first trial at which the two elements are presented together, and is virtually at maximum strength at this time. Then why does it often require many trials before the subject responds correctly in a consistent fashion? The problem appears to be one of rapid forgetting, produced by processes of interference, rather than a problem of slow acquisition.

Some of the most convincing evidence on this topic comes from studies of short-term memory (STM) using the Peterson and Peterson (1959) technique. This technique consists of presenting a subject with a word or nonsense syllable, preventing him from rehearsing for some fixed interval (usually by having the subject perform some rapid mathematical computations), then testing for recall of the item. Using this technique, a number of studies have found that a well-practiced subject will show virtually perfect recall of a nonsense item if tested within a second or two after the item has been removed from sight; thereafter, the probability of correct retention drops in a fairly regular fashion so that by 18 seconds after the item has been removed, there is only about 20% probability of correct recall (e.g., Murdock, 1961). The item was obviously *learned*; it was not retained. The evidence suggests that forgetting of such items is due to interference from previously acquired items; and that the closer these items are to each other in the cognitive space, the greater the likelihood of interference-induced forgetting (e.g., Wickens, Born, & Allen, 1963).

Stimulus differentiation. The second learned element in our multifactor molecule of learning is the degree to which the functional stimulus has been differentiated. As was pointed out earlier in this chapter, Gibson's research has shown that experience with a stimulus leads to the differentiation of this stimulus from other stimuli, in the environment, with which it might possibly be confused. What effect does such differentiation have on behavior? With greater stimulus differentiation, the subject is more likely to recall the correct response. This is because such differentiation protects the learned system of associations from disruption which might be produced by competing representational items nearby in the cognitive space.

Response differentiation. It has previously been suggested that the distinction between stimulus and response is arbitrary from the point of view of their characteristics as points in the cognitive space. If we present Representation 1 in an attempt to elicit Representation 2, then 1 is the stimulus and 2 the response; however, if we present 2 in an attempt to elicit 1, then 2 is the stimulus and 1 is the response. If the point which functions as the stimulus is capable of developing differentiational properties, then it seems reasonable to assume that the point which functions as the response should also be capable of developing similar properties.

The evidence indicates that response differentiation does indeed occur (e.g., Saltz, 1961; Saltz & Felton, 1968). The data suggest that increased response differentiation, like increased stimulus differentiation, reduces the effects of interference acting on a learned system. This shows itself as a more rapid rise in the probability of a correct response as a function of practice.

Systematic resistence to interference ("boundary strength"). Even if both the stimulus and the response are very well differentiated, the "learning curve" may rise relatively gradually under conditions where there is a great deal of interference from other systems of learned elements. It appears that the system of elements as described (viz., the association, the differentiated stimulus, and the differentiated response) must develop a resistance to interference from other systems in the cognitive space. The degree of such resistance to interference has been referred to as the "boundary strength" of the system of associated, representational points in the cognitive space.

Later in this chapter additional assumptions from the human memory area will be introduced as appropriate. For the time being, the assumptions introduced above will suffice to start our reconsideration of the phenomena of instrumental learning and conditioning.

CONSEQUENCES FOR INSTRUMENTAL LEARNING AND CONDITIONING

One-Trial Learning

Classical conditioning. If the position taken above is applicable to classical conditioning, then it would follow that conditioning is a situation in which we would expect the learning curve to be close to asymptote except for the operation of various uncontrolled sources of interference. The first question to be answered, then, is: Do we have any reason to believe that interference is a factor in conditioning? While the typical accounts of conditioning do not discuss this issue, several investigators have presented evidence to suggest that interference is indeed operating. Mateer's (1918) classic account of her early attempt to produce Pavlovian conditioning in this country is an example. According to Mateer, the young children whom she tried to condition were likely to respond to almost any random stimulus, which preceded the UCS, as though it were the CS. In effect, Mateer described the conditioning situation as one in which the organism must distinguish between those stimuli which would be regularly followed by the UCS, and those which would not.

Voeks (1954) set about to control as many of these potentially interfering stimuli as she could in an eyelid-conditioning study. Subjects were placed in a soundproof room to insure against extraneous auditory stimulation. Further, she attempted to control for *internal* stimulus factors: Just prior to the CS onset, Voeks signaled her subjects, and they held their breaths to control cues from breathing; and they depressed two keys, one with each hand, to control for kinesthetic sensations in the arms and hands. Under these conditions, Voeks reports that half her subjects invariably made the conditioned response after once doing so. Most of the other subjects also had flat learning curves, with only one or two failures to emit the CR after the first CR was emitted.

One problem does exist, in the Voeks data, for the position outlined above. While most subjects showed jumps from chance to 100% performance in one trial, this trial was often *not the first test trial.* The theory derived from verbal learning data suggests that the CS-CR association should have been formed as virtually maximum strength after the first CS-UCS pairing. What factors might account for the delay in production of the first CR? One possibility resides in an aspect of the procedure used by Voeks. She attempted to habituate the alpha response to the CS prior to the onset of conditioning by presenting the CS a number of times without the UCS. Some of the recent Russian literature on conditioning (e.g., Sokolov, 1963) suggests that this type of procedure results in extinction of the orienting response to the CS; extinction of the orienting response to a stimulus typically impedes the acquisition of any response to the stimulus.

One final question must be raised with regard to the Voeks study. Does it involve V-form, C-form, or both forms of conditioning? Since this distinction was not salient in 1954 when Voeks published her study, the appropriate measures were not collected to answer this question.

Note that the issues of stimulus and response differentiation did not arise in the Voeks study. A study by Grant, Levy, Thompson, Hickok, and Bunde (1967) is extremely important in that it did manipulate variables relevant to differentiation. Before proceding, it should be pointed out that the subjects in this study proved to be V-form conditioners.

The Grant et al. study was one of classical, differential eyelid conditioning. The subjects were presented one of two stimuli on each trial. Stimulus 1 was always followed by the UCS; Stimulus 2 was never followed by the UCS. Different categories of stimuli were used as the CSs for different groups of subjects. For Group A, both CS-1 and CS-2 were words; for Group B the stimuli were unfamiliar geometric forms; arabic numerals and spelled numbers were also used as stimuli for some of the other groups. After 60 trials of differential conditioning with one set of stimuli, subjects were then transferred to a second set of stimuli from the same category as the first set, and were given an additional 40 trials of transfer training. Each subject received three such sets of transfer trials.

Let us now consider this experiment in terms of our initial theoretical approach. Words are known to be highly differentiated items (e.g., Saltz & Felton, 1968); unfamiliar geometric forms are known not to be. Let us concentrate on these two unambiguous groups, A and B, then. Turning to the CR, it is reasonable to assume that the naive experimental subject had had little experience with eyelid closure in anticipation of a puff of air to the eye. At the onset of original learning, at least, we can assume that the CR is relatively undifferentiated; by transfer set 1, it should be more differentiated.

Turning to Group A, in which CS-1 and CS-2 were real words, we would expect relatively gradual learning in the 60 original learning trials. The stimuli were well differentiated, but the responses were not. By the first transfer task, however, the V-form CR can be assumed to be relatively well differentiated. Thus, by the first transfer set, our subject encounters a new pair of words as stimuli—but they are, after all, real words, and therefore well differentiated, and the CR is well differentiated; conditioning should be extremely rapid.

Group B, on the other hand, encounters a poorly differentiated set of geometric forms as stimuli in original learning, and the CR is relatively poorly differentiated; therefore, original learning should be relatively slow. By the first transfer trial, the CR is relatively well differentiated, but a new set of undifferentiated unfamiliar forms is introduced as the CS's; thus acquisition in the first transfer task should be gradual.

Figure 2 summarizes the relevant data from Groups A and B in the Grant et al. study. As can be seen, learning is relatively gradual in the original set of 60 trials for both Groups. However, by the first transfer task, Group A, with words as stimuli, shows virtually perfect performance from the first block of trials. Grant et al. report that actually the curve jumps to virtual perfect performance on the first test trial after the CS and UCS were paired. As can be seen in Figure 2, this trend is fairly consistent over transfer tasks 2 and 3.

On the other hand, Group B, with a new set of unfamiliar forms as stimuli in the first transfer task, displays relatively gradual acquisition on this transfer task as well as on the second and third transfer tasks. (The other groups, it might be noted, fall between Groups A and B in transfer performance.)

The Grant et al. design is interesting because it permits isolating the effects of stimulus differentiation from those of response differentiation. In Group A, since the stimuli are well differentiated, the gradual learning in the original learning task must be attributed almost completely to lack of response differentiation. This seems particularly likely since, on the first transfer task, when the CR is relatively well differentiated, learning jumps to virtually perfect levels on the first test trial despite the fact that a new set of well-differentiated stimuli was substituted for the stimuli of the original learning task.

For Group B, on the other hand, neither stimuli nor responses were well differentiated during original learning. Yet performance here is very comparable to that of Group A. This suggests that the combined effects of poor stimulus and poor response differentiation are not much different from the effect of one of these alone. Since the data of Group A suggest that by the first transfer task the CR is well differentiated, the gradual learning shown by Group B on the first transfer task must be attributable almost completely to poor stimulus differentiation.

In short, the Grant et al., data support the utility of our molecule of learning as a reasonable approach to V-form conditioning.

Instrumental learning. The conditioning data provide strong support for the notion of virtually perfect trial 1 formation of the association, as well as

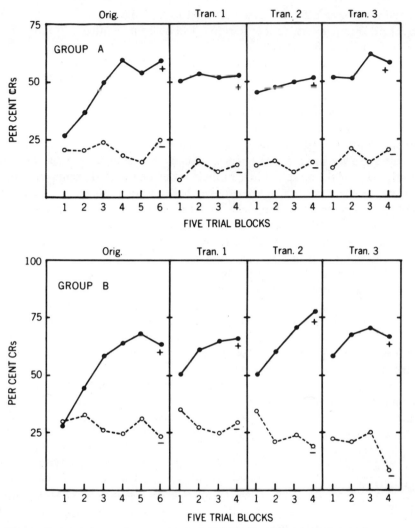

FIG. 2. Percentage of CRs to reinforced (+) and nonreinforced (−) stimuli on successive five-trial blocks in original learning (*Orig.*) and the three successive transfer discrimination learning (*Tran.*) tasks. (Taken from Grant, Levy, Thompson, Hickok, & Bunde, 1967. Reproduced with permission of the American Psychological Association.)

evidence for the utility of the concepts of stimulus and response differentiation. Note, however, that the particular data at issue involved human subjects and V-form conditioning. When we turn to the animal literature in instrumental learning, the data are not as clear. There are, no doubt, a number of reasons for this (see Saltz, 1971). First, it is particularly difficult, in animal data, to determine whether the animal learned, then forgot, or never learned at all. An animal runs down a T-maze and finds food in a particular location; on the next trial he does not return to that location. Did he learn and then forget, or did he fail to learn in the first place?

It is also difficult to distinguish learning from thinking in the rat. The animal may recall where he last found food, yet not realize that food will be placed there again on the next trial. (Again, the distinction between learning is made in a more systematic fashion in Saltz, 1971.)

One aspect of the human memory formulation is clearly relevant to even the simplest instrumental learning. The instrumental learning situation characteristically involves massive interference. A number of studies have displayed this clearly. One of the most dramatic of these is Cotton's (1953) examination of rat behavior in the straight alley. Here the rat has to learn nothing more than to run straight ahead to find food—the animals decisions about aspects of the *apparatus,* to which he should respond, have been reduced to virtually zero. Then what are the sources of interference? Many of these are internal. The rat may stop and groom himself, may turn around and retrace, and so forth. When Cotton disgarded all trials on which the rats made *overt* responses which competed with forward motion toward the goal, he obtained a curve for running speed that was extremely flat across trials. If we accept running speed as an index of learning, this suggests that the main effect of practice trials in the alley is to reduce the effects of interference; further, if we disgard the effects of interference from early trials, we find that learning, as indexed by speed, is virtually asymptotic after the first few trials.

There are several problems with this analysis. First, while some studies have obtained data similar to Cotton's (e.g., Pereboom & Crawford, 1958), others have found gradual increments in the speed curves even after disgarding trials on which competing responses were clearly evident (e.g., Marx & Brownstein, 1963). The second problem is related to the fact that such studies have attempted to control only *overt* manifestations of interference. We know that interference tendencies may disrupt behavior even when these tendencies are not strong enough to emerge as discrete responses. For example, strong internal cues to grooming could slow an animal's running speed even if these cues did not result in overt grooming. Thus the studies which controlled overt competition are encouraging for the position that the laws of human memory may be applicable for instrumental learning, but these studies are far from definitive on the subject.

A study by Saltz, Whitman, and Paul (1963) took a somewhat different approach from that of Cotton in analyzing the genesis of interference in the runway. We started by analyzing the prerequisites for runway performance into several distinct cognitive systems, each of which is necessary for appropriate performance, but which must be differentiated from one another because, if they occur in the wrong sequence, performance will be disrupted. Put very concretely, the rat must *run* in the alley if he is to reach the goal; he must *stop running* in the goal box if he is to eat. Thus running and not running are two competing systems which must be differentiated if the animal is to perform appropriately in the alley. From this point of view, the greater the difference in external cues for the alley as opposed to the goal box, the easier the rat's task should be in differentiating his competing responses. The study tested this notion very simply. Animals were trained either to run in an alley which was painted the same color as the goal box (viz., white alley, white goal box; or black alley, black goal box); or they were trained to run in an alley painted a color which was different from that of the goal box (viz., white alley, black goal box; or black alley, white goal box). The results were straightforward and strong: The learning curve, measured in running speed, rose much more quickly when the alley and goal box were painted in *different* colors.

Let us briefly compare these results with expectations from a theory that assumes learning is the gradual development of associative strength between a stimulus and response as a function of number of reinforced trials. Amsel (1958) had speculated on just the sort of study we later performed, using the Hullian theory as the basis for his thinking. His reasoning took the following form. If the alley and goal box are the same color, the expectation of reinforcement which develops in the presence of food in the goal box will generalize to the alley; this expectation (the Hullian r_G-s_G is assumed to be the basis for the magnitude of reinforcement variable (K) and to have motivational properties (performance = H x K). Therefore, running in the alley was predicted to be faster, by Amsel, if the alley and goal box were painted the *same* color than if they were painted different colors.

At this point the reader has very likely anticipated the next suggestion that will be made concerning runway performance. The Saltz, Whitman, and Paul study shows that rate of improvement in runway performance is a function of the degree of differentiation of alley cues from goal box cues. Could this be, in part at least, the basis for the effect of magnitude-of-reinforcement on performance in the alley? If there is no reinforcement, there is relatively little difference between alley and goal box cues. A small amount of reinforcement produces a large difference in cue value, since the rat will make radically different responses in the presence of food from those made in its absence. Above this minimum, increasing magnitudes of food produce differentially more vigorous and persistant eating behavior that is increasingly different from behavior in the alley.

Before leaving the topic of acquisition rate in instrumental learning, it should be pointed out that animals and people are, after all, somewhat different neurologically. It is quite possible that humans form associations that have virtually 100% strength at trial 1, while the rat does not. The rat, in general, appears to have a poorer memory than man, and this could be the basis of the difference. On the other hand, it appears that much of learning in both rat and man consists of the differentiation of competing cognitive systems.

Osmotic Effects Between Cognitive Systems

There is reason to suggest that osmotic effects may occur between cognitive systems: The longer two systems coexist very close to each other in the cognitive space, the greater the tendency for these systems to merge and interfere with one another. I have previously suggested (Saltz, 1971) that this type of mechanism may be the basis for proactive inhibition in human forgetting. In this chapter, it will be suggested that just this same mechanism may operate in instrumental learning situations.

Let us start with the evidence for an osmotic effect as this is found in human forgetting of verbal materials. Newton and Wickens (1956), in an extremely well-controlled study, examined the retention of a paired-associates list, List 1, after a 48-hour interval. The osmotic effect was produced, in the experimental groups, by a second list, List 2, in which the stimuli were identical with those of List 1, but the responses were different. List 2 was learned either immediately after learning List 1, 24 hours after learning List 1, or 47 hours after learning List 1. In other words, the two lists coexisted in the cognitive space for either 48 hours, 24 hours, or 1 hour, respectively, before the test for recall of List 1. This study was well controlled in that a comparable set of control groups was also tested; the controls differed from the experimental only in that Lists 1 and 2 were completely unsimilar in either their stimulus or response terms.

The results were nicely consistent with the assumption that osmotic processes were at work. Compared to the control groups, retention of List 1 decreased systematically as a function of the length of time that Lists 1 and 2 coexisted in the cognitive space.

Incidentally, it should be pointed out that the Newton and Wickens data are inconsistent with an attempt to predict forgetting on the basis of a theory based on the notions of experimental extinction and spontaneous recovery. This latter theory assumed that learning List 2 should lead to extinction of the List 1 responses (since these responses would be elicited by the stimuli, but would not be correct). With time, these List 1 responses should spontaneously recover, leading to progressively better recall of List 1. Thus the best List 1 recall should occur when List 2 was learned immediately after List 1 (and 48 hours before List 1 recall), since this would permit the greatest amount of time for spontaneous recovery. The poorest List 1 recall should occur when List 2 was learned 47 hours after List 1 (and immediately before the test for List 1 recall), because this would provide the least time for spontaneous recovery. As we saw, the data were exactly opposite from that predicted on the basis of the extinction-recovery theory.

Turning to the data from instrumental learning, several studies suggest that osmotic effects are to be found in the white rat. First I would like to describe a study from our laboratories at Wayne (Saltz & Asdourian, 1963) since this study was designed explicitly to examine the hypothesis of osmotic processes. In effect, the study was concerned with whether anxiety, developed in one cognitive system, could spread, as a function of time, to other cognitive systems. The general design of the study took the following form. Animals were trained to run down an alley to a goal box for food; then half the animals were shocked directly in the original goal box, and half were shocked in a goal box which was similar but not identical to the original. If the anxiety spreads from one system to another as a function of time, then we would expect that shortly after shock, animals shocked in the original goal box would run down the alley more slowly than animals shocked in a box that only resembled the original goal box; after a period of time, however, anxiety should spread from the cognitive representation of the shocked-box to that of the original training box, and both groups should tend to run as slowly as if they had been shocked in the original goal box.

The results were strongly in support of an osmotic function. One hour after shock, the rats shocked in the original goal box ran the alley in 71.21 seconds, while those shocked in the similar box required only 48.03 seconds to run the alley. However, equivalent groups tested 22 hours after shock did not differ significantly in running time (75.08 and 94.19 seconds, respectively).

A second aspect of the Saltz and Asdourian data also supported the interpretation that an osmotic mechanism was operating to determine the behavior of these animals. It will be recalled that Saltz et al. (1963) showed that running speed in an alley is related to the animals' ability to differentiate alley cues from goal box cues. If this is accepted, then one could assume that animals who ran faster during original, preshock training should be better able to keep competing systems from interfering with one another than animals who ran more slowly in original training. How can the data be analyzed to test this prediction? Recall that the analysis of the Saltz and Asdourian data, summarized above, shows that massive amounts of anxiety-spread occurred between 1 hour and 22 hours after shock for those rats which had been shocked in a box *similar* to the original goal box. This indicates that we can use these 1-hour rats as a base line against which to compare the performance of the 22-hour rats. To this end, 1- and 22-hour rats which had been shocked in the *similar* box were matched on asymptotic *preshock* speed in running the alley. Then the difference in *postshock* test performance was calculated for each matched pair: the size of the difference is an index of the amount of anxiety-spread between 1 and 22 hours after shock for rats at that particular level of preshock performance.

As predicted by the osmosis theory, the index indicated much larger amounts of spread for rats whose speed scores were low during preshock performance (i.e., rats who developed little resistance to interference between competing systems) than for rats with rapid preshock performance. The correlation between preshock speed and amount of anxiety spread was *rho* = −.68 which, for 18 pairs of animals, is highly significant statistically.

Several other investigators have reported studies which support the predictions we have made based on the assumption of an osmotic process. McAllister and McAllister (1962) report coming across the effect unexpectedly in a study of avoidance training. That the effect is not restricted to anxiety responses is clearly shown in a study of instrumental behavior reported by Perkins and Weyant (1958). It should be noted that these investigators have interpreted their data as indicating that *stimulus generalization* increases as a function of time. Several points should be made with regard to the stimulus generalization interpretation. First, stimulus generalization is a *description* of the data, not an *explanation*. When a response learned to one stimulus is elicited by a second, similar stimulus, we call this state of affairs *generalization*. Neither Perkins and Weyant nor McAllister and McAllister used any known characteristics of stimulus generalization to *predict* the increase in generalization as a function of delay between training on one stimulus and testing on a second, similar stimulus. In contrast, the osmotic process can be used as a mechanism for *predicting* this increase in generalization as a function of time.

Second, even at an empirical, descriptive level, an interpretation in terms of stimulus generalization appears to have nothing to say about the relationship between individual differences in learning ability (as indexed by preshock speed in Saltz and Asdourian, 1963) and the extent to which generalization will increase as a function of time. As was seen above, the osmotic notion appears to have been very successful in making such predictions in the Saltz and Asdourian study.

Note that to this point the discussion of osmotic mechanisms has centered on instrumental behavior. Yet it has probably already occurred to the reader that there are clear implications for classical conditioning in the data discussed above. The anxiety response developed in the goal box can safely be assumed to be a conditioned response to the goal box stimuli. Subsequent avoidance behavior in the alley was obviously mediated by the conditioned anticipation of shock in the goal box. With these considerations in mind it appears that the osmotic effect must consist of a spread of the conditioned anxiety response.

Is the osmotic function one that has general applicability in the area of instrumental learning, or is it an effect of relatively restricted interest? At present it is difficult to say. We have seen that potentially it could be the basis for the mechanisms behind proactive inhibition in human verbal learning, and there is good reason to believe that proactive inhibition may be the most important factor in much of human forgetting. On the other hand, forgetting has not been an issue of great interest in laboratory studies of instrumental learning. For the most part, such forgetting has been studied by training an animal, then removing him from the laboratory situation and placing him in some other environment (e.g., his home cage in the case of the pigeon or rat, or "out to pasture" in the case of sheep) for a period of time, then returning him to the laboratory for a retention test. Under these circumstances, little forgetting is found. However, if forgetting is largely due to interference processes, such tests may provide very misleading indices of the amount of forgetting that occurs in the animal's natural state. This is because the laboratory environment is quite different from the environment in which the animal found himself both before and after the laboratory experience. Therefore the possibility of finding forgetting produced by interference is markedly reduced.

Finally, with regard to applicability, Saltz and Asdourian have suggested that the osmotic processes may be basic to a relatively commonly observed clinical phenomenon. Phobic responses at times are found to start with fear of one specific aspect of the environment; they then may spread to other aspects of the environment. The osmotic process may provide a mechanism to account for such spread. In addition, the individual differences aspect of the osmotic process may account for the difference between those phobics who show such a spread and those who do not.

A Stage Theory for Discrimination Learning?

In a chapter as short as the present one, it is necessary to be very selective in the topics covered. The issue of whether a stage theory is necessary for discrimination learning is an appropriately relevant one with which to conclude for several reasons. For one, it illustrates an aspect of the cognitive space theory that was not so obvious in the previous sections. For another, implicit in this issue is a question that has been very central to the present chapter: Do we need different sets of basic laws to account for learning in rats and men? This question arises in discrimination learning because, at the behavioral level at least, there are marked qualitative differences in the discrimination learning of rats and men. In the present chapter the suggestion shall be explicated that these qualitative differences in behavior can be predicted on the basis of a theory that assumes the same basic processes operate in rats and man.

Since the scope of the present chapter does not permit an exhaustive review of the discrimination literature, we shall concentrate on two areas in which qualitative differences in behavior have been consistently reported. These areas are: the reversal-shift behavior, and the performance during the precriterion phase of discrimination learning.

Reversal shift. Let us first consider the reversal-shift problem. It is well known that animals have great difficulty learning the reversal of a previously acquired discrimination. For example, consider the situation in which the animals were first trained that they would be fed if they ran to the black side of a T-maze, but not if they ran to the white side. Next the discrimination was reversed so that food was to be found in the previously empty white side of the maze, while there was no longer any food on the previously rewarded black side. Why is this reversal shift so difficult to learn? According to a theory like that of Spence (1936), the acquisition of the approach tendency to black in the first phase was due to the gradual increments in association which accrued with successive reinforcements of the correct response (viz., the response of approaching black, in this example). In the reversal phase, association of approach to black is still strong and must be extinguished; the association for the new correct response, approach to white, is at first very weak since it has not previously been reinforced.

Turning to adult human subjects we find a dramatic qualitative difference in performance. Such subjects learn the reversal shift almost immediately. Much of the initial research on this topic was done by H. H. Kendler and T. S. Kendler and is summarized in a recent review (Kendler & Kendler, 1970). It is important to note that this rapid reversal cannot simply be attributed to the fact that humans learn faster than animals in general. This is shown by the performance of a control group in most of the studies by the Kendlers. This group learned a nonreversal shift. For example, consider a situation in which adults learned to chose a black stimulus but not a white in original training; the black might be large or small, with size varying randomly and being an irrelevant dimension as far as reinforcement is concerned. The *nonreversal* shift would involve shifting to one of the stimuli in the previously irrelevant size dimension; for example, in phase 2, the subject might be rewarded for choosing the larger stimulus: Note that in choosing the larger stimulus the subject must ignore the black-white dimension, since sometimes the large stimulus would be black, sometimes white. Compared to the reversal shift, the nonreversal shift proves to be very difficult for adults to learn.

To make the comparison between animals and adult humans complete, Kelleher (1956) has shown that rats learn a *nonreversal* shift more quickly than they learn a reversal shift. Clearly, rats and men behave very differently in such situations!

Is this difference in behavior strictly a species difference? No! One of the most fascinating aspects of the Kendler and Kendler (1970) research on reversal shift has been the finding that children form a link between rats and adult humans. Under the age of six, most children behave like the rats in that reversal shifts are more difficult than nonreversal shifts. After the age of six, more and more children show the adult pattern of reversal shifts *easier* than nonreversal.

The Kendlers have proposed what is essentially a stage theory to account for the data. They have suggested that discrimination learning in animals and young children follows the general theoretical model outlined by Spence (1936): that is, that such learning consists of the gradual developing associative strength between the correct stimulus and the relevant response; reversal learning involves the gradual extinction of the discrimination learned in phase 1, and the gradual development of association for the new S-R association. For human adults, on the other hand, a new set of additional processes comes into play, namely, the mediation mechanism. The assumption is made that when the adult learns the relevant discrimination, the external stimulus (e.g., a black card) evokes some relevant internal response (e.g., the verbal response, "color") which has cue properties; it is this internal cue which is associated to the overt response of selecting the black card as correct. A reversal shift permits the subject to use the same mediated response he learned in phase 1; he has merely to attach a new overt response to the mediated cue (e.g., he says, "Color," which is still correct, and must merely learn to choose the white card rather than the black). In the nonreversal shift, on the other hand, the subject must extinguish the previously acquired mediated response, in addition to extinguishing the overt response.

In short, the Kendlers propose a discontinuity of processes between rats and young children on the one hand, and older humans on the other.

Precriterion phase. The second area to be examined is that of the precriterion phase in discrimination learning. Precriterion learning curves for animals and adult humans have been found to differ dramatically. In animals, most studies find relatively gradual increments in performance before the animals respond at anywhere near 100% correct performance. A number of such studies are summarized by Kimble (1961, Ch. 12). On the other hand, human adults tend to show all-or-none learning curves. Bower and Trabasso (1964), and Levine, Miller, and Steinmeyer (1967), for example, find that adults perform at a chance level, with no sign of increments in performance, until the criterion block of trials; from this point on, the subjects make virtually no errors.

Again, as in the reversal-shift problems, young children appear to represent a link between rats and adults. Suppes and Ginsberg (1963) found strong evidence for gradual increases in probability of correct response during the precriterion period of discrimination learning when they reanalyzed several previously published studies involving 5- and 6-year-old children. This discrepancy between animals and humans raises the intriguing question as to whether there may be a communality in mechanisms between behavior observed in reversal-shift learning and the corresponding discrepancy in precriterion behavior. We have obtained some preliminary data on this issue in our laboratory at Wayne. Recall that in the reversal-shift data, 6 years of age appears to be the breaking point between ratlike and humanlike behavior: children younger than six tend to show the difficulty with reversal shift which is characteristic of rats; children older than six tend to show the facility with solving reversal-shift problems which is characteristic of human adults. If similar mechanisms are operating in the precriterion phenomena, we would expect to find a similar breaking point at around 6 years of age. Data from two unpublished studies, conducted at Wayne, are relevant to this issue. (One of these was performed by Mark Felton, the other by Shiela Lampert, 1972, of our Department.) In these two studies, employing completely different stimulus materials, we compared the precriterion performance of 4- and 8-year-olds (viz., 6 ± 2 years). Suppes and Ginsberg (1963) have suggested that the most sensitive test of precriterion data involves Vincentizing the data for each subject separately into quartiles, and this was done in both studies. In each of these studies we found a statistically significant tendency toward gradual increments in precriterion performance for the 4-year-olds. The 8-year-olds, on the other hand, showed no deviation from chance behavior during the precriterion trials.

How can we account for the difference between rat/child behavior as opposed to adult human behavior in precriterion learning? A number of psychologists (e.g., Kendler & Kendler, 1970) have suggested that the gradual increments found in rats and young children may indicate that these organisms learn discriminations in accordance with the Spence (1936) model of gradual increments in associative strength. Suppes and Ginsberg (1962) have suggested that children may tend to learn the discrimination task as though it consisted of a set of independent stimuli, rather than learning that a common basis of response is to be found in the various stimuli (i.e., they learn the task as though it were a list of paired associates). If each item is learned independently, this could lead to a learning curve that shows gradual improvement in correct responses across trials.

Turning to performance in adult human subjects, a number of psychologists (e.g., Restle, 1962) have proposed hypothesis-testing models in which nothing is learned until the subject tests the correct hypothesis concerning which aspect of the stimulus display will lead to consistently correct discriminative responses. Once the adult has the correct hypothesis, his learning curve jumps from chance to perfect performance.

In short, different mechanisms have been called into being to account for precriterion performance in rats, in children, and in adults.

Cognitive space model. Can a single set of assumptions be developed to handle the phenomena cited above? In this section, we shall examine some notions that move in this direction.

A number of studies, from the Wayne laboratories as well as from other sources, suggest that there are developmental trends with regard to the extent of the cognitive space which the organism can bound, or organize, into a single cognitive system. This leads to a marked tendency for children to have concepts which, from an adult point of view, are fragmented. Let us consider some examples of this tendency. Saltz and Sigel (1967) showed children pairs of pictures, each picture being that of a boy's face. The children were asked: Are these both pictures of the same boy, or of different boys? When the youngest children erred, it was in the direction of saying that two pictures were of *different* boys, when actually they were of the same boy. With increasing age, this tendency gradually disappeared; college-age subjects actually showed a slight tendency to say that two pictures were of the same boy, when actually they were of different boys. In other words, younger children tended to fragment the stimulus environment into more boys than actually existed, by dividing some of the boys into two.

At a somewhat more conceptual level, a similar tendency was found with regard to language concepts in a study by Saltz, Soller, and Sigel (in press). Here children were shown a set of 72 pictures and were asked to pick out, successively, those pictures which showed food, clothing, animals, and several other concepts. Consistent with the Saltz and Sigel study, younger children tended to have much more fragmented concepts than older children. For example, younger children considered clothing to be those things that fit on the body, and the body meant the human trunk, *sans* head or limbs; thus shoes, hats, and gloves were not considered clothing. Similarly, food was interpreted as referring to things eaten at mealtime; therefore there was a tendency not to include ice-cream cones or lollypops, though cake on a plate *was* included. The tendency toward fragmentation of concepts by young children can be found in many other studies (e.g., Annett, 1959).

If children do, indeed, fragment the cognitive space more than adults do, what implications would this have for the reversal-shift and precriterion data cited above? Let us consider the reversal shift first. Concept fragmentation would lead a child to learn several subconcepts in place of the single basis of discrimination which determines adult behavior. For example, if the correct response involved responding to a black stimulus, the young child might fragment the cognitive space into two subconcepts: black-large-left and black-small-left as one subconcept, black-large-right and black-small-right as the other. Note that if these where the relevant stimuli for discrimination behavior, reversal of reinforcement from black to white would, first of all, involve extinguishing the response to *two* discriminanda, since black-left would form the basis of one discriminandum, black-right the basis of a second. This fact in itself would retard the child in his learning of the reversal shift. But there is more than this involved. If black-left and black-right were two subconcepts, shifting from black to white would not be a simple reversal from one stimulus on a given dimension to a second stimulus on the same dimension since, *for the child,* two different dimensions are relevant, *color plus position.*

The issues are very similar for precriterion performance. If black is the relevant cue to correct performance, the adult will respond at a chance level as long as he remains unaware of this; once he notices that black is relevant, he can jump to perfect performance as long as he responds to this cue. The child, on the other hand, has organized his cognitive space into several subconcepts with regard to the relevant discriminanda; he must learn each of these separately. Therefore his performance could not jump from chance to perfect performance in one trial.

Before we present some of the evidence supporting this interpretation, several points must be emphasized. First, note that this position is not the same as that of Suppes and Ginsberg (1962), who suggest that the child treats each stimulus instance as discrete and unrelated to every other stimulus, and simply learns, in a rote manner, which stimuli to respond to and which not to respond to. Instead, the cognitive space position states that organisms *organize* discriminanda into units but that these units are smaller than optimal in size. Second, note that the present position assumes that the size of these fragmented units *increases* with age.

The position outlined above makes the basic assumption that there is one set of processes at work for rats, children, and adults in reversal shift and precriterion performance. The qualitative differences in behavior among these types of organisms is accounted for by the developmental changes in a variable that is continuous, in its operation, across all the organisms: that variable is the degree of fragmentation which the organism imposes on the cognitive representation of the relevant discriminandum. No new processes are invoked at age six to account for qualitative changes in behavior.

What data can we present in support of the cognitive space position? We have already seen that there are data in support of the proposition that children form fragmented concepts, and that this fragmentation decreases with age. Further, the unpublished work of Felton and by Lampert (1972), cited earlier, indicates that the qualitative changes between children and adults in reversal shift and in precriterion performance occur within approximately the same age interval; this supports the contention of a common basis for both these types of qualitative changes.

Another aspect of the unpublished experiment by Lampert (1972) goes even further in supporting the fragmentation explanation. Lampert (1972) examined the suggestion made by Suppes and Ginsberg (1962) that young children learn discrimination tasks as a series of paired associates. Suppes and Ginsberg came to this conclusion after fitting the discrimination learning data of 5- and 6-year-old children to two different models: one model assumed that the children learned that one critical cue was sufficient to determine correct performance (e.g., choose the black); the other model assumed that children learned which of the independent stimuli to choose, and which not to choose (e.g., the combination black-small-left is responded to independently of black-large-right without realizing that black, per se, is a sufficient cue).

Following the discrimination learning, Suppes and Ginsberg tested their subjects to determine if a generalized discrimination had been acquired, or if indeed the children had learned the task as a set of discrete responses to discrete stimuli. The test consisted of presenting new stimuli containing the critical cue. While some children were able to respond correctly to these new stimulus complexes, many could not. Apparently, at least some subjects had learned more than independent paired associates.

Note that the paired-associates learners represent the limiting case of our fragmentation notion, and we would not expect such extreme fragmentation except in the case of the very youngest children. Instead, we would expect larger subconcepts to develop of the sort described earlier in this chapter. Suppes and Ginsberg did not, of course, examine their data for the existence of such intermediate-sized cognitive units.

How do we investigate whether the young children are learning paired associates or subconcepts? The critical manipulation in the Lampert study involved arbitrarily calling one of the instances incorrect, which would normally be considered correct. For example, if black were the relevant cue, all stimulus instances involving black would normally be considered correct; in the type of manipulation used by Lampert, one of the instances containing black would be arbitrarily considered as a noninstance of the discriminandum (e.g., black-small-left might be considered a noninstance, while black-small-right, black-large-left, and black-large-right were considered correct discriminanda).

If children were learning the stimuli as a paired-associates list, the arbitrary designation of one stimulus as incorrect would have little effect on learning. Further, that stimulus should not be more difficult to learn than any of the others. Instead, Lampert found that the stimulus which had been arbitrarily designated as incorrect was the most difficult to learn for both 4- and 8-year-old children. At both ages, the last error before criterion was almost always the arbitrarily designated stimulus. This effect was, statistically, strongly significant.

Thus, despite the fact that the 4-year-old children typically show gradual increments in performance during the precriterion period, they are learning discrimination units that are larger than the single stimulus—in short, they appear to be learning fragmented subconcepts.

What is the status of the fragmented-subconcepts notion, vis-à-vis our understanding of the qualitative discontinuities in behavior between rat/child, on the one hand, and human adult on the other? Clearly, in this section we have *stated* an issue, we have not *resolved* it.

CONCLUSIONS

This section started with the assumption that psychologists in the areas of instrumental learning and conditioning have not spent enough time trying to analyze the characteristics of the learning variables, per se. Instead, they have tended to concentrate on relating a single practice variable to various motivational variables in an attempt to predict behavior. This focus on the relationship between practice and motivation has been valuable, but it has left many questions unanswered.

On the other hand, psychologists in the areas of human verbal learning and higher mental processes have been developing more complex notions concerning the structure of learning. In the present chapter we have examined several attempts to relate these notions back to the areas of the instrumental learning and conditioning. How useful will these attempts prove to be? Only time will tell. However, potentially at least, they provide several sets of mechanisms which, in interaction with one another, open broad possibilities for predicting complex behavior patterns.

REFERENCES

Amsel, A. The role of frustrative nonreward in noncontinuous reward situations. *Psychological Bulletin,* 1958, **55**, 102–119.

Annett, M. The classification of instances of four common class concepts by children and adults. *British Journal of Educational Psychology,* 1959, **29**, 223–236.

Bower, G. H., & Trabasso, T. R. Concept identification. In R. C. Atkinson (Ed.), *Studies in mathematical psychology.* Stanford, Calif.: Stanford University Press, 1964.

Cerekwicki, L. E., Grant, D. A., & Porter, E. C. The effect of number and relatedness of verbal discriminanda upon differential eyelid conditioning. *Journal of Verbal Learning and Verbal Behavior,* 1968; **7**, 847–853.

Coppock, W. J. Preextinction in sensory preconditioning. *Journal of Experimental Psychology,* 1958, **55**, 213–219.

Cotton, J. W. Running time as a function of amount of food deprivation. *Journal of Experimental Psychology,* 1953, **46**, 188–198.

Gibson, E. J. A systematic of the concepts of generalization and differentiation to verbal learning. *Psychological Review,* 1940, **47**, 196–229.

Grant, D. A. A preliminary model for processing information conveyed by verbal conditioned stimuli in classical conditioning. In A. H. Black & W. F. Prokasy (Eds.), *Classical conditioning II: Current theory and research*. New York: Meredith, 1972.

Grant, D. A., Levy, C. M., Thompson, J., Hickok, C. W., & Bunde, D. C. Transfer of differential eyelid conditioning through successive discriminations. *Journal of Experimental Psychology*, 1967, **75**, 246–254.

Guthrie, E. R. Conditioning as a principle of learning. *Psychological Review*, 1930, **37**, 412–428.

Guthrie, E. R. *The psychology of learning*. New York: Harper, 1935.

Hull, C. L. The conflicting psychologies of learning. A way out. *Psychological Review*, 1935, **42**, 491–516.

Hull, C. L. *Principles of behavior*. New York: Appleton-Century-Crofts, 1943.

Kelleher, R. T. Discrimination learning as a function of reversal and nonreversal shifts. *Journal of Experimental Psychology*, 1956, **51**, 379–384.

Kendler, H. H., & Kendler, T. S. Developmental processes in discrimination learning. *Human Development*, 1970, **13**, 65–89.

Kimble, G. A. *Hilgard and Marquis' conditioning and learning*. New York: Appleton-Century-Crofts, 1961.

Lampert, S. *The psychological structure of concepts in children and the nature of structural changes occurring with age*. Unpublished masters thesis, Wayne State University, 1972.

Levine, M., Miller, P. I., and Steinmeyer, H. The none-to-all theorem of human discrimination learning. *Journal of Experimental Psychology*, 1967, **73**, 568–573.

Marx, M. H., & Brownstein, A. J. Effects of incentive magnitude on running speeds without competing responses in acquisition and extinction. *Journal of Experimental Psychology*, 1963, **65**, 182–189.

Mateer, F. *Child behavior: A critical and experimental study of young children by the method of conditioned reflexes*. Boston: Badger, 1918.

McAllister, W. R., & McAllister, D. E. Postconditioning delay and intensity of shock as factors in the measurement of acquired fear. *Journal of Experimental Psychology*, 1962, **64**, 110–116.

Murdock, B. B., Jr. The retention of individual items. *Journal of Experimental Psychology*, 1961, **62**, 618–625.

Newton, J. M., & Wickens, D. D. Retroactive inhibition as a function of the temporal position of the interpolated learning. *Journal of Experimental Psychology*, 1956, **51**, 149–154.

Pereboom, A. C., and Crawford, B. M. Instrumental and competing behavior as a function of trials and reward magnitude. *Journal of Experimental Psychology*, 1958, **20**, 244–261.

Perkins, C. C., Jr., & Weyant, R. G. The interval between training and test trials as a determiner of the slope of generalization gradients. *Journal of Comparative and Physiological Psychology*, 1958, **51**, 596–600.

Peterson, L. R., & Peterson, M. J. Short-term retention of individual verbal items. *Journal of Experimental Psychology*, 1959, **58**, 193–198.

Restle, F. The selection of strategies in cue learning. *Psychological Review*, 1962, **69**, 329–343.

Saltz, E. Response pretraining: Differentiation or availability? *Journal of Experimental Psychology*, 1961, **62**, 538–587.

Saltz, E. *The cognitive bases of human learning*. Homewood, Ill.: Dorsey Press, 1971.

Saltz, E., & Asdourian, D. Incubation of anxiety as a function of cognitive differentiation. *Journal of Experimental Psychology*, 1963, **66**, 17–22.

Saltz, E., & Felton, M. Response pretraining and subsequent paired-associate learning. *Journal of Experimental Psychology*, 1968, **77**, 258–262.

Saltz, E., & Sigel, I. E. Concept overdiscrimination in children. *Journal of Experimental Psychology*, 1967, **73**, 1–8.

Saltz, E., Soller, E., & Sigel, I. E. The development of natural language concepts. *Child Development*, in press.

Saltz, E., Whitman, R. N., & Paul, C. Performance in the runway as a function of stimulus differentiation. *American Journal of Psychology*, 1963, **76**, 124–127.

Sokolov, E. N. *Perception and the conditioned reflex.* London: Pergamon Press, 1963.

Spence, K. W. The nature of discrimination learning in animals. *Psychological Review*, 1936, **43**, 427–449.

Spence, K. W. *Behavior theory and conditioning.* New Haven: Yale University Press, 1956.

Spence, K. W., & Taylor, J. A. Anxiety and strength of the UCS as determiners of amount of eyelid conditioning. *Journal of Experimental Psychology*, 1951, **42**, 183–188.

Suppes, P., & Ginsberg, R. A. Application of a stimulus-sampling model to children's concept formation with and without correction of responses. *Journal of Experimental Psychology*, 1962, **63**, 330–336.

Suppes, P., and Ginsberg, R. A. A fundamental property of all-or-none models, binomial distribution of responses prior to conditioning, with application to concept formation in children. *Psychological Review*, 1963, **70**, 139–161.

Tolman, E. C. *Purposive behavior in animals and men.* New York: Appleton-Century-Crofts, 1932.

Underwood, B. J. Retroactive and proactive inhibition after five and forty-eight hours. *Journal of Experimental Psychology*, 1948, **38**, 29–38.

Voeks, V. W. Acquisition of S-R connections: A test of Hull's and Guthrie's theories. *Journal of Experimental Psychology*, 1954, **47**, 137–147.

Wickens, D. D., Born, D. G., & Allen, C. K. Proactive inhibition and item similarity in short-term memory. *Journal of Verbal Learning and Verbal Behavior*, 1963, **2**, 440–445.

3

REIFICATION AND REALITY IN CONDITIONING PARADIGMS: IMPLICATIONS OF RESULTS WHEN MODES OF REINFORCEMENT ARE CHANGED[1]

David A. Grant
University of Wisconsin – Madison

This chapter will deal with certain specific inadequacies in the paradigms or didactic diagrams that are commonly used by psychology teachers in instructing students respecting classical and instrumental conditioning. These inadequacies were pinpointed in eyelid-conditioning experiments when the mode of reinforcement was shifted from instrumental reward or classical instrumental avoidance training to classical reinforcement and when the mode of reinforcement was shifted from classical to instrumental reward or classical instrumental avoidance training. The experiments themselves were performed to investigate some of the implications of the Soviet psychology of volition in the context of eyelid conditioning. Because certain inadequacies of the conditioning paradigms can be fairly clearly specified, it is possible in this chapter to propose certain changes and elaborations of the diagrams which should improve the diagrams for didactic purposes, for the planning of research, and for interpreting of research findings.

THE SOVIET PSYCHOLOGY OF VOLITION AND THE TRANSFER OF CONDITIONED RESPONSES

The general topic of transfer of training is very important to psychological learning theory, and, in practice, an understanding of transfer is crucial to the success of all education and training programs. The Soviet psychology of volition requires certain very specific kinds of transfer of conditioned responses, and

[1] Preparation of this paper and the research reported were supported in large part by USPHS research grant MH 06792. Additional support was provided by the National Science Foundation and the Wisconsin Alumni Research Foundation.

because the theory and methodology of conditioning is relatively well developed, investigation of transfer in the context of conditioning should prove to be feasible and should contribute generally to our knowledge of transfer of training.

The Soviet account of the development of voluntary control of behavior involves a sequence of transfers of conditioned responses to different conditioned stimuli and the preservation of the conditioning under changed modes of reinforcement (Luria, 1961; Pavlov, 1955). To summarize this account briefly, a response that cannot be performed voluntarily is first conditioned classically to an initial CS which might be nonverbal, involving the first signaling system only, or verbal, which would involve the first and second signaling systems (Ivanov-Smolensky, 1956). After initial conditioning, the CR may be transferred to a new CS which might be a verbalization supplied by the experimenter or the subject. The second CS could then be reduced to a subvocalization by the subject, which would still evoke the CR. With continuing performance of the CR to the subvocalization, a further change in the CS occurs so that the subject may no longer be aware of any subvocal activity, but the CR will still be performed "voluntarily" to unspecifiable internal conditioned stimuli. That is, the CS-CR association will have dropped out of the second signaling system.

The foregoing account of the development of voluntary control of a response requires: (a) that a CR can readily be transferred from the control of one CS to the control of another CS, and (b) that the CR will not extinguish, but will be preserved when the mode of reinforcement has been shifted from the original classical conditioning to some other mode of reinforcement, such as instrumental reward or instrumental avoidance. As an example, vomiting is not normally under voluntary control. In a child, however, nausea and vomiting can occur when it is being fed under circumstances of intense emotional conflict with its parents. In this situation the nausea can readily be conditioned to stimuli that normally occur at mealtime. If the conditioned nausea and vomiting responses enable the child to escape from an aversive feeding situation or to avoid the unpleasant consequences of failing to obey his parents' demands at mealtime, the child may readily learn to facilitate rather than to inhibit the conditioned nausea; and if these tactics are successful in controlling the parents' behavior, the child may further learn to vomit under many circumstances when it is subject to parental discipline. Thus the initial involuntary reflex comes under voluntary control, first by being conditioned to situational stimuli, then by transferring to overt and subvocal verbalization with instrumental avoidance reinforcement preventing the extinction of the conditioned nausea.

THE COMMON DIDACTIC DIAGRAMS OF CONDITIONING

Instructors and many textbooks of psychology use slight variations of the paradigms shown in Table 1 for classical conditioning, classical instrumental avoidance training, and instrumental reward training. In these diagrams the

TABLE 1

Diagrams Commonly Used to Instruct Students about Conditioning

Conditioning procedure	Pattern of reinforcement	Didactic paradigm or diagram
Classical conditioning	All trials reinforced; i.e., UCS follows CS	CS ⇌ OR (to CS) ↘ CR UCS ⟶ UCR
Classical instrumental avoidance training	UCS follows CS if no CR; UCS omitted if CR occurs	CS ⟶ CR (omission of aversive UCS)
Instrumental reward training	Reward given on trials when CR occurs	CS ⟶ CR (reward)

learned response is often indicated by the common acronym for a conditioned response, CR. The use of this acronym for the learned response in classical, instrumental avoidance, and instrumental reward paradigms would seem to imply that the second requirement for the Soviet psychology of volition could readily be met; that is, a response conditioned under one mode of reinforcement would be available and would be performed when the mode of reinforcement was changed. The research to be reported indicates, however, that these paradigms should be elaborated and corrected because they can be seriously misleading.

In general, teachers and investigators recognize that paradigms should inform and instruct their students, clarify their own research planning, and aid in the interpretation of their research results. Mature investigators and teachers recognize, however, that paradigms can misinform their students and can confuse and mislead the investigator in his research planning and in the interpretation of his research results. Most investigators in the area of conditioning recognize that the diagrams in Table 1 are oversimplifications, and they use very different and more elaborate diagrams to aid them in their research. Typically, research findings reveal the oversimplification of diagrams used initially, and the diagrams are corrected and elaborated so that the initial paradigm becomes progressively more useful and more adequate in accounting for psychological phenomena. As an example of the evolution of paradigms, the A-B, A-C and the A-B, C-B transfer diagrams have evolved into an enormous and diverse progeny of paradigms that are used in the investigation of verbal transfer and interference and in the instruction of students of verbal learning (Grose & Birney, 1963; Kausler, 1966). Curiously enough, however, in spite of the vast research on classical conditioning, the venerable diagrams of Table 1 with only slight variations continue to appear in elementary textbooks and in textbooks on the psychology of learning.

The diagrams in Table 1 will be explained in terms of procedures used in our laboratory. With classical conditioning (Fleming & Grant, 1966), the CS is always presented visually. It might be a word, a visual form, or simply the illumination of a ground-glass window. Initially, the CS usually elicits a short latency eyelid response and probably other orienting reactions. During the training phase, the CS is always followed by presentation of the UCS, a corneal air-puff, which elicits a sharp, complete eyelid closure, the UCR. Following a number of paired presentations of the CS and the UCS, a new eyelid closure begins to appear with a latency of 200 milliseconds or more but anticipatory to the presentation of the UCS. A given subject will usually give an eyelid CR that shows one of two topographies, the C-form or the V-form (Hartman & Ross, 1961). (The C-form is a gradual incomplete closure of limited duration, and the V-form is a more abrupt, complete, and prolonged closure of the eyelid.) Accordingly, the subjects may be classified as Vs or Cs (Grant, 1972).

Classical instrumental avoidance training (Hansche & Grant, 1965; Hellige, 1972) is given by adjusting the recording equipment so that a relay is triggered by any eyelid response that would be scored as a classical CR if classical reinforcement were being used. The relay will eliminate delivery of the air-puff on all trials when a CR with the proper latency and amplitude occurs. On trials when no CR occurs, the air-puff UCS will be delivered to the subject's cornea.

With instrumental reward training the air-puff is never used. The recording equipment is arranged so that the relay triggered by the eyelid response will produce illumination of a light bulb and will operate an electric counter 1/2 second after the response. The subjects have been told that this signifies a correct response, but they are not told just what a correct response might be. Operation of the light and the counter is thus given a symbolic reward value. On trials when no CR is performed, the symbolic reward is not given the subject (Cerekwicki & Grant, 1967).

TRANSFER OF THE CR TO A NEW CS WHEN THE MODE OF REINFORCEMENT IS UNCHANGED

The first experiment to be reported tests the first requirement of the Soviet account of the acquisition of voluntary control, i.e., that a CR can readily be transferred from the control of one CS to the control of another CS. In this experiment (Grant, Levy, Thompson, Hickok, & Bunde, 1967), the eyelid response was first differentially conditioned to an initial pair of conditioned stimuli, where the CS+ was reinforced 30 times with the air-puff, and the CS− was given 30 nonreinforced trials, randomly interspersed with the reinforced trials of CS+. After the initial differential conditioning, a new pair of stimuli became CS+ and CS−, and they were given 40 trials of differential reinforcement. Then a third new pair of stimuli were similarly reinforced, and finally a fourth pair were employed, so that there were four successive conditioned discriminations involved in the experimental procedure. In the primary experiment five groups of subjects were employed. The stimuli were visually presented unrelated words, or Vanderplas and Garvin (1959) random shapes, or the numerals 0 through 9, omitting 1 and 8, or the same numbers spelled out. For four of the groups the successive pairs of differential stimuli were all of the same type, that is, all were pairs of words, or pairs of numbers, etc. The fifth group received a mixed sequence of pairs of differential stimuli. First they were differentially conditioned to a pair of visual forms, next to a pair of numerals, third to a pair of spelled numbers, and finally to a pair of words. All of the

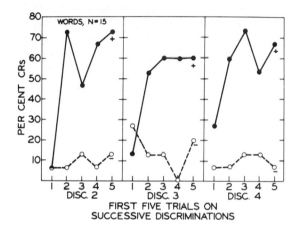

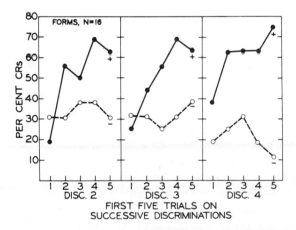

FIG. 1. Transfer of conditioned discrimination to new pairs of differential conditioned stimuli. CR performance to CS+ and CS− on the first five trials of the second, third, and fourth discriminations in the Grant, Levy, Thompson, Hickok, and Bunde (1967) experiment.

differential stimuli were readily discriminable, and only the Vanderplas and Garvin forms were unfamiliar.

During the first discrimination, the CR itself had to be learned, as well as the contingencies between the differential stimuli and the reinforcement. In the second, third, and fourth discriminations, because the CR had already been learned and was available, the subject had simply to familiarize himself with the new differential stimuli and, on the basis of the differential reinforcement contingencies, establish associations between the new differential conditioned stimuli and the CR. Acquisition of the first discrimination was rather gradual because of the necessity for response learning, whereas transfer to the new pairs of differential stimuli in Discriminations 2, 3, and 4 was quite rapid, especially with the familiar, unrelated words which are highly distinctive stimuli.

Figure 1 shows some of the data from the experiment. In Figure 1 are plotted the percent CRs to CS+ and CS− *trial by trial* for the first five trials of the second, third, and fourth discriminations, respectively. The upper panel shows the results when words were used as differential stimuli, and the lower panel shows the results when the unfamiliar random forms were used. It is obvious that with words, after one reinforcement of CS+ and one nonreinforcement of CS−, the discriminative performance is almost at asymptote. This shows that when the stimuli are familiar and distinct, the transfer of a differential CR from one pair of stimuli to another pair is virtually immediate. The transfer is not quite so rapid with the unfamiliar forms, because the subject must familiarize himself with the new stimuli. The results of the Grant et al. (1967) experiment would seem to indicate that the first requirement of the Soviet psychology of volition−that the CR readily transfers from one CS to another−is met, as such transfers do indeed take place in the context of differential eyelid conditioning.

CR PERFORMANCE TO THE ORIGINAL CS
WHEN THE MODE OF REINFORCEMENT
IS CHANGED

As stated earlier, a second requirement of the Soviet account of the acquisition of voluntary control over a response is that the response, conditioned by one kind of reinforcement procedure, must continue to be performed when the mode of reinforcement is changed. The implications of the conditioning paradigms of Table 1 are such that one would expect: (a) *symmetry of transfer,* that is, more or less the same amount of transfer of conditioning as the reinforcement is changed from any one kind to any other kind; and (b) *progressive transfer,* that is, that the amount of transfer of conditioning from the first mode of reinforcement to the second mode of reinforcement should be a progressively increasing function of the number of reinforcements with the first mode of training. Such predictions are implied by the use of the common acronym for the conditioned response, CR, in each of the three diagrams.

To investigate whether or not symmetric and progressive transfer does occur, two experiments were performed in which the experimental designs and procedures followed the same pattern. In each, there were two stages of reinforcement. In Stage I, the subject received 0, 5, 10, or 20 reinforcements by either classical, instrumental reward, or classical instrumental avoidance training. Then in Stage II the subjects received 60 more training trials with the same CS as in Stage I, but with the mode of reinforcement changed to one different from that employed in Stage I. In the first experiment (Grant, Knoll, Kantowitz, Zajano, & Solberg, 1969), one-half of the subjects were shifted from classical to instrumental reward training, CL-IR, and the other half of the subjects were shifted from instrumental reward to classical reinforcement, IR-CL. Some of the results of this experiment are shown in Figure 2.

In the upper panel of Figure 2 the percent frequency and the amplitude of instrumental responses of the CL-IR groups during the second stage of the experiment are plotted as a function of the number of classical reinforcements given in Stage I. It is clear that the frequency and amplitude of instrumental responses during Stage II is an increasing function of the number of classical reinforcements given in Stage I. The upper panel indicates, therefore, that classically conditioning the eyelid response makes available in Stage II a CR that transfers readily and facilitates subsequent instrumental conditioning performance. This interpretation is also consistent with the fact that there was a clear tendency for a subject to give a CR with the same topography during the instrumental reward stage as he had learned to give during the classical reinforcement stage, even if its topography were of the C-form, which is rarely produced by instrumental reward training.

The lower panel of Figure 2 shows the percent conditioned responses during the classical conditioning stage for Vs and Cs during acquisition and extinction as a function of the number of contingent instrumental reinforcements in Stage I for the IR-CL groups. In Panel 2 it is clear that neither for the Vs nor for the Cs is there an orderly increase in the percent of classical CRs in Stage II as the function of an increasing number of instrumental reinforcements in Stage I. Furthermore, the trial-by-trial plots (not shown) during Stage II of the IR-CL groups were unusual in that they did not show a progressive acquisition of the classical CR by the Vs. And the somewhat more usual increasing acquisition functions for the CRs of the Cs were not correlated with the number of instrumental reinforcements during Stage I. Finally, there was no correlation between the CR response topography in the classical training of Stage II with the CR topography during the instrumental training of Stage I.

Thus, the results of this experiment show an asymmetry in transfer of conditioning when the mode of reinforcement is changed. Although there is progressively greater transfer to instrumental conditioning as the number of classical pretransfer reinforcements increase, there is no such orderly or progressive increase in transfer to classical conditioning as a function of the number of pretransfer instrumentally reinforced responses.

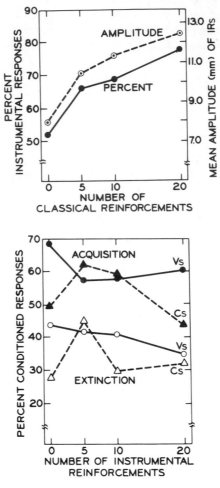

FIG. 2. Stage II conditioning performance as a function of the number of Stage I reinforcements with a different reinforcement technique. The upper panel shows percent responses with Stage II instrumental reward training following 0, 5, 10, or 20 Stage I classical reinforcements. The lower panel shows responses with Stage II classical conditioning reinforcement following Stage I instrumental reward reinforcements. (Data from Grant, Kroll, Kantowitz, Zajano, & Solberg, 1969.)

In the second experiment (Hellige, 1972), one-half of the subjects received 0, 5, 10, or 20 classical reinforcements during Stage I, which were followed by 60 trials of classical instrumental avoidance training during Stage II (CL-AV groups). The other half of the subjects received 0, 5, 10, or 20 classical instrumental avoidance reinforcements during Stage I, and these were followed by 60 trials of classical reinforcement during Stage II (AV-CL groups). Some of the results of this experiment are presented in Figure 3. In the upper panel the percent avoidance CRs during the first 10-trial block of Stage II are plotted separately for Vs and Cs as a function of the number of Stage I classical reinforcements for the CL-AV groups. In the lower panel the percent classical

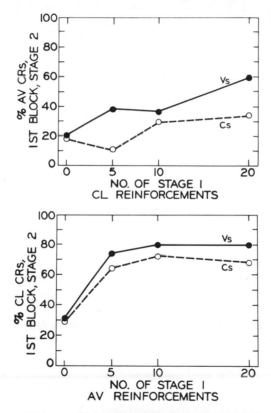

FIG. 3. Conditioning performance on the first 10-trial block of Stage II as a function of the number of Stage I reinforcements with a different reinforcing technique. The upper panel shows percent responses with Stage II classical instrumental avoidance reinforcement following 0, 5, 10, or 20 Stage I classical reinforcements. The lower panel shows the percent CRs with Stage II classical reinforcement following Stage I classical instrumental avoidance reinforcements. (Data from Hellige, 1972.)

CRs during the first 10-trial block of Stage II are plotted separately for Vs and Cs as a function of the number of Stage I avoidance reinforcements for Groups AV-CL. The data in the upper panel show that response rate during the initial block of avoidance training trials in the CL-AV groups was a progressively increasing function of the number of pretransfer classical reinforcements. After the first 10-trial avoidance block, however, the percent avoidance CRs converged to about the same value for all four groups (see Figure 4) so that at the end of the experiment all groups were giving avoidance CRs at about the same rate.

The lower panel shows that during the first 10-trial block of Stage II the percent classical CRs for both Vs and Cs increased from 30% for those subjects who had received no avoidance reinforcements on Stage I to a more or less constant level of from 63 to 68% for Cs and from 73 to 80% for Vs who had received 5, 10, or 20 avoidance reinforcements in Stage I. In other words, as few as 5 avoidance reinforcements appeared to be almost as effective as 20 avoidance reinforcements in improving classical conditioning performance during Stage II. Thus the Hellige experiment, like that of Grant et al. (1969), showed fairly orderly symmetric and progressive transfer from classical to the instrumental mode of reinforcement, but the transfer from classical instrumental avoidance reinforcement to classical reinforcement appeared to be more orderly and progressive in the Hellige experiment than was the transfer from instrumental reinforcement to classical reinforcement in the Grant et al. (1969) experiment.

The results of the Grant et al. (1969) and the Hellige (1972) experiments may be summarized by stating that in the context of eyelid-conditioning contingencies, the second requirement for the Soviet account of the acquisition of voluntary control is met when the initial conditioning is by classical reinforcement and the transfer is to classical avoidance reinforcement or positive instrumental reinforcement. If the initial conditioning is by means of classical avoidance training and the transfer is to classical reinforcement, there is good evidence for positive transfer, but the adequacy of transfer from instrumental reward training to classical reinforcement is questionable. It should be noted, however, that in the Soviet account it is extremely unlikely that transfer from other modes of reinforcement to classical reinforcement would ever be required.

The fact that with eyelid conditioning CR performance will continue when the mode of reinforcement is changed from classical to instrumental reward or classical instrumental avoidance, combined with the fact that a CR differentially conditioned to one CS+–CS– pair of stimuli will transfer quickly to a new CS+–CS– pair, suggests strongly that two of the crucial requirements for the validity of the Soviet account of acquisition of voluntary control of a response have been met. Although responses other than the eyelid response may show special complicating features, the basic required transfers of conditioning processes seem to take place quite readily.

DIFFICULTIES WITH THE CONDITIONING PARADIGMS

The detailed results of the Grant et al. (1969) and Hellige (1972) experiments show that CR transfer when the mode of reinforcement is changed is not as simple and straightforward as the oversimplified didactic paradigms of Table 1 would imply. The keys to the difficulties with the didactic diagrams are the asymmetries in Stage II CR performance that were obtained with four different kinds of reinforcement changes, CL-IR, IR-CL, CL-AV, and AV-CL. The asymmetries in transfer of conditioning pinpoint the difficulties with the paradigms and also suggest simple corrections and elaborations of them which should make them more valuable for instructing students and for planning and interpreting research on the different reinforcement procedures used in conditioning.

Two of the differences in Stage II performance have been described earlier, and to these a third difference would be added. The first asymmetry in Stage II performance was that although the Stage II performance of the CR in the CL-IR shift was a progressively increasing function of the number of pretransfer classical reinforcements, the Stage II performance CR in the IR-CL shift was not. In the Grant et al. (1969) experiment there was even some indication of a negative transfer effect during CL training following the largest number (20) of pretransfer instrumental reward reinforcements. The second difference is between Stage II CR performance with instrumental reward and classical reinforcement following 0, 5, 10, and 20 classical reinforcements and classical avoidance reinforcements, respectively. Whereas the Stage II CRs with instrumental reward were a progressively increasing function of the number of pretransfer classical reinforcements, the Stage II CR performance with classical reinforcement showed no increase as the number of pretransfer avoidance reinforcements was increased from 5 to 20. The third difference to be described was between the set of acquisition curves for the instrumental responses in Stage II of the Grant et al. (1969) experiment and the set of acquisition curves for the avoidance responses of Stage II of the Hellige experiment. In both experiments, Stage II acquisition followed 0, 5, 10, or 20 pretransfer classical reinforcements. These differences in the learning curves are diagramed in Figure 4. In the upper panel of Figure 4 the set of acquisition curves for the four CL-IR groups are diagramed roughly, with percent instrumental responses as a function of successive 10-trial instrumental reinforcement blocks. The parameter is the number of pretransfer classical reinforcements. In the lower panel the set of acquisition functions for the avoidance responses in the CL-AV groups are plotted similarly for the six 10-trial avoidance training blocks. It will be noted that the acquisition curves for the instrumental responses are roughly parallel, so that the initial superiority of the subjects who have received 20 classical reinforcements in Stage I over the performance of the other groups is retained throughout the 60 trials of instrumental reward training. In contrast, although the CR performance on the initial block of avoidance training was a progressively increasing function of the number of Stage I classical reinforcements, thereafter all four

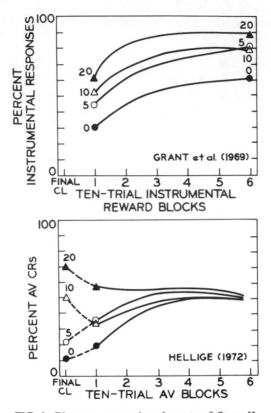

FIG. 4. Diagrams comparing the sets of Stage II acquisition functions for responses conditioned with instrumental reward reinforcement following 0, 5, 10, or 20 Stage I classical reinforcements (*upper panel*; from Grant, Kroll, Kantowitz, Zajano, & Solberg, 1969) with the Stage II acquisition functions for responses conditioned by classical instrumental avoidance reinforcement following 0, 5, 10, or 20 Stage I classical reinforcements (*lower panel*; from Hellige, 1972).

curves tend to converge to a common asymptote. Thus the progressive positive transfer effect from classical training appeared only on the initial Stage II blocks.[2]

Examination of the details of the experiments and the eyelid-response tracings obtained revealed the probable reasons for the three departures from the

[2] It should be noted that with the experimental conditions and instructions used in our laboratory, eyelid conditioning with classical instrumental avoidance reinforcement is apparently an automatic process that requires no cognitive mediation on the part of the subject. Among over 180 subjects who have received avoidance training, only one was able to report postexperimentally that performance of an eyelid response led to the omission of the air-puff (Grant, 1972).

prediction that symmetric and progressive transfer of conditioning should occur during Stage II, when the mode of reinforcement had been changed, as a function of the pretransfer reinforcements during Stage I. First, the anomalous IR-CL transfer can probably be traced in part to: (a) asymmetries in the instructions at the Stage I–Stage II transition between the IR-CL shift and the CL-IR shift procedures, and (b) problems with the topography of the instrumentally conditioned CR. The records show that the topography of these CRs is often ineffective in avoiding the air-puff UCS during Stage II, although the topography had been quite adequate to trigger the instrumental reinforcement equipment during Stage I. With 20 instrumental reinforcements in Stage I, the response topography was so thoroughly learned that it was resistant to change so as to become more effective in avoiding the puff during Stage II classical reinforcement. In short, with instrumental reward reinforcement the CR that was learned was not the same response as the CR that is usually learned with classical reinforcement. The common acronym CR in the Table 1 diagrams is therefore misleading and easily leads to reification; the acronyms should not be the same in all three diagrams.

Second, to account for the failure of 10 and 20 avoidance reinforcements, as compared with 5 avoidance reinforcements, to produce progressively better responding in Stage II classical training, requires consideration of the number of trials during Stage I training where the CR was not performed. These trials result in the delivery of a classical reinforcement to the subject. The four AV-CL groups, in addition to receiving 0, 5, 10, and 20 avoidance reinforcements, also received, on the average, 0, 9.3, 13.4, and 16.8 classical reinforcements, respectively, on Stage I trials when the CR was not performed. Thus, each of the three groups receiving avoidance reinforcements also received enough classical reinforcements to produce maximal associative strength (Kimble & Dufort, 1956),[3] so that it is not surprising that their subsequent CR performance during Stage II was very similar. Because the classical reinforcements during classical avoidance conditioning of the eyelid are thought to be a significant feature in response acquisition (Kimble, 1961; Kimble, Mann, & Dufort, 1955; Logan, 1951; Hellige, 1972), these classical reinforcements must be included explicitly in the paradigm for classical avoidance training procedures.

Third, the fact that learning curves for the response with instrumental reinforcements following classical reinforcement remain more or less parallel, whereas the acquisition curves for the CR under avoidance reinforcement following classical reinforcement converge, requires consideration of the differences between the reinforcement schedules for instrumental reward training on the one hand and classical instrumental avoidance training on the

---

[3] It should be noted that the experimental results upon which Kimble and Dufort based their notion, that in classical eyelid conditioning perhaps as few as three to five reinforcements are sufficient to produce maximal associative strength, have proved difficult to replicate (Ross & Hartman, 1965, pp. 185–186), suggesting that the original findings require a certain combination of subject characteristics and experimental conditions.

other hand. With instrumental reward training, every single response is reinforced in the same way, that is, with a symbolic reward. With instrumental avoidance training, however, there is both an adding and subtracting feature. Each performance of a CR involves successful avoidance of the air-puff and presumably an avoidance reinforcement. However, at the same time, each performance of an avoidance CR eliminates one classical reinforcement with the air-puff, and this should have an extinction effect. The higher the percent avoidance responses, the more classical extinction trials are being given, so that one might expect an equilibrium to occur between the effect of avoidance reinforcement and the effect of classical extinction processes. This equilibrium would account for the convergence of the curves in the Hellige experiment.

The fact that the avoidance response has a double function of providing an avoidance reinforcement and a classical extinction trial must also be shown explicitly in the paradigm for classical instrumental avoidance training by distinguishing between the two types of trials, those on which an avoidance CR is performed and those on which an avoidance CR is not performed.

CORRECTION AND ELABORATION OF THE CONDITIONING PARADIGMS

Note that it is first desirable to make an explicit distinction between instrumental avoidance training where the aversive stimulus to be avoided will normally evoke a UCR that is highly compatible with the required avoidance response, and the case where the aversive reinforcement will normally evoke a UCR that is unrelated to the required avoidance response. The former will be called *classical instrumental avoidance training,* and the latter will be called simply *instrumental avoidance training.* In avoidance experiments the apparatus can be arranged so that almost any response arbitrarily selected by the experimenter will produce omission of the aversive stimulus, and will by definition be the avoidance response. This response may or may not be related to the UCR evoked by the aversive stimulus itself. If the UCR to the aversive stimulus is highly compatible with the avoidance response, the aversive stimulus is essentially a classical UCS for the avoidance response, and omission of the UCS should produce a classical extinction effect. If the UCR to the aversive stimulus is unrelated to the avoidance response, omission of the aversive stimulus need not produce a classical extinction effect.

The diagrams of conditioning are presented in Table 2, revised in such a way as to correct for the inadequacies described in the preceding section of this chapter. The only revisions in the diagrams for classical reinforcement: (*a*) place the CS, CR, UCS, and UCR in the temporal relationship usually found in conditioning experiments; and (*b*) indicate that the UCR is a complex of responses of which the CR (usually) is a component.

The paradigm for classical instrumental avoidance training makes explicit the fact that two kinds of trials may occur: (*a*) an avoidance trial, where the CR

TABLE 2

Revised Diagrams of the Conditioning Procedures

Conditioning procedure	Pattern of reinforcement	Didactic paradigm or diagram
Classical conditioning	All trials reinforced; i.e., UCS follows CS	CS ⇄ OR (to CS) ⟶ CR UCS ⟶ UCR complex (incl. CR)
Classical instrumental avoidance training	Avoidance reinforcement and classical extinction trial	CS ⟶ avoidance response (AR) ⟶ no UCS
	Classically reinforced trial	CS ⟶ no avoidance response ⟶ UCS Note: also UCS = produced drive
Instrumental reward training	Reinforced trial	CS ⟶ instrumental response (IR) ⟶ reward
	Nonreinforced trial	CS ⟶ no instrumental response ⟶ no reward

occurs and the UCS is omitted, making it an avoidance reinforcement and a classical extinction trial; and (b) a classically reinforced trial, where the CR does not occur, so that a classical reinforcement with the UCS is given the S. It should also be noted that, with classical instrumental avoidance training, omission of the UCS on an avoidance reinforcement trial may reduce UCS-produced drive, and inclusion of the UCS on a classically reinforced trial may increase UCS-produced drive (Spence, 1958). As the avoidance response can be arbitrarily selected by the experimenter, it is designated as an AR rather than a CR, because it may bear no resemblance to the CR in classical conditioning. Of course in classical instrumental avoidance training the AR will necessarily resemble the classically conditioned CR to some extent. It is clear from the revised paradigm of classical instrumental avoidance training that two kinds of conditioning and extinction may be taking place simultaneously and that their reinforcement effects may be opposed to each other. The avoidance reinforcement involves classical extinction, and the classical reinforcement involves avoidance extinction, although the avoidance extinction would presumably not take place unless the aversiveness of the UCS were inescapable.

The paradigm for instrumental reward training has also been elaborated to make explicit the fact that two types of trials occur, reinforced trials and nonreinforced trials. The response to be rewarded may be arbitrarily defined, so that it is designated an IR rather than a CR, as it may bear no resemblance to the classically conditioned CR. It is clear from the instrumental reward training paradigm that in it, as opposed to the paradigm for classical instrumental avoidance training, only a single reinforcement process is involved, so that there will be no opposition between two modes of reinforcement with instrumental reward training.

Consideration of the revised diagrams of the conditioning processes in Table 2 suggests a nice analogy between the three conditioning procedures and the kinetics of three common chemical reactions. Classical conditioning is similar to a simple first-order reaction where Molecule A is being converted to Molecule B. Classical instrumental avoidance training is analogous to a first-order reaction where there is an opposing back reaction; that is, Molecule A is converted to Molecule B at a certain rate, and Molecule B is converted back into Molecule A at another rate. Instrumental reward training is analogous to a monomolecular autocatalytic reaction where the conversion of Molecule A to Molecule B takes place at a rate which is proportional to the concentration of Molecule A remaining and to the proportion of Molecule B which has been produced by the reaction; that is, the presence of Molecule B catalyzes the reaction of Molecule A into Molecule B. (See Appendix for more detail.) The analogy is good because an instrumental response must be performed in order to obtain the reward. With progressive reinforcement the rate of emission of instrumental responses will increase, so that the rate at which rewards are received and the rate at which further conditioning takes place will also increase initially until asymptotic levels are approached. If the initial rate of performing the instrumental response were zero, no learning could take place with this type of reinforcement. Similarly, if autocatalysis is required for a chemical reaction, no reaction will take place unless the initial concentration of Molecule B is greater than zero. With continuous instrumental reward reinforcement, the learning process should proceed to a maximum asymptote, just as would be the case with classical reinforcement. Responses learned by classical instrumental avoidance training, however, should not reach the same high asymptote as those learned by classical training because of the back action, that is, the fact that occurrence of an avoidance response involves a classical extinction trial. What will be reached is an equilibrium dependent upon the relative potency of avoidance trials in reinforcing the avoidance response and the potency of classical extinction trials in extinguishing the avoidance response. In the case of the eyelid response, the extinction back action is evidently quite considerable in classical instrumental avoidance training, so that typically an asymptotic performance with this mode of reinforcement is considerably lower than that with classical conditioning (Logan, 1951; Kimble, 1961; Kimble & Dufort, 1956; Moore & Gormezano, 1961, 1963; and Hansche & Grant, 1965). With other responses, the back action of the extinction process might be minimal or completely absent. This would be particularly true if the UCR to the aversive stimulus was unrelated to the required avoidance response.

It is the writer's opinion that diagrams like those in Table 2, rather than the commonly used diagrams of Table 1, should be employed in instructing students respecting the nature of the conditioning processes. Further elaboration and correction of the revised diagrams will doubtless be required by the results of further research. Two-stage experiments in which the mode of reinforcement is shifted should be especially useful in elaborating and correcting the paradigms of Table 2.

APPENDIX

In a *first-order* chemical reaction, Molecule A, originally present in Concentration a, is totally converted to Molecule B. If x is the momentary concentration of Molecule B, the rate of decrease in the concentration of Molecule A is given by the differential equation:

(1)
$$\frac{d(a-x)}{dt} = -kt$$

Solution of this equation yields the negatively accelerated exponential increase in the concentration of Molecule B, $x = a(1 - e^{-kt})$, which is analogous to conditioning with classical reinforcement.

In an *opposed first-order* chemical reaction, Molecule A is converted to Molecule B at a rate, $k_1(a-x)$, that is proportional to the concentration of A; and Molecule B is converted back into Molecule A at a rate, $k_2 x$, that is proportional to the concentration of B, giving a net rate of formation of Molecule B of:

(2)
$$\frac{dx}{dt} = k_1(a-x) - k_2 x$$

This reaction reaches an equilibrium concentration of Molecule B, $x_{eq} = \dfrac{a k_1}{k_1 + k_2}$, so that complete conversion of all A molecules to B molecules does not take place. This chemical reaction is analogous to conditioning with classical instrumental avoidance reinforcement.

In a *monomolecular autocatalytic* reaction, the rate of increase in the concentration of Molecule B is proportional to the remaining concentration of Molecule A and is also proportional to the concentration of Molecule B, which acts as a catalyst as well as a product of the reaction. The rate of formation of Molecule B is given by:

(3)
$$\frac{dx}{dt} = k(a-x)x$$

so that it is obvious that at time zero, there must be some B molecules present in order for the reaction to begin. If the initial concentration of Molecule B is x_0, Equation (3) yields the solution:

(4)
$$x = \frac{a}{1 + \left\{\dfrac{a-x_0}{x_0}\right\} e^{-kt}}$$

The autocatalytic reaction is analogous to conditioning with instrumental reward reinforcement, where the rate of performance is the analog of the concentration of Molecule B. The rate of performance of the instrumental response that is rewarded serves a double function; it is a product of the learning, and it produces the reinforcer, so that with increasing response rate, the rate of reinforcement increases, which increases the amount of learning and the rate of performance of the rewarded response. For learning to take place, the initial rate of performance of the instrumental response must not be zero, or no learning can occur.

REFERENCES

Cerekwicki, L. E., & Grant, D. A. Delay of positive reinforcement in instrumental eyelid conditioning. *Journal of Experimental Psychology,* 1967, **75**, 360–364.

Fleming, R. A., & Grant, D. A. A comparison of rate and contingency of classical and instrumental reinforcement upon the acquisition and extinction of the human eyelid CR. *Journal of Experimental Psychology,* 1966, **72**, 488–491.

Grant, D. A. A preliminary model for processing information conveyed by verbal conditioned stimuli in classical conditioning. In A. H. Black & W. F. Prokasy (Eds.), *Classical conditioning II: Current research and theory.* New York: Appleton-Century-Crofts, 1972.

Grant, D. A. Cognitive factors in eyelid conditioning. *Psychophysiology,* 1973, in press.

Grant, D. A., Kroll, N. E. A., Kantowitz, B. H., Zajano, M. J., & Solberg, K. B. Transfer of eyelid conditioning from instrumental to classical reinforcement and vice versa. *Journal of Experimental Psychology,* 1969, **82**, 503–510.

Grant, D. A., Levy, C. M., Thompson, J., Hickok, C. W., & Bunde, D. C. Transfer of differential eyelid conditioning through successive discriminations. *Journal of Experimental Psychology,* 1967, **75**, 246–254.

Grose, R. S., & Birney, R. C. *Transfer of learning.* New York: Van Nostrand, 1963.

Hansche, W. J., & Grant, D. A. A comparison of instrumental reward and avoidance training with classical reinforcement technique in conditioning the eyelid response. *Psychonomic Science,* 1965, **2**, 305–306.

Hartman, T. F., & Ross, L. E. An alternative criterion for the elimination of "voluntary" responses in eyelid conditioning. *Journal of Experimental Psychology,* 1961, **61**, 334–338.

Hellige, J. B. *Transfer of eyelid conditioning from classical to instrumental avoidance reinforcement and vice versa*. Unpublished masters thesis, University of Wisconsin, 1972.

Ivanov-Smolensky, A. G. *Works of the Institute of Higher Nervous Activity: Pathophysiological Series*. Vol. 2. Moscow: Academy of Sciences, USSR, 1956. (Trans., Israel Program for Scientific Translations for the NSF, USA, 1960.)

Kausler, D. H. *Readings in verbal learning: Contemporary theory and research*. New York: Wiley, 1966.

Kimble, G. A. *Hilgard and Marquis' Conditioning and learning*. New York: Appleton-Century-Crofts, 1961.

Kimble, G. A., & Dufort, R. H. The associative factor in eyelid conditioning. *Journal of Experimental Psychology*, 1956, **52**, 386–391.

Kimble, G. A., Mann, L. I., & Dufort, R. H. Classical and instrumental eyelid conditioning. *Journal of Experimental Psychology*, 1955, **49**, 407–417.

Logan, F. A. A comparison of avoidance and non-avoidance eyelid conditioning. *Journal of Experimental Psychology*, 1951, **42**, 390–393.

Luria, A. R. *The role of speech in the regulation of normal and abnormal behavior*. New York: Liveright, 1961.

Moore, J. W., & Gormezano, I. Yoked comparisons of instrumental and classical eyelid conditioning. *Journal of Experimental Psychology*, 1961, **62**, 552–559.

Moore, J. W., & Gormezano, I. Effects of omitted versus delayed UCS on classical eyelid conditioning under partial reinforcement. *Journal of Experimental Psychology*, 1963, **65**, 248–257.

Pavlov, I. P. *Selected works*. Trans. by S. Belsky. Moscow: Foreign Languages Publishing House, 1955.

Ross, L. E., & Hartman, T. F. Human-eyelid conditioning: The recent literature. *Genetic Psychology Monographs*, 1965, **71**, 177–220.

Spence, K. W. A theory of emotionally based drive (D) and its relation to performance in simple learning situations. *American Psychologist*, 1958, **13**, 131–141.

Vanderplas, J. M., & Garvin, E. A. The association value of random shape. *Journal of Experimental Psychology*, 1959, **57**, 147–154.

4

A COGNITIVE THEORY OF AVOIDANCE LEARNING[1]

Martin E. P. Seligman and James C. Johnston[2]
University of Pennsylvania

In this chapter we review some of the problems that face existing theories of avoidance learning, and then propose a cognitive model which we believe successfully accounts for more of the relevant data. We discuss three different kinds of theories.

1. *Two-process fear mediation theory* is treated at greatest length. We find that difficulties in verifying the mediation of fear have led to formulations that make fewer and fewer predictions. Even the more flexible versions, however, cannot be reconciled with the great resistance to extinction of avoidance and the concomitant absence of fear.

2. *Two-process aversion theory,* it will be argued, is silent about many important avoidance phenomena, particularly those involving fear, and is also incompatible with very high resistance to extinction.

3. *Discriminative stimulus theory* we find to be formulated in a manner that leaves it silent about so many phenomena that it risks becoming a vehicle only for a posteriori description, not prediction.

Our avoidance theory contains two components: one cognitive and one emotional. The cognitive component relies on the constructs of expectancies and

[1] Supported by PHS grants MH 19604 to M. Seligman, MH 19989, and an NSF graduate fellowship to J. Johnston.
[2] We thank R. Bolles, H. Gleitman, R. Hendersen, R. Herrnstein, S. Mineka, and P. Rozin for many helpful comments on drafts of the chapter. We are also deeply grateful to two of our colleagues, F. W. Irwin and R. L. Solomon: Without the prodigious work of Solomon over the last two decades, there would be little data in the field of avoidance to theorize about. Without the conceptual framework provided by Irwin's cognitive theory, and without his patience and generosity at several stages in the writing of the chapter, there would be little theory we could offer.

preferences and is the primary mechanism supporting the avoidance response. We discuss a number of phenomena, particularly high resistance to extinction and the effects of response blocking, which are accounted for by this component of the theory alone. The emotional component consists simply of the classical conditioning of fear according to known Pavlovian laws. By adding this component, our theory can be made to account for many remaining avoidance phenomena, including the course of observed fear itself.

DIFFICULTIES WITH PREVIOUS AVOIDANCE THEORIES

Miller (1948) viewed cognitive accounts of avoidance learning as unnecessary and even profligate. Why talk about cognition if a perfectly adequate account of avoidance can be given without it? Unfortunately, all alternative accounts of avoidance that we know of are seriously flawed. In the following sections, the difficulties facing three of the most favored contemporary avoidance theories will be reviewed. In many places we attempt to meet an alleged difficulty by constructing a rejoinder in the spirit of the theory under discussion. We hope to make it clear which difficulties can be overcome and which cannot.

TWO-PROCESS FEAR MEDIATION THEORY

The most popular theory of avoidance over the last 20 years has been a variant of general two-process theory in which classically conditioned fear mediates instrumental avoidance responding (Mowrer, 1947; Solomon & Brush, 1954; Soltysik, 1963; Rescorla & Solomon, 1967; Maier, Seligman, & Solomon, 1969). This theory has two key premises:

1. By classical conditioning, when a CS is paired with an aversive US (such as shock), the CS comes to elicit the conditioned response of fear.

2. Fear motivates the avoidance response. When the response is made, the CS terminates, fear is reduced, and the avoidance response is reinforced by this fear reduction.

This kind of theory eliminates the apparent forward-lookingness of avoidance. Rather than responding to ward off a shock in the future, an "avoider" is actually escaping from fear-evoking stimuli in the present.

Two-process fear mediation theory has recently come under heavy attack (Herrnstein, 1969; Bolles, 1970; D'Amato, 1970). Problems facing the theory are of three kinds: difficulties in specifying CSs; difficulties in verifying the existence of appropriate fear CRs; and difficulties in accounting for the very high resistance to extinction of most avoidance responding.

The Elusiveness of the CS

The crucial construct, fear, is asserted to be a Pavlovian CR, so its presence during avoidance must be produced by a Pavlovian CS. But identifying the effective CS has not been straightforward. In conventional avoidance training, of course, the onset and offset of the external CS present no trouble for fear theory. The CS is always on prior to the response and is therefore available for fear elicitation; it always terminates after the response, allowing fear reduction to occur. In the trace avoidance paradigm, however, the external CS terminates after a brief fixed time interval. CS termination occurs prior to responding and is independent of it. At first glance, this paradigm presents problems for fear theory. Avoidance should not be acquired because there is no CS around to evoke fear immediately prior to responding, and there is no CS termination after responding to provide reinforcement by fear reduction. Since dogs and rats *do* acquire trace avoidance conditioning (e.g., Kamin, 1954) albeit somewhat falteringly, the range of allowable CSs must be broadened. Fear theory might make the same move made by Pavlov (1927) to handle classical trace conditioning. If the memory trace of the external signal were the operative CS, the evocation of fear to motivate responding could be provided for. But how could reduction of fear by CS termination be handled? The memory trace of the external CS would not do, since there is no reason that the memory trace should terminate when the response is made.

A more promising move is to make the CS a compound of the memory trace *and* "internal stimuli" (Sidman, 1953; Dinsmoor, 1954; Anger, 1963) provided by proprioceptive, visual, and kinesthetic feedback from the avoidance response (hereafter designated "r") and from all other responses (hereafter designated "r̄"). Feedback from r̄ is paired with shock and should become a fear-evoking CS. Feedback from r is paired with no shock and should therefore elicit no fear. Thus engaging in r̄ after the external signal is turned off will elicit fear. Making r will reduce this fear, reinforcing r.

Similar problems arise, of course, for a fear theory account of Sidman avoidance. Making r postpones the shock for some number of seconds (the response-shock interval). If no response occurs, shocks are presented at some fixed interval (the shock-shock interval). By responding consistently with interresponse times smaller than the response-shock interval, the subject can avoid shock altogether. In spite of the fact that no external CS is presented, animals learn to avoid readily on this schedule (e.g., Sidman, 1953). A two-process fear theory can now postulate another compound CS: feedback from not having made the response (r̄) together with the length of time since the preceding response (see Anger, 1963). Increasing lengths of time in the presence of r̄ elicit increasing fear; making r terminates the compound CS and reduces fear. To account for Sidman avoidance, fear theory needs very little over and above what it needed for trace avoidance. It now gives the animal the ability to keep track of time since his last response. This assumption is not unreasonable since related assumptions are probably needed to explain scalloped responding on fixed-interval schedules.

Similar considerations account for Kamin's (1956) finding that rats could learn to avoid the US in spite of the fact that response-contingent CS termination was independent of responding. While this study makes it appear that CS termination is not necessary for avoidance, only *external* CSs were independent of responding. Feedback CSs, already needed to explain trace and Sidman avoidance, would explain Kamin's results equally well. Feedback CSs from r̄ are available to elicit the fear that motivates r; making r terminates these CSs and reduces fear. The fact that Kamin's rats did not learn to avoid as well as control rats which had both external CS termination and avoidance of the US contingent on the response need only lead a fear theorist to assert that terminating an entire compound of external and internal CSs is more fear-reducing than terminating only the feedback component.

Herrnstein (1969) discusses the elusiveness of the CS at length and adds some data of his own (Herrnstein & Hineline, 1966) which he argues are much more difficult for two-process theory to handle. While we are sympathetic with much that Herrnstein has to say, we think that the Herrnstein and Hineline data add no problems for two-process theory that were not there already. Herrnstein and Hineline's rats were exposed to two densities of shock—high and low. If they bar-pressed, they were shifted immediately from the high to the low shock density schedule. There were no external CSs correlated with the schedules. As Herrnstein (1969) noted, "The shock-free interval following a response is, on the average, greater than the shock-free interval measured from any other point in time. The average shock-free interval gradually shrinks back to its original value as time since a response increases [p. 59]." The rats eventually learned to respond although it took them thousands of trials. Herrnstein asserted that this kind of experiment puts two-process theory on the horns of a dilemma. Either two-process theory can formulate no plausible conditioned stimulus, or "the notion of a conditioned stimulus has retreated out of the range of empirical scrutiny [p. 57]." This is a serious overstatement: 1. two-process theory *can* plausibly postulate a CS to handle such experiments, *and* 2. the existence of such a CS is testable.

1. A plausible CS is the feedback from r̄ relied on earlier. Shocks are USs for the CR of fear. The feedback from r̄ regularly precedes shock. Hence, fear will be classically conditioned to r̄. The fact that the interval between r̄ and shock fluctuates around some average interval need not handicap fear conditioning (e.g., Rescorla & LoLordo, 1965, experiment 1). The feedback from responding (r) also regularly precedes shock, but at a considerably longer interval. In accordance with the principle of inhibition of delay, this longer CS-US interval should lead to periods of lower fear *immediately* after the response. The longer interval may also lead to weaker fear conditioning *overall*. Thus conditioned fear elicited by feedback from r should be smaller than that elicited by feedback from r̄; hence making r should reduce the fear level.

We can see no important additional assumptions that fear theory needs to make here. That feedback from r̄ and r could become conditioned fear stimuli is already necessary to account for trace and Sidman avoidance conditioning. That fear can be conditioned with a probabilistic US has been demonstrated

(Rescorla, 1966). That a longer average CS-US interval would have produced greater inhibition of delay particularly after thousands of trials is likely (e.g., Kimmel, 1965; Seligman & Meyer, 1970), and the alternative assumption that weaker CRs would result from longer average intervals is at least plausible. That reduction of fear intensity from high to low is a reinforcer is highly likely.

Herrnstein (1969, p. 59) asserts that the reinforcer is the reduction in shock rate itself, not reduction of fear. This implies an ability of the animal to integrate over time to determine relative rates. While animals may well be able to make such a determination (e.g., Seligman, Maier, & Solomon, 1971), two-process fear theory does not even need this assumption to account for the results. A difference in shock rates is equivalent to a difference in average CS-US interval in the Herrnstein and Hineline (1966) study, and no new principles are needed to account for interval effects.

2. Herrnstein seems to feel quite strongly that a willingness to postulate such CSs takes the notion of conditioned stimulus out of the realm of testability. Elsewhere he claims that inferring the existence of such stimuli is an exercise in "sheer tautology [Herrnstein, 1969, p. 59]." We are puzzled by this claim. The hypothesis that these CSs are operative can be tested by traditional methods. A stimulus is a fear CS when it comes to evoke a fear CR. One could measure heart rate or any of the supposed fear indices following r and r̄ in the Herrnstein schedule. The two-process account under discussion suggests that heart rate will be higher following r̄ than following r, and that heart rate will lower consequent to r. Alternatively, if the animals were on a concurrent appetitive schedule, suppression should have been greater during r̄ periods than periods following r. The results of these tests are not logically implied by the data from which the CSs were inferred, and therefore their postulation is not a tautological exercise.

It is somewhat surprising that Herrnstein implies that postulation of such feedback CSs is tautological; for he ends this section of his paper by recounting evidence which he correctly considers to be an empirical "assault" on such CSs: Taub and Berman (1963, 1968) have found that monkeys could maintain trace avoidance responding even when locally or spinally deafferentated. These monkeys were deprived of (a) visual feedback from the response (the arm was hidden), (b) external CS feedback (the external CS was trace), and (c) proprioceptive and kinesthetic feedback. One yeoman monkey even persisted, albeit sleepily, without any of these and also without his cranial parasympathetic system and his vagal system. While the performance of the monkeys was *disrupted* considerably by deafferentation, they came to avoid sufficiently well to make dubious the assumption that feedback CSs are necessary to mediate avoidance responding.

To account for these results, a fear theorist would need a new source of stimuli to serve as CSs. If feedback existed from commands to the motor system to make r and r̄ (Teuber, 1967) it might be able to serve as the CS. Except for the change in the type of feedback CSs relied on, the account could remain unchanged and very much alive. In this form, the theory would now be still more difficult to test. One can easily imagine, however, that physiologists might be able to deprive animals of even these CSs.

The foregoing arguments about the elusiveness of the CS were directed at the question of whether CS termination is *necessary* for avoidance learning. Fear theory has also been criticized on the grounds that CS termination is not *sufficient.* In Kamin's study (1956) referred to above, one group of rats could terminate the CS, but not prevent the US. They acquired the avoidance response considerably less strongly than rats which could both terminate the CS and prevent the US, and only slightly better than control rats which could do neither. This data need not bother a two-process fear theorist greatly. Kamin argued that when the CS is terminated, but shock still occurs, the animal is punished with some delay by shock onset. This should decrease the probability of the "avoidance" response. We prefer to conceive of the experiment as failing to meet fully the fear-reduction requirements deemed necessary for reinforcement by two-process theory. Since both the continuation of the external CS (when the animal fails to respond) and the noncontinuation of the external CS (when the animal responds) are paired with shock, both could elicit fear. Similarly, feedback from r and r̄ are both paired with shock and should elicit fear. So neither terminating the external CS nor responding will reduce fear. Therefore the two-process requirements for acquisition and maintenance of fear are simply not met.[3] In general, the paradigm of CS-escape with noncontingent delivery of USs *cannot* meet the reinforcement requirements of fear theory. By definition, if US presentation is noncontingent, the stimuli facing an animal after r and r̄ will lead to shock with equal probabilities and will be equally fear provoking. So fear reduction contingent on r will not occur. An alternative way of assessing the effectiveness of only the CS-termination contingency is to omit the US entirely and use a CS which acquired its fearfulness prior to the experiment. This was done long ago (Miller, 1951), and it was found that animals can learn to escape such a CS before fear extinguishes.

In summary, there is no reason to believe that the CS-escape mechanism proposed by two-process fear theory is not *sufficient* to produce avoidance responding. The considerations advanced earlier, however, leave the fear theorist with a somewhat elusive account of the *necessity* of the CS. The class of stimuli postulated as CSs has progressively expanded to include: (*a*) the internal feedback from not responding, (*b*) the passage of time since the last successful response, and (*c*) feedback from commands to the motor system. The animal's reliance on such CSs may be difficult to test, but mere difficulty of testing by no

---

[3] In Kamin's study, the group that can only terminate the CS shows some acquisition of "avoidance" responding. On escape trials, the CS terminates along with the shock; termination of both external and feedback CSs is paired with no shock. To the extent that the animal fails to discriminate between escape and avoidance conditions, these CSs in "avoidance" may provide some fear reduction. Bolles, Stokes, and Younger (1966) confirmed Kamin's results and also found that omitting the US-escape contingency reduced the number of "avoidance" responses markedly.

means justifies the claim that the theory has "passed over the line into irrefutable doctrine [Herrnstein, 1969, p. 67]." Gravity waves, whose existence is crucial to field theory, are also immensely hard to measure experimentally, but such difficulties do not take the question of *their* existence "over the line into irrefutable doctrine." In any case, two-process fear mediation theory makes predictions about other aspects of avoidance and indeed has been found wanting on other empirical grounds.

The Elusiveness of the Fear CR

Two-process theory holds that whatever the CS might be, a CR of fear motivates avoidance responding, and the termination of that fear reinforces responding. If this fear CR could be readily identified, the CS would become much less elusive: the CS would be the internal or external event whose onset reliably preceded the evocation of the fear CR and whose offset reliably preceded the reduction of the fear CR. Considerable data have been obtained about the extent to which various autonomic and behavioral measures of fear correlate with avoidance. After an extensive review of the literature, Rescorla and Solomon (1967) concluded that "in summary, we have not yet identified any peripheral CRs which are necessary to mediate avoidance behavior [p. 169]." We know of no development since 1967 which changes their conclusion. For example, claims that heart rate accelerates maximally during the CS up to the point of responding and then decelerates immediately on the making of the response have not held up under empirical scrutiny (Black, 1959; Soltysik, 1960; Bersh, Notterman, & Schoenfeld, 1956; Wenzel, 1961). Space does not permit a review of the literature on peripheral concomitants of the fear CR.

The absence of peripheral CRs is especially striking in an animal which has learned to avoid asymptotically (i.e., is no longer receiving any shocks). Such animals may actually look nonchalant before and after the CS and make the avoidance response with aplomb (Solomon & Wynne, 1954; Maier, Seligman, & Solomon, 1969). There is often no autonomic arousal to the CS (Black, 1959), and imposing the CS onto appetitive behavior produces no suppression (Kamin, Brimer, & Black, 1963). There is simply no reason to believe that any peripheral fear CR mediates the avoidance response.

Rescorla and Solomon (1967) did not conclude from these considerations that two-process theory was in deep trouble. Rather, they suggested that fear might be a *central state,* with various observable peripheral events only occasionally associated with responding. They asserted that "what concomitance we do observe between instrumental behavior and peripheral CRs is due to mediation by a common central state [p. 170]." It seems from this statement that whenever concomitance is observed, this is supposed to constitute support for the fear mediation hypothesis. Yet they clearly wish *failures*[4] to observe

---

[4] Failure of concomitance between CER and avoidance (Kamin et al., 1963) also does not count against the central fear hypothesis. Rescorla and Solomon (1967) suggest that

(Footnote continued p. 76)

peripheral CRs concomitant with avoidance responding *not to disconfirm* the fear mediation hypothesis. We do not see how they can have it both ways without considering data on a basis of "heads we win, tails don't count." Rescorla and Solomon were apparently uncertain about how to cope with this problem. At one point they themselves suggest that looking for concomitance "becomes an irrelevant strategy." Yet they do not seem prepared to give up the connection between peripheral CRs and the central fear state; for in characterizing their theory in the concluding sentence of the paper, they again emphasize "that the concomitance we do observe between peripheral CRs and instrumental responding is mediated by a common central state [p. 178]."

If we are correct that Rescorla and Solomon's version of two-process theory can be neither confirmed nor disconfirmed on the basis of concomitance evidence, the appeal of such a theory diminishes considerably. When the fear CR was said to be peripheral, and concurrent measurement was a relevant strategy, the principle of fear mediation could be directly tested. Fear CRs themselves could be measured while avoidance responding was actually in progress. The mediation of Pavlovian fear could then be confirmed independently of avoidance responding. When we give up the measurement of mediating CRs, we are left with only one dependent measure—the avoidance response—from which to confirm both the Pavlovian and instrumental postulates of two-process theory. Where we once had two kinds of dependent variables to draw conclusions about two different processes, Rescorla and Solomon now leave us with only one.

If neither manipulation of external CSs nor observation of peripheral CRs will provide a critical test of two-process fear theory, what predictions from the theory remain to be tested? For Rescorla and Solomon the critical remaining claim is that whatever central state mediates avoidance must obey the laws of Pavlovian conditioning. One way they suggest of testing this assumption is to independently condition animals to respond to Pavlovian CSs and then impose these on avoidance responding. For example, Rescorla and LoLordo (1965) trained dogs to avoid on a Sidman schedule. They then imposed onto this schedule a CS+ and a CS− which had been paired with shock and no shock, respectively, in a separate Pavlovian procedure. The avoidance rate increased during CS+ and decreased during CS−. Rescorla and LoLordo assert that this finding confirms two-process theory on the following grounds: "If a CS+ is a Pavlovian excitor, then conditioned fear should be augmented by its presence and the instrumental responding rate should increase above the normal rate. In contrast, if CS− is a Pavlovian differential inhibitor, then it should actively suppress conditioned fear and the instrumental responding rate should decrease below the normal rate [p. 173]."

"the CER experiment is not an adequate index of the conditioned fear reaction. After all, there does not exist a closely reasoned account of the fact that the CER procedure produces *suppression* of the appetitively maintained operant. Why should we not instead find rate increases [p. 169]?"

While Rescorla and LoLordo's results provide some comfort to two-process theory, their clear implications are quite limited. Such data do indicate that CSs established by Pavlovian procedures can modulate ongoing avoidance responding. *What they do not show is that the state responsible for mediating avoidance in the first place obeys Pavlovian laws, much less that this state is central fear. They do not even show that the modulating effects of probe CSs are due to raising or lowering levels of whatever state was already present.* While Rescorla and LoLordo's data are certainly consistent with two-process theory, they also seem consistent with a number of alternative hypotheses including the cognitive one we will present later in this paper.

We are sympathetic with Rescorla and Solomon's review: The lack of concomitance between peripheral CRs and responding does suggest that avoidance is mediated by a central state. But we think there are several candidates for that state other than Pavlovian fear: (*a*) conditioned aversion, (*b*) the state underlying the ability to form a discriminative stimulus for avoidance, and (*c*) the expectations that responding leads to no shock and that not responding leads to shock.

Although modifications of two-process fear theory have tended to restrict its empirical implications, it is not untestable. We now turn to evidence which we believe shows that mediation of avoidance *cannot* be due to a Pavlovian CR, because the Pavlovian law of extinction is violated.

The Elusiveness of Extinction

Avoidance is, by and large, a remarkably persistent behavior. Animals will commonly respond for hundreds of trials without receiving a shock. Experimenters have often given up trying to extinguish the animal before the animal has given up responding. Just how difficult avoidance is to extinguish probably depends on a number of parameters.

Figure 1 presents the classic extinction curve for 13 dogs trained in a two-way shuttlebox to avoid intense shock by Solomon, Kamin, and Wynne (1953). The mean latency of responding was still getting shorter 200 trials after the last US was received. Solomon and Wynne (1954) also reported that "in return for a few intense shocks during acquisition of avoidance, dogs gave back as many as 650 avoidances without showing any sign of extinction [p. 359]." Similarly, Seligman and Campbell (1965), using a one-way shuttlebox, found that their rats were still avoiding with short latencies after 150 extinction trials. As Figure 2 shows, the latencies seem to be lengthening slightly but are still considerably shorter than the CS-US interval. While very high resistance to extinction seems to be the rule (e.g., F. R. Brush, 1957; Black, 1958; Miller, 1951; Baum, 1970), sometimes more rapid extinction is observed. For example, Figure 3 shows extinction curves for Kamin's (1954) dogs run under trace avoidance procedures. With a 2-second CS followed by trace intervals of 20 or 40 seconds before shock, the dogs extinguished within about 50 trials. It should be noted that the more difficult the response was to learn, the more readily it extinguished. The groups

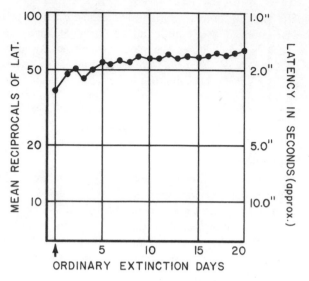

FIG. 1. Mean response latency as a function of number of days of standard extinction, with 10 trials per day. (From Solomon & Wynne, 1954.)

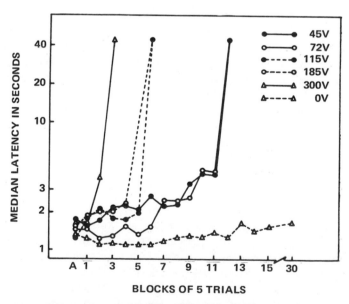

FIG. 2. Median response latency for 0.15-sec.-duration punishment groups. Only the bottom curve (0 volt–unpunished group) is relevant to the effectiveness of standard extinction. (From Seligman & Campbell, 1965.)

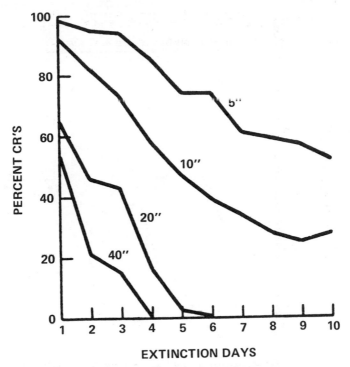

FIG. 3. Percentage of avoidance responses by extinction days (10 trials per day) as a function of CS-US interval. (From Kamin, 1954.)

with 5- or 10-second trace intervals were still showing some avoidance responding after 100 extinction trials. We cannot pinpoint the parameters that make extinction of avoidance more likely to occur, but we suspect the following to be relevant: preparedness or naturalness of the response (Bolles, 1970; Seligman, 1970), trace versus delay CS (Kamin, 1954), and reflexiveness of the response (Turner & Solomon, 1962). We can safely assert, however, that under a wide variety of conditions, avoidance responding is extremely resistant to extinction.

In contrast, classically conditioned responses extinguish very readily. Most Pavlovian CRs (e.g., salivation, GSR, eyelid) extinguish within several dozen nonreinforced trials. Figure 4 presents extinction data for CER established with different intensities of shock in rats (Annau & Kamin, 1961). Even with exceedingly intense shock for rats (2.91 milliamperes) extinction occurred within 40 trials. With less intense shock, extinction occurred even more rapidly. Church and Black (1958) found that classically conditioned heart-rate changes in the dog largely extinguished within 10 trials, with substantial extinction occurring after the very first shock omission. These results contrast strikingly with F. R. Brush's (1957) study of avoidance extinction in dogs. He varied intensity of shock from very mild to intense and found that all groups were still

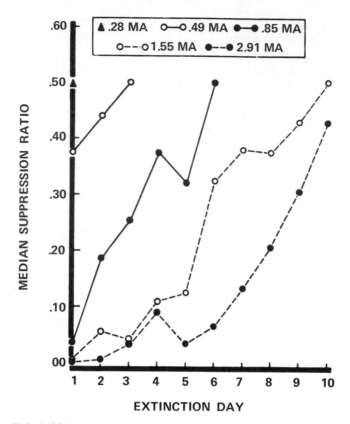

FIG. 4. Median suppression ratio by extinction days (four trials per day) as a function of US intensity. (From Annau & Kamin, 1961.)

reliably avoiding after 200 extinction trials. We know of no form of classical conditioning, not excepting fear conditioning, which even approaches the usual resistance to extinction of avoidance.

The relative inextinguishability of avoidance responding was recognized as a serious problem for two-process theory by Ritchie (1951) and by Solomon and Wynne (1954). Since then it seems to have been swept under the rug, at least for theoretical purposes. The fact that animals apparently avoid fearlessly during extinction (Solomon & Wynne, 1954; Black, 1959; Kamin et al., 1963) has been dealt with by Rescorla and Solomon (1967) by making fear a central state. The deeper problem is that if any fear CR—either peripheral or central—*were* present, it would seem to violate the Pavlovian law of extinction.

On those trials in which a response occurs in the presence of the CS, no shock occurs. So, we have a Pavlovian extinction trial: the fear-evoking CS complex is paired with no shock. Fear to the CS should decrease monotonically, and extinction of the response in the presence of the CS should take place at about the rate of the Pavlovian fear extinction. After several dozen occurrences of the CS without the US, fear should be reduced to near zero. If the central state motivating the response were Pavlovian, as Rescorla and Solomon claim, avoidance would extinguish rapidly.

Conservation of Anxiety

Solomon and Wynne (1954) have proposed the principle of conservation of anxiety as a reply to this difficulty. After noting the very short latencies at which their dogs responded during extinction, they suggest that "the subject removes himself from the presence of the CS so rapidly that the CS is *almost* ineffective. . . . The occurrence of a rapid instrumental response to the CS would prevent peripheral anxiety reactions from occurring; *if nonreinforced exercise of a CS-CR relationship is the necessary condition for extinction,* then the extinction of the associational linkage between the CS and at least this portion of the anxiety reaction cannot take place [p. 359]."

This move does not help. If the CS is not on long enough to elicit the CR, there will be no fear to motivate responding and, of course, no fear reduction to reinforce responding. If the CS is on just long enough to elicit a little bit of CR, there will be fear to motivate the response, and fear reduction to reinforce it. However, this must also be an extinction trial, since an effective CS is followed by no shock.[5]

We propose the following principle: *Any minimum CS which is sufficiently fear evoking to provide for the motivation and reinforcement of the avoidance response exposes the animal to an effective CS paired with no US, which is a Pavlovian extinction trial.*

We are aware of four principles which two-process fear theory might invoke to get off the horns of the dilemma and conserve conservation of anxiety: intermittent extinction, partial irreversibility, titration, and protective inhibition.

1. *Intermittent extinction.* This is our label for the species of conservation of anxiety originally proposed by Solomon and Wynne (1954). They conceded that fear could not be present on every trial to motivate the response because fear would then extinguish long before animals gave up responding. They proposed that fear was only elicited on those trials in which animals waited to respond until unusually long into the CS-US interval. On these occasions the animal could be exposed to a long CS which had not yet been extinguished, so fear would be elicited. Making the response would terminate this fear, and the resulting reinforcement would serve to maintain the response on a partial

---

[5] It does not matter whether the necessary condition for a Pavlovian extinction trial is either (*a*) a CS followed by no US, or (*b*) a CS followed by the CR and no US. The avoidance extinction trial in which some minimal CR is elicited by the CS and followed by no shock meets both conditions. For two-process fear theory, the motivation of the response demands that a CR be present, and if so, both (*a*) and (*b*) are fulfilled.

reinforcement basis. Such a version of conservation of anxiety would rather clearly be unacceptable to present-day two-process fear mediation theory which emphasizes the motivating effect of fear rather than limiting itself to the reinforcing effect of fear reduction. In addition, Solomon and Wynne note that their mechanism would only postpone extinction of the CR. It *is* being elicited intermittently and *will* eventually extinguish. Solomon and Wynne recognized that such an explanation would not account for resistance to extinction of as long as 650 trials.

2. *Partial irreversibility.* Solomon and Wynne, in addition, proposed that the Pavlovian extinction problem might be met head on simply by assuming that fear CRs based on highly traumatic USs never wholly extinguish. Annau and Kamin's (1961) experiment, referred to earlier, shows that even very intense shock is not sufficient to produce high resistance to extinction of CER. Furthermore, F. R. Brush (1957) demonstrated that even with a nontraumatic US (0.7 milliampere shock versus 10 milliamperes for Solomon and Wynne), avoidance responding does not extinguish within 200 trials. Traumatic USs are therefore not necessary for high resistance to extinction.

3. *Titration.* Let us represent the "almost effective" CS in the usual signalized avoidance paradigm as the compound $(T \cdot \bar{r}_t)$, where T represents the external signal (conventionally a tone), $\bar{r}_t$ represents the feedback from not responding, during the time, t, since the onset of the tone. At the beginning of extinction the tone need only be on for a very short length of time $(T \cdot \bar{r}_{t_1})$, to elicit a minimal CR to motivate the response. $T \cdot \bar{r}_{t_1}$ is now paired with no shock and will indeed extinguish. But all that will happen is that the animal will wait a bit longer when he will face $T \cdot \bar{r}_{t_2}$ where t_2 is an instant longer than t_1. If the increments in t are small enough, extinction will be very slow indeed. This argument depends on an implausibly high degree of precision in an animal's responding. It also requires an implausibly low level of generalization of extinction across compound CSs differing only by a fraction of a second in the r_t component. The titration model also predicts a gradual increase in latency which does not fit the Solomon et al. (1953) data.

4. *Protective inhibition.* Konorski (1948) and Soltysik (1963) have argued that the response is a conditioned inhibitor of fear during extinction and protects the CS from extinction. Here is how this argument goes: The animal is exposed to two different kinds of trials in avoidance training. On acquisition trials on which he avoids, he receives $T \cdot \bar{r}_{t_x} + r \rightarrow$ no shock. In other words, when the tone (T) comes on, he does not respond $(\bar{r}_{t_x})$ for some interval less than the CS-US interval; then he does respond (r), and no shock occurs. On trials in which he fails to avoid, he receives $T \cdot \bar{r}_{t_x} + T \cdot \bar{r}_{t_y} \rightarrow$ shock. This merely represents the fact that the animal does not respond during the CS-US interval $(t_x + t_y = \text{CS-US interval})$. On extinction trials, of course, as long as the animal continues to avoid, he receives $T \cdot \bar{r}_{t_x} + r \rightarrow$ no shock. Because r is paired with the nonoccurrence of shock, it should become a conditioned inhibitor of fear. By the hypothesis of protective inhibition, when a fear eliciting $T \cdot \bar{r}_{t_x}$ is

followed by a conditioned inhibitor (r) and the compound is not followed by shock, extinction of fear to $T \cdot \bar{r}_{t_x}$ alone is retarded. Intuitively, the claim might be that since all of the information about the safety of the compound is attributed to r, when $T \cdot \bar{r}_{t_x}$ is presented alone it will still evoke fear.

There are good empirical reasons to believe that this move will not work. Konorski and Soltysik based their argument on experiments in which the conditioned inhibitor preceded or was simultaneous with the CS to be protected. In avoidance, however, the inhibitor, r, necessarily must follow the CS. In addition, Konorski and Soltysik were generalizing from results obtained with food rather than shock. Two experiments have attempted to mimic protective inhibition as it is alleged to occur in avoidance paradigms. Using dogs, LoLordo and Rescorla (1966) found that when the conditioned inhibitor follows the conditioned excitor in time, extinction of fear to the CS proceeds at the same rate whether or not a conditioned inhibitor is present. No protective inhibition at all was observed.

Using a CER on the baseline procedure in rats, Johnston, Clayton, and Seligman (unpublished data, 1972) attempted to follow the course of protection from extinction. In a "protective inhibition group" a tone was first paired with shock for 20 trials. The tone here was intended to be analogous to $(T \cdot \bar{r}_{t_x})$. Then 48 trials were given in which the tone was *followed* by a light (analogous to r) and then no shock. A standard extinction control group first received 20 tone-shock pairings, then received the 48 tone–no shock trials with the light omitted. A third group received 20 tone-shock pairings and then 48 trials with a light *preceding* the tone and no shock. In all cases, after observing the course of extinction through 48 trials, the tone was tested alone. We found no evidence for protection from extinction in the "protective inhibition" group. Both the course of extinction while the light was still present, and the final level observed only when the tone was presented, were virtually identical to the standard extinction control performance. When light *preceded* tone, marginal protection was observed.

To summarize, our results and those of LoLordo and Rescorla suggest that protection from extinction is nonexistent when the inhibitor follows the conditioned fear stimulus as it must in avoidance paradigms. If the central state motivating avoidance is Pavlovian, it should extinguish when the animal responds to the CS and receives no shock.

The attempt to avoid the extinction dilemma by relying on protection from extinction was surely a long shot to begin with. The animal must continue to become afraid to a $CS_1(T \cdot \bar{r}_{t_x})$ alone (to motivate avoidance responding) at the same time that the compound $CS_1 + r$ comes to evoke no fear. Protection of CS_1 from extinction must occur while this very CS_1 is eliciting a CR. There was no reason to have hoped that protection could occur under these circumstances. In part, the reason that a preceding or simultaneously presented conditioned inhibitor provides protection for a CS may be precisely because the CR is inhibited.

To recapitulate, Rescorla and Solomon (1967) proposed that a central Pavlovian CR mediates avoidance. Such a hypothesis is *prima facie* incompatible with the fact that avoidance does not extinguish under conditions where Pavlovian fear should extinguish. The conservation of anxiety hypothesis has been proposed to keep fear present even under apparent extinction conditions. We have been able to reject four different versions of this claim. Perhaps, efforts in this direction were misguided since most animals at asymptote show no signs of being afraid anyway.

Must two-process fear mediation theory be abandoned entirely? Or might there be some way to save the broad outlines of it while jettisoning the claim that asymptotic responding is motivated by fear? Two principles occur to us that might be tacked onto a fear theory to handle asymptotic avoidance: safety signal reinforcement, and automatization.

Safety signal reinforcement. Stimuli that have been paired with the absence of shock become safety signals. They inhibit ongoing avoidance behavior (Rescorla & LoLordo, 1965); they do not disrupt and may even enhance ongoing appetitive responding (Hammond, 1966; Seligman, 1968); and they reinforce instrumental responding (Weissman & Litner, 1969). Bolles (1970) has proposed that CS termination and feedback from avoidance responding become safety signals since they are paired with no shock (cf. Denny and Weisman, 1964). Once such safety signals have been established, they may provide positive reinforcement to maintain avoidance responding. The animal may continue to respond during extinction because safety signals *positively reinforce* responding, and not because fear elicited by the CS is reduced. It should be noted that when safety signals are appended to two-process theory, some transition must occur between the early phase of acquisition governed by fear and long-term maintenance governed by safety. The hypothesis of such a transition would not be entirely *ad hoc*, since safety signals probably develop more slowly than danger signals in the avoidance situation (Bolles, 1970). One of the possible obstacles to be overcome by a safety signal account of asymptotic avoidance is that it must make the following claim: *Stimuli which are paired with no shock retain their positively reinforcing safety properties long after motivating fear has extinguished.* Safety signals must continue to be maintained by being paired with the absence of shock, even when former danger signals no longer evoke fear. Very little data exist on the course of extinction of safety signals as a function of extinction of danger signals. Grossen (1971) reported that safety signals affected appetitive responding only in fear-eliciting situations. The claim that safety signals reinforce asymptotic avoidance would gain markedly in plausibility if it could be demonstrated that animals will work to receive a safety signal in the absence of any ambient fear. This seems unlikely in the light of Grossen's evidence.

Unfortunately, grafting safety signals onto two-process theory exchanges one difficulty for another. While resistance to standard extinction procedures can be accounted for, the phenomenon of extinction by response blocking now becomes a mystery. Response blocking is an effective technique for extinguishing avoidance. In this procedure, a reliably avoiding animal is penned up, and the avoidance response is made unavailable. He is then exposed for a time to the CS without shock. Later the response is made available again, and the CS is turned on in a standard extinction procedure. If the animal's resistance to extinction is reduced, response blocking is said to have succeeded. The initial results on response blocking were contradictory: Solomon, Kamin, and Wynne (1953) found the technique ineffective with dogs, but Page and Hall (1953), Page (1955), and Schoenfeld (1950) found it successful with rats. It is possible that both short CS exposures and lack of generalization from glass-barrier to no-glass-barrier conditions may have contributed to this discrepancy. Since then the results have uniformly shown the technique to be effective in both dogs and rats (Black, 1958; Carlson & Black, 1960; Polin, 1959; Baum, 1966; Shipley, Mack, & Levis, 1971; and see also Baum, 1970, for review). Traditional two-process theory will account for the fact that avoidance is extinguished by forcibly exposing the animal to the CS while responding is blocked. This is a simple Pavlovian extinction of fear procedure: the external CS and feedback from $\bar{r}$ are presented without the US of shock. Since fear of the compound CS extinguishes, avoidance responses are no longer motivated or reinforced. (This, of course, is unfortunately the same reasoning which would lead two-process fear theory to predict rapid extinction by standard procedures.)

The safety signal hypothesis, however, undercuts two-process theory's account of response blocking. If it is only the positive reinforcement of the response provided by a safety signal which maintains avoidance, and fear has dropped out, there is no fear CR to be extinguished. Since the compound CS is not fear evoking anyway, pairing it with no shock should be irrelevant. *The safety signal view is silent on why pairing the external CS and nonresponding with no shock should break up avoidance.*

Automatization. Kimble and Perlmuter (1970) have suggested that asymptotic avoidance responding is governed by the principle of "automatization." In their sense, automatization refers to the process by which well-practiced responses come to be initiated without direct motivational antecedents. Like safety signal reinforcement, an automatization account of asymptotic avoidance would hold that fear was not responsible for response initiation during extinction, even though it might have been during early acquisition.

Unfortunately, like the safety signal view, automatization allows two-process theory to explain resistance to extinction, but undermines its explanation of response blocking. Why should exposing the animal to external and feedback CSs paired with no shock break up automatization? An automatization theorist might reply that response blocking works because it disrupts the flow of responding (with a barrier) rather than because it exposes the animal to shock-free CSs. But why should the *particular* technique of exposure to CSs with r unavailable be *particularly* effective? If the disruption argument is not to become hopelessly ad hoc, it must lead to the prediction that *any* manipulation which leads to a significant change in response requirements will facilitate extinction. Consider a hypothetical experiment in which dogs are trained to jump a high hurdle to avoid. The hurdle is then raised off the ground so that the dog must walk under it to the safe side rather than jump. Such disruption of the flow of responding should, according to the automatization principle, facilitate extinction. We doubt that it would. Baum (1970) observes that when rats are response-blocked, they frantically try to get to the other side by any means they can. In addition, Miller (1951) demonstrated that rats would learn a new response to escape the CS. Such reports suggest that asymptotic avoiders are not merely carrying out an automated action sequence.

In summary, attempts to graft either safety signal reinforcement or automatization mechanisms onto two-process theory do not look very promising. If not, the theory's inability to account for the marked resistance to extinction of avoidance appears to us to be fatal. This flaw is particularly serious because the theory has come to be formulated in a manner which makes it difficult to test the key assumptions about the role of the CS and CR. We must reject two-process fear theory.

TWO-PROCESS AVERSION THEORY

Schoenfeld (1950), Sidman (1953), and Dinsmoor (1954) have proposed accounts of avoidance that have some resemblance to two-process fear mediation theory already discussed. As before, two kinds of conditioning are invoked. By respondent (classical) conditioning, stimuli which have been paired with shock become "noxious" or "aversive." The removal of an aversive stimulus then provides reinforcement of preceding responses according to the laws of operant conditioning. The critical difference between this type of aversion theory and fear mediation theory lies in the logical nature of the concepts of "fear" and "aversiveness." Fear has clearly been used as a hypothetical construct (Mac-Corquodale & Meehl, 1948) uniting a variety of observable phenomena. The list of empirical *manifestations* of fear that have been suggested is long and open-ended: urination, defecation, howling, freezing, jumping, GSR changes, heart-rate and blood-pressure changes, suppression of ongoing appetitive behavior, facilitation of ongoing avoidance behavior, etc. On the other hand, "aversiveness" is used in quite a narrow and specific way. As Dinsmoor indicates most clearly, what it means to this theory for a stimulus to become aversive is exactly, and only, that termination of this stimulus will now increase the probability of preceding behaviors. The fact that an aversive stimulus has other behavioral or physiological consequences is viewed as entirely incidental and not a part of what it *means* for the stimulus to be aversive. Unlike fear theory, aversion theory says nothing at all about anything going on *inside* the organism—"aversiveness" is simply a shorthand expression that summarizes what happens if such a stimulus is terminated.[6]

---

[6] Such theories speak explicitly only of the *stimulus* as having become aversive. However, it is obviously the animal that has changed and not the stimulus. We are reminded of

(Footnote continued p. 87)

It should be clear to the reader that the term *aversion* is being used in a way that amounts to little more than a rearranged description of observed behavior. The only testable consequence of the alleged respondent conditioning phase is the success of the operant conditioning phase. Like Rescorla and Solomon's central fear theory, aversion theory must infer the effects of both types of conditioning from only one type of dependent variable, the operant response.

As the formal similarity of the two theories might suggest, the problems with aversion theory are much the same as those with a central fear account. Most importantly, the failure of avoidance to extinguish readily cannot be accounted for. One of the very few testable consequences of aversion theory's rather descriptive account is that aversion must at least follow the descriptive laws that apply to respondent conditioning *in general*. One of these is the law of extinction. Aversion theory is not consistent with the unusually high resistance to extinction of avoidance.

Difficulties with identifying the CS are not critical, because aversion theory has the same moves available to it as other two-process theories. As a result of these moves, though, the CS can no longer be an experimenter-controlled variable. The usefulness of this kind of functional account is therefore diminished. Since aversion theory makes no pretense of observing *directly* the alleged effects of respondent conditioning, it cannot be disconfirmed by lack of concomitance found between peripheral CRs and avoidance. On the other hand, it is completely incidental that fear is involved in avoidance at all. The fact that heart-rate increases and CER seem to be concomitant with the early acquisition of avoidance (Black, 1959; Kamin et al., 1963) is unaccounted for. The influence of independently established CS+ and CS− on Sidman baseline (Rescorla & LoLordo, 1965) is unaccounted for. The fact that animals become visibly afraid when prevented from responding during extinction (Baum, 1970) and when they give long latency-avoidance responses (Solomon & Wynne, 1954) is unaccounted for. We find two-process aversion theory inadequate.

DISCRIMINATIVE STIMULUS THEORY

Herrnstein (1969) has formulated an account of avoidance that dispenses not only with fear, but with aversion as well. External signals are not said to become aversive; rather they become mere discriminative stimuli which "set the occasion" for the avoidance response. They are merely cues that the animal is now in that subset of the session during which responding produces reinforcement. The only other role for external signals is that their response-contingent offset may help the animal to "discriminate the avoidance contingency" (D'Amato, Fazzaro, & Etkin, 1968; D'Amato, 1970). Reinforcement for the

---

Mowrer's quip that if such theories are to be understood literally, we could take a stimulus that had been made aversive in conditioning one animal and use its termination to reinforce a naive animal's behavior.

response is provided not by the removal of a conditioned negative reinforcer (the CS) but rather by the absence of shock itself (a special case of reduction in shock density—reduction to a zero level).

Given the limited role played by external signals according to this account, the theory can actually draw strength from the elusiveness of the CS. In addition, like aversion theory, it has no problems with the elusiveness of the CR. While for aversion theory no CR was observable, since conditioned aversion had no properties other than its capacity to reinforce responding, the discriminative stimulus account has no CR because it has no classical conditioning. Also, like aversion theory, discriminative stimulus theory says nothing about fear at all, and evidence that fear *is* present under some circumstances is simply ignored. In addition to the evidence of this kind cited previously, Herrnstein would not have predicted one piece of evidence which aversion theory did: animals can be taught to escape from a CS previously paired with unavoidable shock (Miller, 1948; Brown & Jacobs, 1949).

We believe that Herrnstein's theory suffers from more serious problems. Like two-process theories, it does not account for the fact that avoidance responding persists in the face of standard extinction procedures. To see how this phenomenon might be handled, we need to examine further the nature of reinforcement of the avoidance response. Herrnstein has asserted that "reduction in shock rate" is the reinforcer. In most traditional experiments, the reduction is presumably to zero. In this case, Herrnstein's account seems to converge with the common operant conditioning assertion that "nothing happening" can be a negative reinforcer. Reynolds (1968) has argued that omission of a shock in an otherwise regular sequence of shocks is itself an event with behavioral consequences, on the analogy of a clock that fails to tick on schedule. So far this sense of "nothing happening" is in the spirit of the definition of a negative reinforcer as a stimulus whose *removal* increases the probability of a response. Both the "nothing happening" and the "reduction in shock rate" accounts seem to share an implicit contrast with other events. "Nothing happening" will not be a reinforcer unless something aversive has happened in the past, and a low shock rate will only be a reinforcer if the shock rate has been higher in the past. So far as we know, no one has tried to spell out exactly what the conditions are under which the appropriate "contrast" is present. The extreme resistance to extinction of avoidance responding would seem on the face of it to eliminate any contrast. Since the animal has not received any shocks for hundreds of trials, why should making the event of "no-shock" contingent on responding provide any contrast to maintain reinforcement? "Nothing happening" as it occurs in extinction seems remote from the notion of reinforcement by *removal* of a stimulus. As we shall suggest below, the most plausible contrast seems to be provided by an *expectation* that the event of shock (or a higher shock rate) would occur *if* the animal did not respond.

Surely this kind of contrast cannot be appealed to by a discriminative stimulus theorist. We do not know what else might be appealed to, but in any case it seems unlikely that a principled answer will emerge. Rather, after appropriate parametric studies are done, those conditions under which otherwise neutral events maintain behavior on which they are contingent, will be said to be just the conditions necessary to provide the proper contrast. The discriminative stimulus account is fundamentally a descriptive framework, not a predictive hypothesis. Surely if the data revealed rapid extinction of avoidance, discriminative stimulus theory could accommodate itself with equal ease.

It seems very likely that an ad hoc solution will also be required to account for the deterioration of avoidance after response blocking. We shall suggest below that an expectancy that not responding will lead to shock, handles the phenomenon nicely—this expectancy is directly disconfirmed. Discriminative stimulus theory does not say this, of course, and we do not know what other account they could give. It might be asserted that competing responses are being reinforced by no shock during the response blocking, and then competing responses undermine the avoidance response. However, Black (1958) has shown that curarization of animals provides for effective response blocking—indeed the most effective variety known. This paradigm provides, to say the least, far from optimal circumstances for reinforcing competing responses.

Alternatively, response blocking might be asserted to provide just the right recent history as background so that "nothing happening" will no longer be a reinforcer. In any case we think that the effectiveness of response blocking would never have been *predicted*. Discriminative stimulus theory would find itself equally unembarrassed if response blocking failed to produce rapid extinction.

Discriminative stimulus theory finds itself in the position of only restating the data in the form of "functional" relationships. We have found that it is simply silent about many major phenomena of avoidance learning. Surely it is worth striving to find a theory which fits the way the world is, and would *not* fit radically different worlds equally well. We now turn to our attempt to state such a theory.

THE COGNITIVE THEORY

Cognitive Precursors

Before presenting our theory, we would like to say a few words about its historical antecedents. Avoidance learning has long been recognized as a relatively favorable domain for cognitive theorizing. Hilgard and Marquis (1940), Osgood (1950), and Ritchie (1951) are among those who have taken a cognitive view of avoidance. Ritchie's views are of particular interest. He claimed two decades ago that high resistance to extinction presented a problem for prevalent S-R reinforcement theories. The purported problem was speculative, however, since he did not yet have data showing that classically conditioned fear extinguishes much more rapidly than avoidance. As an alternative to the S-R accounts, Ritchie suggested that extinction data could be readily handled by Tolmanian S-S expectancies. Ritchie contended that an animal in a traditional one-way shuttlebox avoidance situation expects to be shocked after some seconds in the start box, and expects not to be shocked in the goal box. During extinction, an asymptotically avoiding animal will leave the start box before he expects shock to arrive, so this expectancy will never be disconfirmed. One way to disconfirm it, Ritchie suggested, would be to block the response during extinction, and expose the animal to the start box through the time he expected shock to arrive. Ritchie noted Solomon and Wynne's (1950) preliminary report of a failure to extinguish dogs with response blocking and was willing to put his theory on the line as predicting that these early indications would not be upheld. Presumably, he would find modern data on response blocking much more congenial.

After a long dormant period, cognitive theory has recently emerged anew in an especially attractive form. In 1971, Francis W. Irwin published *Intentional Behavior and Motivation: A Cognitive Theory*. This book is, in our opinion, a signal achievement. Irwin has shown that a great deal of behavior can be handled in a single coherent framework relying on only two kinds of postulated states—*preferences* between outcomes, and *act-outcome expectancies*. Act-outcome expectancies are well-defined descendents of Tolman's (1932) "means-ends" relations. In a given situation, an animal is said to come to expect that a given act (a)—rather than some alternative act—will lead to a given outcome (o). A sufficient condition for making an act a_1 is having both (1) expectations that, in the situation at hand, a_1 leads to o_1, while a_2 leads to o_2,[7] and (2) a preference of o_1 to o_2. Irwin presents rigorous empirical criteria for diagnosing the presence of such expectancies and preferences.

Our theory is stated within Irwin's situation-act-outcome (SAO) framework and uses a variant of Irwin's notation. We discuss in the appendix the relation of our theory to Irwin's approach.

Introduction to Our Theory

While we have called our account a cognitive theory, it actually has two components: one cognitive, the other emotional. The cognitive component makes use of pairs of act-outcome expectancies and a corresponding preference between outcomes.

In our theory, an expectancy is a hypothetical construct: a state of the organism which represents (stores information about) contingencies between responses and outcomes in a given situation. The general form of this three-term expectancy is S:rEo, which is read, "It is expected that in a given situation (S) a given response (r) leads to a given outcome (o)." A preference is also a hypothetical construct: a state of the organism which controls the choice of response on the basis of outcomes expected. The general form of the preference

---

[7] See Appendix for a more precise account of Irwin's expectancies.

is $o_1 Po_2$ which is read "one outcome (o_1) is preferred to another outcome (o_2)."[8]

The emotional component is based on classically conditioned fear as a response elicitor. Reinforcement by fear reduction plays no role in the theory.

Our exposition of the theory will be as follows. We will (I) present the cognitive component of the theory and (II) discuss empirical consequences that can be derived from it alone. We will then (III) present the theory's emotional component and (IV) discuss the additional empirical consequences that follow from a combination of the two components. We will next (V) discuss how our theory covers some further phenomena with the addition of subsidiary premises congenial to the theory. Lastly, (VI) we will mention some residual phenomena which our theory cannot easily explain.

I. The Cognitive Component

This part of the theory postulates that an animal has one preference and during avoidance learning acquires two related expectancies.

1. The animal prefers no shock ($\bar{s}$) to shock (s); that is, $\bar{s}Ps$.

2. The animal expects that if he responds within a given time (r_t, where t is the length of the CS-US interval in signalized avoidance, or the R-S interval in unsignalized avoidance), no shock ($\bar{s}$) rather than shock (s) will occur; that is, $r_t E\bar{s}$.

3. The animal expects that if he does not respond within the appropriate time ($\bar{r}_t$),[9] shock (s) rather than no shock ($\bar{s}$) will occur; that is, $\bar{r}_t Es$.

4. Expectancies are strengthened when they are confirmed, and weakened when they are disconfirmed. Thus $r_t E\bar{s}$ is confirmed when r_t is followed by $\bar{s}$, and disconfirmed when it is followed by s; $\bar{r}_t Es$ is confirmed when $\bar{r}_t$ is followed by s, and disconfirmed when it is followed by $\bar{s}$.[10]

5. Holding constant the preference for $\bar{s}$ rather than s, the *probability* of r_t is a monotonically increasing joint function of the strengths of both $r_t E\bar{s}$ and $\bar{r}_t Es$.[11]

II. Empirical Implications of the Cognitive Component Alone

Extinction. According to the rules of the cognitive component, r_t will decrease in probability when at least one of the following occurs: (a) $r_t E\bar{s}$ is

---

[8] See discussion in Appendix of our notation and its relation to the SAO framework.

[9] Technically we prefer to use $\bar{r}_t$ to refer to *making* another response that is a member of the set of responses consisting of all responses except r_t; $\bar{r}_t$ and r_t then refer to exclusive and exhaustive sets of responses.

[10] Clearly the theory will eventually have to be refined so that appropriate attention by the animal is a necessary condition for augmenting the strength of an expectancy. See item 3 in the section on unsolved problems below.

[11] It may be that $r_t E\bar{s}$ must have some minimal strength before increasing the strength of $\bar{r}_t Es$ will have any effect on responding. Future analysis of failure to acquire avoidance may show this to be the case.

disconfirmed, (b) $\bar{r}_t$Es is disconfirmed, or (c) $\overline{s}$Ps is weakened. The following phenomena can thus be accounted for:

1. Avoidance is extremely difficult to extinguish by the conventional procedure of omitting shock: $r_t\overline{Es}$ continues to be confirmed; $\bar{r}_t$Es is not disconfirmed because $\bar{r}_t$ is never made and the contingency never sampled; $\overline{s}$Ps is unchanged.

According to our theory, the high resistance to extinction of avoidance is not dependent on any special properties of aversive outcomes (as was the case with Solomon and Wynne's (1954) principle of partial irreversibility). It might be expected that if an animal on an appetitive schedule never sampled disconfirmation of the expectation that not responding leads to no reinforcement, high resistance to extinction would also be obtained. Schoenfeld (this volume) found that this is indeed true. He put pigeons on an acquisition schedule in which they received grain at the end of a period of time if they had pecked a key during that interval. The birds were then shifted to an extinction schedule in which grain arrived at the end of the period whether or not key pecking occurred. Schoenfeld's pigeons failed to extinguish noticeably for as long as the schedule was continued. This experiment can be treated in a manner very similar to avoidance. The pigeon acquires the expectation that responding during the interval (r_t) leads to food (fd) r_tEfd—and that not responding during the interval ($\bar{r}_t$) leads to no food ($\overline{fd}$)—$\bar{r}_t$E$\overline{fd}$. The pigeon has a preference fdP$\overline{fd}$. As in avoidance "extinction," the animal continues to respond during Schoenfeld's appetitive "extinction" schedule because the first expectancy continues to be confirmed, the second expectancy is not disconfirmed, and the relative preference for outcomes remains unchanged.

2. The efficacy of standard avoidance extinction procedures will, according to our theory, be a function of how likely the animal is to sample disconfirmation of $\bar{r}_t$Es. Anything that prevents an animal from producing r_t with total reliability should lead to more sampling and faster extinction. For instance, more sampling of disconfirmation and faster extinction should occur if the animal is required to make a "heavy-weight" response, e.g., one that is physically difficult to perform in the allotted time interval. We would also predict that an analysis of individual response records for a given experiment would show that less reliable responders at the start of extinction will reach a strong extinction criterion unusually fast.

At our present level of understanding we are largely ignorant of independent variables that produce greater or lesser sampling of $\bar{r}_t$. For the moment it is true that our theory can only assert that "weak responding leads to even weaker responding," (cf. Beecroft, 1971).

3. Omitting the avoidance contingency by allowing shock to occur (regardless of whether the animal responds) while continuing the CS-termination contingency, should produce extinction considerably faster than the standard procedure; $r_t\overline{Es}$ would be disconfirmed. So far as we know, this implication of our theory has not been tested yet.

4. Response blocking should facilitate extinction (e.g., Baum, 1970). In response blocking, r_t is prevented, and $\bar{r}_t$Es is therefore directly disconfirmed. The more disconfirmation to which the animal is exposed, the more effective the procedure should be, as Baum (1969) has reported.

Unlike two-process theory, our theory asserts that *response extinction* occurs independently of Pavlovian *fear extinction*. It is therefore entirely possible according to our account that after response blocking some animals could still be afraid of the CS even though the avoidance response had entirely extinguished. Baum (1970) has reported observing this phenomenon.

5. Punishing the avoidance response by shock should facilitate extinction because r_tĒs is disconfirmed and replaced by r_tEs. Evidence on this point is not yet decisive. F. R. Brush (1957) and Seligman and Campbell (1965), for example, have found punishment to be effective, but Brown (1969) has reviewed the contrary evidence.

6. The strength of s̄Ps should be greater the longer the animal spends in the shock-free compartment. Reynierse and Rizley (1970) reported higher resistance to extinction (and superior acquisition) with longer shock-free reinforcement.

Acquisition

1. If s̄Ps (no shock is preferred to shock), acquisition will not occur. Very low shock intensities do not produce acquisition.

2. Circumstances which facilitate the occurrence of initial r_t's will facilitate avoidance acquisition. Once the avoidance response starts being made, the expectancy r_tĒs will be confirmed, and the probability of r_t will increase. As before, this assertion is at present largely a statement that an animal must start making the avoidance response to learn to avoid—scarcely surprising. It does suggest looking at individual response records (see, e.g., Solomon & Wynne, 1953) to see if the acquisition curve is a sensible function of number of previous confirmations of r_tĒs.[12] Furthermore if we have independent means of predicting when r_t will be emitted, more impressive predictions become possible. The emotional component of our theory provides a start in this direction.

3. CS termination with no avoidance of shock should not produce much acquisition of r_t because r_tĒs is disconfirmed.[13] Kamin (1956) obtained

---

[12] Obviously if the animal responds too well, too early, it is in principle possible that $\bar{r}_t$Es will never become very strong. This seems rarely to be a relevant consideration in experiments so far conducted. When it is, the acquisition curve will be affected by individual differences in exposure to confirmations of this expectancy. In any case, a start at fitting acquisition data can be made in cases where $\bar{r}_t$Es can be sensibly considered asymptotic for all animals by the time of the first avoidance response.

[13] Some acquisition might occur if the animal prefers no fear to fear, and comes to expect that turning off the CS leads to less fear (see below). Since a US follows even when the CS has been turned off, however, fear will soon develop to the trace of a CS that has been recently escaped. Thus very little change in fear would be achieved, and the response would be acquired feebly if at all.

evidence for moderate acquisition under these circumstances, but Bolles, Stokes, and Younger (1966) have found virtually no acquisition when the contaminating effects of an escape contingency are removed. This is true even when the response is occurring with a relatively high base-line frequency.

4. A US avoidance contingency alone, without escape or CS-termination contingencies, should lead to acquisition if the response is emitted with enough probability to achieve reasonable confirmation of $r_t E\bar{s}$ (e.g., Bolles et al., 1966).

5. Avoidance learning need not be accompanied by fear at all. Only a preference for the nonaversive outcome is necessary. Ray (1972) and Grant (this volume) have reported that instrumental avoidance of air-puffs can be acquired by rats and men. There are no indications that subjects are actually afraid of the air-puff in these experiments. Unlike Rescorla and Solomon, we take the absence of peripheral fear signs as presumptive evidence that no fear is present.

6. Our theory accounts for Herrnstein and Hineline's (1966) finding that animals can learn to avoid an increase in shock density. The theory requires only that animals have the (quite plausible) preference for low shock density over high shock density. The theory then holds as before, with "low shock density" substituted for $\bar{s}$ and "high shock density" for s.

7. Our theory holds that punishment (passive) avoidance is produced in the same way as active avoidance. The only difference is that the animal acquires expectations rEs and $\bar{r}E\bar{s}$; his preference for $\bar{s}$ now causes $\bar{r}$ to be made. The roles of r and $\bar{r}$ are simply reversed from the active avoidance paradigm.

8. Under appropriate circumstances, animals can learn to respond to terminate a CS previously paired with shock but now shock-free (e.g., Miller, 1951). Pairings of the CS and shock should have established the expectation $\bar{r}Es$. When the shock is turned off and the animal is allowed to sample r, he will acquire the expectation that, during the CS, $rE\bar{s}$. This effect should depend on having a high enough initial probability so that $rE\bar{s}$ will become established, before the animal waits through enough CSs to lose the $\bar{r}Es$ expectancy.

III. The Emotional Component

1. Fear is classically conditioned to a CS paired with shock.

2. Fear is classically extinguished to the CS when the CS is not followed by shock.

3. Fear can be indexed by autonomic responses and skeletal responses elicited by the CS. These skeletal responses may, with some probability, include the specified avoidance response or similar responses.

It should be noted that we are *not* offering a new analysis of the classical conditioning process. In particular, we are *not* asserting that it is mediated by expectancies of any kind.[14]

It should be noted that fear reduction plays no reinforcing role in our account. Fear serves only in the elicitation of responses.

[14] Classical conditioning *might*, in fact, be mediated by expectancies of some kind, but our theory is neutral on this point.

It is not critical for our theory whether fear is considered to be peripheral or central. If it is the latter, however, it must at least be reliably indexed by peripheral skeletal and autonomic responses.

IV. Implications That Follow from the Cognitive and Emotional Components of the Theory Together

Extinction. 1. Fear, as indexed by autonomic responses, and CER will not be present during asymptotic acquisition or extinction (e.g., Black, 1959; Kamin et al., 1963). According to our theory, fear has classically extinguished to those *durations* of external and feedback CSs that have not been followed by shock. In fact, animals typically are *not* afraid of the CS that is controlling their asymptotic avoidance response (Maier et al., 1969; Solomon & Wynne, 1954).

2. Fear may be observed when long latency responses occur (Solomon & Wynne, 1954). This is because the animal now exposes himself to a duration of the CS which has not previously been classically extinguished by pairing with shock. Aside from eliciting fear, such a long latency trial is a classical extinction trial to this longer duration of the CS. Eventually no fear should be produced by even long-latency responses.

3. Fear should be observed during response blocking itself (e.g., Solomon et al., 1953; Baum, 1970). The animal is exposed to longer durations of the CS than had previously been classically extinguished during avoidance training.

4. As mentioned earlier, our theory permits the avoidance response to extinguish during response blocking without extinction of the fear CR (Baum, 1970). Extinction of the fear CR occurs when enough CS–no shock pairings have occurred for classical extinction. Disconfirmation of $\bar{r}_tEs$ also requires CS–no shock pairings, but there is no reason why effective disconfirmation could not proceed at a faster rate than fear extinction.

5. We have already stated that factors which provide the animal with experience disconfirming $\bar{r}Es$ will lead to faster avoidance extinction. One way for this to occur is if r_t is "unnatural"—that is, not similar to any part of the animal's species-specific defense repertoire (Bolles, 1970). In this case the animal will tend to emit other more natural responses which are incompatible with r_t and serve as effective instances of $\bar{r}_t$. If independent ethological observation is used to define the SSDR, there need be no circularity in a prediction that SSDR-incompatible responses will extinguish more readily.

Acquisition. 1. As noted earlier, circumstances which facilitate the occurrence of initial r_t's will facilitate the acquisition of avoidance. Initial r_t's should be facilitated if they are classically elicited by a fear-evoking CS or if they are part of an animal's SSDR. In either case the probability that r_t will be made, and $r_tE\bar{s}$ confirmed, increases.

2. If r_t is part of an animal's SSDR, avoidance conditioning will be retarded by any factor that retards classical conditioning of fear. Elicitation of early responses will be delayed. Evidence suggests that in fact techniques which can be

presumed to suppress fear do retard avoidance acquisition. Sympathectomy, adrenalectomy, and administration of tranquilizers should lead to less effective avoidance learning because they retard the emission of the early avoidance responses elicited by fear (e.g., Wynne & Solomon, 1955).

3. Concomitance of peripheral fear CRs and skeletal avoidance responses should be observed early in acquisition. Since fear elicits early r_t's, we would expect that the moment of onset of a peripheral CR would closely precede making the avoidance response. On the other hand our theory says nothing about the moment of onset of fear *reduction*, and we would not predict that making the avoidance response would reliably precede the decline of peripheral CRs. Black (1959), studying heart-rate acceleration in dogs, has reported just such a pattern of results in early acquisition: the *onset* of a peripheral fear CR reliably precedes making the avoidance response, but this response is not closely followed by a reliable decline of the peripheral fear CR. We have not carried out a serious review of the huge literature that has accumulated on this topic, but we believe that a reevaluation of it with an eye toward only elicitation concomitance is in order.

4. CER to the CS will be seen early in avoidance because CER is also an index of fear (Kamin et al., 1963).

5. Autonomic fear CRs, and CER to the CS, will not be found late in acquisition (Black, 1959; Kamin et al., 1963). Fear has classically extinguished since the CS is never followed by shock if the animal responds reliably.

V. Additional Phenomena Accounted for by the Theory with Subsidiary Assumptions

As presented thus far, the theory we are proposing consists of two components based on act-outcome expectancies and on classically conditioned fear. Relying only on core assumptions of the theory, we have attempted to show that it accounts for much of the salient and reliable empirical evidence on avoidance. In the next section we will show that some additional avoidance phenomena can be handled by our theory with the addition of subsidiary assumptions that we consider to be readily compatible with our approach. Other theories of avoidance, we believe, also need subsidiary assumptions to cover many of these phenomena.

1. Animals respond with latencies considerably shorter than the CS-US interval in signalized avoidance (e.g., Solomon et al., 1953).

This phenomenon can be handled within our theory if we assume that *fear (f) and no fear ($\bar{f}$) can be outcomes in act-outcome expectancies and that no fear is preferred to fear.* Fear and no fear, like shock and no shock, or food and no food, are events about which animals can display preferences. Any such event can serve as an outcome in an act-outcome expectancy. As stated previously, fear is elicited by classical conditioning at some duration t^* of the CS (where t^* is the time from CS onset to fear onset, $t^* \ll$ CS-US interval). Presumably the precise duration of t^* follows the law of inhibition of delay (Pavlov, 1927). The animal acquires two expectations about fear during avoidance learning—that responding in less than t^* leads to no fear—$r_t * E f$—and that not responding in less than t^* leads to fear—$\bar{r}_t * E f$. These two expectancies, together with a preference for no fear rather than fear, are sufficient to produce the avoidance response in less than t^*—that is, a short latency response. So the animal responds with a short latency to *avoid* fear, just as he responds to avoid *shock*. Reinforcement by fear reduction plays no role in this explanation.

If t^* is defined as the interval between the last response and fear onset, this account also explains why interresponse times in Sidman avoidance are considerably shorter than the R-S interval (e.g., Rescorla & LoLordo, 1965).

2. Church, Brush, and Solomon (1956) have found evidence that trace avoidance conditioning may show less resistance to extinction than delay conditioning.

According to our theory, during the *situation* defined by the intertrial interval (ITI), $\bar{r}$Es is disconfirmed when $\bar{r}$ is followed by no shock. It seems to us important that the ITI and the CS offset–US interval are both silent in trace conditioning, but that only the ITI is silent in delay conditioning. Like other learning theories, ours needs a *stimulus (situation) generalization principle.* In this particular case it is reasonable to suppose that in trace conditioning the animal will generalize from the silent ITI to the silent CS offset–US interval. We can therefore expect $\bar{r}_t$Es to be subject to continuing weakening due to generalization from the ITI situation. This means that the probability of making the response will be lowered for trace conditioning, and extinction can develop more rapidly.[15]

In addition, it has been found that the longer the silence in the CS offset–US interval of trace avoidance conditioning, the lower the resistance to extinction (Kamin, 1954; E. S. Brush, 1957). Following the situation generalization principle just set forth, the longer the interval of silence, the more the CS-US interval will be confusable with the ITI, and the more weakening of $\bar{r}$Es will occur.

Katzev (1967) and Katzev and Hendersen (1971) reported that delaying CS termination but retaining shock avoidance in extinction reduces resistance to extinction. In addition, the longer the CS remained on after the animal responded, the less the resistance to extinction. Again following the situation generalization principle, the situation in the presence of the CS *after* the animal has responded is confusable with the situation in the presence of the CS *before* he has responded. After he responds, the animal is in the presence of the CS for an additional time period, and no shock occurs. He should therefore disconfirm the expectancy $\bar{r}$Es in the presence of the CS after responding. This should

---

[15] For present purposes it makes little difference in which direction the generalization occurs. If the ITI is treated as similar to the CS-US interval, the strength of $\bar{r}_t$Es will be mistakenly decremented. If the CS-US interval is treated as similar to the ITI, $\bar{r}_t$ will be made, and the animal will encounter disconfirmation directly.

generalize to the r̄Es expectancy in the situation where a CS is on prior to responding. The probability of responding will decline as this expectancy is reduced in strength. Further, the longer the CS remains on after responding, the more powerful this generalization effect will become, and the faster extinction will proceed.

3. When the escape response is the same as the avoidance response, acquisition is facilitated. The conditioned fear response has already been assumed by theorists (e.g., Solomon and his collaborators) to have many elements in common with the unconditioned response to shock. Feedback from these two responses should be similar enough for some *generalization between escape and avoidance* situations to develop. Such generalization will raise the probability of the initial r_t's and so facilitate acquisition.

4. Rescorla and LoLordo (1965) have found that ongoing avoidance responding is increased by probe CS + s and decreased by probe CS − s. The effect of probe CSs can be handled by our theory in either of two ways: (*a*) by modulation of act-outcome expectancies, or (*b*) by modulation of fear as a response elicitor.

(*a*) In the Rescorla and LoLordo procedure, animals are penned up on one side of the shuttlebox and exposed to a CS+ paired with shock and a CS− paired with no shock. During the CS+ the animal cannot make r, and is shocked. The expectancy r̄Es in the presence of the CS+ should be established. The base-line avoidance rate should *already* be a function of r̄Es where the controlling situation does not specify presence or absence of an external CS. When the CS+ is now imposed onto ongoing avoidance, it is plausible to assume that, for this compound situation, the situation specifications of both expectancies are met and both are in force. It is also plausible that *the expectation r̄Es in the compound situation will draw strength from both separately established expectations.* We are not prepared to specify a precise pooling function. However, the r̄Es expectation from the Pavlovian training should be extremely strong; we are confident that most plausible pooling functions would produce a r̄Es expectancy in the compound situation stronger than the r̄Es expectancy in the Sidman situation by itself. In accord with I. 5. in the discussion of the cognitive component above, an increase in the strength of the r̄Es expectation should be reflected in a higher probability of making r at any moment and a higher overall response rate.

Conversely, during Pavlovian CS− training, the animal makes r̄ and is not shocked. He will therefore develop an expectation that r̄Es̄. When the CS− is imposed onto a Sidman schedule, we again have a compound situation, in which pooling of expectations about the consequences of r̄ is hypothesized. In this case any reasonable pooling function should result in the CS− situation expectation r̄Es̄ *weakening* the contrary Sidman situation expectation r̄Es. Thus response rate should be lowered by a CS−.

Rescorla (personal communication, 1972) has suggested that this explanation may not be adequate to explain CS+ effects when Pavlovian training is conducted while the animal is not penned up and can respond freely (e.g., Rescorla, 1967). In this procedure, although $\bar{r}Es$ is strengthened, $r\bar{E}s$ is weakened because it is disconfirmed. No increase in rate to CS+ might then be expected. Before accepting the criticism and turning to a different explanation of probe CS + s, we will need to see more fine-grained data than are available. Does the delivery of shocks actually follow a response only infrequently? Do CS + o work unusually poorly (well) in animals for whom shock followed responses unusually frequently (infrequently). If the answer to both of these questions is yes, then our explanation of the effects of probe CS + s seem adequate even for unconstrained animals.

(b) An alternative fear-modulation account of CS+ effects is possible if we add the assumption that *an increase in fear elicits the dominant defensive response*. When the CS+ is turned on, classically conditioned fear occurs and would thus increase the probability of barrier jumping.[16]

This account of CS+ effects is testable. Autonomic concomitants of fear should be good predictors of the elicitation of responding during CS+. Correlation of avoidance responding and peripheral indices of fear is, of course, a valid strategy according to our theory. Furthermore, the concomitant measurement data that already exist are quite consistent with classically conditioned fear as an elicitor of responding. Several other predictions follow from this assumption. Other ways of increasing fear during asymptotic responding should increase response probability. Fear-eliciting drugs (e.g., adrenalin) and free shocks imposed on a well-learned avoidance baseline should correlate with the increased rate (e.g., Baum, 1967).

[16] Since our theory contends that the ambient fear level is near zero at asymptote, CS-effects must still be accounted for by lowering the strength of the ambient expectancy ($\bar{r}Es$). Moreover, it is not implausible that the CS+ increase and the CS− decrease may result from different mechanisms—in this case, CS+ from fear induction, and CS− from lowering the strength of $\bar{r}ES$. LoLordo (1967) trained dogs to avoid shock on a Sidman schedule. A CS which predicted loud noise increased the rate, but a CS which predicted absence of noise did not decrease the rate. According to the hypothesis we are presenting here, CS+ for noise increased fear, eliciting the response; CS− had no effect because signalized information about absence of noise did not change the expectations about shocks which were controlling baseline responding.

When inhibitory effects of CS− on avoidance are found, we would rely on concurrent measurement of fear indices to determine whether the decrease in avoidance rate was due to lowering expectations of shock or a decline in fear level. We are committed to the view that asymptotic responding on a simple avoidance schedule is not generated by any fear at all. So when a CS− trained *off the baseline* is imposed onto asymptotic avoidance in which shocks are no longer being received, we must predict that no fear is present to be reduced, and lowering of fear will not accompany lowering of avoidance rate. Modulating effects of off-the-baseline conditioned inhibitors should operate through lowering the $\bar{r}Es$ expectation. During *on-the-baseline* conditioning (LoLordo, 1967; Rescorla, 1967), however, the animal is still frequently shocked, and some fear may be present during avoidance and may be contributing to the control of the avoidance rate. Under these conditions, it would be possible for a CS− lowered avoidance rate to be accompanied by lowered fear. At any rate, concurrent measurement is the relevant strategy for deciding whether fear modulation or expectation modulation is operative in probe effects on avoidance.

VI. Unsolved Problems

It would be nice to be able to end here. Unfortunately several avoidance phenomena remain which our theory cannot easily explain. Handling them would seem to require additional premises of an ad hoc variety that would not be merely natural adjuncts to our central principles. Some of the phenomena to be discussed are simply failures to obtain phenomena which typically *are* in accord with our predictions. The rest are unusual cases which, as far as we know, no theory of avoidance yet advanced can handle in a principled manner.

1. Punishing the avoidance response does not always facilitate extinction and may even produce "vicious circle" behavior (Brown, 1969). We know of no coherent explanation of this significant, but rather hard to obtain phenomenon, in anyone's theory of avoidance.

2. With certain classes of responses (e.g., wheel turning in the rat), successfully acquired avoidance responding mysteriously degenerates into escape (Coons, Anderson, & Myers, 1960; Anderson & Nakamura, 1964). We do not explain this.

3. Evidence already exists suggesting that mere exposure to response-outcome contingencies may not be sufficient for expectations to develop. Animals may have to pay attention to the relevant events.[17] D'Amato et al. (1968) have shown that an external signal imposed after an avoidance response facilitates acquisition. Presumably this helps the animal to pay *attention to the relevant response* rather than to other responses made during the CS-US interval. We are not yet certain what theoretical mechanism(s) should be added to our theory to effectively handle attentional phenomena (cf., for instance, Sutherland & MacKintosh, 1971).

Turner and Solomon (1962) have collected evidence that "reflexive" kinds of responses will never be acquired in spite of numerous pairings with no shock. Furthermore, Bolles (1970) presents evidence that the operant level of a response may not predict how well it will be acquired as an avoidance response. It is possible that different responses may be differentially prepared (Seligman, 1970) to be acquired for avoidance, and that such preparedness is not a function of how probable the response is initially. Alternatively, we might have to merely restrict the class of acquirable avoidance responses to nonreflexive or "intentional" (cf. Irwin, 1971) responses to handle the Turner and Solomon, and the Bolles data.

4. Tolman and Gleitman's (1949) "latent learning" study is important for any theory of avoidance to handle and has been unduly neglected by recent theorists. Rats were first trained in a T-maze in which a left turn led to food in one distinctive compartment (c_1) and a right turn led to food in another distinctive compartment (c_2). They were then placed in c_1 and shocked. When

---

[17]Cf. footnote 10.

returned to the start box of the maze, animals now reliably ran to c_1 and not c_2. Extra premises seem necessary to handle this phenomenon.[18]

5. "Learned helplessness" effects, in which inescapable shock retards escape and avoidance learning (e.g., Seligman et al., 1971) are not explained by this theory. Some additional assumptions would be necessary (e.g., animals might acquire an expectation with special disruptive consequences that shock is independent of responding and not responding).

Concluding Remarks

Even readers who feel that this theory handles avoidance data more completely than its rivals, may feel uneasy about it for other reasons. A number of objections that have been raised about previous cognitive theories might be raised about ours as well: (*a*) that the theory's terms are used loosely, (*b*) that it is conceptually profligate, (*c*) that it is only a verbal restatement of existing noncognitive accounts, and (*d*) that it leaves the animal "lost in thought."

Looseness. Cognitive theories have frequently been accused of relying on vague terms, with no behavioral criteria for their use. We believe that this criticism does not apply to the key terms of our theory: SAO expectancies and preferences. Irwin (1971) has presented tight behavioral criteria for diagnosing such expectancies and preferences, and these criteria are met in the avoidance situation. Simplifying somewhat, we rely on the following diagnostic criteria to provide presumptive evidence that the appropriate expectancies are operative: (*a*) Suppose that no shock ($\bar{s}$) is made contingent on a response (r_t); that shock is made contingent on not making this response ($\bar{r}_t$); and that an animal exposed to these contingencies learns to perform r_t rather than $\bar{r}_t$. (*b*) Suppose further (to control for response biases) that if the role of the responses is inverted so that s is made contingent on r_t and $\bar{s}$ is made contingent on $\bar{r}_t$, the animal learns to perform $\bar{r}_t$. In this case, presumptive evidence is present that the animal has expectancies in (*a*) that $r_t E\bar{s}$ and $\bar{r}_t Es$; and in (*b*) that $r_t Es$ and $\bar{r}_t E\bar{s}$. While such data also provide presumptive evidence for a preference of $\bar{s}$ to s, this preference

---

[18] Tolman and Gleitman's experiment could be accounted for by attributing to an animal the S-S expectancy that being in c_1 leads to shock, plus the ability to make the "syllogistic" inference that if $r_{left} Ec_1$, and c_1 leads to shock, then r_{left} leads to shock. Thus a new act-outcome expectancy, $r_{left} Es$, might be acquired without direct experience. We have chosen not to take this step, in keeping with our desire not to proliferate mechanisms. On the other hand, evidence may eventually demand an S-S interpretation of animal avoidance learning. One major stumbling block to such an account is to come up with a mechanism for *using* S-S expectancies to make responses. SAO expectancies are theoretically easier to work with because the response term occurs in the expectancy, and the addition of the relevant preference is sufficient for the response to occur. In addition, some account of the relationship of S-S expectancies to classical conditioning would be needed.

Alternatively, it might be supposed that by experience with c_1 paired with shock, and c_2 paired with no shock, the animal comes to prefer c_2 to c_1 ($c_2 Pc_1$). Since the animal expects $r_{left} Ec_1$ and $r_{right} Ec_2$, he will turn right (Irwin, 1971, p. 62). Since we are not prepared to state the laws of *acquired* preferences and defend the ramifications of such a move, we can only offer this as a possible explanation.

can be tested independently of the particular expectancies at issue by doing another experiment in which r' and r̄' are substituted as responses.

The reader should note that the empirical consequences of our theory have been derived from explicitly stated properties of our key terms, rather than "surplus meaning" from their ordinary language uses. This is not to deny that such surplus meaning may prove to have heuristic value in suggesting new research (e.g., exploring information-processing strategies in animal learning).

Profligacy. It is easy to understand why cognitive theories are often accused of being conceptually profligate. At the time Ritchie proposed his S-S expectancy theory, he was choosing from Tolman's (1949) pharmacopoeia which included six types of learning. By contrast, the conceptual framework we are relying on is virtually ascetic. The acquisition of only one kind of expectancy (an act-outcome expectancy) is postulated, and the only other "learning" employed is classical conditioning of fear; yet a wide variety of avoidance phenomena can be successfully accounted for. Parsimony is difficult, if not impossible, to quantify. We would not wish to try to count up premises of our own and competing theories even if these were available in axiomatic form, which they are not. We feel, however, that our theory is no more complex even than the theories we have criticized for not dealing with vast bodies of data.

Verbal recasting of traditional noncognitive accounts. It might be argued that our theory is not really different from previous noncognitive reinforcement accounts. This impression may be created when the reader notices that our terms "situation," "response," and "outcome" have parallels, albeit roughly, in the terms "stimulus," "response," and "reinforcement" used in many previous theories. Indeed the most critical differences between our cognitive theory and previous noncognitive theories lie not in the factors in the learning situation that are considered relevant, but in the way these factors govern behavior.

1. We share the assertion with two-process theory that fear directly influences the occurrence of initial "avoidance" responses, by eliciting them. After that, we part company. According to two-process theory avoidance responses continue to be motivated by fear and reinforced by fear reduction. According, to our theory, *learned* avoidance responses come to be controlled by the expectations $r_t E \bar{s}$ and $\bar{r}_t Es$ and the preference $\bar{s}Ps$; the response would be made even in the absence of fear. Even our account of short-latency responding, which relies on expected outcomes of fear and no fear, does not converge onto two-process theory's account. Neither the actual occurrence of fear (for motivation) nor the occurrence of fear reduction (for reinforcement) is relied on in our account.

2. Aversion theory, apart from ignoring fear-related phenomena handled by our fear component, does not converge on an equivalent treatment of phenomena handled by our cognitive component. For aversion theory, it is the aversiveness of the CS which is being escaped, not the dispreferred outcome which is being avoided. The differing empirical consequences of this claim are

highlighted by different predictions about standard extinction procedures. Aversion theory must predict that avoidance responding disintegrates when classically conditioned aversion is extinguished. For our theory, extinction requires disconfirmation of at least one of the governing expectancies, which should not occur for an animal responding reliably in a standard extinction paradigm.

3. Discriminative stimulus theory agrees that it is the outcomes, shock and no shock, that are critical for avoidance, not CS escape. The theory makes no precise specification, however, of the conditions under which outcome events will or will not provide reinforcement. Vagueness of the theory is highlighted by its compatibility with almost any results from standard extinction and response-blocking paradigms. Thus we do not find that discriminative stimulus theory makes assertions that are flatly incompatible with our theory. Rather discriminative stimulus theory fails entirely to specify the means by which extinction and avoidance occur and thus is not at all equivalent to our theory, which does.

Some readers may wonder why we wish to label our theory "cognitive". Unlike the competing theories reviewed, ours attributes to an avoiding animal the capacity to store (in the form of expectancies) and use information about the relation of his actions to other events in the world. The animal can even properly be said to have acquired knowledge. It should be emphasized that such terms as "cognitive" and "knowledge" are not terms that are used *in* the theory itself, but we believe they can be intelligibly used to characterize important aspects of the way the theory functions.

"Lost in thought." Cognitive theories relying on S-S expectancies have quite properly been accused of leaving the animal "lost in thought" because they have not been able to specify how such expectancies could generate the relevant response. This problem is not present for our theory. By postulation, the presence of two SAO expectancies $S:a_1 Eo_1$ and $S:a_2 Eo_2$, and a preference $o_1 Po_2$, is a sufficient condition for the response a_1 to be made in the presence of S with a certain probability. It should be noted that this theoretical device exactly parallels the way in which Hull got the response out:

Habit strength $_S H_R$ "carries its response (R) built-in," waiting for appropriate motivational conditions (D) and stimulus conditions (S) to cause it to be produced. Similarly, expectations themselves already specify a response which is activated if preferences are appropriate and the situation occurs. The "mechanism" is parallel in both cases—by fiat!

SUMMARY

We have reviewed several previous theories of avoidance learning. Two-process fear mediation theory was explored at greatest length and criticized for failing to account for the extraordinary persistence of responding under standard extinction procedures. Several variants of this theory were found to be incapable of handling this evidence while at the same time explaining why response blocking *does* produce a rapid decline in responding. Two-process aversion theory was also found to be unable to acount for extinction data and, in addition, to be silent about fear-related phenomena in avoidance. Discriminative stimulus theory was found to be silent about an even wider range of phenomena.

We have proposed a cognitively oriented theory with two components. The cognitive component assumes that a subject has a preference for no shock over shock, and acquires two expectancies: that responding leads to no shock, and that not responding leads to shock. Behavioral criteria for diagnosing such expectancies and preferences were adapted from considerations advanced by Irwin (1971). According to the theory, the presence of the stated preference and pair of expectancies is a sufficient condition for responding to occur. The principles of the cognitive component were shown to account successfully for the troublesome data on the effects of extinction and response-blocking procedures, as well as some other extinction and acquisition data.

The theory also includes an emotional component based on the elicitation of responses by classically conditioned fear. The addition of the fear component extends our theory to cover most of the major facts of acquisition and extinction of avoidance. Several additional facts are handled with minor subsidiary principles such as stimulus generalization and pooling of separately established expectancies. Finally, we note several other phenomena which are not accounted for by this theory or by any of its competitors.

APPENDIX

The Relationship of the Cognitive Theory of Avoidance to F. W. Irwin's Theoretical Framework

We are greatly indebted to Irwin's (1971) development of a framework for cognitive theorizing. There are several ways in which we deviate from Irwin's formulation. In our theory the logical status of expectancies is different. In Irwin's system, expectancies are simply behavioral dispositions. The assertion, in his system, that an animal has certain expectancies is logically of the same form as the assertion that a match is flammable (Irwin, 1971, p. 106). If certain empirical criteria are met, it is simply true, *by definition,* that an animal has expectancies. Irwin has even been able to assert (p. 107) that data already obtained make it a *fact* that some animals have expectancies. For us, on the other hand, expectancies are hypothetical constructs in a theory (MacCorquodale & Meehl, 1948). While the theory implies that certain data should be obtained, such data would not, conversely, imply that the theory is true. We cannot preclude the possibility that other theories might explain the same data without relying on expectancies. Since the existence of expectancies is not a matter of definition for us, if confronted with a superior theory we might well conclude that animals do not have expectancies.

More technically, we are using expectancies which differ from Irwin's in several respects:

1. For Irwin, a situation is not included in the specification of an expectancy. Rather a situation specifies the circumstances in which an expectancy can be observed to operate. In our theory, a representation of the situation is considered to be a part of the structure of an expectancy itself. We say the animal expects that in a given situation an act leads to an outcome. For Irwin *in a given situation* the animal expects that an act leads to an outcome. There are several advantages to our formulation: Rather than treating separately the acquisition of an act-outcome expectancy and the development of a tendency for it to be present only in the appropriate situation, we handle both with a single structure—a situation-act-outcome expectancy. We also believe that our formulation has some heuristic value in that it makes the situation itself explicitly a matter for animal cognition. This might facilitate further development of cognitive theory to handle more complex phenomena (e.g., attention to different dimensions of situations, and S-S learning).

2. Irwin's expectancies are of the form $a_1 a_2 Eo_1$, which is read, "The animal expects that one act (a_1) rather than another act (a_2) leads to an outcome (o_1)." When expectancies correctly reflect the contingencies, such an expectancy should be generated by contingencies for which $p(o_1/a_1) > p(o_1/a_2)$. Our expectancies are of the form $S:a_1 Eo_1 o_2$, which is read, "The animal expects that in a given situation (S) an act (a_1) leads to one outcome (o_1) rather than another (o_2). In the body of the paper we omit the situation term since it is the CS onset throughout. The o_2 is also suppressed since it is $\bar{o}_1$ throughout—the class of all other outcomes. We have used responding (r) and not responding ($\bar{r}$) for specific acts, shock (s) and no shock ($\bar{s}$) for specific outcomes. Strictly speaking, our type of expectancy $a_1 Eo_1 o_2$ should be generated by contingencies for which $p(o_1/a_1) > p(o_2/a_1)$. In a case such as the one we are dealing with, where both outcomes are exhaustive and mutually exclusive it can be shown that our pair of expectancies $a_1 Eo_1 o_2$ and $a_2 Eo_2 o_1$ should be generated under the same set of circumstances as Irwin's expectancies, $a_1 a_2 Eo_1$ and $a_2 a_1 Eo_2$, and *vice versa*. Thus $a_1 Eo_1 o_2$ should be generated only if $p(o_1/a_1) > p(o_2/a_1)$, and $a_2 Eo_2 o_1$ should be generated only if $p(o_2/a_2) > p(o_1/a_2)$. If o_1 and o_2 are exhaustive, then $p(o_1/a_1) > .5$, $p(o_2/a_1) < .5$; $p(o_2/a_2) > .5$, $p(o_1/a_2) < .5$. So $p(o_1/a_1) > p(o_1/a_2)$ which should generate $a_1 a_2 Eo_1$, and $p(o_1/a_2) > p(o_2/a_1)$ which should generate $a_2 a_1 Eo_2$.

Although these two kinds of expectancies would develop in rigorously parallel fashion in the limited cases with which this paper deals, we prefer to employ single-act expectancies, partly for expositional purposes. If one were to use Irwin's type of expectancies in a theory of avoidance *acquisition* (which Irwin himself does not do), the strengths of both $r_t \bar{r}_t E\bar{s}$ and $\bar{r}_t r_t Es$ would be affected whenever either r_t or $\bar{r}_t$ was made (in fact $r_t \bar{r}_t E\bar{s}$ and $\bar{r}_t r_t Es$ would be incremented or decremented in lockstep fashion). On the other hand our expectancy $r_f E\bar{s}s$ is affected only when the animal responds, and $\bar{r}_f E s\bar{s}$ is affected only when the animal fails to respond. The effects of responding and not responding are thus stored separately; the probability of responding is of course still a joint function of both expectancies. In addition to expositional ease, we feel that having animals store separate expectancies about the outcomes of individual acts, rather than storing likelihood ratios directly, will permit greater theoretical flexibility for dealing with more complex tasks. In particular, our expectancies seem to be better suited than Irwin's for handling experiments in which an animal has available a large number of responses, each associated with a different outcome probability. Another problem is how to account for what an animal has learned when effectively only one response class is available (e.g. in Miller's (1951) experiment, the class of all responses available during CS-US pairings leads to shock). Irwinian "alternative act" expectancies seem not to apply here. Our "single response class" expectancies do apply, and we can thus parsimoniously rely on the same analysis used to account for standard avoidance (see section II-8).

REFERENCES

Anderson, N. H., & Nakamura, C. Y. Avoidance decrement in avoidance conditioning. *Journal of Comparative and Physiological Psychology*, 1964, **57**, 196–204.

Anger, D. The role of temporal discrimination in the reinforcement of Sidman avoidance behavior. *Journal of the Experimental Analysis of Behavior*, 1963, **6**, 477–506.

Annau, Z., & Kamin, L. J. The conditioned emotional response as a function of intensity of the US. *Journal of Comparative and Physiological Psychology*, 1961, **54**, 428–432.

Baum, M. Rapid extinction of an avoidance response following a period of response prevention in the avoidance apparatus. *Psychological Reports*, 1966, **18**, 59–64.

Baum, M. Perseveration of fear measured by changes in rate of avoidance responding in dogs. Unpublished doctoral dissertation, University of Pennsylvania, 1967.

Baum, M. Extinction of an avoidance response following response prevention: Some parametric investigations. *Canadian Journal of Psychology*, 1969, **23**, 1–10.

Baum, M. Extinction of avoidance response through response prevention (flooding). *Psychological Bulletin*, 1970, **74**, 276–284.

Beecroft, R. S. Patterns in avoidance extinction. *Psychonomic Science*, 1971, **23**, 53–55.

Bersh, P. J., Notterman, J. M., & Schoenfeld, W. N. Extinction of a human cardiac-response during avoidance-conditioning. *American Journal of Psychology*, 1956, **59**, 244–251.

Black, A. H. The extinction of avoidance responses under curare. *Journal of Comparative and Physiological Psychology*, 1958, **51**, 519–524.

Black, A. H. Heart rate changes during avoidance learning in dogs. *Canadian Journal of Psychology*, 1959, **13**, 229–242.

Bolles, R. C. Species-specific defense reactions and avoidance learning. *Psychological Review*, 1970, **77**, 32–48.

Bolles, R. C., Stokes, L. W., & Younger, M. S. Does CS termination reinforce avoidance behavior? *Journal of Comparative and Physiological Psychology*, 1966, **62**, 201–207.

Brown, J. S. Factors effecting self-punitive behavior. In B. A. Campbell & R. M. Church (Eds.), *Punishment and aversive behavior*. New York: Appleton-Century-Crofts, 1969. Pp. 467–514.

Brown, J. S., & Jacobs, A. The role of fear in the motivation and acquisition of responses. *Journal of Experimental Psychology*, 1949, **39**, 747–759.

Brush, E. S. Traumatic avoidance learning: The effects of conditioned stimulus length in a free-responding situation. *Journal of Comparative and Physiological Psychology*, 1957, **50**, 541–546.

Brush, F. R. The effects of shock intensity on the acquisition and extinction of an avoidance response in dogs. *Journal of Comparative and Physiological Psychology*, 1957, **50**, 547–552.

Carlson, N. J., & Black, A. H. Traumatic avoidance learning: The effects of preventing escape responses. *Canadian Journal of Psychology*, 1960, **14**, 21–28.

Church, R. M., & Black, A. H. Latency of the conditioned heart rate as a function of the CS-US interval. *Journal of Comparative and Physiological Psychology*, 1958, **51**, 478–482.

Church, R. M., Brush, F. R., & Solomon, R. L. Traumatic avoidance learning: The effects of CS-US interval with a delayed-conditioning procedure in a free-responding situation. *Journal of Comparative and Physiological Psychology*, 1956, **49**, 301–308.

Coons, E. E., Anderson, N. H., & Myers, A. K. Disappearance of avoidance responding during continued training. *Journal of Comparative and Physiological Psychology*, 1960, **53**, 290–292.

D'Amato, M. R. *Experimental psychology: Methodology, psychophysics and learning.* New York: McGraw-Hill, 1970.

D'Amato, M. R., Fazzaro, J., & Etkin, M. Anticipatory responding and avoidance discrimination as factors in avoidance conditioning. *Journal of Experimental Psychology*, 1968, **77**, 41–47.

Denny, M. R. and Weisman, R. G. Avoidance behavior as a function of length of nonshock confinement. *Journal of comparative and physiological Psychology*, 1964, **58**, 252–257.

Dinsmoor, J. A. Punishment. I. The avoidance hypothesis. *Psychological Review*, 1954, **61**, 34–46.

Grossen, N. E. Effect of aversive discriminative stimuli on appetitive behavior. *Journal of Experimental Psychology*, 1971, **88**, 90–94.

Hammond, L. J. Increased responding to CS– in differential CER. *Psychonomic Science*, 1966, **5**, 337–338.

Herrnstein, R. J. Method and theory in the study of avoidance. *Psychological Review*, 1969, **76**, 49–69.

Herrnstein, R. J., & Hineline, P. N. Negative reinforcement as shock-frequency reduction. *Journal of the Experimental Analysis of Behavior*, 1966, **9**, 421–430.

Hilgard, E. R., & Marquis, D. G. *Conditioning and learning.* New York: Appleton-Century-Crofts, 1940.

Irwin, F. W. *Intentional behavior and motivation: A cognitive theory.* New York: Lippincott, 1971.

Kamin, L. J. Traumatic avoidance learning: The effects of CS-US interval with a trace-conditioning procedure. *Journal of Comparative and Physiological Psychology*, 1954, **47**, 65–72.

Kamin, L. J. The effects of termination of the CS and avoidance of the US on avoidance learning. *Journal of Comparative and Physiological Psychology*, 1956, **49**, 420–424.

Kamin, L. J., Brimer, C. J., & Black, A. H. Conditioned suppression as a monitor of fear of the CS in the course of avoidance training. *Journal of Comparative and Physiological Psychology*, 1963, **56**, 497–501.

Katzev, R. Extinguishing avoidance responses as a function of delayed warning signal termination. *Journal of Experimental Psychology*, 1967, **75**, 339–344.

Katzev, R., & Hendersen, R. W. Effects of exteroceptive feedback stimuli on extinguishing avoidance responses in Fischer rats. *Journal of Comparative and Physiological Psychology*, 1971, **74**, 66–74.

Kimble, G. A., & Perlmuter, L. C. The problem of volition. *Psychological Review*, 1970, **77**, 361–384.

Kimmel, H. D. Instrumental factors in classical conditioning. In W. Prokasy (Ed.), *Classical conditioning.* New York: Appleton-Century-Crofts, 1965.

Konorski, J. *Conditioned reflexes and neuron organization.* Cambridge: Cambridge University Press, 1948.

LoLordo, V. M. Similarity of conditioned fear responses based upon different events. *Journal of Comparative and Physiological Psychology,* 1967, **64**, 154–158.

LoLordo, V. M., & Rescorla, R. A. Protection of the fear-eliciting capacity of a stimulus from extinction. *Acta Biologiae Experimentalis,* 1966, **26**, 251–258.

MacCorquodale, K., & Meehl, P. E. On a distinction between hypothetical constructs and intervening variables. *Psychological Review,* 1948, **55**, 95–107.

MacCorquodale, K., & Meehl, P. E. Edward C. Tolman. In W. K. Estes (Ed.) *Modern learning theory.* New York: Appleton-Century-Crofts, 1954.

Maier, S. F., Seligman, M. E. P., & Solomon, R. L. Pavlovian fear conditioning and learned helplessness effects on escape and avoidance behavior of (a) the CS-US contingency and (b) the independence of the US and voluntary responding. In B. A. Campbell & R. M. Church (Eds.), *Punishment and aversive behavior.* New York: Appleton-Century-Crofts, 1969.

Miller, N. E. Studies of fear as an acquirable drive. I. Fear as motivation and fear reduction as reinforcement in the learning of new responses. *Journal of Experimental Psychology,* 1948, **38**, 89–101.

Miller, N. E. Learnable drives and rewards. In S. S. Stevens (Ed.), *Handbook of experimental psychology.* New York: Wiley, 1951.

Mowrer, O. H. On the dual nature of learning: A re-interpretation of "conditioning" and "problem-solving." *Harvard Educational Review,* 1947, **17**, 102–148.

Osgood, C. E. Can Tolman's theory of learning handle avoidance training? *Psychological Review,* 1950, **57**, 133–137.

Page, H. A. The facilitation of experimental extinction by response prevention as a function of the acquisition of a new response. *Journal of Comparative and Physiological Psychology,* 1955, **48**, 14–16.

Page, H. A., & Hall, J. F. Experimental extinction as a function of the prevention of a response. *Journal of Comparative and Physiological Psychology,* 1953, **46**, 253–255.

Pavlov, I. P. *Conditioned reflexes.* London: Oxford University Press, 1927.

Polin, A. T. The effect of flooding and physical suppression as extinction techniques on an anxiety-motivated avoidance locomotor response. *Journal of Psychology,* 1959, **47**, 253–255.

Ray, A. J., Jr. Shuttle avoidance learning and performance: Electric shock and air-stream aversive stimulation compared. Paper presented at the meeting of the Eastern Psychological Association, Boston, April 1972.

Rescorla, R. A. Predictability and number of pairings in Pavlovian fear conditioning. *Psychonomic Science,* 1966, **4**, 383–384.

Rescorla, R. A. Inhibition of delay in Pavlovian fear conditioning. *Journal of Comparative and Physiological Psychology,* 1967, **64**, 114–120.

Rescorla, R. A., & LoLordo, V. M. Inhibition of avoidance behavior. *Journal of Comparative and Physiological Psychology,* 1965, **59**, 406–412.

Rescorla, R. A., & Solomon, R. L. Two-process learning theory: Relationships between Pavlovian conditioning and instrumental learning. *Psychological Review,* 1967, **74**, 151–182.

Reynierse, J. H. and Rizley, R. C. Relaxation and fear as determinants of maintained avoidance in rats. *Journal of Comparative and Physiological Psychology,* 1970, **72**, 223–232.

Reynolds, G. S. *A primer of operant conditioning.* Glenview, Ill.: Scott Foresman, 1968.

Ritchie, B. F. Can reinforcement theory account for avoidance? *Psychological Review,* 1951, **58**, 382–386.

Schoenfeld, W. N. An experimental approach to anxiety, escape, and avoidance behavior. In P. J. Hoch & J. Zubin (Eds.), *Anxiety*. New York: Grune & Stratton, 1950. Pp. 70–99.

Seligman, M. E. P. Chronic fear produced by unpredictable electric shock. *Journal of Comparative and Physiological Psychology*, 1968, 66, 402–411.

Seligman, M. E. P. On generality of the laws of learning. *Psychological Review*, 1970, 77, 406–418.

Seligman, M. E. P., & Campbell, B. A. Effects of intensity and duration of punishment on extinction of an avoidance response. *Journal of Comparative and Physiological Psychology*, 1965, 59, 295–297.

Seligman, M. E. P., Maier, S. F., & Solomon, R. L. Unpredictable and uncontrollable aversive events. In F. R. Brush (Ed.), *Aversive conditioning and learning*. New York: Academic Press, 1971. Pp. 347–400.

Seligman, M. E. P., & Meyer, B. Chronic fear and ulcers in rats as a function of the unpredictability of safety. *Journal of Comparative and Physiological Psychology*, 1970, 73, 202–207.

Shipley, R. H., Mack, L. A., & Levis, D. J. Effects of several response prevention procedures on activity, avoidance responding, and conditioned fear in rats. *Journal of Comparative and Physiological Psychology*, 1971, 77, 256–270.

Sidman, M. Avoidance conditioning with brief shock and no exteroceptive warning signal. *Science*, 1953, 46, 253–261.

Solomon, R. L., & Brush, E. S. Experimentally derived conceptions of anxiety and aversion. In M. R. Jones (Ed.), *Nebraska Symposium on Motivation*, 1954, 4, 212–305.

Solomon, R. L., Kamin, L. J., & Wynne, L. C. Traumatic avoidance learning: The outcomes of several extinction procedures with dogs. *Journal of Abnormal and Social Psychology*, 1953, 48, 291–302.

Solomon, R. L., & Wynne, L. C. Avoidance conditioning in normal dogs and in dogs deprived of normal autonomic functioning. *American Psychologist*, 1950, 5, 264.

Solomon, R. L., & Wynne, L. C. Traumatic avoidance learning acquisition in normal dogs. *Psychological Monographs*, 1953, 67 (4, Whole No. 354).

Solomon, R. L., & Wynne, L. C. Traumatic avoidance learning: The principles of of anxiety conservation and partial irreversibility. *Psychological Review*, 1954, 61, 353–385.

Soltysik, S. Studies on the avoidance conditioning. II. Differentiation and extinction of avoidance reflexes. *Acta Biologiae Experimentalis*, 1960, 20, 171–182.

Soltysik, S. Inhibitory feedback in avoidance conditioning. *Boletin del Instituto de Estudios Medicos y Biologicos*, Universidad Nacional de Mexico, 1963, 21, 433.

Sutherland, N. S., & MacKintosh, N. J. *Mechanisms of animal discrimination learning*. New York: Academic Press, 1971.

Taub, E., & Berman, A. J. Avoidance conditioning in the absence of relevant proprioceptive and exteroceptive feedback. *Journal of Comparative and Physiological Psychology*, 1963, 56, 1012–1016.

Taub, E., & Berman, A. J. The effect of massive somatic deafferentation on behavior and wakefulness in monkeys. In S. J. Freedman (Ed.), *The neuropsychology of spatially oriented behavior*. Homewood, Ill.: Dorsey Press, 1968.

Teuber, H.-L. Lacunae and research approaches to them. In J. C. Eccles (Ed.), *Brain and conscious experience*. New York: Springer-Verlag, 1967. Pp. 182–216.

Tolman, E. C. *Purposive behavior in animals and men*. New York: Appleton-Century, 1932.

Tolman, E. C. There is more than one kind of learning. *Psychological Review*, 1949, 56, 144–155.

Tolman, E. C., & Gleitman, H. Studies in learning and motivation. I. Equal reinforcements in both end-boxes, followed by shock in one end-box. *Journal of Experimental Psychology*, 1949, 39, 810–819.

Turner, L. H., & Solomon, R. L. Human traumatic avoidance learning: Theory and experiments on the operant-respondent distinction and failure to learn. *Psychological Monographs,* 1962, **76** (40, Whole No. 559).

Weisman, R. G., & Litner, J. S. Positive conditioned reinforcement of Sidman avoidance behavior in rats. *Journal of Comparative and Physiological Psychology,* 1969, **68,** 597–603.

Wenzel, B. M. Changes in heart rate associated with responses based on positive and negative reinforcement. *Journal of Comparative and Physiological Psychology,* 1961, **54,** 638–644.

Wynne, L. C., & Solomon, R. L. Traumatic avoidance learning: Acquisition and extinction in dogs deprived of normal peripheral autonomic functioning. *Genetic and Psychological Monographs,* 1955, **52,** 241–284.

5
DOES TELEOLOGY HAVE A PLACE IN CONDITIONING?

W. Horsley Gantt
*V. A. Hospital, Perry Point, Maryland, and
Johns Hopkins University Medical School*

I am not going to attempt to settle a problem that could not be settled by Aristotle, Leibnitz, and the prominent people that have taken up this question of what role is played by teleology in our life and in the universe. I have a much more limited position, and that is to retrace some of the evolution in my personal thinking over 40 years of work in this field of the study of behavior by the method of the conditional reflex, which was taught to me by Pavlov during my years in Russia.

I recognize that in the study of behavior we have two universes confronting us. One is the external universe, the external environment, which has been studied most intensively since the time of John Locke, who said that we come into the world as a *tabula rasa,* and that later everything is cued to experience. In his footsteps there have been prominent people who have elaborated his themes, such as Helvetius and Condorcet, and, more recently in our generation, John B. Watson and Skinner.

However, there is another universe which is much more interesting and much more complex—the *internal universe* which we carry around with us within our skins, which is bounded by our skins, and which is certainly much more complex than all the total nonorganismal universe, exclusive of the boundary of our skins. I want to say, however, that my thinking has ranged from a somewhat, if not mechanistic point of view, at least rather fatalistic point of view, to a later point of view which has emerged not (I think) on account of my age, but rather on account of the facts I have seen in the laboratory.

To review the Pavlovian work—a theme mentioned by David Grant (this volume)—Sechenov, who was called the father of Russian physiology, gave a theoretical basis to the study of behavior by the method of the conditional reflex when he wrote, in 1863, *Reflexes of the Brain.* Now this was not directed really to the external universe and the environment, but to the internal universe. Sechenov got his idea, I think, for the statement that thinking and our psychical life were reflex in character from his study of internal inhibition. He had been studying in the frog inhibition which came from putting sodium chloride on the optic thalamus. From that he derived the idea that our whole mental life was related to the inhibition of reflexes.

Now Pavlov did not derive his concept of the conditional reflex directly from Sechenov's work, but nevertheless it fitted in to a certain extent. Pavlov's conditional reflex concept came from what he saw during his study of the physiology of the gastrointestinal system in the normal animal. By using the unanesthetized, normal, healthy dog, he was able to see that this animal formed new reactions during its life to the elements of the environment around it. This study began about the time Pavlov won the Nobel Prize (which was not for the conditional reflex, but for the physiology of the digestive system), i.e., around the turn of the century, and continued until Pavlov's death 36 years later in February, 1936.

I worked with Pavlov from 1922 to 1929, and I saw him twice after that—in 1933, when I visited him in his laboratory in Russia, and again at the time of the International Physiological Congress in 1935, in Leningrad and Moscow.

Pavlov emphasized through his physiological studies the purpose of physiology; e.g., he showed that the gastric juice was secreted in proportion to the work that it had to do, a different composition, a different amount depending on whether the dog received meat, bread, or milk. And he showed that furthermore, the conditional reflex which was formed to a signal for separate foods was parallel to the unconditional reflex in its composition. He emphasized that this was the *purpose* of the reaction—to digest the food the dog would receive. He also mentioned in the first lecture of his book, *Lectures on Conditional Reflexes* (1928), that the salivary secretion was purposeful in that it had to do with the kind of food, as well as with division of the food; e.g., if you put the same substance, silicon dioxide, into the mouth of the dog in the form of pebbles, there is little secretion, but if it is divided in the form of sand there is a copious secretion which Pavlov said was related to the purpose of getting the sand out of the mouth, rinsing it out. He also noted, in the use of the pain conditional stimulus (CS) when you use a faradic shock as a conditional stimulus, that this can serve as a CS for food as long as the stimulus is not strong enough to injure the bone which underlies the skin. Pavlov pointed out how purpose comes into this reaction and into the study of human psychoses. (He took up the study of psychiatry at age 80, about my age now.) He tried to relate the clinical symptoms to the laboratory work; he theoretically assumed that schizophrenia was a protective inhibition, that it was due to the fact that the human had been subjected to what we call supramaximal stimuli, and that the excessive stimulations produced a state of inhibition which Pavlov had found in his dogs. This inhibition, characteristic of schizophrenia, protects the organism from further harmful stimulation. Here we see that Pavlov, though considered a mechanist by some people, emphasized in all his cases how purpose came into the reaction of the organs.

In the beginning of my work I was not so conscious of this teleology; I was more impressed with the fatalistic kinds of reactions which occurred, and which were exemplified by the study of the conditional reflex.

But if everything occurred according to purpose and teleology, we would be able, without doing experiments, to predict what would happen to the organism. We can't do this all the time because we do not know, we do not have the total view of what is teleological. Sometimes the organism shows what is teleological, but what it will do is not easy to predict. It is easier after the reaction occurs to say whether it seemed to be teleological or not.

In my study with my collaborators over the years, I have been impressed by the physiological as rather mechanistic reactions; e.g., if you give a certain amount of food for the conditional reflex salivary secretion, you get a regular exponential curve. You *could not predict* this; the unconditional reflex gives a linear curve, and it is not explained by teleology.

In the study of the reflex arc, which I began in my laboratory with R. B. Loucks, a National Research Fellow, back in the 1930s, and with a medical student, J. S. Light, in 1936, we began to study what part of the reflex arc was essential for the formation of the conditional reflex. By elimination successively of the different parts of the reflex arc, both on the conditional reflex side and also on the unconditional reflex side, we could eliminate the external sense organ, the afferent nerves that brought in the sensation of pain, by placing the stimulus successively on the posterior nerve roots, the posterior columns, in the cerebellum (with W. J. Brogden), and finally in the motor area of the brain. We were using this as an unconditional stimulus and in every case getting a movement, and this could be conditioned just as easily as if you applied a painful stimulus to the skin, even though in the case of the cerebellum there was not any evidence of pain. And on the conditional stimulus side you could apply the stimulus to the area striata of the visual area of the cortex instead of using a light falling on the eye.

In all of these cases it appeared to me that the function was inherent in the structure and that, given a certain structure and applying a certain stimulus, you would, in an inevitable fatalistic way, get the same kind of reaction, and that you could form the conditional reflex independently of the external environment by using all of the stimuli applied within the central nervous system. This then made it appear that the conditional reflex was a function of structure, and that we did not see any special relationship in what the organism did that could be ascribed to purpose, that it was comprehensible as a kind of mechanistic reaction.

Also, in the study of the experimental neurosis, it was always puzzling to me—and still is—why, when a dog gets a conditional stimulus, where the inhibitory one is very close to the excitatory one, based on food: why does the dog not simply neglect the one that he can't differentiate, and why does he have to become neurotic? It appears that the neurosis is formed on this principle of difficult differentiation. But it is difficult to see any underlying teleological principle in the formation of that neurotic state. Also, since then we have been studying the cardiac conditional reflex (I began studying this in 1939 with W. C. Hoffmann, of Oslo, 25 years before it became the vogue). In the study of the cardiac conditional reflex, I never heard of instrumental or operant and classical conditioning until 6 or 7 years ago, because Pavlov used what is now called instrumental conditioning as well as what is now called classical conditioning; he used them according to what he wanted to work with. Hence I never heard of the classical conditional reflex until I had a psychological student, James J. Lynch, working with me who informed me of that difference. Pavlov didn't know the difference because he used both.

Now, in the study of the cardiac conditional reflex, if we give a constant reinforcement, a painful stimulus, a signal for the pain to the foot the dog is going to get, why does the dog, when you reinforced that signal for the inevitable shock hundreds of times, perhaps a thousand times, still lift his foot to the signal, although he can never avoid the shock that is going to follow? Now it would seem there again that if the dog is simply acting according to the effect and with some kind of purpose in mind, that it is no use to lift the foot because he still gets the shock whether he lifts his foot or not. All of these experiments made it appear that the conditional reflex is a kind of phenomenon which occurs according to the structure of the nervous system and of the organism, and that it occurs within these systems in a fatalistic way.

When I began to study the cardiac conditional reflex in 1939 (Gantt & Hoffman, 1940), I canvassed a number of physiologists to ask whether they would predict there would be a cardiac change when the dog was listening to a signal for a very small amount of food, 1 gram of food. Seven of the ten that I asked said there would not be any change in the heart rate. My opinion was also more on that side because it did not appear, if you looked at it physiologically, that there would be any use for the heart rate to go up perceptibly simply to provide the salivary secretion for a very small amount (1 gram) of food. Very little physiological energy is required for secretions for that small amount of food.

However, I did not feel that I knew the answer or I would not have done the experiment. We did the experiment with various amounts of food to see whether the heart rate went up to the signal, and from that came the cardiac conditional reflex.

This early work (Gantt, Hoffman, & Dworkin, 1947; Dykman & Gantt, 1951a, 1951b) was done with W. C. Hoffmann, from Norway, and also with Dr. Roscoe Dykman, who is now in Little Rock, Arkansas, and there have been many collaborators of mine who have worked on this problem of the cardiac conditional reflex, both measuring blood flow and blood pressure.

The next question that occurred to me was, Does the heart go up simply to food in an amorphous kind of way, or does the heart make this differentiation the same way it is made with the secretion of the salivary conditional reflex in proportion to the amount of food that the dog is going to get? I could not predict this; you have to go to the experiment to find out, but it occurred that the cardiac rate goes up precisely to the amount of food that the dog is going to get; the blood pressure also goes up to the amount of food that the signal signalizes. This is a precise relationship.

In psychiatry I did not go along with the current psychiatric explanations that everything could be explained by some use to the organism, e.g., kleptomania, the results of Masserman, who was able to cure his neurotic cats by letting them drink the proper amount of alcohol. His cats were superior to my dogs, because my dogs didn't do that; the most stable ones took the most alcohol. So here was a kind of breakdown, too, in the use of the drug being used. I was also impressed in the study of the cardiac conditional reflex that there is a big difference between the cardiac reactions and the more superficially observed and specific ones, such as salivary secretion and the CR movement, in that the cardiac CR will generally, not always, form after one repetition (Newton & Gantt, 1966). If you give food once to a hungry dog, or if you give a strong shock once, on the second repetition you will see an increase in heart rate to the signal, but this does not hold for the salivary nor for the motor condition. The dog has formed a cardiac conditional reflex—not always, but more than it does not—to one episode.

This gave me the idea of the difference in conditioning the different systems which I call schizokinesis (Gantt, Dykman, & Peters, 1952; Gantt, 1953), and it also represents in my opinion, because the cardiac conditional reflex is very difficult to eradicate once it is formed, a kind of a built-in disharmony of the body which is covered by the term *schizokinesis*.

I went along with the general idea which was elaborated chiefly by Bykov in Russia during his study of the autonomic nervous system, that every function in the body could become a conditional reflex by simply using the conditional signal and following that by the unconditional stimulus, just as you do with salivation in the food response, or with the pain stimulus, or motor movement. Bykov worked especially with the kidney, as well as with a large number of other organs. Having translated his book (Bykov, 1957), I felt he was right at that time. I did not know then that he had gotten some different results from mine; e.g., with acetylcholine he reported that he got a heart rate change; Teitelbaum and I could not get any heart rate change (and acetylcholine slows the heart; thus you can't get slowing of the heart as a conditional reflex to the injection of acetylcholine) (Teitelbaum, Gantt, & Stone, 1955). Also, we worked very early, Loucks and I (Gantt, Katzenelbogen, & Loucks, 1937), with hyperglycemia in adrenaline, and we could not condition the hyperglycemia to the injection of adrenaline.

Now in a number of cases where we studied such functions as bradycardia produced by acetylcholine and hyperglycemia, it appeared that there was a dividing line which was responsible for the conditioning. The principle that I have elaborated over the years, and still am working on to see if I can find an exception, is that reactions which occur because of peripheral stimulations involving the central nervous system in their product cannot become conditional reflexes. I have not found an exception yet. A coworker asked me, "Why are you still working on that? You showed that 20 years ago." I said, "Well, I am not satisfied; there may be some exceptions somewhere." So, I am still working on the principle of peripheral and central excitation in forming the conditional reflex to see if there is any exception.

Briefly, it appears that if an excitation involves the central nervous system, such as food in a hungry dog, or such as pain, where both involve the central nervous system, the reaction can become conditioned. But if you produce a change in heart rate, e.g., by the injection of acetylcholine (slowing), or by injection of atropine (acceleration), these changes cannot be conditioned. It is impossible in our experiments to form a conditional reflex because the stimulus acts at the peripheral nerve ending; it does not produce its effect through the central nervous system. Of course there can be feedback to the central nervous system, but that is not sufficient for the formation of the conditional reflex.

A decade ago I began a study of what Bykov had worked on. I firmly believed in his experiments with renal diuresis, i.e., giving the dog a large amount of water and preceding that by a conditional stimulus. Bykov had some very beautiful, as recorded, experiments showing that the renal diuresis, the increase of urine, could be formed to the dog's drinking or injecting water into the dog's stomach or into the rectum; and furthermore Bykov showed that this had a double control. If you took out the hypophysis, you would still get the conditional diuresis; if you left the hypophysis and cut the renal nerves, you would still get it; but if you took away both controls, you would not get any renal conditional reflex. In the book that I translated (Bykov, 1957) are very precise, beautiful diagrams that show this. Now I began with two dogs simply as a kind of interesting experiment to confirm Bykov. One kidney in each dog was transplanted to the neck of the dog, and the other was extirpated, so that one kidney would do the whole work for the dog which had no nerves going to it because we had severed the nerves. It had only the blood supply assured by connecting the carotid artery to the renal artery and the jugular vein to the renal vein when the kidney was transplanted.

To my surprise, I could not get any conditional diuresis in this dog; and according to Bykov, through the hypophysis and hormones we should get a conditional diuresis. Not being able to get it in these two dogs with cervical kidneys, we studied dogs with a normal kidney in situ, taking out the other kidney and bringing the ureter from the kidney to the surface of the abdomen so that you could collect the urine without going through the bladder. The bladder is another organ, and its contraction has been reported as conditioning; and I am inclined to agree that the bladder can be conditioned, but that is not kidney secretion. And now (with my collaborators Andrew Livingston, Frances Watt Baker, from Durham, Dr. Perez-Cruet, and some others), in about 8 years working with various dogs measuring the various electrolytes, measuring the specific gravity, creatinine, protein, osmolality, volume, we have not been able to see a single element that we have measured, become a conditional reflex. The curve is perfectly flat. There is no evidence whatever of any conditional reflex diuresis. Also using phloridzin (Livingston & Gantt, 1968), which causes sugar in the urine, there is no evidence of any conditioning to the injection of phloridzin. Using pitressin, which inhibits diuresis, we were unable to get any conditional reflex to injection of this substance, though Bykov reported obtaining an inhibitory conditional reflex to pitressin.

If you measure heart rate, however, the heart rate becomes conditioned to giving the thirsty dog water to drink. Here you get another evidence of schizokinesis. One organ is being conditioned, but the other is not. And the heart rate becomes conditioned not only to giving a thirsty dog water to drink, but also to when the person appears before the dog the heart rate goes up, and that is a condition that can become a cardiac conditional reflex independently, viz., to the presence of the person. The person is a great stimulus for the heart rate of the dog, and you can form a conditional reflex to the presence of the person in the dog as easily as you can with food or with pain. Now, we got the heart rate conditioned to the drinking of water and to the presence of the person, but there was absolutely no change in the renal secretion to the drinking of this water. There was some slight evidence of inhibition of urine formation to a painful stimulus.

The inability to form a conditional reflex diuresis really began to astonish me, and I began to think, "Have I been wrong about the conditional reflex all these years?" It didn't make so much difference to me that other people were wrong, but that I had been wrong after that period of working with the conditional reflex was another matter. I felt it was really not the way it should be; and I was much more tolerant of people like Neal Miller and his assertions than I would have been otherwise when I thought of the big mistake that I could make. Realizing this makes me much more tolerant of people who have not worked as long as I, who I think are making gross errors (clinging to clichés and stereotyped thinking).

Now then, the first question is, who is right about the renal secretion? That is the fundamental question, and that is the reason I have been working for 10 years to see if I can be wrong about it; and there is certainly controversy about the renal secretion. It has been reported, as I said, by Bykov (1957) as being conditioned, and it has been reported in this country by Hofer (1963) in humans; it has also been reported by Neal Miller (Miller & DiCara, 1968). There have been some people who have repeated these experiments and have been unable to get it. For example, back in the early 1930s renal experiments were performed according to Bykov's method in the laboratory of E. K. Marshall (Personal communication, 1932) at Johns Hopkins; he was not able to get any renal diuresis. Corson (1971) at Ohio State has not been able to get a positive renal secretion. Hofer, working with humans, reported a small conditional diuresis; but urine was collected from the bladder, so he does not know whether he is conditioning the bladder or the kidney. Also these were medical students who were being paid for this work, which makes it somewhat suspect.

I began to look at what is the function of the kidney in the body. First, it is a question of whether the secretion of the kidney is reflex at all. It is subject to a number of controls; it has nerves, but exactly what the nerves do is not clear. The great expert, Irvine Page, said no one knows exactly what the nerves do. The kidney is under a number of chemical controls; it is also responsive to the composition of the blood. If you look at the function of the kidney, it is to balance the fluid of the body, and to maintain that fluid. If you compare the function of the kidney with the gastrointestinal secretions, you find a marked difference. The saliva, the gastric juice, pancreatic juice, in the human can amount to as much as several gallons of these fluids in one day. But what happens? Suppose you do not get the food signalized? There is no damage done to the body because all of this fluid is in the intestine and it is reabsorbed, nothing is lost—electrolytes, water, etc., nothing is lost from the body. There may be a slight waste of energy rather than of substance, but not very much. Now with the kidney: suppose the kidney would begin secreting to signals for water and it did not get water. The more thirsty the animal is, the greater would be the conditional reflex, if we judged by salivation and gastric juice and hunger; so the greater the thirst, the greater would be the conditional diuresis. The kidney then would be throwing off substances of which it is very much in need for the body economy.

What happens to the urine when it is secreted by the kidney? Compare that to the gastrointestinal secretions. When the urine reaches the pelvis of the kidney, it does not enter the system anymore: it goes on down into the bladder, and it is not reabsorbed by the bladder; so once it is secreted by the kidney and beyond the tubules, it is not reabsorbed but is lost completely.

It is an entirely different physiological situation whether the kidney will form a diuresis as a conditional reflex and whether there is a motor conditional reflex to the signal for pain or the gastrointestinal secretions as conditional reflexes. And if you look at the explanation in the function, it would appear then that the kidney's primary function is to balance the fluids in the body and to keep this balance, to maintain this integration for the health of the organism—as Claude Bernard (1865) pointed out—to maintain the equilibrium. Bernard pointed out that not only with the kidney but also with other functions—e.g., the blood composition—the body maintains a constancy of the *milieu interieur* as regards both temperature and composition of the blood, which he said is a prerequisite for a free and independent existence in life. Now the kidney would be violating this if it began forming diuretic CRs.

This brought me to the idea which is certainly a revolutionary one in my thinking about the conditional reflex as a stereotyped mechanistic reaction—the idea that teleology for the physiological functions of the body is maintained by the organ which you are working with. The cardiovascular reactions, the gastrointestinal, prepare the system for what is to come. But the kidney does not need that kind of preparation for the ingestion of water because it has plenty of time; it is a slow-acting organ which can take hours to throw out the excess water necessary; its function is entirely different from that of the heart or salivary gland.

Figure 1 shows the dog with the kidney in his neck—the kidney has been transplanted to the neck; that was the only kidney this dog had. He lived for

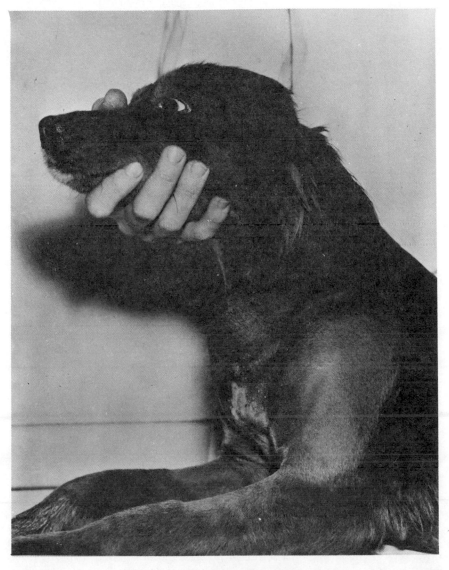

FIG. 1. Dog with kidney transplant in neck.

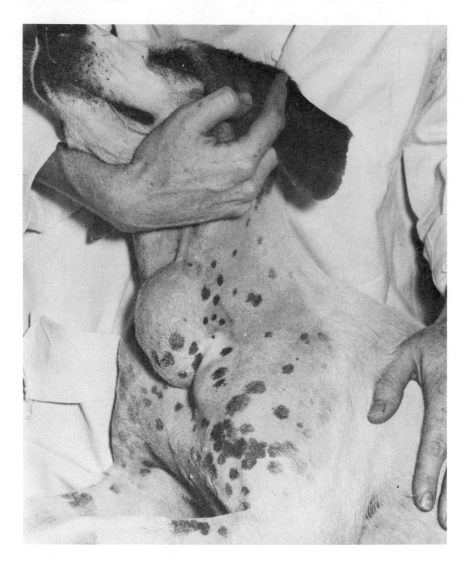

FIG. 2. Dog with kidney transplant in neck.

about 4 years in the laboratory after this transplant. Figure 2 shows another dog with a similar transplant. One can see he was in good health. Figure 3 shows the results when the dog drank fluid (milk or water) and the increase in the amount of secretion to the drinking of that fluid. Here the signal for that which you see is a perfectly flat line; there is no secretion of urine to the signal or to being in the same room or confronted by the same person who brings the water to the dog. There is no conditional secretion in these various curves. You can see in what we are measuring—electrolytes, volume, osmolality—that there is a very definite change in the solid line which is the drinking of the fluid, but there is no evidence whatever of any conditional reflex after working with these dogs for 2 years. Figure 4 shows in all these curves the same thing; there is no conditioning, no rise in the sodium or potassium; there is no evidence of a conditional reflex. Figure 5 shows the dog with an externalized ureter; just as for the dog with the cervical kidney, there is no conditional diuresis, although to the drinking of water over a period of 2 hours there is a large amount of water, a liter or sometimes more. There is a good unconditional diuresis, but there is no evidence of a conditional diuresis. Figure 6 shows a dog on the stand for collection of urine. When the dogs are placed in a familiar room or a new room to see whether there is any effect of the room where the dog has been given water to drink, we see that there is practically no difference. So if we use the surroundings as the conditional stimulus instead of a bell, and if we also use giving the dog a small amount of water to drink as a conditional signal, in none of these cases is there any regular evidence whatever, of any conditional diuresis. We could pick out perhaps some protocols which would show some evidence; but when averages are used over long periods, it isn't seen.

There are perhaps some controversial gaps about conditioning. For example, we tried conditioning the balancing mechanism of the dog, the vestibular response. If a galvanic current is passed through the external auditory meatus of the dog, you get the dog to fall over if he is blindfolded. We were able to form that as a conditional reflex. It is not possible to see any purpose served by the

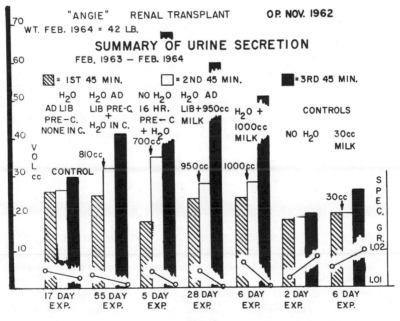

FIG. 3.

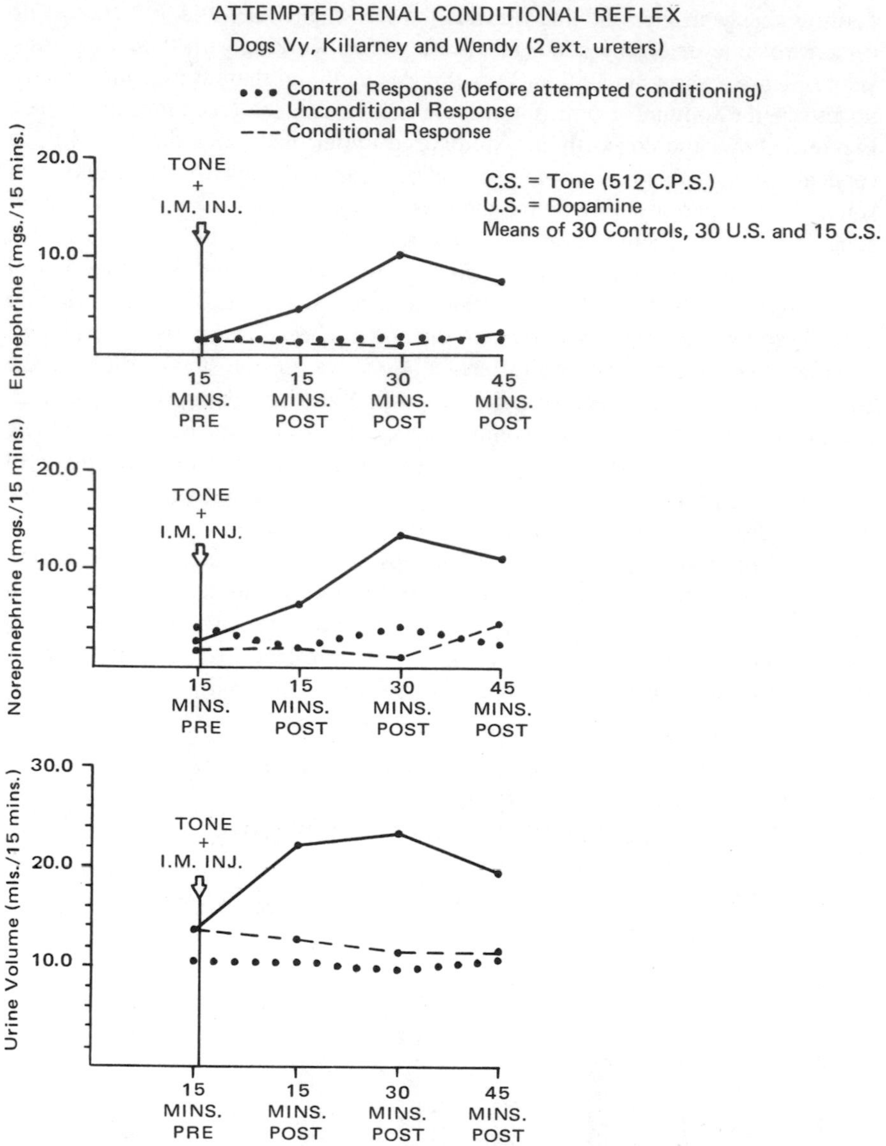
ATTEMPTED RENAL CONDITIONAL REFLEX
Dogs Vy, Killarney and Wendy (2 ext. ureters)
• • • Control Response (before attempted conditioning)
—— Unconditional Response
- - - Conditional Response
C.S. = Tone (512 C.P.S.)
U.S. = Dopamine
Means of 30 Controls, 30 U.S. and 15 C.S.
Epinephrine (mgs./15 mins.)
20.0
10.0
TONE + I.M. INJ.
15 MINS. PRE
15 MINS. POST
30 MINS. POST
45 MINS. POST
Norepinephrine (mgs./15 mins.)
20.0
10.0
TONE + I.M. INJ.
15 MINS. PRE
15 MINS. POST
30 MINS. POST
45 MINS. POST
Urine Volume (mls./15 mins.)
30.0
20.0
10.0
TONE + I.M. INJ.
15 MINS. PRE
15 MINS. POST
30 MINS. POST
45 MINS. POST

FIG. 4.

dog's falling over. But it is necessary to point out that the dog normally balances through three mechanisms—his vision, his proprioceptive system, and also his vestibular apparatus. Now if you use a pathological stimulus such as the galvanic current, and if you knock out his other two mechanisms, then you can form the vestibular loss of balance to a conditional stimulus, which does not seem to serve any purpose. But this is a pathological animal.

If we try to draw conclusions from these various—and what seem to be somewhat controversial, contradictory—experiments, in which the kidney is the chief one to which I find the principal exception where it is impossible to form any conditional response, it would appear to me then that these conclusions are justifiable. If you take a system such as the cardiovascular in the rewarding of food with the gastrointestinal secretions, the respiratory and the cardiovascular are supporting the organism, furnishing energy for something that has happened, or that is happening or may happen; the secretions are providing secretion for the acceptance of food or are aiding in digestion, and the lifting of the dog's leg is to avoid the painful shock. The fact that in these dogs this purpose is not always accomplished is not against the principle which I call *organ-system responsibility*. This principle does not mean that a given system will make the discrimination of when a reaction is useful and when it is not. It may, for example, pathologically continue to secrete gastric juice in the presence of a gastric ulcer, and to cause death by bleeding. It may continue to produce hypertension and high blood pressure, which is injurious to the person.

But although the system cannot make the differentiation, according to any *individual* reaction, as to when it is useful and when it is not useful, in the main *that system is conditionable if the conditional reflex usually serves some end or*

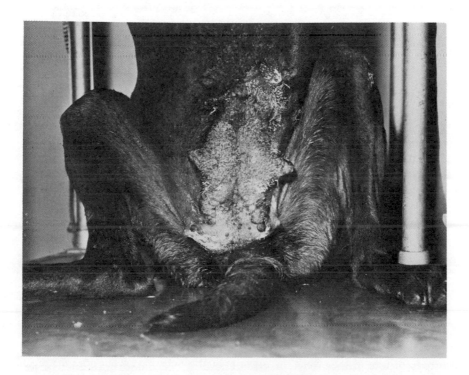

FIG. 5. Dog with externalized ureter.

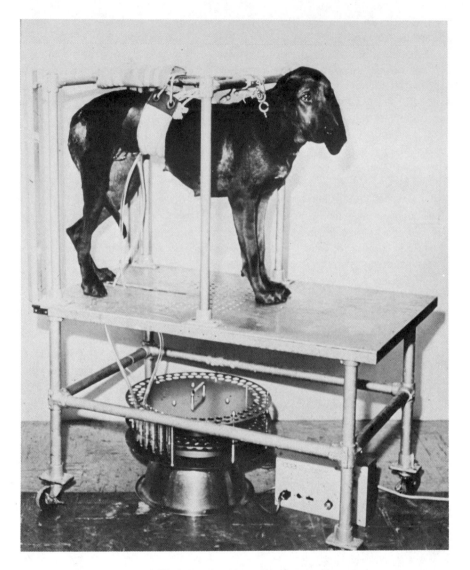

FIG. 6. Dog in urine-collection stand.

purpose in the economy of the organ. However, with the kidney we see that it would never, as far as we can understand, be of any value to begin secreting and throwing out these substances to the signals that appear, before they are actually present in the system. And my idea of organ-system responsibility, then, means that one is justified in making this differentiation, according to the physiological purpose or use, of that work the organ is in the body for. What does the organ do in the body?

The kidney has the function of maintaining homeostasis through constant composition of the blood and the various tissues and of getting rid of toxins. It is not concerned with making quick short changes simply to what goes on in the external environment, with the exception sometimes of shutting down its function. Such cessation of function can quickly be compensated for in the next few hours. The kidney is not very responsive to the external universe, it is concerned primarily with the internal universe and with maintaining a homeostatic balance within.

Organ-system responsibility and the principle of teleology does not mean that we can always make a prediction according to logic, according to teleology; we do not know precisely the teleology of the organ or of the individual. We only know a little about it. So we cannot, as the great physicists—Einstein and Planck—have done, sit down with a few figures and, without performing an experiment, make predictions and come out with great laws. You cannot do that with a biological organism because of the tremendous number of factors which are at work. So you have to go to the dog and do the experiment to find out what happens; you cannot bypass the experiment simply by the principle of organ-system responsibility. This leads me to the conclusion, however, that I, as well as other people, can be very wrong by adhering to a stereotyped paradigm without looking at the underlying function of the physiology of that system with which you are working. And although it seems very popular and very alluring to say that everything can become conditioned, that you can cure heart disease, and that you can regulate every autonomic function in the body by the simple bell-and-food paradigm, I think that we have to exercise wisdom, look more at the physiology, and understand what are the organs doing—what are they for—and, thus, get rid of stereotyped thinking (of which I must say I have been guilty over a number of years). We must look toward new experiments that will open new frontiers, and not say that everything is always for the best in this best of all possible worlds.

REFERENCES

Bernard, C. *Introduction a l'etude de la Medecine Experimentale*. Paris: 1865.

Bykov, K. M. *The cerebral cortex and the internal organs*. Trans. & ed. by W. H. Gantt. New York: Chemical Publishing, 1957.

Corson, S. A. Cardiovascular and visceral conditioning. Paper presented at the Fifth World Congress of Psychiatry, Mexico City, December 1971.

Dykman, R. A., & Gantt, W. H. A comparative study of cardiac conditioned responses and motor conditioned responses in controlled "stress" situations. *American Journal of Psychology*, 1951 (July), 6(7), 263.

Dykman, R. A., & Gantt, W. H. A comparative study of cardiac and motor conditional responses. *American Journal of Physiology*, 1951 (December), 167 (3).

Gantt, W. H., Katzenelbogen, S., & Loucks, R. B. An attempt to condition adrenalin hyperglycemia. *Bulletin of The Johns Hopkins Hospital*, 1937 (June), 9(6), 400–411.

Gantt, W. H., & Hoffmann, W. C. Conditioned cardiorespiratory changes accompanying conditioned food reflexes. *American Journal of Psychology*, 1940 (May), 129(2), 360–361.

Gantt, W. H., Hoffmann, W. C., & Dworkin, S. The cardiac conditional reflex. *Abstracts of Communications,* International Physiological Congress, Oxford, 1947 (July), **17**, 15–16.

Gantt, W. H., Dykman, R. A., & Peters, J. E. Experimental tachycardia. *American Medical Association,* Chicago, 1952. (Exhibit).

Gantt, W. H. The physiological bases of psychiatry: The conditional reflex. In J. Wortis (Ed.), *Basic problems in psychiatry.* New York: Grune & Stratton, 1953. Pp. 52–89.

Hofer, M. A., & Hinkle, L. E. Production of conditioned diuresis in man. *Journal of Clinical Investigation,* 1963, **48**(9).

Livingston, A., & Gantt, W. H. An attempt to condition components of urine formation in dogs. *Conditional Reflex,* 1968, **3**(4), 241–253.

Miller, N. E., & DiCara, L. V. Instrumental learning of urine formation in curarized rats: Changes in renal blood flow. *American Journal of Physiology,* 1968, **215**, 677–683.

Newton, J. E. O., & Gantt, W. H. One-trial cardiac conditioning in dogs. *Conditional Reflex,* 1966, **1**(4), 251–265.

Pavlov, I. P. *Lectures on conditioned reflexes.* Trans. by W. H. Gantt. New York: International Publishers, 1928.

Sechenov, I. M. *Reflexes of the brain.* St. Petersburg (USSR): 1863.

Teitelbaum, H. A., Gantt, W. H. & Stone, S. Cardiac conditional reflexes can be formed to centrally motivated states (pain) but not to peripherally acting stimuli (acetylcholine). *Journal of Pharmacological and Experimental Therapeutics,* 1955 (January), **113**(1). (Abstract)

6
SECOND-ORDER CONDITIONING: IMPLICATIONS FOR THEORIES OF LEARNING[1]

Robert A. Rescorla[2]
Yale University

Pavlov (1927) reported that a stimulus repeatedly followed by food not only comes to produce a conditioned salivary response, it also can be used as a reinforcer to establish conditioned salivation to another neutral stimulus. He termed the latter conditioning "higher-order" conditioning because it did not involve presentation of the original reinforcer, but only presentation of a stimulus which had previously been followed by that reinforcer. Although he viewed such conditioning as derivative, he thought it obeyed laws substantially similar to those of "first-order" conditioning.

However, examination of the literature on higher-order conditioning reveals that the concept has met with mixed reviews. On the one hand, it has been applauded by theorists and others who would employ Pavlovian conditioning as an explanation for more complex behaviors. For instance, it is widely used in conjunction with the notion of incentive motivation, to account for the presence of learned motivations early in an instrumental response sequence, far from the eventual goal. And it has been employed in a large number of settings to account for learning in the absence of immediate, unlearned reinforcers. That is to say, theorists who would make use of Pavlovian conditioning principles to generate less primitive behaviors have found the notion of higher-order conditioning extremely useful for extending the domain of those conditioning principles. On the other hand, experimentalists have often been harsh in their criticism of the notion of higher-order conditioning. Their attitude stems largely from the

[1] The preparation of this paper and the experiments reported here were supported by grants from the National Science Foundation.
[2] Thanks are due to Mrs. Barbara Steinfeld for aid in data collection and analysis.

127

paucity of firm demonstrations of higher-order conditioning of any reasonable magnitude.

This situation with regard to higher-order conditioning is typical of traditional American attitudes toward Pavlovian conditioning. Theorists of learning have been more than glad to adopt (sometimes with considerable distortion) selected elementary principles of conditioning, but rarely have those principles met with extensive investigation in their own right. This has led to a kind of ambivalence about the status of Pavlovian conditioning principles which is particularly apparent in the case of higher-order conditioning. As theorists we would like to use that concept, but as experimentalists bound by data, we find little justification for doing so.

One purpose of the present paper is to reconcile these contradictory views of the value of higher-order conditioning. We will first attempt to provide a somewhat more convincing demonstration that substantial higher-order conditioning can be obtained in a standard Pavlovian setting. We will then explore the kinds of associations involved in higher-order conditioning and suggest an interpretation with considerable theoretical implications for our understanding of learning processes. Finally, we will explore the relation of higher-order conditioning to a number of other learning paradigms. Again the analysis will reveal implications for our general theories of the learning process. For simplicity, our discussion will focus mainly upon the most elementary case of higher-order conditioning, second-order conditioning.

AN ILLUSTRATIVE STUDY

The assertion that a stimulus, S_2, produces a response as a result of second-order conditioning requires that two principle conditions be met: (a) the ability of S_2 to produce the response must depend upon the relation which was arranged between S_2 and some reinforcer (S_1), and (b) the ability of S_1 to serve as a reinforcer must depend upon some prior relation between it and a primary reinforcing event (US). The first condition is designed to insure that the response produced by S_2 results from associative processes; if the relation between S_2 and S_1 is irrelevant to the response produced by S_2, we would not be inclined to take the occurrence of that response as evidence of conditioning. The second condition is designed to insure that the response observed to S_2 is second-order in character; if S_1 required no prior treatment to serve as a reinforcer, then the conditioned response to S_2 would simply be an example of first-order conditioning.

A recent study in our laboratory was intended to meet these requirements (Rizley & Rescorla, 1972). We employed a conditioned suppression procedure in which conditioning is indexed by disruption of an ongoing operant behavior. Four groups of eight rats each were initially trained to bar-press on a VI food reinforcement schedule; they then received various Pavlovian fear conditioning treatments. The groups were labeled to indicate their Pavlovian treatments in three successive phases, where a "P" indicates paired presentation, a "U" unpaired presentation, an "N" no trials, and an "E" extinction. During the first conditioning phase, three groups (PPN, PPE, and PUE) each received eight paired presentations of a 10-sec. flashing light and a 1-ma. 0.5-sec. foot shock, superimposed on their bar pressing. A fourth group (UPE) received eight lights and eight shocks delivered according to an "explicitly unpaired" procedure.

After this first-order conditioning, a second phase employed the light as a reinforcer in an attempt to establish second-order conditioning to an 1,800-Hz. tone. Three groups (PPN, PPE, and UPE) received six conditioning trials consisting of a 30-sec. tone followed immediately by the 10-sec. light. A fourth group (PUE) received the same number of tones and lights, but they were unpaired. No shocks were delivered during this phase. By the end of this second phase, Groups PPN and PPE had both received initial pairing of the light with shock and then pairing of the tone with light. Groups PUE and UPE had received the same number of events, but the pairing relation has been omitted in one of the two phases. Thus it is the degree to which the tone disrupts responding in the groups during this second phase that is of interest in assessing the presence of second-order conditioning. Treatment during a subsequent third phase will be described later.

The left panel of Figure 1 describes the development of second-order conditioning during Phase II. The data are presented in terms of a suppression ratio of the form $A/(A + B)$, where A is the response rate during the tone, and B is the rate in a comparable period prior to its onset. Thus a ratio of 0 indicates no responding during the CS (good conditioning) while one of 0.5 indicates similar rates of responding during the CS and pre-CS period (little conditioning).

It is clear from the figure that Groups PPE and PPN both developed marked suppression over the six second-order trials. By the final two trials they were reliably more suppressed than either of the control groups (Mann-Whitney U's < 2, p's $< .01$). Their difference from Group PUE indicates that a paired relation between tone and light during Phase II was necessary to produce conditioning; their difference from Group UPE indicates that the light acquired its reinforcing power by prior pairing with the shock. It is also of interest to note that Group UPE showed more suppression than did Group PUE. The former group received pairing of the tone and light during Phase II, but no prior conditioning of the light. This result may indicate that the light is a mildly aversive stimulus, itself capable of producing some first-order conditioning of the tone. This result emphasizes the necessity of control procedures such as those used here.

The results of this experiment indicate that under properly controlled conditions, it is possible to produce substantial second-order conditioning. Indeed, the conditioning of the tone in Groups PPE and PPN was as rapid and complete as may be obtained by first-order conditioning using an electric-shock US.

Throughout the remainder of this paper we will see repeated demonstrations that strong second-order conditioning occurs with the conditioned fear response.

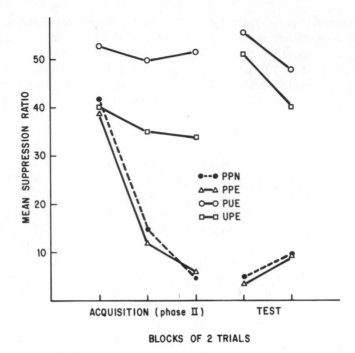

FIG. 1. Mean suppression ratio during the second-order stimulus. Extinction of the first-order stimulus intervened between acquisition and test of the second-order stimulus.

But it is well to just note that there are supporting results to indicate that second-order conditioning both is obtainable and follows laws roughly similar to those of first-order conditioning. In our laboratory, Neal Silverman has compared delay, trace, simultaneous, and backward second-order conditioning in a conditioned suppression setting. His results paralleled those of first-order conditioning, with delayed conditioning being superior to trace conditioning; neither his backward nor his simultaneous procedures generated substantial suppression. Similarly, McAllister and McAllister (1964) have found forward second-order conditioning superior to backward conditioning in a shuttlebox setting. And Anderson and his colleagues (e.g., Anderson, Plant, Johnson, & Vandever, 1967; Johnson & Anderson, 1969) have accumulated evidence for second-order fear conditioning in a number of different situations. Finally, Kamil (1969) has begun exploring second-order conditioning using conditioned suppression.

Given that second-order conditioning of such magnitude is easily produced, we can now turn to the study of the kinds of processes it involves. As we hope to demonstrate in subsequent sections, this study reveals second-order conditioning to be a very useful tool in understanding associative processes. Its investigation uncovers new ways to study traditional questions as well as raising a number of important theoretical issues on its own.

THE NATURE OF SECOND-ORDER CONDITIONING: WHAT IS LEARNED?

One of the most interesting questions one may ask about second-order conditioning concerns the kinds of associations which it represents. In a typical second-order conditioning experiment, S_1 is paired with the US, and then S_2 is regularly followed by S_1. As a consequence, S_2 comes to evoke a CR; but what associations are being formed within the organism? Three quite different conceptualizations have historically been given. (a) One obvious alternative is that second-order conditioning results in associations between S_2 and S_1. S_2 then evokes a CR because S_1 does so and S_2 is associated with S_1. This interstimulus association interpretation seems implied by the often-used statement that in second-order conditioning the first-order stimulus comes to function as a US. (b) A second alternative has been suggested by Konorski (1948). It seems plausible that during first-order conditioning, S_1 becomes associated with some representation of the US. When S_2 is followed by S_1, S_1 reactivates the US representation and gives an opportunity for S_2 to become associated with it. Thus, although S_2 is not followed by the US, it is followed by the activation of some "memory" of the US. Thus both S_1 and S_2 develop associations with a representation of the US, but not necessarily with each other. (c) A third plausible interpretation views second-order conditioning as S-R learning. Since S_1 reliably evokes a CR in the presence of S_2, a direct association could be formed between S_2 and the CR (cf. Hull, 1943).

The S_2-S_1 Possibility

One feature which distinguishes the first account from the other two is the assumption that the ability of S_2 to evoke a CR is dependent upon the continued elicitation of the CR by S_1. Thus S_2 produces a CR following second-order conditioning only because S_1 does so. Consequently, should extinction of the response to S_1 follow upon the establishment of second-order conditioning to S_2, we would anticipate loss of the conditioned response to S_2 as well. Neither of the alternative interpretations makes that prediction.

We have carried out several experiments examining this prediction. Our first attempt employed the groups for which second-order conditioning is shown in Figure 1. Following acquisition of second-order conditioning, Groups PPE, UPE, and PUE each received twenty 10-sec. nonreinforced presentations of the light (S_1) superimposed on bar pressing, in an attempt to extinguish its CR. Group PPN simply bar-pressed during this time. The question of primary interest was whether these different treatments of the first-order CS would produce a difference in second-order conditioned responding in Groups PPE and PPN. The right-hand portion of Figure 1 shows the results of test presentations of the tone following this treatment; it is clear that extinction of the response to light had no measureable effect upon second-order responding to the tone. This suggests that the response to S_2 does not depend upon maintenance of conditioning to S_1. However, this result must be interpreted with some caution, since the first-order extinction period of this experiment was not extensive and no demonstration was provided that first-order responding actually differed in Groups PPN and PPE after extinction of the light.

A second experiment, correcting these shortcomings, provided a more powerful test of the S_2-S_1 hypothesis. Two groups of eight rats each were given initial VI bar-press training and then received eight first-order conditioning trials with the 1,800-Hz. tone (S_1). Each tone was 10 seconds long and terminated in a 0.5-sec. 0.5-ma. foot shock. Then each group received second-order conditioning with a 30-sec. light CS (S_2). Each of eight trials terminated with a 10-sec. presentation of the tone. Following second-order conditioning, the eight animals of Group E received 12 nonreinforced 10-sec. presentations of S_1 on each of 3 days; the animals of Group C simply continued bar pressing during this time. On the next 2 days, two test procedures were administered. On the first test day the light was superimposed on bar pressing to assess any differences in second-order conditioning. On the second day the tone was presented during bar pressing to establish that extinction had produced a difference between the groups in first-order conditioned responding.

Figure 2 shows the acquisition of second-order conditioning to the light in the two groups; the groups did not differ at this stage. More importantly, following intervening extinction of the tone, the light test still revealed no difference between Groups E and C in second-order responding. Finally, the subsequent assessment of the tone showed Group C to have considerably more first-order conditioning than did Group E ($U = 6, p < .01$). It is especially worth noting that following extinction, Group E showed substantially more second-order conditioning than it did first-order conditioning.

These results, together with additional experiments reported by Rizley and Rescorla (1972), indicate that continued maintenance of the first-order conditioned response is not necessary for continued control over behavior by the second-order stimulus. Apparently, once second-order conditioning is established, it becomes independent of the first-order stimulus upon which it was based.

A recently completed experiment emphasizes this independence of the second-order CR. Notice that after extinction of the first-order CR in the previous experiment, the animals showed a larger CR to S_2 than to S_1. If the response to S_2 is independent of that to S_1, we should be able to use S_2 to reinforce S_1, even though S_2 originally received its value from S_1. The second-order CS should be useable as a reinforcer for its own original reinforcer. To examine this possibility, we ran two groups treated similarly to those described in the previous experiment. After bar-press training, two groups of

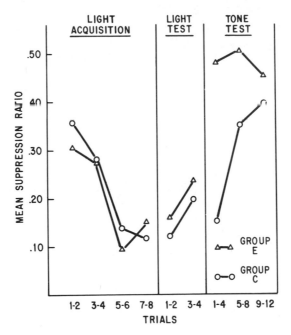

FIG. 2. Mean suppression ratio during second-order conditioning of the light and final testing of the light and tone. Extinction of the first-order tone followed acquisition of suppression to the light.

eight rats each received eight pairings of a 30-sec. light (S_1) with a 1-ma. 0.5-sec. foot shock. They then received eight second-order conditioning trials in which a 30-sec. tone (S_2) was followed by the 30-sec. light. Next both groups received 24 nonreinforced extinction trials with the light. Finally, Group E received four presentations of the light (S_1) followed by the tone (S_2) on each of 3 days; Group C received unpaired presentations of the light and tone. The question of interest is whether S_2 can serve as a reinforcer for S_1 in Group E during this final phase of the experiment. To increase the sensitivity of detection of this effect, S_1 was only incompletely extinguished. The reinforcing effect of S_2 can then be displayed as retardation in the rate of extinction of S_1.

Figure 3 shows the results of the final phase of this experiment, during which Group E received S_1 followed by S_2. Although both groups showed intermediate suppression to the light at the beginning of this phase, as training progressed, Group C extinguished more rapidly than did Group E. By the final four-trial block there was a reliable difference between the groups ($U = 14, p < .05$). This suggests that indeed second-order conditioning is sufficiently autonomous to reinforce its own previous reinforcer.

As a set, these experiments indicate that second-order conditioning is not dependent upon its first-order antecedent for the production of a conditioned response. This suggests that the first account of second-order conditioning is

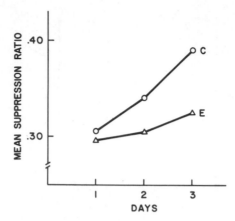

FIG. 3. Mean suppression ratio to S_1 when it is followed by S_2 (Group E) or unpaired with S_2 (Group C).

incorrect. Second-order conditioning does not seem to reflect an association between the two stimuli.

The S_2-US Possibility

In the preceding experiments we argued that degrading the value of S_1 did not change the value of S_2; from that we concluded that second-order conditioning does not critically involve an S_2-S_1 association. An analogous manipulation involving the US can provide us with information relevant to the possibility that second-order conditioning involves an association between S_2 and a representation of the US. If the US is involved in second-order conditioning, then degrading the value of the US after conditioning should attenuate the second-order CR. In a recent series of experiments in our laboratory, we have found it possible to produce such a degradation of the US by habituation procedures. Using a loud noise as a US in a conditioned suppression situation, we have found that habituation of that US prior to conditioning reduces its potency as a Pavlovian reinforcer.

In one recent experiment, (Rescorla, in press) we used this information to examine the possibility that associations with the US are involved in second-order conditioning. Two groups of 16 rats each were given initial bar-press training on a VI schedule of food reinforcement. They then received eight first-order conditioning trials, superimposed on that bar pressing. During each trial, a 30-sec. CS terminated in a 2-sec. 112-dB. noise. Then all animals received eight second-order conditioning trials in which a second 30-sec. CS was followed by 30 seconds of the first-order stimulus. Half the animals received a flashing of the house light as the first-order CS and a 1,800-Hz. tone as the second-order CS; for the other half the stimuli were interchanged. Following second-order conditioning, half the animals received habituation of the noise US. While confined to chambers discriminably different from the Skinner boxes, these animals received three sessions during each of which 36 two-second noise USs were given. The control animals received no habituation. Finally, all animals were returned to the Skinner boxes and given two presentations each of the first- and second-order CSs during each of four test sessions. The data of primary interest here are the amounts of suppression elicited by the stimuli on this final test.

FIRST ORDER CS

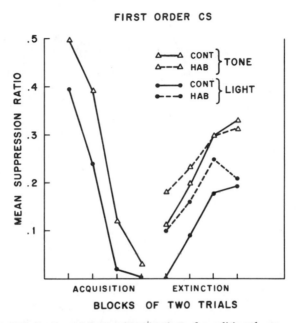

FIG. 4. Acquisition and extinction of conditioned suppression to the first-order CS paired with a noise US. Data are shown separately for groups receiving tone and light as the CS. Habituation of the noise US intervened between acquisition and extinction in the groups labeled *hab*.

Figure 4 shows the results of acquisition and extinction tests with the first-order CS, separated according to light and tone. Good first-order conditioning was found with both stimuli; the superiority of the light as a CS is typical of our laboratory, even when shock is the US. Following habituation of the noise US, extinction testing of the first-order CS revealed an attenuation of its CR (Wilson χ^2 = 4.5, df = 1, $p < .05$). Light remained superior to tone as a CS, but within each modality US habituation attenuated the CR. This reduction in first-order conditioned responding has been confirmed in a number of other studies in our laboratory. These findings with the first-order CS indicate that the noise is a potent US, but that its habituation following conditioning does produce sufficient degradation to attenuate the first-order CR.

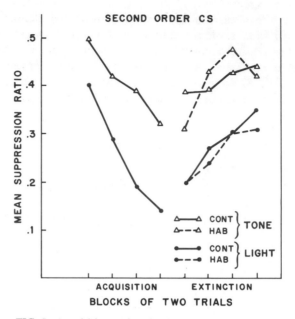

FIG. 5. Acquisition and extinction of conditioned suppression to the second-order CS. Data are shown separately for the groups receiving the tone and light as the second-order CS. Habituation of the noise US intervened between acquisition and extinction in the groups labeled *hab.*

Of more concern in the present context are the results for the second-order CS, shown in Figure 5. Substantial second-order conditioning occurred during acquisition; again the light was superior to the tone as a CS. This superiority continued in the extinction test following US habituation. However, there was no evidence within either stimulus modality that US habituation attenuated the second-order CR.

These results imply that the integrity of the US is not critical to the continued performance of a second-order CR. This suggests that what is learned in second-order conditioning is not an association between S_2 and the US. It may also be noted that this experiment provides additional evidence against the S_2-S_1 possibility. Habituation of the US did attenuate the ability of S_1 to produce a response; however, this attenuation did not affect the ability of S_2 to produce a response. Apparently whether S_1 is devalued by extinction (as in the previous experiments) or by habituation of the US (as in this experiment), its value is irrelevant to that of S_2.

The present experiments have equally important implications for the character of first-order conditioning. Just as the failure of US-habituation to affect S_2 may be taken as evidence against S_2-US association, so the success of that habituation in attenuating the response to S_1 may be taken as evidence for the importance of an S_1-US association. This possibility has been developed in more detail elsewhere (Rescorla, in press, b).

The experiments described in this section and in the preceding one may also have implications for certain practical applications of conditioning models. One common application interprets phobias as examples of Pavlovian conditioned fear reactions. The present results suggest that to the degree that such phobias involve second-order conditioning, they may continue long after both the original US and the intervening CS have lost their power. That is, they may become functionally autonomous of their origins. This autonomy may contribute heavily to the apparent irrationality of many phobic reactions. It also suggests that attempts to remove those phobias are best directed at the fear-eliciting stimuli themselves, not at their antecedents.

The S_2-R Possibility

The preceding experiments indicate that first- and second-order conditioning are independent in several important senses. First, the level of responding to a first-order stimulus is manipulable independently of that to second-order stimuli based on it. Secondly, while the first-order CS does appear to become associated with the stimulus following it (the US), the second-order CS does not become associated with its consequent stimulus (the first-order CS). More theoretically, first-order conditioning does seem partly to involve learning about the US, but second-order conditioning does not.

One remaining possibility is that second-order conditioning is S-R in character, that S_2 becomes associated with the CS which is repeatedly evoked by the first-order CS. This possibility is consistent with the outcomes of all of the experiments reported above. According to an S-R account of second-order conditioning, the response to S_2, once established, should be unaffected by either extinction of S_1 or habituation of the US. If this alternative is correct, then first-order conditioning would be S-S and second-order conditioning S-R in nature. Casually speaking, in first-order conditioning the animal may learn that he will receive a US following the CS; after second-order conditioning he may remember that he was afraid following the CS, without remembering the sources of that fear. Unfortunately, we have no additional experiments at present which provide more direct evidence on this possibility. But in any case, the study of second-order conditioning raises anew the apparently buried issue of S-R versus S-S interpretations of conditioning, it suggests a new experimental approach to that issue, and it offers a tentative compromise solution.

Whether or not one agrees with the possibility that first- and second-order conditioning differ with regard to the S-R versus S-S dichotomy, the independence of the two processes may create important analytic problems for the study of conditioning. As we will discuss in more detail later, it is common to acknowledge that an extended stimulus presentation may be conceptualized as a sequence of partially discriminable stimuli. This is true whether the stimulus in question is relatively neutral (a CS) or not (a US). Such a conceptualization permits one portion of a stimulus sequence to act as a reinforcer for earlier portions. Consequently, even in what is purportedly simple first-order conditioning, some parts of the CS may receive second-order conditioning from other parts of the CS or even from parts of the US itself. If first- and second-order conditioning are separate processes, this may result in multiple sources of responding even in simple conditioning. It is of interest to speculate that such a complication may account for the incomplete attenuation of the first-order CR when the US is habituated. Since US habituation apparently leaves intact second-order conditioning, it would not attenuate any such second-order conditioning which had occurred to the first-order CS during initial conditioning.

ADDITIONAL IMPLICATIONS OF SECOND-ORDER CONDITIONING

Our exploration of the character of second-order conditioning has raised some general issues about the nature of the conditioning process. In the following sections we consider a number of more specific issues raised by the phenomenon of second-order conditioning.

Relation to Sensory Preconditioning

There is a close parallel between the second-order conditioning experiment and the sensory preconditioning experiment. In second-order conditioning, S_1 is first paired with a US, and then S_2 is paired with S_1; finally, S_2 is presented to see what response it evokes. The sensory preconditioning experiment differs only in that it interchanges the first two steps of the experiment: first S_2 and S_1 are paired, then S_1 is paired with the US, and finally S_2 is tested. It is therefore of interest to ask whether the same kinds of processes are involved in sensory preconditioning as in second-order conditioning.

Consequently, we recently carried out a sensory preconditioning experiment with two aims in mind: (a) To adequately demonstrate the phenomenon of sensory preconditioning. Historically, sensory preconditioning has been viewed with even more skepticism than second-order conditioning, and so we thought such a demonstration to be in order. (b) Secondly, we wished to explore the effects of extinction manipulations similar to those performed above in the second-order conditioning paradigm. What effect would extinction of S_1 have if it were interposed just prior to testing of S_2; would it leave the response to S_2 intact in sensory preconditioning as it had for second-order conditioning?

This experiment is moderately complicated in design and has been reported in detail elsewhere (Rizley & Rescorla, 1972); consequently only the broad outline will be given here. Two groups of rats received a straightforward sensory preconditioning treatment in a conditioned suppression situation. They first received S_2-S_1 pairings, and then had S_1 paired with shock. One of these groups then received repeated nonreinforced presentations of S_1 to produce extinction;

the other did not. Finally, both groups were tested for sensory preconditioning by a savings procedure in which S_2 was conditioned by pairings with shock. Three control groups were run to assess the magnitude of sensory preconditioning and to insure that the S_1-shock pairings as well as the S_2-S_1 pairings were necessary to obtain the observed effects.

The results indicated that sensory preconditioning may be obtained in this setting. This agrees with several recent studies in other laboratories (e.g., Tait, Marquis, Williams, Weinstein, & Suboski, 1969). However, the suppression was substantially smaller than that one observes in comparable second-order conditioning experiments. A more sensitive savings test was indeed necessary to detect sensory preconditioning. Of equal interest, interposing extinction of S_1 completely eliminated the response to S_2. Evidently the ability of S_1 to produce a CR is important to sensory preconditioning in a way it is not for second-order conditioning.

One interpretation of these results is that sensory preconditioning involves the processes its originators thought, S-S learning. On this interpretation, S_2-S_1 associations are formed in sensory preconditioning, but not in second-order conditioning. Consequently in the former, but not the latter, the state of S_1 is important to the response to S_2. However, such a difference in explanation of two apparently related procedures is both distressing in its complexity and post hoc.

A somewhat more consistent account of the two procedures can be given within an S-R framework. According to traditional S-R interpretations of sensory preconditioning (Osgood, 1953; Coppock, 1958), during the initial S_2-S_1 pairings, S_2 comes to evoke the responses which S_1 normally produces. Furthermore, those responses have stimulus consequences (say, S_1'), so that after the first stage, S_2 produces both the behaviors usually produced by S_1 and the stimulus consequences of those behaviors. During the second phase, S_1 is paired with the US; however, during that conditioning S_1 continues to produce its own responses and their stimulus consequences (S_1'). As a result, both S_1' and S_1 become capable of producing a conditioned response. Then during the final test, S_2 evokes the response-consequences of S_1, and as a result it evokes S_1'; but since S_1' produces a response, so does S_2. Notice that according to this account the ability of S_1' to produce a CR is critical to the ability of S_2 to do so. Consequently, if we interpose extinction of S_1 (and thus of S_1') before testing S_2, we should expect to observe no sensory preconditioning.

According to this S-R account, the situation is quite different in second-order conditioning. In that case, S_2 is regularly followed by the CR (since S_1 regularly evokes it) and thus may become directly associated with the response. The continued ability of S_1 or S_1' to evoke a response is then unnecessary for S_2 to produce a test response. Thus within the same framework, the S-R interpretation predicts both the sensitivity of sensory preconditioning and the immunity of second-order conditioning to the effects of extinguishing S_1. This strengthens the conclusion of the previous section that S-R connections are involved in such conditioning paradigms.

Whichever interpretation one favors, it is clear that the ability of S_1 to produce a CR at the time it is paired with S_2 is of no minor importance. The resulting response to S_2 is not only substantially stronger, but also less dependent upon the response to S_1. The learning about sequences of neutral stimuli apparently is importantly different from the learning about ones of affective consequence.

Relation to Conditioned Inhibition

The second-order conditioning paradigm is also related to another important conditioning paradigm—conditioned inhibition. In a conditioned inhibition paradigm, two kinds of trials are presented: S_1 reinforced, and an $S_1 S_2$ compound nonreinforced. In some variations of this procedure, S_2 precedes S_1 during nonreinforced compound trials. The typical outcome of this procedure (cf. Konorski, 1967; Pavlov, 1927; Rescorla, 1969) is that S_2 develops the ability to inhibit the conditioned response normally evoked by S_1. That is, the result of this paradigm is opposite to that of the second-order conditioning paradigm. Despite the fact that the procedures engaged in by the experimenter are highly similar, the second-order conditioning experiment enables S_2 to evoke a response, while conditioned inhibition training endows S_2 with the power to inhibit the CR. An understanding of this difference in outcome is clearly of importance for the understanding of both second-order conditioning and conditioned inhibition.

Several procedural differences between the paradigms might be expected to be important. (a) First, investigators of conditioned inhibition have typically employed a relatively large number of trials before assessing the inhibitory power of S_2; in contrast, investigators of second-order conditioning have typically looked for conditioning after only a few trials. (b) Secondly, Pavlov (1927) has argued that the degree to which S_2 continues during the presentation of S_1 is of importance. He comments that he was unable to obtain second-order conditioning if the two stimuli overlapped; rather, the result was conditioned inhibition. (c) Finally, partly because of the difference in number of S_2-S_1 trials used with the two paradigms, experimenters have differed in whether they continue to present S_1 reinforced trials. Those investigating conditioned inhibition have often given reinforced presentation of S_1 intermingled with the $S_2 S_1$ trials; on the other hand, those examining second-order conditioning have avoided the continued reinforcement of S_1, presumably fearing the charge of subtle first-order conditioning of S_2 if the reinforcer is continued in any capacity. It seems unlikely that continuing to reinforce S_1 when it is presented alone would attenuate the development of second-order conditioning to S_2, but this is a dimension along which such studies have differed.

We recently performed an experiment designed to permit observation of both second-order conditioning and conditioned inhibition within the same setting, as well as to examine the importance of these variables. We used a simple conditioned suppression procedure in which two groups of rats received both S_1

reinforced and $S_2 S_1$ nonreinforced trials. Each conditioning session involved the superimposition of four conditioning trials upon the bar-press performance. On the first 2 days, all trials involved the presentation of a 10-sec. flashing light (S_1) terminating in a 0.5-ma. 0.5-sec. foot shock. Thereafter S_1 reinforced and $S_2 S_1$ nonreinforced trials were intermixed. On one trial of each day, a 10-sec. flashing light (S_1) terminated in foot shock. On the remaining three trials, a 1,800 Hz. tone (S_2) was presented together with S_1 and the compound was nonreinforced. In Group I, S_2 onset preceded S_1 by 30 seconds and terminated with the onset of S_1. The treatment of Group II was identical, except that S_2 continued during the 10 seconds of S_1. Because these treatments were administered during bar pressing, it was possible to observe the response to S_2 as a function of number of conditioning trials.

The left-hand side of Figure 6 shows the course of conditioning during the first 30 seconds of S_2, plotted in blocks of three trials. It is clear that both groups initially developed substantial conditioned suppression. This suggests that indeed intermingled S_1-reinforced trials do not prevent the development of second-order conditioning to S_2. However, as conditioning proceeded, both groups showed attenuation of the suppression evoked by S_2. Furthermore, the magnitude of that attenuation was greater in Group II, the group for which S_2 overlapped S_1. By the eighth day of conditioning, this difference was reliable ($U = 13$, $p < .05$). This suggests that although Pavlov was incorrect in asserting

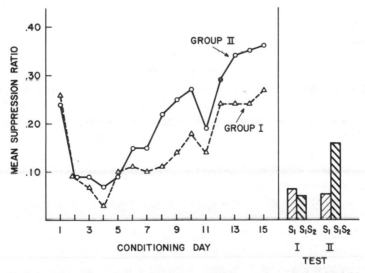

FIG. 6. The course of second-order conditioning and conditioned inhibition. The left-hand panel shows the change in suppression to a tone which precedes a nonreinforced light. For Group II the tone overlapped the light; for Group I it did not. The right-hand panel shows the results of test presentations of the light alone and light-tone compound.

that second-order conditioning is not obtainable when S_2 and S_1 overlap, he was correct in believing that the overlap interferes with that conditioning. It may be noted in passing that it is widely believed that with first-order conditioning procedures, overlap facilitates, rather than retards, the development of an excitatory CR. This appears not to be the case for second-order conditioning.

Although the course of conditioning indicated a loss of suppression to S_2, it did not provide evidence directly relevant to the issue of conditioned inhibition. Consequently, we terminated conditioning after 15 days and carried out a summation test for conditioned inhibition. The logic of this test is that S_2 is identified as an inhibitor of fear if its presentation disrupts the suppression which a known response elicitor would have produced in its absence (Rescorla, 1969). Consequently, we compared the response to S_1, a known fear elicitor, when it was presented alone and when it was preceded by S_2. Because the two groups had received experience with different S_2 durations during conditioning, we tested each group with each S_2 duration. Thus the summation test involved two nonreinforced presentations of each of three kinds of trials: S_1 presented alone for 10 seconds, S_1 when preceded by a 30-sec. S_2, and S_1 when preceded by a 30-sec. S_2 which additionally continued during S_1. The right-hand side of Figure 6 shows the results of this test. Both groups showed substantial and equal suppression to S_1. Furthermore, within each group, S_2 duration had little effect; consequently, the two kinds of compound test trials have been combined. It is clear that in Group II, preceding S_1 with S_2 attenuated the response to S_1; however, in Group I presentation of S_2 had no measurable effect. Statistical comparisons revealed that within Group II, the compound trials gave less suppression than did S_1 alone (Wilcoxon $T = 0, p < .05$); furthermore, Group II responded reliably more on compound trials than did Group I ($U = 14, p < .05$). It should be noted, however, that administration of several additional test sessions did reveal some evidence for inhibition to S_2 in Group I. Because testing involved some trials on which S_2 overlapped S_1, it is difficult to know whether Group I actually controlled a small amount of inhibition because of its conditioning treatment, or whether that inhibition developed during the testing itself. In any case, this study indicates that both second-order conditioning and conditioned inhibition are observable in the same setting, but that their appearance is a function of number of trials and degree of stimulus overlap. For a related result, see Herendeen and Anderson (1968).

It is of interest to ask what kind of a theory would permit repeated exposure to the same training conditions to yield first conditioned excitation and then conditioned inhibition. Our own thinking favors accepting the implication of earlier studies that first- and second-order conditioning occur independently of one another, although both can lead to the development of suppression. Early in the application of this procedure, S_2 is repeatedly followed by an effective first-order stimulus, S_1, and consequently may be expected to develop second-order conditioning. Because S_1 retains its power through separate reinforcement, and because S_2 is regularly followed by S_1, at this stage there is no reason to expect that this second-order conditioning will disappear; rather there is every reason to expect that we have arranged adequate conditions for its maintenance.

On the other hand, we know from many other studies in which S_2 is coterminous with S_1 and the compound nonreinforced, that we may expect S_2 to acquire first-order conditioned inhibition. Rescorla and Wagner (1972) have provided a quantitative model of conditioning which adequately explicates this finding. According to that theory the condition for the development of conditioned inhibition to a stimulus is that a conditioned response be evoked in its presence but that no reinforcement ensue. That is, conditioned inhibition develops whenever the associative strength evoked in the presence of a stimulus is too high to be appropriate to the subsequent US. This condition, too, is clearly satisfied by S_2 in the current paradigms; it is a stimulus in the presence of which considerable associative strength is evoked by S_1, but which is never reinforced.

It therefore seems reasonable to expect that the development of (first-order) conditioned inhibition becomes superimposed upon the second-order conditioning of S_2. Considerable other work with conditioning (see Rescorla & Wagner, 1972) indicates that in such settings the learning rate parameters for the development of conditioned inhibition are quite low. Consequently, it seems reasonable to expect that we would first observe the second-order conditioned response and only later see the development of conditioned inhibition. Furthermore, it is plausible that the actual presence of S_2 at the time of nonreinforcement would maximize the development of inhibition to it. Presumably this accounts for the superior development of inhibition in Group II over Group I in the present study. This is not to say that terminating S_2 prior to S_1 onset will prevent the development of inhibition to S_2; indeed, there are available studies which would contradict such an assertion (Rescorla & LoLordo, 1965; Rescorla, 1969). However, when S_2 terminates before S_1 onset, there are only the trace aftereffects of S_2 present during nonreinforcement, and we may well expect these to generalize only partially to S_2 itself.

Once S_2 comes to produce conditioned inhibition, it will attenuate the fear response produced by S_1. Consequently, on $S_2 S_1$ trials, S_2 will be followed by a stimulus which has less ability to provoke a fear response. If, as we have suggested earlier, second-order conditioning involves S-R learning, then we would expect this to result in some extinction of the second-order conditioned response. Such extinction would reflect itself in the observed attenuation of responding to S_2 as conditioning proceeds.

In summary, one account of such experiments is as follows: Initially, S_2 develops second-order conditioning because it is followed by the fear-producing S_1. Because S_2 is presented with an adequate fear elicitor and nonreinforced, however, it gradually develops conditioned inhibition. That inhibition attenuates the response to S_1, which in turn makes it a less potent reinforcer and thus allows extinction of the second-order conditioning to S_2.

This is only a very general account of the relationship between second-order conditioning and conditioned inhibition. However, the assumption that first- and second-order conditioning processes exist independently side by side does provide a plausible account of the occurrence of both excitatory and inhibitory outcomes and of the variables which affect their occurrence.

SOME COMMENTS ON SECOND-ORDER CONDITIONING DURING SEQUENTIAL PRESENTATION OF STIMULI

In all of our previous discussions we have dealt with second-order conditioning under conditions where the first-order stimulus is the only active reinforcer. Even in the case of the conditioned inhibition paradigm, although S_1 was reinforced when presented alone, the only reinforcement present at the time of second-order conditioning was S_1; the original US was carefully omitted. But theoretically and empirically many of the situations in which second-order conditioning occurs involve the eventual delivery of the US. That is to say, many situations arranging the conditions for second-order conditioning actually involve the sequential presentation of stimuli which eventually terminate in the US. Thus we may expect stimuli early in the sequence to benefit both from the eventual primary reinforcement and from the second-order conditioning of subsequent stimuli in the sequence. This point has been made especially clear by Wickens (1965), who used second-order conditioning to account for different levels of conditioning to sequentially presented stimuli.

One point to notice about such situations is that the available data (e.g., Williams, 1965; Rescorla, 1967; Scheuer & Keeter, 1969) indicates that with extensive training the early stimuli in a sequence preceding the US actually lose their ability to evoke a response. It seems reasonable to assume that this loss is analogous to that obtained in the conditioned inhibition paradigm discussed in the preceding section. That is to say, inhibition of delay and similar phenomena represent the development of conditioned inhibition superimposed upon the earlier developing second-order conditioning.

However, our earlier discussions have emphasized evidence that second-order conditioning and first-order conditioning are independent processes. If this is the case, should it not be possible to arrange it so that stimuli early in a sequence preceding a US actually receive more total conditioning than do later stimuli? The stimuli early in the sequence have not only a somewhat delayed US as a source for first-order conditioning; they also have later stimuli as a source for second-order conditioning. In contrast, a stimulus just preceding the US has a perhaps more favorable relation to the US for first-order conditioning but has no opportunity to acquire second-order strength. Indeed, one might think that by multiplying the possibilities of second-order conditioning he could essentially multiply without limit the power of a sequence-terminating US.

Under some circumstances this superior conditioning of earlier stimuli in the sequence apparently occurs. For instance, early in long delay conditioning, the onset of a CS evokes a greater conditioning response than do later parts of that stimulus (Rescorla, 1967). In addition, one may interpret some of the findings in support of informational variables in conditioning (e.g., Egger & Miller, 1962, 1963) as consistent with this prediction. There stimuli early in a sequence preceding a US often control a greater conditioned response than do later stimuli; one interpretation is that those earlier stimuli are favorably placed for second-order conditioning and also close enough to the final US to obtain considerable conditioning from it (cf. Rescorla, 1972).

But there is a process which apparently prevents second-order conditioning from multiplying the conditioning of early stimuli without limitation. This is the phenomenon of blocking, first investigated in detail by Kamin (1968, 1969). Kamin has demonstrated with simultaneously presented compound stimuli terminating in reinforcement, that previous training on one stimulus will attenuate conditioning of other stimuli in the compound. This ability of one stimulus to block conditioning to another stimulus has been explored in detail and has received a reasonably successful theoretical treatment from Rescorla and Wagner (1972). According to that account, USs preceded by conditioned CSs are relatively ineffective as reinforcers.

A related effect may be expected to occur with sequentially presented stimuli. To the degree a stimulus late in a sequence preceding a US becomes conditioned, it will be able to produce second-order conditioning of earlier stimuli, but it will also block first-order conditioning of those stimuli. That is, because the later stimuli are conditioned, they will attenuate the effectiveness of the US and thus attenuate first-order conditioning of stimuli earlier in the sequence. Thus, there is a trade-off between first- and second-order conditioning in such situations. To the degree a later stimulus becomes conditioned it can serve as a good second-order conditioner, but to that same degree it will interfere with first-order conditioning of earlier stimuli.

This reasoning has received support from a recent series of experiments carried out in our laboratory. We have found that interpolating an already-conditioned CS between a target CS and the US will attenuate conditioning to that target stimulus. Furthermore, that attenuation is greatest when the interpolated stimulus precedes the US but is in an unfavorable position for setting up second-order conditioning to earlier stimuli. Such experiments provide evidence for blocking in sequential stimulus compounds. But more important for the present discussion, they indicate that although second-order conditioning may be expected to benefit stimuli early in a sequence, that effect may be more than compensated for by the loss in first-order conditioning due to blocking. Because of this, the assumption that first- and second-order conditioning result in independent associations for a CS need not imply virtually unlimited conditioning to stimuli early in a sequence.

One may extend the analysis of sequential stimulus presentations a step further. We have noted in earlier sections that one can consider a single stimulus presented for a long period as conceptually divisible into partially discriminable subparts. This means that a CS of extended duration may actually produce second-order conditioning within itself. Some attributes of the CS which are present primarily at stimulus onset may receive second-order conditioning from aspects which are also present at the time of US delivery.

One reason that we might have some hesitancy about accepting such an implication is that it smacks of simultaneous conditioning. Depending upon how the long CS is conceptually divided, the kind of second-order conditioning we are discussing might actually rely upon conditioning from one stimulus to another when their onsets are simultaneous. Simultaneous conditioning is another of those Pavlovian concepts which have fallen into empirical disfavor. However, Heth and Rescorla (in press) have recently reported convincing data to indicate that simultaneous fear conditioning does occur in first-order conditioning paradigms. Without giving a detailed discussion here, the key to that demonstration is the arrangement that the CS and US onsets are simultaneous but that the CS terminates prior to the US. Under these circumstances considerable first-order conditioning occurs to the CS.

This kind of stimulus relationship may be exactly the one conceptually applicable to second-order conditioning within long delay CSs. That is, we may think of certain aspects of such a stimulus as only being present with the CS onset, whereas other aspects may persist throughout the duration of the CS. One case of within-CS second-order conditioning (presumably the weakest case) would involve the second-order conditioning from such durational stimuli to onset stimuli. The two stimuli are initiated together, but the stimulus to receive second-order conditioning terminates first. This is exactly the second-order analogue to the Heth and Rescorla first-order procedure.

To see whether second-order conditioning could occur with this kind of relationship, we recently carried out a conditioned suppression experiment similar to those reported above. Three groups of eight rats each (Groups F, S, and U) received a 60-sec. light terminating in a shock, in order to establish it as a first-order CS. A control group (Group C) received the light and shock unpaired. Then, during a subsequent second-order conditioning phase, Group S (simultaneous) received nonshocked trials on which a 30-sec. tone overlapped the first half of the 60-sec. light. The control group from Phase I received the same treatment; Group F (forward) received the tone for 30 seconds prior to the 60-sec. light, and Group U (unpaired) received the light and tone in an explicitly unpaired procedure. These latter two groups were included to determine the limits of good second-order conditioning (a forward relation in Group F) and poor conditioning (an unpaired control procedure in Group U). The critical issue was how much conditioning we would observe in the critical group which received simultaneous onset of the first- and second-order stimuli.

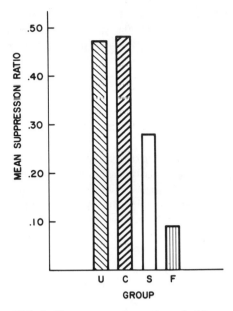

FIG. 7. Mean suppression ratio evoked by a second-order conditioned stimulus on a single test trial. Groups F and S received forward and simultaneous second-order conditioning, respectively. Groups U and C received control treatments.

After eight second-order conditioning trials, a single 30-sec. test presentation of the tone alone was superimposed upon bar pressing in all four groups. Figure 7 shows the mean suppression ratio on that test. Neither of the control groups (Group C and U) showed evidence of fear to the CS, while Group F showed strong suppression to the tone. Of most interest, however, is the substantial conditioning in Group S. Group S was reliably more suppressed than either of the controls (U's = 7, 8; p's < .01) but less suppressed than Group F ($U = 1$, $p < .01$). Apparently with such stimulus arrangements substantial simultaneous second-order conditioning may be obtained. These data make more plausible the notion that internal second-order conditioning within a long delayed CS may be an important process. Even stimuli presented simultaneously with a first-order stimulus accumulate some second-order conditioning.

There is also one anomalous phenomenon which may be made comprehensible by this analysis. Several authors (cf., Eysenck, 1968; Rohrbough & Riccio, 1970) have reported that under some circumstances the initial effect of nonreinforced presentation of a first-order CS is not to produce extinction but rather to enhance the conditioning controlled by that stimulus. It seems possible that such enhancement is due to second-order conditioning from one part of the CS to another, thus increasing the total amount of conditioning the stimulus controls. Apparently, in this case the magnitude of the second-order conditioning is more than sufficient to offset the decrement in first-order conditioning produced by nonreinforcement. One might expect this to occur early in conditioning, when second-order conditioning could produce substantial increments, but before first-order conditioning is so advanced that nonreinforced presentations produce substantial decrements (cf. Rescorla & Wagner, 1972). It is of interest to note that the reports of this "self-reinforcement" enhancement have all come from situations involving relatively few trials prior to the "self-reinforcement" trial.

In any case, this example illustrates that consideration of the effects of second-order stimuli may lead to unexpected consequences for many experimental paradigms. Even the time-honored extinction paradigm may actually have quite different effects if the conditions for second-order conditioning are manipulated.

CONCLUSION

The aim of this paper has been multiple. First we have wished to rehabilitate the notion of higher-order conditioning; to that end we have presented demonstrations that it is both substantial and reliable in its occurrence. We have also provided some evidence concerning the nature of associations in second-order conditioning, suggesting that stimuli-response associations may be involved. Furthermore, those experiments have indicated that first-order conditioning may be of quite a different sort than second-order conditioning; the two kinds of conditioning may be both empirically and theoretically more independent than has normally been thought.

We have also considered a number of implications of second-order conditioning for other conditioning paradigms. These considerations provided some understanding for the related phenomena of sensory preconditioning and conditioned inhibition. Finally, we have dealt with some implications of second-order conditioning for sequential stimulus situations and pointed to some unusual predictions made from such an analysis.

The results observed here indicate that second-order conditioning can play a substantial role in governing behavior. Furthermore, its presence may need to be taken more seriously in a number of apparently simple conditioning situations.

REFERENCES

Anderson, D. C., Plant, C., Johnson, D., & Vandever, J. Second-order aversive classical conditioning. *Canadian Journal of Psychology,* 1967, **21,** 120–131.

Coppock, W. J. Pre-extinction in sensory preconditioning. *Journal of Experimental Psychology,* 1958, **55,** 213–219.

Egger, D. M., & Miller, N. E. Secondary reinforcement in rats as a function of information value and reliability of the stimulus. *Journal of Experimental Psychology,* 1962, **64,** 97–104.

Egger, D. M., & Miller, N. E. When is a reward reinforcing? An experimental study of the information hypothesis. *Journal of Comparative and Physiological Psychology*, 1963, **56**, 132–137.

Eysenck, H. J. A theory of the incubation of anxiety/fear responses. *Behavior Research and Therapy*, 1968, **6**, 309–321.

Herendeen, D., & Anderson, D. C. Dual effects of a second-order conditioned stimulus: Excitation and inhibition. *Psychonomic Science*, 1968, **13**, 15–16

Heth, C. D., & Rescorla, R. A. Simultaneous and backward fear conditioning. *Journal of Comparative and Physiological Psychology*, in press.

Hull, C. L. *Principles of behavior*. New York: Appleton-Century-Crofts, 1943.

Johnson, D., & Anderson, D. C. Acquisition of a second-order classically conditioned response. *Canadian Journal of Psychology*, 1969, **23**, 174–183.

Kamil, A. C. Some parameters of the second-order conditioning of fear in rats. *Journal of Comparative and Physiological Psychology*, 1969, **67**, 364–369.

Kamin, L. J. "Attention-like" processes in classical conditioning. In M. R. Jones (Ed.), *Miami symposium on the prediction of behavior: Aversive stimulation*. Miami: University of Miami Press, 1968.

Kamin, L. J. Predictability, surprise, attention, and conditioning. In B. A. Campbell & R. M. Church (Eds.), *Punishment and aversive behavior*. New York: Appleton-Century-Crofts, 1969.

Konorski, J. *Conditioned reflexes and neuron organization*. Cambridge: Cambridge University Press, 1948.

Konorski, J. *Integrative Activity of the Brain*. Chicago: University of Chicago Press, 1967.

McAllister, D. E., & McAllister, W. R. Second-order conditioning of fear. *Psychonomic Science*, 1964, **1**, 383–384.

Osgood, C. E. *Method and theory in experimental psychology*. New York: Oxford University Press, 1953.

Pavlov, I. P. *Conditioned reflexes*. London: Oxford University Press, 1927.

Rescorla, R. A. Inhibition of delay in Pavlovian fear conditioning. *Journal of Comparative and Physiological Psychology*, 1967, **64**, 114–120.

Rescorla, R. A. Pavlovian conditioned inhibition. *Psychological Bulletin*, 1969, **72**, 77–94.

Rescorla, R. A. Informational variables in Pavlovian conditioning. In G. Bower (Ed.), *The psychology of learning and motivation*. Vol. 6. New York: Academic Press, 1972.

Rescorla, R. A. The effect of US habituation following conditioning. *Journal of Comparative and Physiological Psychology*, in press. (a)

Rescorla, R. A. A model of Pavlovian conditioning. In V. S. Rusinov (Ed.), *Mechanisms of formation and inhibition of conditional reflex*. Moscow: Academy of Sciences of the USSR, in press. (b)

Rescorla, R. A., & LoLordo, V. M. Inhibition of avoidance behavior. *Journal of Comparative and Physiological Psychology*, 1965, **59**, 406–412.

Rescorla, R. A., & Wagner, A. R. A theory of Pavlovian conditioning: Variations in the effectiveness of reinforcement and nonreinforcement. In A. Black & W. F. Prokasy (Eds.), *Classical Conditioning II*. New York: Appleton-Century-Crofts, 1972.

Rizley, R. C., & Rescorla, R. A. Associations in second-order conditioning and sensory preconditioning. *Journal of Comparative and Physiological Psychology*, 1972, **81**, 1–11.

Rohrbaugh, M., & Riccio, D. C. Paradoxical enhancement of learned fear. *Journal of Abnormal Psychology*, 1970, **75**, 210–216.

Scheuer, C., & Keeter, W. H. Temporal vs. discriminative factors in the maintenance of conditioned suppression: A test of the information hypothesis. *Psychonomic Science*, 1969, **15**, 21–22.

Tait, R. W., Marquis, H. A., Williams, D. R., Weinstein, L., & Suboski, M. W. Extinction of sensory preconditioning using CER training. *Journal of Comparative and Physiological Psychology*, 1969, **69**, 170–172.

Wickens, D. D. Compound conditioning in humans and cats. In W. F. Prokasy (Ed.), *Classical conditioning: A symposium.* New York: Appleton-Century-Crofts, 1965.

Williams, D. R. Classical conditioning and incentive motivation. In W. F. Prokasy (Ed.), *Classical conditioning: A symposium.* New York: Appleton-Century-Crofts, 1965.

7
"CONTINGENCY" IN BEHAVIOR THEORY

W. N. Schoenfeld, B. K. Cole, J. Lang, and R. Mankoff
Queens College

1. A science of behavior has two primary facets: (*a*) to divide the behavior stream into categories for measurement, and (*b*) to classify the operations which influence those behavior categories. A single conceptualization, the "reflex," has become prominent in the experimental analysis of behavior over the last three-fourths of a century, presumably because it contributes to the solution of both problems. The reflex concept, it was supposed, provided an analysis of both the behavior and its controlling influences, attributing causality to a hypothetical, inductively reached connection between the two. Since its introduction two centuries earlier, the reflex concept has been empirically validated and descriptively refined until at present the "response" has become a credible unit of behavior, the "stimulus" a tenable unit of influence upon that behavior, and their interconnection the accepted mediator of that influence.

The analytic power of the reflexes isolated by early investigators was so exemplary and impressive that the reflex became the dominant unit of behavior theory. From this tradition, Pavlov extended the concept to encompass procedures which shifted the effective control of a response from one stimulus to another. He needed only to interject a hypothetical connection between real stimuli and real responses to outline a physiological model of a reflex arc. The interposed connection was equally logical whether the reflex was initially functional, i.e., "unconditional," or was produced only after Pavlov's procedures had been applied, i.e., "conditional." The appearance of the "conditional response" following the "conditional stimulus" forced the inference that a "new reflex" has been formed. Although the particular stimuli and responses varied across many demonstrations, the notion of a mediating interconnection became a preferred and standard inference whereby to realize flexible behavior control. Thus, when "contingency" first entered learning theory, which it did via "operant" conditioning, it took its place without apparent difficulty as an inferred interconnection between the response and stimulus elements of a reflex. A fragment of behavior, preselected for observation, was followed by a stimulus delivered by the experimenter. In deference to the spirit, if not the letter, of the reflex concept, Thorndike summarized the influence of "contingency" in his Law of Effect: by its satisfying or pleasant nature, the "reinforcer," S^R, strengthened the response, R, which produced it. The circle of argument was completed by the affirmation that, when R recurred as a result of this contingent relation, "production" or "procurement" of S^R by R could be inferred. The strengthening was also assumed by Thorndike to be a "stamping in" of a connection between R and S^R (or, as it was later stated, a conditional relation between S^R and subsequent recurrences of members of that R class). The net result was a description of an independent variable relation (R "produces" S^R) inferred from a dependent variable (the recurrence of R). Even Skinner's subsequent simplification of Thorndike's procedures was guided by the "reflex concept." His elaborate review of the history of the reflex (Skinner, 1931) was a preparation for including "voluntary" behavior in the "reflex" schema, even though the exact stimulus antecedent of voluntary responses might be unknown. The control over "voluntary reflexes" was to be obtained, in the absence of known antecedents for R, by arranging a "contingency".[1]

The seeming lack of alternatives to "contingency" for gaining control over voluntary behavior made it appear that it was a necessary ingredient of operant conditioning. Accordingly, contingency became a fixture in experimental designs for operant research, and was a consistent feature of Skinner's massive exploration of intermittent reinforcement. In "regular reinforcement," every R "procured" S^R, that is, R was both necessary and sufficient to "procure" S^R; thereafter, intermittent reinforcement procedures dropped the sufficiency rule but retained the necessity rule according to which a particular response occurrence was still required for "production" of S^R. R continued to "procure" S^R, but the R that did so was one selected from a series of Rs ("ratio" schedules), or one which was the first to occur after a designated period of time ("interval" schedules). Whatever intermittent reinforcement schedule was in effect, S^R did not occur without the necessary "procuring" antecedent R.

The same criterion of necessity was a constant feature of the early work with the t-τ systems. To make contact with the work of other operant reinforcement theorists, continuously variable temporal and probability parameters were used in those systems to describe the range of possible permutations of the sufficiency rule in operant reinforcement schedules. Once this range was successfully treated, the possibility of manipulating necessity immediately emerged. Necessity could be diluted by allowing the probability of S^R to be greater than zero when no R had occurred. This made it possible at once to

---

[1] In Skinner's (1969) latest description, a response-stimulus contingency is still said to exist only when particular changes occur in the dependent variable.

broaden response-stimulus relations to include both "contingency" and "non-contingency," and to describe both types of R→S^R relations with the same systematic parameters.

2. Although the description of their learning experiments in reflex terms seemed natural enough to both Thorndike and Skinner, the "contingency" required to control responses, for which the antecedent stimuli were unknown, did not seem to them derivable from Pavlov's procedure. The latter produced what Thorndike termed "associative shifting," and Skinner, "respondent conditioning." It manipulated stimuli, and accepted the response already under control of one of the stimuli as the behavior to be watched and measured. In contrast, Thorndike's "trial and error" learning, and Skinner's "operant conditioning," seemed to require that the experimenter wait for the selected R to occur. When it did, it was allowed to "produce" S^R and thereby be strengthened. It was not clear that any continuous parameter existed by which the Thorndikian and Pavlovian procedures could be related. Eventually, the sequential positions of R and S^R with respect to each other became the chief theoretical distinction between the two paradigms and the major reason for believing that there are two "types" of conditioning. Thus, E. R. Hilgard (1964) made contingency the distinguishing characteristic of the two procedures: "In instrumental or operant conditioning, the reinforcing stimulus (equivalent to Pavlov's unconditioned stimulus) occurs if, and only if, the instrumental or operant conditioned response occurs; thus the response that is strengthened is that which *produces* or *leads to* the reinforcing stimulus rather than that elicited by the reinforcing stimulus [p. 122; Hilgard's parentheses and italics]."

For better or worse, two-type learning theory has come to be favored over one-type or multi-type theories. The principal support of two-type theory is the inability of theorists to describe the stimulus-response relations of Pavlov's procedure, and the contingency of the Thorndikian-Skinnerian procedure, in the same terms. The distinction between them is usually regarded today as an "operational" one. Increasingly, however, results from the laboratory have blurred even that distinction, the last upon which a rigid separation of learning into "types" depends. In striving to incorporate these new laboratory facts, the prospect of a unified theory has opened again.

3. The relation between R and its S^R in operant conditioning which is called "contingency" can be stated without implying "procurement" or "production." It is any rule by which an experimenter imposes a conditional probability between R and S^R in that temporal sequence, and thereby forces a dependence of the distribution of S^{R}s in time upon the distribution of Rs in time. If this dependence holds in any measure whatever, a "contingency" between R and S^R is said to exist in corresponding measure. It is the extension of this contingency that gives humor to the renowned cartoon: (*See top following page*) A reverse contingency is added to complement the usual one, extending the sequential dependency from R and S^R alone to two Rs, one from each organism in the rat-experimenter dyad. By replacing the experimenter's solitary situation

"Boy, have I got this guy conditioned! Every time I press the bar down he drops in a piece of food."

[*Used by permission of* JESTER, *Columbia College.*]

with reciprocity between the rat and experimenter, each organism becomes entitled to make the same inference from the behavior of the other.

The phase lag which operant conditioning imposes upon temporal distributions of R and S^R through the conditional relations it calls "contingency" may be inverted. That is to say, the distribution of S^R can also determine the distribution of R. Indeed, in any case where operant conditioning is "successful," the inversion must have occurred, else the experimenter would conclude that he had erred in his choice of R, of subject, of S^R, or of some other factor crucial for the conditioning. He would thereupon alter his experiment until it worked. The fallback to a pragmatic criterion of contingency (as well as of other experimental design features) invites two comments. First, it reflects the practical interest which marked operant conditioning from its birth (Schoenfeld & Cole, 1972). Skinner's demonstrations of behavioral control were all-important in the history of the science because the very possibility of such a science hinged on the success of those demonstrations. Yet the demonstrations did not constitute a behavior science. They only enabled it. The pragmatic fact that the demonstrations "worked" did not substitute for behavior science, they only gave the science a future. One might well have asked, "*What* worked?" The answer that it was "reinforcement" and the "contingency" of S^R upon R—that is to say, the pragmatic and simple operational answer—compromised the power of the independent variables they had so dramatically confirmed. Second, the pragmatic criterion was identical with that of E. R. Guthrie. Erasing the differences between Guthrie and Skinner was a service to theory, but at the same time nourished the suspicion that whatever criticisms were valid for one theory are equally valid for the other (Mueller & Schoenfeld, 1954). It was a historical curiosity, not unknown in other sciences, that the identity between the two theories was overlooked or concealed sufficiently to allow one to prosper while the other languished.

In any event, once the conditional probability of "S^R given R," or $S^R|R$, is considered at all, the reverse case of $R|S^R$, wherein the temporal distribution of S^R determines the temporal distribution of R, cannot be excluded. No logic is violated, either when this dependency also is labeled "contingency," or when an experiment incorporates the dependency of R upon S^R in its design. Indeed, Pavlov's procedure was grounded upon the latter by reason of its antecedent manipulations of independent variables. He dealt with an R that he knew was reliably produced by a given "unconditional" S. The constraints which his procedure imposed on the variety of data he obtained were immediate: the procedure was by force a trial-by-trial one, because the experimenter paced the presentation of S; because behavioral control was somehow "passed" to an accompanying "conditional" S, the UCS qualified as a "reinforcer" (as in Hilgard's foregoing statement); the measure of conditioning was seldom expressed in terms of response rate, as is conventional with the "free" operant, because the time phase relations between S (either UCS or CS) and R (either UCR or CR), combined with the pacing of S presentations independently of R, constricts the range through which response rate can vary. Finally, where Pavlov dealt with an R already under control of a stimulus he could manipulate experimentally, Skinner began with an R which he did not control but over which his procedure could establish control. Yet there was a similarity between them. For Pavlov, successful conditioning was indicated by a shift of control to a new stimulus which initially had no control over the measured R; and similarly, Skinner judged himself successful when he gained control over an R with a stimulus which initially had not controlled that particular R. The original control of R by other Ss was not explicitly measured in Skinner's experiment, and it was not entertained as an empirical question whether the new stimulus control which substituted for the original stimulus control was a serious parallel of Pavlov's finding. While both paradigms involved "contingency" from the start, in that both imposed an interdependency upon response-stimulus temporal distributions, opposite temporal directions seemed to be involved. Even that apparent opposition fades when proper weight is given to several additional considerations. For example, *all* Pavlovian conditioning is discriminative to some degree (i.e., the CR comes under differential control of some stimuli as against others), but equally, all operants come under similar discriminative stimulus control as soon as they are "conditioned." Again, if the idealized "free operant" conditioning experiment is a limiting case of a trial-by-trial procedure, then by the same token the idealized "classical" conditioning experiment may be a limiting case of response rate control (cf. Logan & Ferraro, 1970; Jenkins, 1970; Schoenfeld, Cole, et al., 1972).

If what we have said thus far about "contingency" is correct, then the conventional picture of that relation is not complete. Extreme cases of conditional probability between R and S^R can and do strain the credulity of theorists, who are for that reason apt rather to give separate names and treatment to variations of "contingency." For example, when extreme delays of reinforcement are employed, it is difficult to honor even a *de facto* definition of "contingency". This weakness of theory is correctable only if it is acknowledged that all the parameters of "contingency" are continuous, and that special or extreme values of those parameters fall along the same continua as the routine and familiar ones.

4. In view of the seeming procedural differences that lent credibility to two-type learning theory, the demise of "contingency" as the genie of operant conditioning may be said to have begun with Skinner's (1948) demonstration of "superstitious conditioning." In that study, clock-scheduled S^Rs were delivered to pigeons without reference to the behavior in progress at the time of S^R delivery. Most of the subjects developed a pronounced stereotypy in their ongoing behavior, but the particular pattern was different for individual animals. From an "operational" point of view, what had been demonstrated was that "operant" conditioning could occur without contingency. Yet Skinner reached the opposite conclusion. He assumed that although no experimental "contingency" existed, an effective "contingency" could be inferred from the observed response stereotypy, to wit, a contingency between the R and the S^R that had occurred after it, even if only by happenstance. As we have stated elsewhere," . . . it was possible to salvage the concept (of contingency) by appeal: (*a*) to the fact that the behavior stream is continuous; (*b*) to the inference that a reinforcer, even when applied without preselection of a response, must be contingent upon some response; and (*c*) to the presumption that whatever response is in the proper temporal relation to the reinforcer takes the impact of the 'contingency' and emerges as the conditioned response. To rescue contingency in this way, however, is to rob it of at least part of its meaning, because every reinforcement schedule must then be asserted as being contingent, or, conversely, that no schedule can be said to be noncontingent [Lachter, Cole, & Schoenfeld, 1971, p. 233] ."

Regardless of how the "superstition" demonstration is viewed, it made two things clear: first, that "contingency," conventionally described as "procurement" and "production," could be adequately stated in temporal terms alone; and second, that operant conditioning was possible without it, that is, without an experimentally specified dependence of the temporal distribution of S^R upon the temporal distribution of R. Skinner (1948) recognized these points, at least in part:

> To say that a reinforcement is contingent upon a response may mean nothing more than that it follows the response. It may follow because of some mechanical connection or because of the mediation of another organism; but conditioning takes place presumably because of the temporal relation only, expressed in terms of the

order and proximity of response and reinforcement. Whenever we present a state of affairs which is known to be reinforcing at a given level of deprivation, we must suppose that conditioning takes place even though we have paid no attention to the behavior of the organism in making the presentation [p. 168]."

From the experimenter's standpoint, "contingency" was conceded as not being necessary for "superstitious" operant conditioning. But Skinner felt it imperative to stand *in loco columbae* as well, and from that position temporal succession and "contingency" were indiscriminable. By implication, the experimenter would confront the same indiscriminability should he try to distinguish between the behaviors produced by the two procedures.

The drama of the "superstition" experiment lay in the actual conditioning of an R which was not preselected by the experimenter and which did not "produce" S^R. The procedure waived the requirement that a *given* R occur if an S^R were to be delivered, but simply awarded the status of necessary antecedent, as well as that of sufficient antecedent, to *any* R which changed in the manner called "conditioning." Every consideration of the "superstitious conditioning" procedure pointed to one conclusion: if a premarked R, with a high operant level, were exposed to the noncontingent procedure, the probability of superstitiously conditioning that R would be high, and would vary directly with the frequency of that R. Such a result would be an apparent contradiction in terms: the superstitious conditioning of a preselected R (Schoenfeld, 1972). Seemingly paradoxical, the contradiction forces behavior theory to recognize that conditioning of any R involves many parameters, including the initial frequency of that R, the schedule of S^R, and the temporal relation of Rs to S^Rs. But contingency is not one of those parameters. As "procurement," contingency is certainly dispensable; and contingency *per se* is equally dispensable in its raw meaning, that is, when it means no more than the limiting values of temporal parameters which comfortably fit the linguistic habits of the experimenter, though those same limits may in fact artificially restrict the full range over which the conditional dependency of R and S^R can be quantitatively specified.

5. The common method for proving that "contingency" produces more specific or more predictable behavioral effects than "noncontingency" has been to shift from a functioning "contingent" schedule to a "noncontingent" one. The effects of the shift are observed upon the R to which S^R was initially tied. The result most often reported has been a decrease in R rate below the value maintained on the contingent schedule, often following an initial, but passing, increase in rate. Several comments regarding this method and its outcome may be in order.

First, the finding of a decrease in R rate is not universal. There have been occasional reports (to which we add below) of the indefinite maintenance of an appreciable R rate during prolonged exposure to noncontingent schedules (e.g., Fenner, 1969; Neuringer, 1970). These results have been found with noncontingent deliveries of "free" reinforcement, both "positive" and "negative." That *any* exception is observed to the more commonly reported finding means that our ability to increase, maintain, or reduce R rate awaits only the discovery of the proper values of schedule parameters to obtain the desired result.

Second, the appearance of a rate reduction after a shift from contingent to noncontingent schedules is usually attributed to the increased variability of behavior which immediately precedes noncontingent S^R. Since no constraint is placed on the composition or "topography" of the "behavior stream" which precedes delivery of a noncontingent S^R, the effect of that S^R is often to dilute the frequency of the originally more restricted R category by reinforcing "other" behavior (Schoenfeld & Farmer, 1970). Interpreted this way, the laboratory findings permit new inferences to be drawn from Skinner's original "superstition" demonstration. For example, it may be expected that responses would shift from one stereotyped pattern to another during prolonged exposure to a particular training regimen. The characteristics of the shift, that is, the longevity of a pattern (or, conversely, the rapidity of its dilution) together with the time necessary for another R category to gain predominance, will be functions of the particular noncontingent schedule in force, and will change if and when the schedule is changed. Another implication is that if the schedule parameters are selected to maintain at least some limited R category indefinitely, then prolonging such a regimen should eventuate in "break-run" patterns of that R. Such patterns, depending upon their properties, would alter the chances that a variant of the now stereotyped R will precede subsequent S^Rs, and thereby affect the drift from one stereotyped pattern of behavior to another.

Third, studies wishing to evaluate "contingency" versus "noncontingency" have often tried to match S^R densities under the two conditions. The "noncontingent" schedule was synthesized to conform with the contingent S^R delivery pattern, both in mean $IS^R T$ ("inter-S^R time"; *vide* Farmer & Schoenfeld, 1964) and dispersion. It was thought that differences between contingent and noncontingent procedures could in this way be evaluated separately from schedule effects. But that separation is impossible. The occurrence of the response determines the time of S^R occurrence in conventional "contingent" schedules, and the only precise way to match R-S^R relations that occur when S^R is presented independently of R is to know in advance the pattern of R occurrence as exactly as the delivery pattern of S^R. Since this is never the case, the match is never perfect. Even if it were, nothing but identical effects for "matched" contingent and noncontingent schedules could ever be observed because the *required* pattern of R occurrence would preclude its sensitivity to influence by S^R, and make of that pattern an inappropriate dependent variable for the purpose. Some difference between R and S^R patterning always exists on contingent versus noncontingent schedules, and the force of that difference cannot be ignored. The difference may be minimized (or rendered trivial in a given experiment), however, by experimental procedures of the "variable delay" format described below.

In view of the foregoing, no further dispute seems necessary about the meaning of behavior changes resulting from a shift from contingent to noncontingent schedules. The effects of the shift were initially regarded as emphasizing the influence of temporal variables upon R and S^R. That influence cannot be challenged, but the variables themselves are schedule variables. They should be studied with an eye rather toward bridging the apparent discontinuities between contingent and noncontingent procedures than toward perpetuating the differences between them. Such bridging can be done within the context of the stimulus schedules that subsume those procedures together with all other "schedules of reinforcement."

Once stimulus schedules as schedules take center stage, two considerations emerge quickly regarding the issue of contingent versus noncontingent procedures. First, on noncontingent schedules in which S^Rs are delivered at a regular pace but without a necessary R, (a) an upper limit is set for the length of the R-S^R interval, that interval being the $IS^R T$ itself, and (b) a lower limit of zero is set for the R-S^R interval. Obviously, corresponding statements may be made for noncontingent schedules with irregular IS^RTs. Second, "contingency" in any specified reinforcement schedule is a limiting case of some "noncontingent" schedule.

6. The t-τ systems of reinforcement schedules (Schoenfeld, Cole, et al., 1972) provided a rational transition from "contingency" to "noncontingency", but only after relaxing some of the traditional restrictions upon operant procedures. The distinction between "contingency" and "noncontingency", and the procedural restrictions which derived from it, had been initially adopted in the t-τ systems in order to get quickly to their primary goal of ordering reinforcement schedules. The early success of the systems in doing so also disclosed some problems which became the systems' next concerns. For example, a restriction initially incorporated in the t system to meet the requirement of a specified response-to-be-reinforced, was to make S^R available only for the first R to occur during each presentation of a repeating time cycle. The S^R followed this "first R" immediately. The "contingency" thus provided for many subtle consequences including: (a) that S^R cannot occur just anywhere in a time cycle—instead, the temporal position of R in the time cycle determined the temporal position of S^R in that same cycle; (b) that a stimulus delivered as S^R might have "no effect on behavior" if only the preselected R were observed, but might nonetheless have a variety of strong effects upon other parts of the behavior stream; (c) that the choice of a punctate "R" event (such as a key-peck) made a rate measure virtually inescapable, but ultimately required a comparison of that measure to other estimates of behavior control. These consequences of the commitment to "contingency" were recognized primarily because of the limitations they placed on the manipulation of the temporal parameters of the t system. The τ system was developed to eliminate the problem of ordinal number designation of the R-to-be-reinforced, as well as the problem of the strict temporal position of the R-to-be-reinforced in each time cycle. The flexibility thus gained suggested that a similar flexibility could be obtained in the t system by moving S^R delivery to the end of each time cycle. It was immediately seen

that this change made "reinforcement delay" procedures definable by the parameters of the t and τ systems. In both systems, "delay of reinforcement" can occur and can reach, but not exceed, a maximum value that is specified by the parameter of the length of the time cycle, T or τ.

The topic of reinforcement schedules thus underwent a significant extension. Still other manipulations of schedule parameters suggested that, at certain values, there was no measurable change in R whether "S^R" deliveries were "contingent" or "noncontingent" (Farmer & Schoenfeld, 1966a and 1966b). Finally, the class of stimuli that could serve as S^R was seen to be indefinitely broad when proper attention is paid to parameters such as sense modality, stimulus intensity, and somatic site of application, aside from the scheduling parameters which together are responsible for the behavioral effect called "reinforcement."

From this background, it is evident that manipulations of schedule, and of physical stimulus parameters, go far beyond the concepts of either "contingency" or "reinforcement". The experimenter is free to manipulate these parameters as independent variables without any need to have the subject's behavior modify either the placement of a stimulus in time, or the physical value of that stimulus. "Schedules of reinforcement" by such means become "stimulus schedules" in the widest sense. The t-τ systems, which had taken as their initial goal the ordering of operant contingent reinforcement schedules, ended by generalizing the problem beyond such schedules. Once that extension is made, the t-τ systems are no longer necessary. But, short of liquidating them, the systems may be used to show that all or most of the procedural details of reinforcement scheduling are actually schedule parameters which early explorers of schedules had treated as discontinuous cases and usually as limiting or extreme cases.

The path that led to the broadened domain of "stimulus schedules" leads also to some conclusions about "laws of learning". Long-accepted doctrines of "reinforcement" and "contingency," once they are generalized, demand a more general framework of "laws of learning" to house them. Operant conditioning as a procedure distinct from classical conditioning may also be submerged into the revised vocabulary of behavior theory. The consequence of abandoning such distinctions will be that the untrammeled concepts will serve behavior theory better than when they were protected and isolated by their restricted definitions. The restraints on the concepts will be discarded, but the concepts themselves will have been reforged to provide a more general and more supportive framework for learning theory.

7. If the concept of reinforcement is broadened to include all stimuli, and if "contingency" is dropped from the lexicon of learning theory, then emphasis moves to the temporal relations among the occurrences of R and the intrusions of S (the "reinforcements") into the behavior stream. The viewpoints of the subject and the experimenter will then coincide, and neither will be more "superstitious" than the other. Reinforcement schedules, and systems like t-τ

which undertook to order them, become "stimulus schedules" in which a stimulus sheds its inferred "functions" and reverts to what it is, namely, an energy input function describable in terms of its physical and its scheduling parameters alone.

Once that degree of generality is reached on the stimulus side of behavioral functions, it seems inevitable that further generality will also be sought on the response side. Behavior theory, to date, has almost exclusively chosen its response as a single punctate event, the "R", and has isolated it from the organism's behavior stream, the better to measure its rate, amplitude, latency, or whatever. This choice arose from the idea that all behavior was reflex in character. While that idea made the goal of behavior control achievable by ignoring all but the selected R, at the same time it set the scene for eventual dissatisfaction with the analytical usefulness of isolating R. Ultimately, the experimental analysis of behavior will have to be extended to the continuity and complexity of behavior. An important limitation that comes from isolating R is that it cannot deal with continuity of behavior, i.e., with the fact that behavior is not made up of "Rs" joined together, but is rather a truly integrated stream out of which "Rs" are abstracted. This continuity is hardly a novel idea (cf. Kantor, 1938, 1943; Schoenfeld, 1969) but the experimental analysis of behavior has as yet done little except acknowledge it. One attempt (Schoenfeld & Farmer, 1970) has been made to treat the behavior stream in exhaustive categories of R and not-R (Ɍ), where the latter is defined as the residual content of the stream between R occurrences. But that attempt is not altogether satisfactory because of the procedural constraints that arise when the same techniques that are used to control R are applied to Ɍ.

Another approach to systematic generality that remains to be explored is to start from the accepted fact that any R involves the movement of an organism, or part of it, in space (cf. Skinner, 1938). Present-day theory regards an organism's actual movements as only the incidental "topography" of R, and regularly treats those movements only as a qualitative aspect of R. When reconsidered, however, they will become the all-important quantitative measures of "behavior" expressed in spatial field equations. This will permit theory to treat more and more of the continuous behavior stream as "functions of stimulation," and thereupon to approximate an organism's behavioral condition. Of course, closer approximation to the continuity of behavior will bring with it the need to deal with greater complexity and variability of behavior, the very properties of behavior which the abstracted "reflex" and "R" were intended to conquer. As experimental control is extended to more continuous and inclusive segments of behavior, it will become necessary to find the orderliness within the increasingly apparent variability of behavior. We cannot as yet anticipate what problems await us here, nor what forms their solutions will take. The only certainty is that it is our science's business to find both those problems and their solutions.

8. We have carried out several experiments illustrating the intent of the foregoing discussion.

EXPERIMENT 1: VARIABLE DELAY OF REINFORCEMENT
B. K. Cole, G. D. Lachter and W. N. Schoenfeld

Purpose

To investigate variable delay procedures specified by the temporal independent variables of the t-τ systems.

Experimental Variables

Subjects and response: three pigeons at 80% of *ad libitum* weight; key pecking. S^{+R} (positive reinforcer): mixed grain.   Independent variable: T, or cycle length, at values of 6 and 12 seconds; probability of S^R (p) in T constant at 0.10; presentation of S^{+R} either immediately followed the first response (R) in a T cycle, or was presented at the end of the T cycle in which at least one R had occurred.

Dependent variable: response rate (quantitative data); postreinforcement pause (PS^RP).

Method

After the measured R had been "shaped," subjects were immediately placed on a two-component multiple schedule for 65 successive sessions of 1 hour each, during which each component (indicated by a change in key color) was presented for 30 minutes. These sessions consisted of six blocks of 10 minutes each (three blocks for one component of the multiple schedule, three for the other), and the order of the blocks was randomly permuted between sessions. One component of the multiple schedule presented a random-interval (RI) 60-sec. schedule T = 6 sec., p = 0.10, T/p = 60 sec. mean interreinforcement time, after Farmer, (1963) in which the first R in any T cycle was followed immediately by S^R at probability (p) = 0.10. In the second component the same T and p values were presented, but S^R occurred only at the end of the T cycle in which at least one R had occurred, and then only at p = 0.10, giving a predicted average of one S^R in 10 cycles. This procedure produced limited, variable delays as a function of the value of T. At T = 6 sec., for example, the minimum temporal separation of R and S^R was 0 sec., i.e., immediate reinforcement, and the maximum temporal separation was 6 sec. The actual delay was a dependent variable and a joint function of the limits imposed by the value of T and the rate and distribution of Rs within each T cycle. In the final stage of the experiment, the value of T was changed to 12 sec. (with p held at 0.10, and T/p = 120 sec. becoming the predicted IS^RT) in both components of the multiple schedule. This procedure was in effect for 60 successive experimental sessions.

Findings

At T = 6 sec.:

1. Substantial running rates (S^R time and PS^RP were subtracted from session time prior to rate calculations) developed in both the immediately

reinforced component and the variable delay component. Two of the three subjects consistently responded at lower rates in the variable delay component than they did in the immediately reinforced component. The third subject had equal or lower rates in the delay than in the immediately reinforced component.

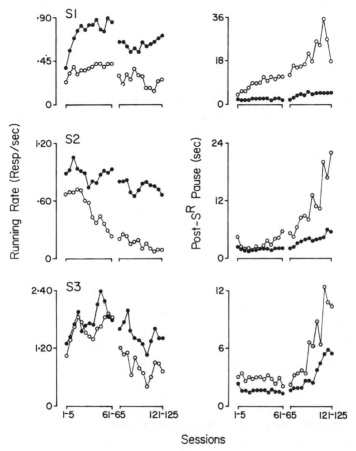

FIG. 1:1 Running rates (S^R time and PS^RP are subtracted from total time before calculating rates) and average PS^RP are shown for three Ss, each exposed to a T (cycle length) value of 6 sec. for the initial 65 experimental sessions and to a 12-sec. T value for 60 additional sessions. Each data point is the mean of five experimental sessions (thus, e.g., the first 13 data points in each function represent the initial 65 sessions, and are followed by 12 data points for the next 60 sessions at the 12-sec. T value). *Filled circles* are used to show data from the contingent component of the two-ply multiple schedule while *open circles* denote data from the variable delay component. (Variable delay provided S^R at the end of a T cycle, with $p(S^R) = 0.10$, only if at least one R had occurred in that T cycle.) The reader should note that the ordinate scales used for individual functions differ between Ss as well as between rate and PS^RP measures for the same S.

2. Average PS^{R}P was greatest in the delay component for all subjects during the 65 sessions at T = 6 sec.

At T = 12 sec.:

1. Response rates remained consistently higher in the immediately reinforced component than in the variable delay component for all subjects (maximum delay now 12 sec.). Greater rate differences between the components were primarily the result of rate decreases in the variable delay component.

2. Mean PS^{R}P increased markedly in the variable delay component for all subjects at T = 12 sec.

3. All subjects showed a combination of decreased response rate and increased PS^{R}P to a degree that some 12-sec. T cycles passed without the necessary response occurrence to sample the S^R probability, p. The net result was a decrease in overall S^R frequency in the variable delay component, and this in turn increased the difference in response measures between the two components.

Discussion

This study illustrated the applicability of schedule parameters as defined with the t-τ systems to behavior control in delay procedures. The parameter changes influenced response rate and PS^{R}P measures. Both immediate and delayed reinforcement procedures were described within the same framework of independent variables as interrelated reinforcement schedules.

EXPERIMENT 2: VARIABLE DELAY AND NONCONTINGENT REINFORCEMENT
J. Lang and R. Mankoff

Purpose

To study the effect of variable delay parameters on a preselected R, and to describe the subsequent maintenance of that R by noncontingent procedures.

Experimental Variables

Subjects and response: five pigeons at 80% of *ad libitum* weight; key pecking. S^{+R}: mixed grain.

Independent variable: T cycle at values of 15, 30, 60, and 120 sec., p(S^R) = 1.0 at all τ values. S^R was presented at the end of each T cycle during which one or more Rs occurred (variable delay). The same T and p values were used in the noncontingent procedures, but a response-independent electronic pulse was substituted for the R that was necessary for S^R occurrence in the variable delay procedure.

Dependent variable: response rate (quantitative data).

Method

Four subjects were each exposed to a four-ply multiple schedule, with T values of 15, 30, 60, and 120 sec. programmed in the presence of: a steady green key light, a flashing red light (5 cps; 100 msec. on, 100 msec. off), a steady red light, and a flashing green light (5 cps, as with flashing red), respectively. Reinforcement was delivered at the end of each T cycle in which one or more Rs had occurred (variable delay procedure) because $p(S^R) = 1.0$ for all components. Each component consisted of ten T cycles, and components were randomly ordered between sessions. After 52 to 56 sessions for individual subjects, the S^Rs were presented noncontingently, i.e., they occurred at the end of each T cycle whether or not an R had occurred in that cycle. This procedure was continued for 55 to 67 sessions.

A fifth subject was given variable delay training at T = 15 sec., $p = 1.0$ for 31 sessions (30 T cycles/session) and then changed to noncontingent delivery of S^R every 15 sec. for the next 31 sessions.

Findings

1. Response rates were a decreasing function of increasing T value for all subjects in the multiple-schedule variable delay procedure. (Figure 2:1).
2. Noncontingent presentation of S^R at the same T and p used in variable delay procedures resulted in maintenance, for 55 or more sessions, of a rate very near or above the rate observed on the variable delay. (Figure 2:1).

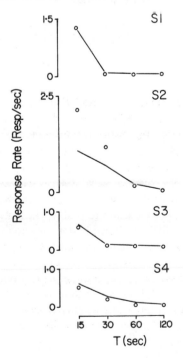

FIG. 2:1 Corrected response rates (S^R time subtracted from total session time before rate calculation) as a function of increasing T values are shown for four individual Ss. All values of T were presented in a four-ply multiple schedule during each experimental session. Randomly permuted orders of the four stimuli which cued the multiple-schedule components were changed from one session to the next. The *solid-line* function gives the average response rate for each component during the last 10 sessions in which the S^R presentation procedures in force were contingent variable delays. The *open circles* at each abscissa value show response rates during the last 10 sessions (of 55 to 67 total sessions for the several Ss) of noncontingent S^R delivery schedules cued in the same multiple-schedule format used with the variable delay procedures. The several T values and the $p(S^R) = 1.0$ provided presentations of noncontingent S^Rs once every 15 sec., 30 sec., 60 sec., and 120 sec. in the four components of the multiple schedule.

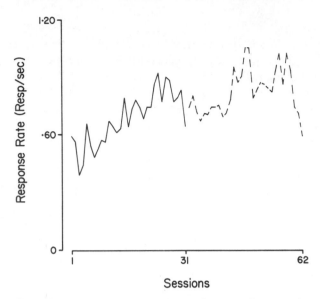

FIG. 2:2 Corrected response rates as a function of consecutive sessions are given for a single *S*. During the initial 31 sessions (*solid line*), a variable delay procedure (T = 15 sec., $p(S^R) = 1.0$) was in effect. For the final 31 sessions (*dashed line* for sessions 32 to 62) S^R was presented independently of R occurrence, and at the identical T and $p(S^R)$ values used for the variable delay schedule.

3. The subject exposed to the single value of variable delay showed the same maintenance pattern as those subjects on multiple schedules of variable delay. (Figure 2:2).

Discussion

Besides confirming the decrease of rate found with increased T in the earlier study (Experiment 1 above) on variable delay, this study illustrated the potential of the variable delay base line for minimizing the disruptive influence of a subsequent shift to noncontingent schedules. Once a stable pattern of responding had developed on a variable delay schedule, producing maximum or near-maximum reinforcement frequency (i.e., when at least one R reliably occurred in all, or nearly all, T cycles), the change to a noncontingent schedule with a similar or identical inter-S^R time ($IS^R T$) distribution to that of the initial schedule maintained the behavior pattern that had developed under the variable delay conditions. Since the variable delay schedule allowed reinforcement to occur other than immediately following a given instance of R, the difference between the behavior pattern reinforced in a variable delay schedule, and the pattern reinforced on a noncontingent schedule with a similar $IS^R T$ distribution, was small.

Both variable delay and noncontingent schedules were accurately definable by the same system of parameters which generated similar temporal distributions of reinforcers for the two schedules.

EXPERIMENT 3: SCHEDULES OF CONCURRENTLY CONTINGENT AND NONCONTINGENT REINFORCEMENT
B. K. Cole

Purpose

To study the effect of varying proportions of contingent and noncontingent reinforcement on maintenance of a preselected R.

Experimental Variables

Subjects and response: four pigeons at 80% of *ad libitum* weight; key pecking. S^{+R}: mixed grain.

Independent variable: T = 6 sec. for both contingent and noncontingent schedules; contingent $p(S^R)$ at values of 0.10, 0.05, 0.025, 0.0125, 0.00625, and 0.0 at various stages of the experiment; noncontingent $p(S^R)$ set at 0.10, 0.05, 0.0125, 0.00625, and 0.0 for various experimental points. The noncontingent schedule was programmed by substituting a response-independent electronic pulse for R of the contingent schedule.

Dependent variable: response rate (quantitative data).

Method

A multiple schedule with two components was used in the initial stage of the experiment. Reinforcements in one component (white key light for three Ss, red for the fourth S) were always contingent with T = 6 sec., $p = 0.10$, T/$p = 60$ sec. The component was presented during three of six 10-min. blocks that comprised an experimental session. The order of 10-min. blocks was randomized between sessions. The other three 10-min. blocks (during a red key stimulus for three Ss, during white for the fourth) also had T = 6 sec., $p = 0.10$, T/$p = 60$ sec., and contingent S^R for the initial 40 sessions. A noncontingent schedule (T = 6, $p = 0.10$, T/$p = 60$ sec.) was then introduced concurrently with the contingent schedule in the latter component for 40 more sessions, thereby doubling reinforcement frequency in that component. Next, while the noncontingent schedule remained in force and unchanged, the p value of the contingent schedule was systematically reduced through the following successive values (40 sessions at each value): $p = 0.05$, 0.025, 0.0125, 0.00625, and 0.0. At the final value, all S^Rs in the component were noncontingent and had an average IS^{R}T of 60 sec.

In the next stage of the experiment, the following schedules were in effect for 30 sessions per experimental condition, and for the entire 60-min. session: noncontingent schedule with T = 6, and $p = 0.10$, 0.05, 0.0125, 0.00625 for successive experimental points.

Finally, the subjects were returned to the multiple schedule for 40 sessions with T = 6, $p = 0.10$ in the contingent component, and T = 6, $p = 0.00625$ in the noncontingent component.

Findings

1. Response rate did not increase when S^R frequency was doubled by the addition of a concurrent noncontingent S^R schedule, but decreased as the frequency of concurrent contingent reinforcement was subsequently decreased.

2. A low rate of response was maintained for 40 or more sessions under a fully noncontingent schedule. (Figure 3:1 for findings 1 and 2).

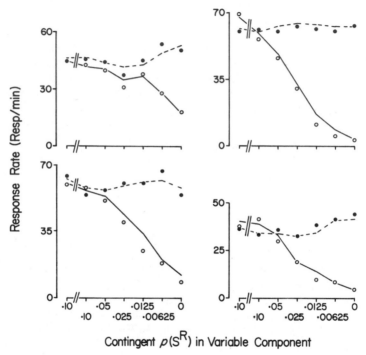

FIG. 3:1 Corrected response rates (S^R time subtracted from session time before rate calculation) are graphed separately for each of four Ss as a function of contingent $p(S^R)$ in one component of a two-ply multiple schedule. The component in which the $p(S^R)$ parameter was manipulated also contained noncontingent S^Rs presented at a constant frequency (T = 6 sec.; noncontingent $p(S^R)$ = 0.10; T/p = 60 sec.) during all experimental points shown except the initial base-line determination (the first abscissa value on each of the four coordinates shown). At the first experimental points both components contained the same predicted contingent S^R frequency. *Solid-line* functions show response rates in the variable multiple schedule component averaged for the entire 40 sessions at each experimental point. *Open circles* represent the average of the last 10 sessions at each point of the independent variable. The *dashed-line* function indicates response rates in the other, unchanging, multiple-schedule component (T = 6 sec.; contingent $p(S^R)$ = 0.10; T/p = 60 sec. throughout the experiment) averaged for 40 sessions at each value of the independent variable. *Filled circles* represent the average of the last 10 sessions of each of the 40-session experimental points.

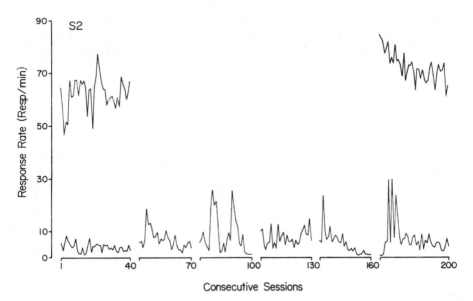

Consecutive Sessions

FIG. 3:2 Corrected response rate of a single representative *S* (*S2* in Experiment 3, Figure 3:1) shown as a function of consecutive sessions in which: (*a*) The multiple schedule composed of a contingent component (T/*p* = 60 sec.) and a fully noncontingent component (also with T/*p* = 60 sec.) was presented for 40 sessions (abscissa values 1 to 40, with the *upper function* showing response rate in the contingent component for each consecutive session, and the *lower curve* showing rates in the noncontingent component. (Sessions 1 to 40 are the successive sessions which were averaged to provide the last point on the Figure 3:1 function for *S2*.) (*b*) Only the noncontingent component of the multiple schedule was presented during each hour-long session. Between 30-session blocks, the noncontingent *p*(S^R) was reduced from *p* = 0.10 (sessions 41 to 70) to 0.05 (sessions 71 to 100) to 0.0125 (sessions 101 to 130) and finally to 0.00625 (sessions 131 to 160). (*c*) The contingent component of the original multiple schedule was reintroduced (sessions 161 to 200) while the noncontingent component was continued at *p*(S^R) = 0.00625. Although the rate in the noncontingent component initially rose and then returned to a characteristic low value, a rate increase in the reintroduced contingent component was interpretable as "contrast" when the upper curve for sessions 161–200 was compared to the upper curve for sessions 1 to 40. (For discussion of the concept of "behavioral contrast" and a review of the relevant findings, the reader is referred to Skinner, 1938; Reynolds, 1961; Terrace, 1966; and Nevin & Shettleworth, 1966.)

3. Further decreases in noncontingent S^R frequency resulted in momentary increases in response rates, often briefly approximating rates seen under contingent reinforcement. (Figure 3:2 for findings 3, 4, 5 and 6).

4. Resumption of a high rate of responding reliably occurred after a prolonged period without S^R, rather than after an R which had preceded a noncontingent S^R.

5. Response rate in the other fully contingent multiple schedule component was approximately the same until the component was later reintroduced.

6. Upon reintroduction of the multiple schedule following the reduction of p in the noncontingent schedule, an increase in contingent response rate resembling that found in "behavioral contrast" was noted in the reintroduced component.

Discussion

This study reported a finding that is common in the current noncontingent literature. When noncontingent reinforcement was substituted for contingent schedules, the decrease in rate of R noted above reliably occurred. Maintenance of the R that had been immediately reinforced occurred only when an R was included in the pattern of behaviors which stabilized between successive S^Rs of the noncontingent schedule. As long as any instances of R were necessary for the immediate presentations of S^R, substitution of noncontingent S^Rs for the contingent ones increased the likelihood that some behavior other than R would immediately precede the noncontingent S^R. The substitution also decreased the likelihood that the new pattern of behavior which eventually stabilized under fully noncontingent reinforcement would include R as part of the final behavior sequence. It was only when the stabilized pattern already included behaviors other than R immediately prior to S^R (such as in the variable delay procedures of Experiments 1 and 2) that the introduction of noncontingent procedures would disrupt the behavior sequence very little, thereby increasing the likelihood that R would continue as a part of the sequence.

These notions of stability and reliability of behavior sequences were additionally supported by the recovery of R rates when frequency of noncontingent S^R was reduced by decreases in the value of p. The shift to earlier behavior patterns, specifically to high rates of R, occurred during IS^RTs which were particularly long relative to earlier IS^RTs. Increases in the time between S^Rs, rather than the fortuitous occurrence of S^R near a particular instance of R, were responsible for the temporary recovery of high R rates. The return to earlier reinforced behavior patterns in the face of extinction (sometimes called "regression") is an indication that the behavior pattern prior to the decrease of p was reliably controlled by the intermittent S^R presentations. With decreased S^R frequency, the variability of that behavior pattern increased until it included the R which had previously been reinforced. The R had merely been reduced in frequency within, or eliminated from, the behavior sequence because the noncontingent S^Rs often followed behavior patterns which did not include R, as well as patterns which did. While decreases in variability, rather than increases, are usually inferred from high R rates, the recovery of the original R rate under these circumstances occurred when behavior became more variable rather than less variable. In addition, the lowered rate after the initial rate increase indicated that a stable pattern was once again reestablished under the new noncontingent S^R frequency, with only incidental inclusion of R as part of the final reliable behavior sequence controlled by the new noncontingent schedule.

The "contrastlike" effect noted when the multiple-schedule base line was reintroduced seemed to favor the position that "contrast" results from decreased

S^R frequency, but the increase and subsequent decrease of R rate in the noncontingent component as well fails to eliminate the possible influence of response rate changes which are also alleged to produce the "contrast" effect. Beyond these factors, however, the increased rate in the contingent component can be treated as the result of adventitious reinforcement of particular high rate variants of R sequences which were produced when S^R frequency was decreased in the noncontingent component. Within each of the two components, there will be differential reinforcement of response variability resulting from reduced S^R frequency in only one component. Rate measures in the contingent component may then vary in the direction labeled "behavioral contrast." Such an effect can occur, however, only when S^Rs control prolonged sequences of behavior rather than isolated responses or a few Rs which immediately precede S^R.

As with the other experiments reported above, this study also specified its parameters within the t-τ temporal framework, and by doing so described both contingent and noncontingent schedules in terms of the same comparable independent variables. This set of studies anticipates the eventual integration of contingent, delay, and noncontingent schedules by means of a unified system within which all "schedules of reinforcement," or stimulus schedules, are described by the same set of experimentally manipulable parameters.

REFERENCES

Farmer, J. Properties of behavior under random interval reinforcement schedules. *Journal of the Experimental Analysis of Behavior,* 1963, 6, 607-616.

Farmer, J., & Schoenfeld, W. N. Effects of a DRL contingency added to a fixed interval reinforcement schedule. *Journal of the Experimental Analysis of Behavior,* 1964, 7, 391-399.

Farmer, J., & Schoenfeld, W. N. Varying temporal placement of an added stimulus in a fixed-interval schedule. *Journal of the Experimental Analysis of Behavior,* 1966, 9, 369-375. (a)

Farmer, J., & Schoenfeld, W. N. The effect of a response-contingent stimulus introduced into a fixed-interval schedule at varying temporal placement. *Psychonomic Science,* 1966, 6, 15-16. (b)

Fenner, D. H. Key pecking in pigeons maintained by short-interval adventitious schedules of reinforcement. *Proceedings of the 77th Annual Convention of the American Psychological Association,* 1969, 831-832.

Hilgard, E. R. Conditioning. In J. Gould and W. A. Kolb (Eds.), *A dictionary of the social sciences.* New York: Free Press (MacMillan), 1964.

Jenkins, H. M. Sequential organization in schedules of reinforcement. In W. N. Schoenfeld (Ed.), *The theory of reinforcement schedules.* New York: Appleton-Century-Crofts, 1970. Pp. 63-109.

Kantor, J. R. The operational principle in the physical and psychological sciences. *Psychological Record,* 1938, 2, 1-32.

Kantor, J. R. An interbehavioral analysis of propositions. *Psychological Record,* 1943, 5, 309-339.

Lachter, G. D., Cole, B. K., & Schoenfeld, W. N. Response rate under varying frequency of non-contingent reinforcement. *Journal of the Experimental Analysis of Behavior,* 1971, 15, 233-236.

Logan, F. A., & Ferraro, D. P. From free responding to discrete trials. In W. N. Schoenfeld (Ed.), *The theory of reinforcement schedules.* New York: Appleton-Century-Crofts, 1970. Pp. 111–138.

Mueller, C. G., & Schoenfeld, W. N. Edwin R. Guthrie. In W. K. Estes et al. *Modern learning theory.* New York: Appleton-Century-Crofts, 1954. Pp. 345–379.

Neuringer, A. J. Superstitious key pecking after three peck-produced reinforcements. *Journal of the Experimental Analysis of Behavior,* 1970, 13, 127–134.

Nevin, J. A., & Shettleworth, S. J. An analysis of contrast effects in multiple schedules. *Journal of the Experimental Analysis of Behavior,* 1966, 9, 305–315.

Reynolds, G. S. Behavioral contrast. *Journal of the Experimental Analysis of Behavior,* 1961, 4, 57–71.

Schoenfeld, W. N. J. R. Kantor's *Objective psychology of grammar* and *Psychology and logic:* A retrospective appreciation. *Journal of the Experimental Analysis of Behavior,* 1969, 12, 329–347.

Schoenfeld, W. N. Problems of modern behavior theory. *Conditional Reflex,* 1972, 7, 33–65.

Schoenfeld, W. N., and Cole, B. K. Behavioral control of intermittent stimulation. In R. M. Gilbert & J. R. Millenson (Eds.), *Reinforcement: Behavioral analysis.* New York: Academic Press, 1972.

Schoenfeld, W. N., & Cole, B. K., with Blaustein, J., Lachter, G. D., Martin, J., & Vickery, C. *Stimulus schedules: The t-τ systems.* New York: Harper & Row, 1972.

Schoenfeld, W. N., & Farmer, J. Reinforcement schedules and the "behavior stream." In W. N. Schoenfeld (Ed.), *The theory of reinforcement schedules.* New York: Appleton-Century-Crofts, 1970. Pp. 215–245.

Skinner, B. F. The concept of the reflex in the description of behavior. *Journal of General Psychology,* 1931, 5, 427–458.

Skinner, B. F. *The behavior of organisms.* New York: Appleton-Century-Crofts, 1938.

Skinner, B. F. "Superstition" in the pigeon. *Journal of Experimental Psychology,* 1948, 38, 168–172.

Skinner, B. F. *Contingencies of reinforcement: A theoretical analysis.* New York: Appleton-Century-Crofts, 1969.

Terrace, H. S. Stimulus control. In W. K. Honig (Ed.), *Operant behavior: Areas of research and application.* New York: Appleton-Century-Crofts, 1966. Pp. 271–344.

8

CONDITIONING OF COVERT BEHAVIOR: SOME PROBLEMS AND SOME HOPES

F. J. McGuigan
Hollins College

Conditioning and learning are today such important theoretical topics largely because of the effectiveness with which the early behaviorists adopted and applied conditioning paradigms in predicting and controlling behavior. Their strategy was, of course, given knowledge of the stimulus, to predict the conditional response; and given control of the stimulus, to manipulate the conditional response. While, in following this strategy, our behavioristic predecessors dealt almost exclusively with overt behavior, they were not oblivious to the importance of the covert (implicit) response. We may note, for instance, the variety of mediational-response constructs in their theories of consciousness, thinking, emotion, and the like (cf. Goss, 1961). They even made courageous experimental efforts to directly measure covert behavior, but their technology was simply not sufficiently advanced (cf. McGuigan, 1970). Principally as a result of remarkable developments in electronics, we now do possess sufficiently powerful psychophysiological techniques with which we can successfully measure covert processes. We should only be prepared for the fact, as pointed out by Davis, Buchwald, and Frankmann (1955), that covert events (because they are smaller and more numerous) are undoubtedly the more difficult to study and to understand. One way of advancing our understanding of covert behavior would be to attempt to extend our laws of conditioning, based on overt behavior, to the covert realm. We shall, thus, seek to determine whether or not our classical and operant conditioning paradigms can also be applied to predict and control covert behavior.

ANTECEDENTS OF COVERT BEHAVIOR

Any external stimulus, regardless of the prevailing environmental condition or the operation being performed by the organism, may have two possible effects:

(*a*) it may produce widespread changes in a variety of regions or systems of the body; or (*b*) it may evoke changes in only a relatively localized region or limited systems of the body. The former will be referred to as a *general stimulus function* and the latter as a *specific stimulus function*. Principally, the two kinds of widespread bodily reactions that have been studied have been called the *orienting reflex* and the *arousal reaction*. Conditional (and discriminative) stimuli evoke the more localized kinds of behavior that we call unconditional and conditional responses. After briefly discussing these classes of behavior, we shall turn to the difficult methodological problem of determining whether a covert response is a component of a widespread bodily reaction or whether it is relatively localized in a given bodily region or system.

The Generalized Function of External Stimuli

The orienting reflex. The orienting reflex, a nonspecific pattern of reactions, is widely held to be the first response pattern of the body to any kind of external stimulus change (i.e., to a novel stimulus). E. N. Sokolov (1963) holds that the function of the orienting reflex is to facilitate the perception of a stimulus, and that its components include eye movements, dilation of the pupils, suppression of respiration, the galvanic skin response, neck movements, and electroencephalographic changes.

E. N. Sokolov (1963) showed that when the orienting reflex commences, there is a reduction of the threshold of *all* sense modalities, thus generally increasing sensitivity to stimuli. On repetition of the evoking stimulus, the orienting reflex habituates (with the exception of components specifically acted on by that stimulus, as in the case of local orienting reactions of the organ of vision to an adequate light stimulus). Perhaps an additional function of the orienting reflex has to do with its role in thought; e.g., Maltzman (1971) cites several studies in which it was shown that orienting reflexes can be self-generated as a consequence of thinking. The orienting reflex thus presumably has a perceptual function when evoked by external stimuli, and functions in thinking when evoked by internal stimuli.

Arousal reactions. Related to the orienting reflex is a generalized function of external stimuli that increase the level of activation of an organism. This heightened state of arousal may be reflected by changes in numerous covert processes such as electroencephalograms, electromyograms, galvanic skin responses, or cardiac activity. Duffy (1962) has studied this topic in great detail and has concluded that while several covert measures generally increase with stimulation, the "organism is not activated as an undifferentiated whole" and that "the organism, even when making no overt response, is in a constant state of flux with respect to both its general level of activation and the activation of its several parts [p. 113]."

Duffy's point is well illustrated by the work of Davis (1957), whose subjects were told to press a key, or to do nothing and to remain as quiet as possible, when a given stimulus was presented. He reported four different response

TABLE 1

Four Response Patterns Evoked by Four Different Stimulus Conditions
(Double Signs Indicate Diphasic Effects)

Response measure	Pattern			
	E-1 (key press)	N (visual and auditory stimuli)	P (complex stimuli)	C (cutaneous stimuli)
Palmar sweating	+	+	+	+
Forearm EMG	+	+	+	+
Pulse rate	+	+ −	−	−
Volume pulse	−	−	−	− +
Pressure pulse		− +	−	+
Finger volume	−	−	−	+
Chin volume		+	−	+
Respiration rate	+	−	−	+ −
Amplitude respiration	+	+	−	− +

Note.—Adapted from Davis (1957).

patterns as a function of four different types of stimuli (Table 1). The E-1 pattern of responses occurred when subjects performed the mild task of paced key pressing. The N pattern was evoked by simple auditory and visual stimuli, while the P pattern occurred to complex stimuli (pictures). The C pattern was the typical reaction to simple cutaneous stimuli. The first two rows of Table 1 indicate that palmar sweating and forearm EMG increased to all four stimulus conditions, while the remaining measures distinguished the various patterns from each other. This general finding is quite important, for it indicates the complexity and widespread nature of covert bodily reactions, it shows that there are relatively unique response patterns as a function of the type of stimulus, and it indicates that there are response measures that increase regardless of the stimulus class. We shall return to this matter later.

In short, novel external stimuli evoke two related kinds of widespread bodily reaction patterns: (*a*) the orienting reflex that facilitates perceptual sensitivity, and (*b*) mobilizing activity of the organism. Both classes consist of patterns of covert processes, though sometimes covert skeletal responses erupt into overt behavior.

The Specialized Function of External Stimuli

In addition to evoking an orienting reflex and arousing the organism, a stimulus may have a more localized effect. Some specific stimulus-localized response connections are, of course, unconditional reflexes that are effective at birth (e.g., acid → salivation). However, more numerous localized responses seem to be evoked by conditional or discriminative stimuli—in the history of any organism, a wide variety of stimuli have no doubt acquired the capacity to evoke a multitude of relatively localized covert (as well as overt) responses. The highly localized responses reported in the classic work of Jacobson (1932), for example, may be assumed to be the product of conditioning. For instance, when a right-handed person imagines lighting a cigarette, a covert response is uniquely measurable in the right arm.

When one considers the scope of covert conditioning, including such as galvanic skin response conditioning, electroencephalographic conditioning, cardiac conditioning, and even phenomena like intestinal conditioning, it becomes immediately apparent that a series of priorities for inquiry must be established. Psychology seems to have been predominantly concerned with behavior that involves skeletal muscle activity. Consequently, the priority here will be to examine the issues in the conditioning of covert skeletal muscle behavior, with the hope that resulting principles will apply to the conditioning of other covert systems. Covert muscle behavior can best be studied with the techniques of electromyography. Hence, we need to assess our knowledge about the conditioning of covert responses that are electromyographically recorded.

IN CONDITIONING, *WHAT* IS CONDITIONED?

Two major methodological problems in the area of covert conditioning are: (*a*) isolating *the* conditional response; and (*b*) distinguishing between a conditional response and a generalized reaction pattern (an orienting reflex or an arousal reaction). The complexity of the first and more difficult problem can best be illustrated with several kinds of studies in which the inference was that a specific, localized reaction was conditioned to one particular stimulus class. The topic (sometimes phrased as the problem of "validating" the conditional response) has received considerable attention, indicating the importance that conditioning researchers attach to it.

Some Examples of the First Problem

Westcott and Huttenlocher (1961) examined the question of cardiac conditioning, and pointed out that, in previous studies, respiratory activity had not been controlled during the conditioning process. In their first experiment these researchers established "that there are profound and reliable effects on cardiac rate attributable to respiratory patterns [p. 355]." The implication is that, in studies of "cardiac conditioning," a respiratory response was actually conditioned such that respiration mediated heart activity. The work of Skinner and Delabarre (in Skinner, 1938) is a case in point. Following Hudgins' (1933) method in his famous experiment on pupillary conditioning, they had a subject say "contract" and a gun was fired to produce strong vasoconstriction. Eventually constriction followed the unreinforced saying of " 'contract'. . .[but] we found that in the case of an apparently successful result the subject was changing the volume of the arm by changing the amount of residual air in the lungs. The depth of breathing was in this case conditioned according to Type R because of the reinforcement of its effect on the volume of the arm. The 'successful' result was obtained many times before the intermediate step was discovered by the subject [Skinner, 1938, p. 114]." To establish that changes in cardiac activity are not merely artifacts of respiratory modifications, respiration needs to be controlled; Westcott and Huttenlocher (1961) did this in their second experiment and provided positive evidence *for* cardiac conditioning. However, there still may be other mediators.

Respiratory activity has been similarly implicated in other studies. For instance, Johnson (1961) found that the nonspecific galvanic skin response is related to changes in respiration. He questions whether this is a causal relation or whether both response changes are due to a third factor, such as level of arousal.

The problem of whether or not brain waves can be instrumentally conditioned is obviously important for several reasons. One reason concerns the question of whether conditioning is basically a response (muscular or glandular) phenomenon and/or a neural process. Among the more recent "successes" in conditioning brain waves is the work of Kamiya (1968). Through a discrimination procedure in which the subject is furnished feedback, Kamiya reports that subjects can learn to control the presence or absence of alpha waves; this phenomenon is called "alpha wave conditioning." Before concluding that this is, however, actually electroencephalographic conditioning, one should study what else besides brain wave changes might be occurring in the subject during the training trials. Kamiya (1968) reports that "people who were relaxed, comfortable and cooperative tended to produce more alpha waves than those who felt tense, suspicious and fearful... [p. 59] ." This observation possibly implicates the muscular state and suggests the possibility that Kamiya's subjects learned to control alpha indirectly by learning certain muscular responses. This interpretation of why alpha waves and alpha blocking occur is an old one. Knott (1939), for example, held that the tensing of muscles with attendant increases in peripheral stimulation produces blocking of the alpha rhythm during "attention." According to this view, then, so-called "alpha conditioning" is mediated by antecedent conditional muscular activity. Hence, it is possible that, had Kamiya electromyographically monitored his subjects, he would have found muscular response changes that preceded (and perhaps controlled) the occurrence and nonoccurrence of alpha waves. Dewan (1968) has actually come up with a most interesting finding in this connection. In Dewan's research, the subject voluntarily controlled alpha activity by manipulating eye position and accommodation (also cf. Fenwick & Walker, 1969; and Mulholland, 1969). The subject was then able to send Morse code signals by means of his electroencephalograms; i.e., short bursts of alpha activity were the dots, while longer bursts were the dashes. If the eye can effectively control brain waves, feedback from other peripheral systems might also be made to serve the same function—or in fact other systems may naturally influence the brain prior to any learning. In a number of studies, it has actually been shown that induced muscular tension enhances evoked potentials from various brain regions, thus empirically implicating the skeletal muscular system as an antecedent of EEG activity (Andreassi, Mayzner, Beyda, & Davidovics, 1970; Dinges & Klingaman, 1972; Eason, Aiken, White, & Lichtenstein, 1964).

The problem of specifying a potential mediator in electroencephalographic or autonomic conditioning is obviously a difficult one. Smith (1954) argued that "galvanic skin response conditioning" is an artifact. Actually, he held, there is skeletal muscle response conditioning; the conditional skeletal response then produces (mediates) autonomic activity, among which is the galvanic skin response. Kimmel and Davidov (1967) sought to test Smith's hypothesis by monitoring electromyograms from both forearms during galvanic skin response conditioning. They failed to find a relationship between electromyograms and galvanic skin responses and thus concluded that Smith's hypothesis was not confirmed. But in view of the complexity of the body's musculature, it seems premature to dismiss Smith's notion by merely sampling electromyograms from two general regions—the critical mediating response may be small and highly localized (perhaps a single motor unit) and extremely rapid (several milliseconds). Looking for such a mediating electromyogram in galvanic skin response conditioning is less likely than finding the needle in the proverbial haystack. It is not that research along the lines of Kimmel and Davidov (1967) is hopeless; merely that a more sensitive and extensive search for a mediating covert response is required before Smith's hypothesis can be dismissed, particularly in view of the fact that Kimmel and Davidov used the rather crude electromyographic recording technique of an ink-writing polygraph.

While much of the focus in "validating" the conditional response has been on galvanic skin response conditioning, "criticisms of galvanic skin response conditioning are not at all unrelated to the validation of conditioned vasomotor change, conditioned cardiac deceleration, the conditioned eyeblink, and conditioned salivation [Kodman, 1967, p. 813]." Kodman continues along the lines that we have developed above: If Smith's hypothesis is true, then the galvanic skin response is "a response from an indivisible sensory-motor system rather than a pure autonomic reaction [p. 816]."

Three more recent examples should suffice to complete the illustration of the possibility that very rapid skeletal muscle activity may mediate the slower autonomic or electroencephalographic events. The first is a study by Cohen and Johnson (1971), who, using a classical conditioning heart-rate paradigm, showed that only those groups of subjects who had significant changes in muscular activity exhibited significant heart-rate changes. They ruled out respiratory rate and amplitude as relevant variables, but the correlation between heart rate and skeletal muscular activity was high. As before, we must ask just what response was conditioned?

Simpson and Climan (1971) have indicated that pupil size during the performance of an imagery task is another autonomic variable that apparently is affected by skeletal muscle activity.

The third example is from Belmaker, Proctor, and Feather (1972), who used a different strategy to test the hypothesis that skeletal muscle tension is a mediator for increases in heart rate. They instructed their subjects to generate inconspicuous muscle tension for a 90-second period. Respiratory pattern changes and surface electromyographic changes were not correlated with heart rate increases, nor were any gross muscle movements observed. Nevertheless, average heart rate during the trials increased about 13 beats per minute over baseline. They concluded that inconspicuous muscle tension is a possible mediator in human operant heart-rate conditioning. (We should note also for a later point on p. 181 that their electromyographic records from an ink-writing polygraph did not indicate the muscular tension that presumably was present.)

Is Curare the Answer?

One strategy for ascertaining the role of skeletal muscle contraction (and feedback resulting from such contraction) in the conditioning of other systems is to completely paralyze the skeletal musculature, usually attempted pharmacologically by administering a neuromuscular blocking drug. In this way the process of conditioning can presumably be studied when the role of the skeletal musculature has been removed. Examples of successful conditioning with curarized preparations have been reported by Solomon and Turner (1962);

Black, Carlson, and Solomon (1962); and DiCara and Miller (1968a). Solomon and Turner, for instance, concluded *"that certain types of transfer of training or problem solving can occur without the benefit of mediation by peripheral skeletal responses or their associated feedback mechanisms* [p. 218, italics in original] ."

The assumptions upon which this strategy of paralysis is based are that the curare used (*a*) is actually effective in producing total paralysis of the skeletal musculature, and (*b*) acts only at the myoneural junction and thus does not affect the central nervous system or peripheral sensory or autonomic mechanisms. The evidence for these assumptions, gained with the use of early impure forms of curare, is ambiguous (Solomon & Turner, 1962). d-tubocurarine, a pure form of curare developed later, was first used in this context by Solomon and Turner (1962), and by Black, Carlson, and Solomon (1962) to conduct improved tests of the central versus peripheral process interpretations of learning and transfer. Since these experimenters necessarily relied heavily on the pharmacological research available at the time for information about the effect of d-tubocurarine on various bodily systems, we should briefly review that pharmacological evidence; as far as I have been able to tell, the three articles they cited still constitute the bulk of our information derived from the study of humans. These are the three articles by Smith, Brown, Toman, and Goodman (1947), by Unna and Pelikan (1951), and by McIntyre, Bennett, and Hamilton (1951).

The pioneering work of Smith et al. (1947) is of special interest to psychologists because findings on one subject resulted in the widely accepted conclusion that individuals remain conscious and can "think" under total muscle paralysis due to curare; therefore, the notion is, muscle activity is not important for thought processes. While one must greatly appreciate this pioneering research, the experiment must be realistically evaluated in light of its methodological inadequacies. Of six shortcomings previously cited, the one with most immediate relevance for the curare-conditioning studies is that the d-tubocurarine used may not have totally paralyzed the skeletal musculature, a point that could be easily decided through appropriate electromyographic monitoring (cf. McGuigan, 1966). Hence, while there may well have been no *overt* responses in the curarized state, important minute (covert) responses still may have occurred (in addition, of course, to autonomic activity). (This experiment was repeated by Leuba, Birch, and Appleton, 1968, but unfortunately did not include the controls suggested by McGuigan, 1966.) This criticism of the Smith et al. (1947) study is also pertinent to the second pharmacological study, cited above, by Unna and Pelikan (1951)—there was no electromyographic monitoring to establish that covert skeletal muscle responses were eliminated. In fact, the amazingly gross measure of grip strength with the hand dynamometer was used as the index of "muscular paralysis," and their graph indicates that even that measure did not decrease to zero under d-tubocurarine; an additional indication of lack of paralysis is that there was never any need for artificial respiration for their subjects. Illustrative of the concern here is Black's

(1967) statement that "in experiments on the operant conditioning of heart rate under curare, it may very well be that electromyographic responses were actually conditioned and that these led to reflexive changes in heart rate [p. 202]." In a personal communication, James Howard suggested a physiological possibility that would fit nicely here. That is that the gamma-efferent system can play a very significant role in conditioning and that the gamma system of fibers may well have a higher threshold than the extrafusal muscle system to the blocking effect of curare (Buchwald, Standish, Eldred, & Halas, 1964). If so, successful conditioning of curarized preparations may have occurred because the covert behavior that remained was due to a still functional gamma-efferent system and its feedback loop. The most sensitive method to determine whether or not the skeletal muscle system is actually paralyzed is to extensively monitor it with sufficiently sensitive electromyographic apparatus.

Regardless of the lack of electromyographic monitoring in these pharmacological investigations, the important question for us concerns conditioning researchers who use curare and their electromyographical findings. I am grateful to Will Millard for helping me in this area of curare and conditioning, and particularly for providing most of the data in Table 2. Our status is that electromyograms were apparently recorded in but three of these autonomic conditioning studies, and in those the electromyographic sampling was limited and quite insensitive (the scales used were from 100 to 300 $\mu v/cm$). (Richard Solomon informs me that, in his research with Black and with Turner, they did employ EMG controls; I very much appreciate Solomon's and Abe H. Black's helpful thoughts on this curare problem, as expressed to me in personal communications.) When one considers that important covert responses may be of the amplitude of several microvolts (see, for example, Figure 7), it is apparent that more sensitive measurement techniques than those of ink-writing polygraphs are required. Even so, close inspection of the sample electromyograms offered by the experimenters cited in Table 2 often do show variations in the curarized preparation; covert behavior of perhaps as much as 20 μv in amplitude may have been occurring in presumably paralyzed animals. Such covert behavior could have important consequences, such as the possibility considered in this context (though rejected) by Black (1965) that the "full occurrence of a response and its associated feedback is not necessary for the modification of that response by operant reinforcement [p. 45]." As a further illustration of how such small-scale skeletal responding can have important consequences, recall that Belmaker et al. (1972) increased cardiac rate in their subjects by instructing them to slightly tense their muscles, yet the electromyographic activity that must have been present was not systematically sensed by their ink-writing polygraph techniques.

In conclusion, conditioning researchers might well find it profitable to improve on their application of this electromyographic control procedure.

Let us now consider the second assumption necessary for successful application of the "curare strategy" (viz., that d-tubocurarine does not affect systems other than the skeletal musculature). Unna and Pelikan (1951) said that,

TABLE 2

Measures Recorded in Experiments on Autonomic Conditioning Using d-Tubocurarine

Experimenter	Subject species	Paradigm (response)	EEG	EMG	EKG
Black, Carlson, & Solomon (1962)[a]	Dog	Classical (heart rate)	−	−	+
Black & Lang (1964)	Dog	Classical (heart rate)	−	+	+
Black & Dalton (1965)[a]	Dog	Classical avoidance (heart rate)	−	+	+
Birk, Crider, Shapiro, & Tursky (1966)	Human	Operant (GSR)	−	−	+
Trowill (1967)	Rat	Operant (heart rate)	−	−	+
Miller & DiCara (1967)	Rat	Operant (heart rate)	−	−	+
DiCara & Miller (1968b)	Rat	Operant (vasomotor response)	−	−	+
DiCara & Miller (1968e)	Rat	Operant avoidance (heart rate)	−	−	+
DiCara & Miller (1968c)	Rat	Operant avoidance (blood pressure)	−	−	+
DiCara & Miller (1968d)	Rat	Operant (vasomotor response)	−	−	+
DiCara & Miller (1968a)	Rat	Operant avoidance (heart rate)	−	+	+
Miller & Banuazizi (1968)	Rat	Operant (intestinal contraction)	−	−	+
Miller & DiCara (1968)	Rat	Operant (urine formation and renal blood flow)	−	−	+
DiCara & Miller (1969a)	Rat	Operant (heart rate)	−	−	+
DiCara & Miller (1969b)	Rat	Operant avoidance (heart rate)	−	−	+
DiCara & Weiss (1969)	Rat	Operant avoidance (heart rate)	−	−	+
Hothersall & Brener (1969)	Rat	Operant (heart rate)	−	−	+
DiCara & Stone (1970)	Rat	Operant (heart rate)	−	−	+
Fields (1970)	Rat	Operant (blood pressure)	−	−	+
Pappas, DiCara, & Miller (1970)	Rat	Operant (blood pressure)	−	−	+
Slaughter, Hahn, & Rinaldi (1970)	Rat	Operant (blood pressure)	−	−	+
Hahn & Slaughter (1971)	Rat	Operant (blood pressure)	−	−	+

[a]Subjects were "partially" curarized.

following administration of d-tubocurarine in six subjects, "no evidence was obtained of any action other than on the neuromuscular junction. . . . In particular no effects on autonomic organs and also none on cerebral functions could be demonstrated [p. 480]." That appears to be the totality of their offering in this regard—Unna and Pelikan did not present any data (nor were any cited) that substantiate that statement, nor did they further discuss the matter of potential central or autonomic nervous system effects of d-tubocurarine. (Except that they indicate that Flaxedil affects blood pressure and pulse rate.) The third pharmacological study cited above was that by McIntyre et al. (1951). In their consideration of this matter of possible brain effects, McIntyre et al. first criticized the above-cited work of Smith et al. (1947) on the grounds that Smith's results came from subjective observations. Following a second criticism having to do with the lack of sensitivity of measurements of muscle activity, McIntyre et al. (1951) concluded that "the balance of evidence establishes beyond doubt that d-tubocurarine is capable of modifying central nervous system activity independently of secondary effects due to hypoxia [p. 301]." It is not too clear, however, what the "balance of evidence" was.

Black et al. (1962) cited several studies in which it was concluded that d-tubocurarine affects the brain, as indicated by EEG measures. Some additional work is consonant with that conclusion. For example, Estable (1959) concluded that curare produces an effect on all cholinergic synapses to varying degrees; Okuma, Fujmori, and Hayashi (1965) reported electrocortical synchronization in animals as a function of the environmental temperature in which the animals received the curare; Amassian and Weiner (1966) and Brinley, Kandel, and Marshall (1958) found an increase in the latency of evoked potentials in curarized animals; and Hodes (1962) reported EEG effects from three different curare compounds (d-tubocurarine, Flaxedil, and succinylcholine). Galindo (1972) implicated both curare and pancuronium. In this same context, I am grateful to James Howard for informing me that curare releases histamine, which causes widespread bodily changes, including increased permeability and dilation of cerebral blood vessels (cf. Douglas, 1970; Koelle, 1960).

The conclusion thus is that d-tubocurarine may possibly have central nervous system effects. Whether or not these effects are direct, or whether they are produced indirectly by such peripheral mechanisms as inadequate artificial respiration parameters or reduction of necessary feedback of sensory, especially proprioceptive, impulses to the CNS is unclear. Unfortunately we lack even primitive data here since none of the conditioning researchers cited in Table 2 apparently monitored electroencephalograms of their subjects. Consequently we do not know whether or not brain activity of their subjects was, by this index, affected (directly or indirectly) by the d-tubocurarine injected. Finally, with regard to the second assumption, while there is something of an indication from the above-cited references that curare affects the brain, other data unambiguously indicate that curare has autonomic effects (cf. Black, 1971; Grob, 1967; Koelle, 1960).

In conclusion, to what extent is the two-fold assumption for the curare strategy justified? First, with regard to the requirement that the blocking agent produces total muscular paralysis, we simply lack sufficient data. Thus the conclusion must be that while it is possible that the "curare-strategy" for removing skeletal muscles as a source of mediation could be effective, even possibly with d-tubocurarine, we do not now possess empirical justification for it. Researchers who study conditioning of autonomic and central nervous system activity by employing this strategy should be encouraged to add to our information by (a) monitoring electromyograms from *several* bodily sites using sensitive equipment, and (b) monitoring electroencephalograms, preferably from more than one location. As things now stand, it cannot be concluded that skeletal muscle responding has been excluded as a possible mediator in the conditioning of brain and autonomic activity.

Second, with regard to the requirement that the muscular blocking agent not affect the brain, we should realize that it is methodologically very difficult to establish a *lack of relationship* (like attempting to "prove the null hypothesis"); this is particularly a problem with such complex variables as d-tubocurarine and central nervous system activity. Nevertheless what electroencephalographic evidence is available seems to indicate that d-tubocurarine may well (possibly indirectly) have central nervous system effects. In the case of curare effects on autonomic activity, the analogy with the test of the null hypothesis is that the assumption has been disproven—curare does have autonomic effects.

While not our major purpose here, it might be of value to relate these conclusions to the question of autonomic conditioning. It is clear that there is successful autonomic conditioning of curarized animals, but there *have* been unsuccessful instances that apparently defy explanation (e.g., Black, 1971; Ray, 1969). The situation seems to be that, under curare, there is partial functioning *and* partial nonfunctioning of the autonomic, of the skeletal muscle, and possibly of the central nervous systems. With this state of affairs, the logical possibilities are sufficiently numerous that one can argue for any of several interpretations. For one, the instances of successes may have occurred because the autonomic system was still (incompletely) functioning, and the failures may have been due to the autonomic interference caused by the curare (cf. Black, 1971, p. 36–37). The same interpretation may be applied to the central nervous system, or even to the skeletal muscle system (see p. 181). One of the logical possibilities (unlikely as it might be) is that the reverse interpretation holds for the brain—that the successful instances of conditioning occurred *because* of the curare; the curare might directly or indirectly inhibit certain cortical functions such that the inhibition allows lower cerebral mechanisms concerned with autonomic functions to allow conditioning to occur.

Conditional Covert Response Patterns

It thus seems that "the curare strategy" has not solved the methodological question posed above. That is, curare has not allowed us to distinguish what the experimenter called "*the* conditional response" from antecedent bodily events that may have been what were "really" conditioned. Perhaps other "strategies" such as electrical stimulation and surgical techniques might be more successful in isolating relevant bodily systems (cf. McGuigan, 1966, p. 294). Illustrative of the stimulation approach would be the work of Penfield (1958). Surgical techniques like those in which Horridge (1965) successfully conditioned an insect without a brain, or the peripheral nerve crushing and deafferentation procedures used by Light and Gantt (1936) and by Taub and Berman (1968), might be useful, though of course not with humans.

Considering its complexity, particularly with humans, not only may this problem be technically unsolvable, but the truth may actually be that a number of bodily processes are indivisible and necessarily participate as a complex conditional response. Perhaps we may thus be *required* to talk not about "*the* conditional response," but about a number of conditional response components that form complex conditional response *patterns*. Hence, when we talk about cardiac conditioning, electroencephalographic conditioning, galvanic skin response conditioning, or even forearm electromyographic conditioning, we perhaps should be emphasizing the *patterns* that were conditioned; such patterns may include a number of essentially simultaneous components *and* their mediating antecedent events. To further complicate the problem of separating critical and uncritical components of the conditional response pattern, we can expect that some adventitious covert behavior gains strength during conditioning. Consequently, an experimenter's definition of a conditional covert response pattern probably would necessarily include some adventitious components. An important research problem would be to ascertain the frequency with which such adventitious components "drop out" as conditioning trials continue, and which kinds might remain as stable parts of the conditional pattern.

It thus seems reasonable to stop using the term "the conditional response" because it tends to blind us as to how really extensive and complex the covert processes are that constitute a conditional pattern. One kind of exception in which we might be able to relatively unambiguously conclude that there was a (single) conditional response, would be with responses that are topographically very well defined, as in the cases of the discrete thumb twitch studied by Hefferline, Keenan, and Harford (1959), the single motor unit recorded with needle electrodes by Basmajian (1963a), or the fine distinction (with needle electrodes) of inverse electromyographic activity in closely associated laryngeal muscles by Faaborg-Andersen and Edfeldt (1958).

Empirical Specification of Conditional Response Patterns

Even though we emphasize *patterns* of responses, such patterns are probably still more localized and limited than widespread arousal reactions. We must thus still consider the second problem stated on p. 177, viz., how to distinguish between conditional response patterns and widespread arousal and orienting reflex reactions. The first step is to ascertain what happens to orienting reflexes and activational patterns during conditioning. Germana's (1968) concept of activational peaking is relevant here. Germana holds that the orienting and arousal reactional processes are essentially the same; they differ only because of stimulus requirements. For example, early in conditioning the novel stimulus evokes an activational pattern which is the orienting reflex; this pattern would habituate rapidly if the subject had nothing to do. But when in conditioning the subject *has* to respond, there is a buildup in the generalized activational level over trials—there is an increase in a number of bodily measures like skin conductance, heart rate, breathing rate, and vasoconstriction. Eventually, when the conditional response has been learned, activational peaking occurs; at this point the various psychophysiological measures reach a maximum. As the subject continues to produce the conditional response, the generalized activational level decreases from the peak to baseline level. The behavioral residue constitutes the conditional response pattern. That is, the conditional response pattern includes those responses from localized regions or systems (including the experimenter's target region in his subject) that persist after the leveling out that occurs following diminution from the activational peak.

To empirically define a specific stimulus-response pattern connection that is formed during conditioning, the experimenter obviously needs to sample a variety of stimuli and responses both before and at the conclusion of conditioning. It should first be shown that the response pattern that is to be conditioned does not occur to a sample of disparate test stimuli prior to conditioning. After conditioning, presentation of the test (nonconditional) stimuli again would establish whether or not there was a single conditional stimulus (assuming controls for stimulus generalization and for cross-modal generalization).

Establishing the uniqueness of the conditional stimulus is relatively straight-forward. The more complex question is on the response side; that is the problem of unambiguously specifying the conditional response pattern, even after activational peaking. For this, we need to simultaneously monitor a number of covert responses throughout conditioning. After conditioning, those responses that do not systematically change when the conditional stimulus is presented obviously do not belong to the conditional response pattern. Those responses that do systematically change when the conditional stimulus is presented constitute the class of potential conditional responses. From this class we will attempt to define the conditional response pattern. Refined analysis of the temporal relationships among these components would provide hints as to what might be mediating what, so that subclasses of the conditional response pattern could be specified. The subclasses might include mediators and their conse-quents; and we perhaps might even learn how to specify adventitious components. Furthermore, such a precise temporal analysis could also suggest routes and mechanisms of information processing; this strategy of studying temporal relations among components of a response pattern is illustrated in Figure 1. For illustration, focus in Figure 1 on the pattern for condition No. 1. The interpretation was that during a thought, a number of feedthrough

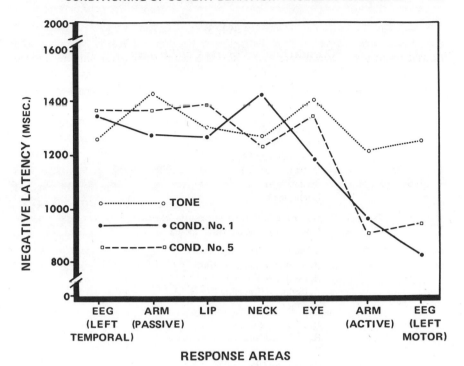

FIG. 1. Relative mean latencies of psychophysiological reactions in various bodily regions. The values presumably occur about the time that the subjects thought "yes" or "no" in answer to a question. The higher the data point on the vertical axis, the earlier in time the response occurred. (From McGuigan & Pavek, 1972.)

("feedback") loops were simultaneously run off involving the left temporal lobe, the passive arm, the lips, the neck, and the eye. Following that processing was a motor "command", the speculation continued, through the cerebral motor area to activate the responding arm.

The methodological point is that patterns of responses in various regions of the body, together with electroencephalographically recorded events, can be plotted along a temporal dimension. Such a set of covert processes can define the conditional covert reaction pattern, in accordance with the reasoning presented above. The next, and most basic, question to which we shall now turn is whether or not covert skeletal responses can actually be conditioned, as we have been assuming.

CAN ELECTROMYOGRAPHICALLY MEASURED COVERT BEHAVIOR BE CONDITIONED?

Classes of Electromyographic Learning Studies

Table 3 represents an attempt to classify the electromyographic conditioning studies (or the electromyographic "conditioning-like" studies) that have been

TABLE 3

Classification of Covert "Conditioning"
Studies Using Electromyography

I. *Classical conditioning*
Prosser & Hunter (1936)
Hunter (1937)
Hilden (1937)
Fink & Davis (1951)
Van Liere (1953)
Fink (1954)
Doehring (1957)

II. *Motor method of speech reinforcement*
Solberg, Tyre, & Stinson (1970)

III. *Operant conditioning*
Hefferline, Keenan, & Harford (1959)
Hefferline & Keenan (1961)
Hefferline & Keenan (1963)
Sasmor (1966)

IV. *Motor unit control*
Harrison & Mortensen (1962)
Basmajian (1963a)
Basmajian (1963b)
Carlsöö & Edfeldt (1963)
Basmajian, Baeza, & Fabrigar (1965)
Basmajian (1962)
Basmajian & Simard (1967)
Simard & Basmajian (1967)
Baginsky (1969)
Fruhling, Basmajian, & Simard (1969)
Petajan & Philip (1969)
Scully & Basmajian (1969)
Simard (1969)
Simard & Ladd (1969)
Thysell (1969)
Sutton & Kimm (1969)
Lloyd & Leibrecht (1971)
Basmajian (1972)

V. *Speech muscle feedback*
Hardyck, Petrinovich, & Ellsworth (1966)
McGuigan (1967)
Hardyck & Petrinovich (1969)
McGuigan (1971)

conducted. Those in the first category were presumed to fit the classical conditioning paradigm, that in the second follows Ivanov-Smolensky's (1956) paradigm, those in the third are covert operant conditioning studies, and the fourth category includes single motor unit training. Category V includes studies in which the effort was to permanently modify speech muscle activity by providing external feedback. We shall now consider each category in greater detail.

Classical Conditioning

The general purpose of the studies in classical conditioning has been to demonstrate that anticipatory electromyographic responses occur to the conditional stimulus. The typical conclusion is that classical conditioning *has* occurred, but the conditional electromyographic response is usually not well defined, being specified as the probability difference of amplitude during stimulus presentation relative to baseline. Furthermore, these studies suffer from lack of three appropriate controls. The first is the failure to simultaneously record electromyograms from a number of bodily locations. The purpose of this control, of course, is to distinguish between widespread bodily arousal and a relatively localized conditional response. For example, Fink (1954), in an admirable experiment for its time, paired a sound stimulus (white noise) with an uninstructed arm response and concluded that the sound became a conditional stimulus that elicited localized covert electromyographic activity in the arm. This finding was important, Fink held, because of the relations holding between covert electromyographic activity and overt behavior, viz., that "overt motor response conditioning may be viewed as a consequence of muscle action potential (EMG) conditioning [p. 68]." To illustrate this control problem, we may note that Fink placed electrodes only on the left arm so that, while he did find that left-arm electromyograms increased during the conditional stimulus interval, that left-arm response might have been but one component of a generalized reaction. The likelihood of this interpretation is increased when one notes that the unconditional stimulus was a 70-decibel tone which, as Van Liere (1953) showed, produces a widespread startle reaction. While Fink used a control group which received the conditional stimulus and the unconditional stimulus noncontiguously, he measured electromyograms during the conditional stimulus interval only so that a general startle pattern would go undetected.

The second of the three control problems arises when the experimenter places electrodes only in the locus of the expected conditional response; the obvious suggestion to the subject is that something important is going to happen in the region of the electrodes; e.g., Fink wanted to mask his interest in a noninstructed left-arm response from his subjects, yet he placed electrodes only at that location. By satisfying the first control problem above (using a number of electrode placements), this second control problem is obviously solved. Otherwise, one could simply use dummy electrodes, as Hefferline et al. (1959) did, though that would still leave unsolved the first problem concerning general arousal.

The third control problem with studies in Table 3 is that the experimenters typically did not sample the behavioral effects of various nonconditional stimuli before and after conditioning (see p. 186). Roessler and Brogden (1943), in their work on vasomotor conditioning, provide an admirable model of this control principle.

In conclusion, there are a number of studies in which it was reported that classical conditioning of relatively localized electromyographic activity was successful; however, due to failure to include appropriate controls, we cannot definitively accept this conclusion.

Motor Method of Speech Reinforcement

It has been traditionally held that this method of conditioning generally fits the classical conditioning paradigm. For example, Solberg, Tyre, and Stinson (1970) used a 40-watt light as the "conditional stimulus," then projected the word "press" as the "unconditional stimulus," whereupon the subject pressed a trigger on a pistol grip ("unconditional response"). However, one might better argue that the motor method of speech reinforcement is actually an operant procedure. Hence, the light is a signal that "press" (a discriminative-stimulus) will occur, whereupon the voluntary response of squeezing (an operant) is emitted. In some experiments, an overt operant has been followed by an explicit reinforcement. Such classification problems as this raise questions about the generality and universal appropriateness of classical and operant paradigms. However, our immediate interest is a more empirical one—we may note that Solberg et al. report an increasing percentage of electromyographic "conditional responses" as a function of trials. The mean terminal conditional response percentage during acquisition, though, was very low, being about 48% for children and 44% for adults. There was no evidence of overt response conditioning, leading them to conclude that while their subjects inhibited overt conditional responses, the more sensitive electromyographic response measure *did* indicate conditioning. During extinction, response level for their adult subjects fell to about that of the control groups, but their child subjects showed relatively large resistance to extinction. There are two major difficulties with their positive conclusion of covert conditioning: (*a*) they did not report any values of electromyographic increases over baseline during the conditional response interval, nor in any other way did they specify what was counted as a conditional response; (*b*) electromyograms were measured only from the arm that was instructed to move, so that "the conditional arm response," rather than being a localized conditional response, could have been generalized tension, or even the result of suggestion due to placement of electrodes in a single region.

We conducted two experiments using the motor method of speech reinforcement. The first was a limited study with James Bertera in which we replicated the Solberg et al. (1970) experiment, though with multiple bodily measurements.[1]

---

[1] For details of the laboratory and recording techniques, see McGuigan and Rodier (1968). For these experiments, stimuli were projected into the subject room from the equipment room by an automatically controlled 35-mm. slide projector.

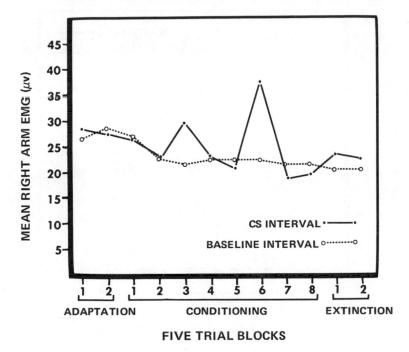

FIG. 2. Amplitude of covert behavior in the right arm during the conditional stimulus interval, relative to a preconditional stimulus baseline interval, as a function of trials.

Experiment I. The subjects were four college students. As an index of possible conditioning, we measured the maximum amplitude of electromyograms during each conditional stimulus period of 1,660 msec. for each subject, and, for comparison, also during a 1,660-msec. baseline period (unsystematically selected during a period between 2 and 4 sec. prior to the conditional stimulus onset.) Mean results for the active arm are presented in Figure 2. While there is some little hint of increased amplitude of right-arm electromyograms during the conditional stimulus period, suggesting a conditional response, the effect is not reliable. Control measures from the left (inactive) arm and the right leg did not significantly increase over baseline values (Figures 3 and 4).

Experiment II. With Jim Bertera we conducted a second study using the motor method of speech reinforcement; in this the subjects (six college females) made a left-arm response on termination of the visual stimulus of a low bar. They similarly made a right-arm response when a high-bar stimulus was terminated (Figure 5). A mild 0.5-second tone occurred simultaneously with the termination of each stimulus as a signal for the arm responses. When raising her arm, the subject also said "past" or "future" to the low and high bars,

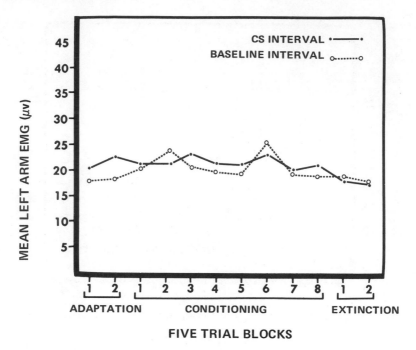

FIG. 3. Amplitude of covert behavior in the left arm during the conditional stimulus interval, relative to a preconditional stimulus baseline interval, as a function of trials.

respectively.[2] The question was whether each arm response would become anticipatory and occur during the presentation of the high ("future") and low ("past") bars. Electromyograms were recorded from both biceps, the right leg, and the lips. Each maximum amplitude was measured during each stimulus presentation, and during each preceding control (baseline) period. During adaptation, in which no unconditional stimulus tone was presented on termination of the stimulus, the high-bar, the low-bar, and a blank slide were presented 3 times each in random order. During conditioning trials, each high-bar, low-bar, and blank slide was presented 20 times in a random order (with, as shown in Figure 5, the tone commencing at slide termination). A mean difference in amplitude of electromyograms during the stimulus and control periods was then computed for each subject, and group means of these differences are presented in Figure 6. We can notice that during conditioning, mean maximum amplitude of electromyograms noticeably increased in both arms during the stimulus presentation intervals, the increase over baseline being significant for the left arm. During the extinction trials (10 randomly ordered

---

[2] The purpose for incorporating these words in this and later experiments was to conduct pilot work in an effort to condition peripheral tracers to Osgood's r_M, in collaboration with Charles Osgood.

presentations of each slide), the subjects were told that the experiment was over but that they should simply sit and observe the slides for another baseline recording. It can be seen in Figure 6 that any possible conditioning effect essentially dissipated. For the reconditioning phase (conducted as for conditioning), biceps electromyograms appropriately increased during the stimulus presentation interval, though neither increase was significant. In a test for generalization, various words with future, present, past, and neutral meanings were read to the subjects; it can be seen that mean arm electromyograms failed to change during each word to any great degree. Five extinction (test) trials for the low bar stimulus and five for the high bar stimulus were imbedded in a final set of conditioning trials. This conditioning series consisted of 10 blank, 10 future, and 10 past slides, in random order. Just as for the extinction phase, there is a hint in Figure 6 of successful conditioning, but the means do not differ significantly from zero. The mean changes for the lip electromyogram and leg electromyogram measures during stimulus presentation relative to control periods were small for all conditions and in no case approached a significant increase over baseline.

We counted the frequency with which each subject had a higher amplitude of his electromyogram during the stimulus intervals, relative to respective control intervals. Strong evidence of conditioning during the conditioning phase was

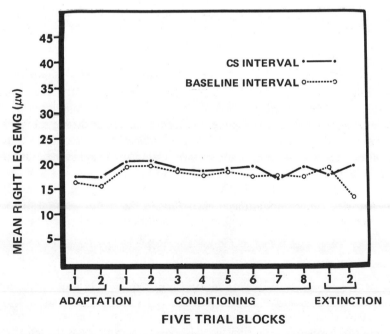

FIG. 4. Amplitude of covert behavior in the right leg during the conditional stimulus interval, relative to a preconditional stimulus baseline interval, as a function of trials.

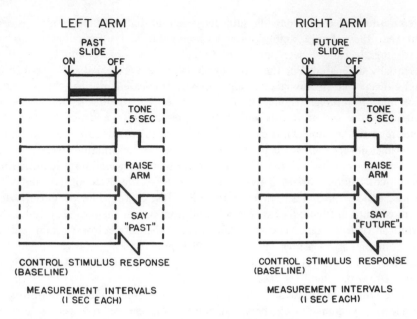

FIG. 5. Paradigm for the biceps electromyographic conditioning experiment. The sequence of stimuli for the right- and left-arm responses and three measurement intervals are specified. Thus there was a control (baseline) interval, followed by a conditional stimulus interval (slide projection). Then, on termination of the slide, the subject heard a tone, raised his arm, and said "future" or "past," as appropriate.

apparent by this criterion for only one subject—that subject responded with a greater anticipatory right-arm electromyogram amplitude on 90% of the future trials and with higher anticipatory left-arm electromyogram amplitude on 85% of the past trials. For reconditioning, the respective values during the stimulus presentation periods were 90% and 90%. This subject is the one who is thus the most responsible for the significant left-arm electromyographic increase to the past stimulus in Figure 6.

There is thus some limited evidence that electromyographically measured covert behavior can be conditioned according to the motor method of speech reinforcement, but there is considerable additional need for research in this area.

Operant Conditioning

The results in Category III with regard to operant conditioning of the thumb twitch can be summarized as positive; i.e., Hefferline and his associates (see Table 3) have shown that a minute muscle response in the thumb can be brought under control through operant means. Of course, multiple measurements would be desirable to establish whether or not the operant is mediated by other responses, even, possibly, by other skeletal muscle activity. A priority research need is to operantly condition other electromyographically defined responses.

Motor Unit Training

The typical procedure here is to record (with needle electrodes) a single motor unit response and transduce the response so that the subject receives external feedback. The feedback is displayed visually and/or auditorally so that, after learning, the single motor unit response appears as a single spike on an oscilloscope and sounds like a "pop" or "click" through a speaker. Within a very few minutes the subject learns to "isolate" the single motor unit (as in response differentiation), produce it "at will," and even emit recognizable patterns for another person, like one of my students who plays "Yankee Doodle Dandy" on his thumb. It is not entirely clear that this learning phenomenon fits any standard conditioning paradigm, though if the feedback functions as a reinforcement, single motor unit training could conceivably fit the operant paradigm.

The data for bringing single motor units under voluntary control are overwhelmingly positive, though again multiple measurements during the response differentiation procedure are usually absent. Regardless, the response is rapidly acquired and can occur in skeletal muscles throughout the body—in preliminary study we sampled and successfully isolated single motor units from the toe up the body through the tongue. However, there evidently has been no

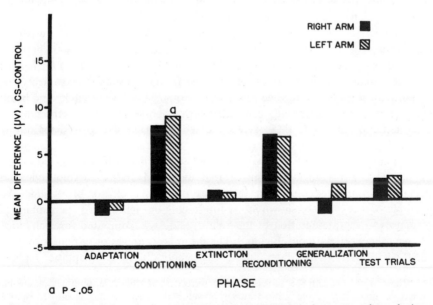

FIG. 6. Mean electromyogram differences (in microvolts) between values during conditional stimulus and baseline intervals. Right- and left-arm responses are presented for the six experimental conditions.

previous effort to bring the single motor unit response under external stimulus control, a task that Anna Rose Childress and I attempted in two experiments in our laboratory with the use of surface electrodes. While training for single motor unit control with surface (as against needle) electrodes can be successful, it is sufficiently laborious that we finally allowed our subjects to define a small-scale response consisting of several motor units, rather than insisting on a single motor unit response.

Experiment I. In our preliminary experiment, the subjects were 10 males or females between the ages of 15 to 25 years.[3] First, surface electrodes were positioned, for electromyograms, on the right and left forearms, and on the base of both thumbs. The subjects then relaxed for the preconditioning (adaptation) phase in which they were shown a random order of 10 slides that either read "click" or were blank. For the training phase, electromyographic signals from the right thumb were transduced through a speaker to provide auditory feedback for the subject. The subjects were instructed to use the feedback to always keep their responses of a constant amplitude and duration. The "click" and blank stimuli were then presented 25 times each in random order. Duration of each stimulus presentation was 1 second, and the interstimulus intervals were (randomly) 6, 7, or 8 seconds.

There was an informal generalization phase in which four of the subjects listened to a series of words read by the experimenter. Some words were also used in conversation. The word "click" was incorporated several times, as were some words that were similar to "click" and some words that were unrelated to "click." At the conclusion of this informal generalization phase, the experimenter reentered the room, gave the impression that the experiment was over (by turning the auditory feedback off), and mentioned that they were going to start recycling the slides for the next subject, but that they would not bother the subject. Twenty extinction trials (feedback off, and the subject presumably not "trying" to respond) were then run with randomized order of "click" and blank slides. The session was *actually* concluded with a debriefing in which the subjects were asked if they felt they were expected to respond to the slides during extinction.

A thumb response was defined as related to a stimulus if it consisted of one or several electromyographic spikes that exceeded 16 μv in amplitude and occurred within 1 second after the onset of the "click" or blank slide. An example of a response is shown in the top tracing of Figure 7. The percentage of responses to the presentation of the "click" slide was computed for each block of five trials, and plotted in Figure 8. The mean percentages of responses to both the "click" and blank slides during the preconditioning (adaptation) phase

---

[3] There were originally 16 subjects, but 4 were dropped because, within a reasonable period of time, they could not adequately develop the response during initial response differentiation training; two more were dropped after the extinction phase, one because he didn't look at the stimuli, and one because he wasn't sure whether or not he was voluntarily responding.

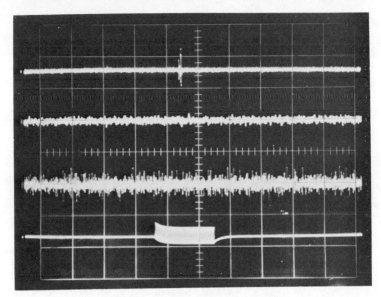

FIG. 7. The "several motor unit response" may be observed in the top trace of electromyographic activity from the right thumb. No hint of a similar response occurs in the left thumb or right arm (#2 and 3 from top). The event marker on the bottom trace shows the stimulus presentation. Horizontal divisions indicate 0.5 seconds. The vertical scale is 20 μv, 50 μv, and 100 μv per division for the three traces reading from the top down.

approximated zero. During the conditioning phase, the percentage of responses to "click" approached 100% and remained relatively elevated during extinction (percentage of responses to the blank slides during conditioning was almost always zero, indicating a good discrimination). During extinction, responses occurred to about 67% of the "click" slides and to 8% of the blank slides, a difference that was significant (A = .162, $p < .05$). During extinction, significantly more responses were made to the "click" slide than during interstimulus (baseline) periods of equal duration, viz., 67% versus 2% (A = .148, $p < .05$).

Upon final debriefing, four subjects said that they interpreted the "extinction set" (i.e., to relax for baseline recordings) as a period in which they were still somehow supposed to respond. Four others said they did not think they were supposed to respond and they were not in any way trying to respond. No differences of note appeared between these two subgroups during the preconditioning or the conditioning phase. More importantly, during extinction trials, the two subgroups responded with approximately the same frequency to both the "click" slides (66% versus 66%) and to the blank slides (8% versus 9%). It is most interesting, then, that these response-frequency data suggest conditioning by both subgroups and do not allow any differentiation between the subgroups. Evidently the small-scale thumb response, through operantlike conditioning,

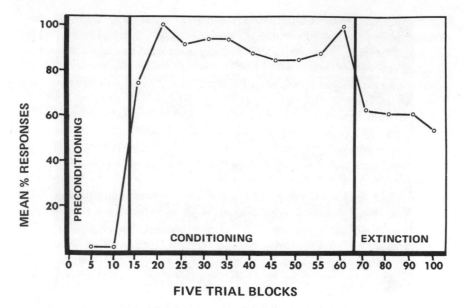

FIG. 8. Percentage of right-thumb responses to the visual presentation of "click" in each block of five trials.

came under external stimulus control so that it occurred "automatically" to the projected word "click."

During the generalization phase, the four subjects responded to various words in the list read to them and during conversation, on the average, 10 times each; a mean of six of these responses were made to the word "click." The four other responses per subject were made to such as the following, some of which are similar to "click," viz., "snap," "smut," "bang," "pop," and "glick." These rather informally collected data carry some suggestion of generalization of the response from the projected word "click" to its use beyond the formal phases of the experiment. These data are, however, no more than suggestive and certainly raise more questions than they answer.

Experiment II. For the second experiment, subjects were 11 male or female volunteers from 15 to 25 years of age. (One was eliminated because he could not adequately relax.) Except as noted, the same general procedure was used as for the previous experiment. The stimuli were those of Figure 5, viz., slides with a black bar near the top identified as future slides, those with a black bar near the bottom (past slides), and blank slides.

After the electrode placements, subjects relaxed while 10 slides in a randomized order of future, past, and blank were presented for the preconditioning phase. For the training phase, auditory feedback was presented from both thumbs. The subjects first developed a response, successively, in each thumb such that each response could be readily produced 10 consecutive times on command. Then they practiced until they could alternately produce the response in each thumb for 10 alternations. Next, each subject said "future" aloud when making the right-thumb response and "past" aloud when making the left-thumb response. When he had successfully completed this added alternation 10 times, the experimenter asked the subject to make the response to the experimenter's random enunciation of "future" and "past." Criterion here was 10 correct responses in each hand.

This training session was concluded by instructing the subject to make the right-thumb response to each future slide, the left-thumb response to each past slide, and no response to the blank slides in the upcoming presentation. The first conditioning trials then started, consisting of future, past, and blank slides in random order. After a 4-minute rest period, there was a second conditioning series in which the subject whispered "future" or "past" as appropriate. Another rest period, followed by 50 more trials in which the subject was told to think "future" or "past" while responding, concluded the conditioning phase.

A generalization phase was informally conducted somewhat as for the first experiment, except that the words "future" and "past" replaced "click." Finally 20 "extinction" trials were run in which the future, past, and blank slides were presented in random order.

The primary results are presented in Figure 9. The number of times that the subjects responded appropriately to the future and past slides was counted for each 10-trial block. The percentage of these combined right- and left-thumb responses for each 10-trial block is plotted in Figure 9; we can note that the curve resembles that of Figure 8. In particular, the fact that the subjects continued to "automatically" respond to the future and past slides during extinction confirms the results of the previous experiment, suggesting that the two small-scale thumb responses were respectively conditioned to the future (high-bar) and past (low-bar) slides. That is, during extinction: (a) the subjects responded with their right thumb to the future stimulus significantly more often than they did to the blank slide (58% versus 12%, A = .153, $p < .05$); (b) the right-thumb response was made to the future stimulus significantly more often than during the baseline period (58% versus 5%, A = .156, $p < .05$); (c) the left-thumb response was made to the past stimulus more frequently than during the baseline period (56% versus 5%, A = .156, $p < .05$); (d) the left-thumb response occurred more often to the past stimulus than to the blank slide (58% versus 12%, A = .181, $p < .05$); and (e) the subjects made relatively few "errors" during extinction, i.e., they responded with their left thumb to the future stimulus only 7% of the time, and with their right thumb to the past stimulus only 12% of the time.

In both Experiment I and Experiment II, no responses were identified in the other regions of the body sampled that were correlated with the thumb responses. Consequently, as hypothesized on p. 185, the thumb response appears to be a highly localized event.

As in the first experiment, then, it appears that these small-amplitude thumb responses came under external stimulus control, but this time there were two responses that were successfully evoked by their respective stimuli.

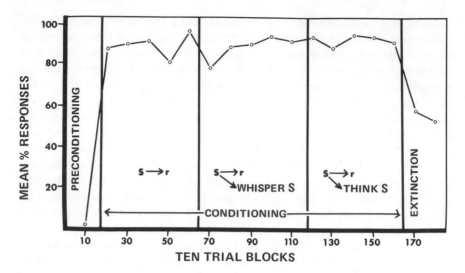

FIG. 9. Percentage of right- and left-thumb responses made to the future and past slides (combined) in each 10-trial block throughout the experiment.

During the generalization phase, the experimenter read a list of 20 words to each subject, following which the subject read the same list aloud. Time-related words (like "tomorrow"), including "future" and "past," appeared eight times on the list. The subjects made thumb responses to an average of 28% of the time-related words read by the experimenter, and to 20% of the time-related words that the subjects themselves read out loud. As in Experiment I, several responses per subject were also made to words that "sounded" like the response (e.g., "click," "pop"). Similarly, during informal conversation an average of about three responses per subject were made to the time-related words. The intent is obviously not to establish a generalization effect, but the fact that any responses occurred in this "extra-experimental" situation is sufficiently encouraging to suggest more serious investigation. Certainly, firm establishment of a generalization effect would be a very valuable phenomenon as well as an additional criterion of successful covert conditioning.

Speech Muscle Feedback

There have been several studies in which auditory feedback from covert oral behavior was furnished to subjects while they were engaged in silent reading. The strategy in these studies was to attempt to permanently reduce amplitude of covert oral behavior ("subvocalization") during reading to see whether or not the reduction actually retarded reading proficiency, as is the popular educational view. The immediate question is whether or not there is learning in the speech musculature under these conditions. The statements offered by Hardyck and his associates (see Category V in Table 3) have been that subvocalization can be permanently eliminated within a very short period of time (about 5 minutes). It is, of course, technologically and theoretically interesting if speech muscle responses that have been used in silent reading for many years can be so rapidly and permanently "extinguished." Our approach to this problem (McGuigan, 1967, 1971) has been to use an "operantlike" paradigm—we transduced electromyographic signals from the reader's chin so that when the signals exceeded an amplitude of 20 μv, a noxious stimulus was presented; the stimulus was removed when the reader's covert oral behavior dropped below 20 μv. The results for one female college subject (Figure 10) show no reduction in amplitude of chin electromyograms until trial 28, when we told her that she was controlling the tone; with some knowledge of the response-feedback contingency, chin amplitude fell, and we were able to shape the response downward quite nicely. The important point here, however, is that chin response amplitude rebounded to about baseline level when the subject later read without feedback. The conclusion, contrary to the widely accepted statements of Hardyck, Petrinovich, & Ellsworth (1966), is that the subject did not learn (in any permanent sense) to control her covert oral behavior in absence of feedback. This finding was confirmed with six other subjects (Figure 11). Figure 12 indicates that a sample of other response measures did not systematically change as a function of feedback condition. Consequently, the response changes were apparently localized in the speech region.

This sample of data thus suggests that we cannot permanently control (condition) gross skeletal muscular activity through these feedback techniques, at least under these experimental conditions.

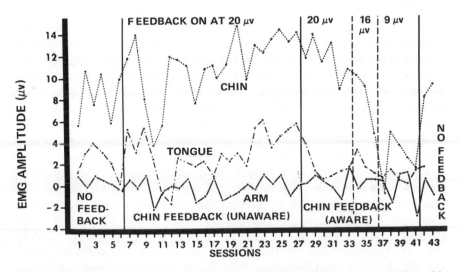

FIG. 10. Amplitudes of electromyograms for each session. Feedback started when chin amplitude exceeded 20 μv during Sessions 7 to 33; thresholds for later sessions were lowered to 16 and 9 μv. (From McGuigan, 1971.)

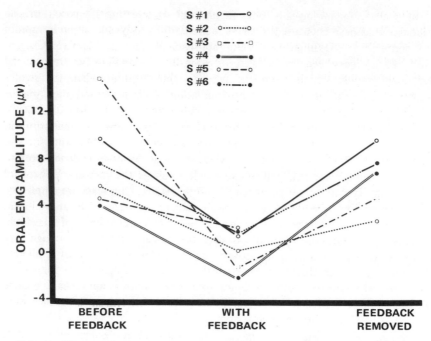

FIG. 11. Effect of feedback presentation and subsequent withdrawal on the triggering covert oral behavior during silent reading. Feedback was from the chin for Subjects 1, 3, 4, and 5, and from the lips of Subjects 2 and 6. (From McGuigan, 1971.)

Conclusion

The results of the studies cited in Table 3 indicate that we *can* modify covert behavior that is electromyographically defined. A major problem, though, is how to systematically conceptualize these various learning phenomena—it has been difficult to fit all the procedures specified for the five categories of Table 3 to standard conditioning paradigms. For example, the motor method of speech reinforcement does not precisely fit either the classical or the operant paradigms. Thus, while the verbal stimulus of "press" has traditionally been called a "conditional stimulus," it has more of the properties of the discriminative stimulus in operant conditioning. Yet, because the motor method of speech reinforcement may well not require a contingent reinforcing stimulus, this method does not unambiguously fit the operant paradigm. Similarly, the procedure for acquiring single motor unit control resembles the operant paradigm, but it has not been established that external feedback from the muscles ("biofeedback") has the properties of a reinforcing stimulus. Perhaps the informative function of the feedback is sufficient for learning. This, a classical problem, became apparent in the traditional knowledge of results studies; then, we asked, to what extent might knowledge of results (or "biofeedback") function merely to furnish information, to what extent might it function as a secondary reinforcer, or to what degree might it serve both an informative and reinforcing function. Systematic study of the relationship between these two contingency variables is called for.

In short, our conclusion for this major section is that, within the limits of the control problems cited therein, covert skeletal behavior has been successfully conditioned in accordance with the principles of classical and operant conditioning. However, some instances of covert learning do not unambiguously fit our paradigms for operant and classical conditioning. Perhaps further study of relevant variables, such as establishing that a reinforcement function of biofeedback is necessary for acquiring single motor unit control, will allow us to universally apply existing principles to account for the modification of all covert behavior. Otherwise, it may be that some covert responses obey as yet unformulated laws of learning.

ON THE FUNCTION OF THE CONDITIONAL COVERT SKELETAL RESPONSE

The early behaviorists hypothesized that covert behavior was critical in such higher mental processes as thinking. Research to date has established that covert

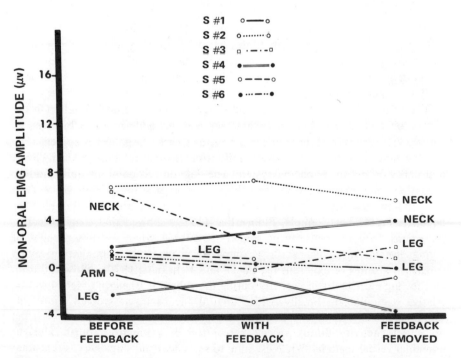

FIG. 12. Amplitude of nonoral response measures during feedback and subsequent nonfeedback reading sessions.

behavior, particularly covert responses of the speech musculature, occur during the performance of linguistic tasks that require thought (McGuigan, 1970). Perhaps by acquiring such covert skeletal responses, we facilitate our performance of linguistic tasks. If so, what is the beneficial facility acquired in the process of covert skeletal muscle conditioning (learning)?

We have previously hypothesized that a function of the rapid, numerous, and minute skeletal responses is to facilitate internal information processing by generating and transmitting a verbal code (McGuigan, 1970). When one reads, for instance, linguistic stimuli are input visually, whereupon coded neural impulses from the eye evoke conditional responses in the speech musculature, as well as elsewhere in the body. Thus evoked, these conditional covert responses form a complex temporal and spatial pattern of neuromuscular events; a large number of parameters are thus available for the formation of verbal codes that can be afferently transmitted, in parallel sequences, to the brain (McGuigan, 1973). A. N. Sokolov (1967) has suggested that such afferently generated codes excite speech regions of the brain. We might expect there to follow a central coordination of the linguistic regions involving intracerebral feedthrough loops; simultaneously efferent impulses descend as components of complex and extensive feedthrough loops involving peripheral mechanisms. (These various loops must be extremely rapid, and continuous.) It is the simultaneous running off of these intracerebral loops and the loops between the brain, the arms, the speech musculature, the eyes, the neck, etc. (as hypothesized for Figure 1 on p. 187), that constitutes the internal information processing activity in which the reader comprehends the prose being read. Similar internal information processing systems, in the form of rapid neuromuscular loops, should function in a similar manner when the linguistic input is in other modalities.

The hypothesis that the speech (and other) musculature does function in the generation and transmission of an abstract code to and from the brain is, of course, very difficult to test. In some way, as Charles Osgood has suggested to me, the task is to show that there is a discriminative correlation between covert oral behavior and the phonemic system. The data on this point are quite limited. Yet, there are some that at least hint at this possibility that the speech musculature covertly responds differentially as a function of the kind of linguistic input. For example, Blumenthal (1959) showed that tongue electromyograms were of significantly greater magnitude when subjects thought of saying alveolars ("lingual words") compared to when they thought of saying labials. In a series of experiments, Locke and Fehr (e.g., 1970) followed this up by showing more covert lip activity during the subvocal rehearsal of labial words, relative to nonlabials. Finally, with Edmund Jacobson, we studied one of his well-relaxed subjects in our laboratory. Our attempt was to record differential lip muscle activity during speech perception as a function of labial versus nonlabial verbal material. While listening to sentences and single words that were loaded with labials, this subject significantly increased integrated lip electromyograms by an average of 2.8 μv over baseline (A = .16, $p < .05$). While listening to comparable nonlabials, however, the mean change in lip electromyograms was only 0.3 μv (A = 1.06, $p > .05$).[4] Response amplitude in the left and right forearms remained essentially unchanged during presentation of the verbal material.

The next priority is for research along these, and other, lines to specify coding systems involved when the speech musculature covertly interacts with the linguistic regions of the brain in carrying out an internal information-processing function.

SUMMARY

The purpose was to determine whether or not our laws of conditioning, derived from the study of overt behavior, are also applicable to covert responses. First, two major methodological problems were considered: (*a*) that of isolating *the* conditional covert response, and (*b*) that of distinguishing between a conditional covert response and such widespread reaction patterns as the orienting reflex and generalized arousal.

With regard to the first problem, "the curare strategy" was examined, and it was concluded that this technique of administering curare has not yet allowed us to unambiguously remove the role of the skeletal musculature during conditioning. The first problem is sufficiently complex, in fact, that it is probably best to universally replace the concept of a single, localized conditional response with that of conditional response *patterns*. With regard to the second problem, researchers seek to specify relatively unique relationships between a conditional stimulus and a conditional covert response pattern; methodologically, the solution is to extensively sample various stimulus and response classes before, during, and at the conclusion of conditioning. As conditioning trials increase, activational peaking diminishes, leaving a "behavioral residue" that includes the conditional response pattern; however, due to technological limitations, this residual pattern may necessarily include mediators, and some adventitious components too.

To assess the available evidence for the conditioning of covert skeletal responses, five classes of studies which employed electromyography were specified. It was concluded that covert skeletal responses *are* modifiable, but, because of methodological shortcomings, we do not yet adequately specify the components that constitute conditional covert response patterns. Of greater importance, while there are instances of covert learning that seem to fit operant and classical conditioning paradigms, other instances of covert learning may obey as yet unformulated laws.

Concerning the function of conditional covert behavior, we have hypothesized that covert responses, particularly those of the speech musculature, facilitate the performance of linguistic tasks. In particular, complex temporal

---

[4] Thanks to Debbie Mitchell for help with this subject.

and spatial patterns of conditional covert oral responses may function in the generation and transmission of abstract verbal codes which are neurally conducted to and from the linguistic regions of the brain. Numerous, rapid feedthrough loops thus operate between peripheral mechanisms like the speech musculature and the brain, in addition to intracerebral loops that function in central coordination. These loops may be activated to internally process information that one receives from external verbal material.

A test of this hypothesized function of covert oral responses is to show that there is a discriminative correlation between covert oral responses and the phonemic system. Some limited data indicate that there *is* uniquely heightened covert lip activity during the processing of external verbal material loaded with labial words. It may thus be that, for example, lip activity helps to encode incoming labial words so that critical information is thereby afferently carried to the linguistic regions of the brain.

REFERENCES

Amassian, V. E., & Weiner, H. The effect of (+)-tubocurarine chloride and of acute hypotension on the electrical activity of the cat. *Journal of Physiology*, 1966, **184**, 1–15.

Andreassi, J. L., Mayzner, E. S., Beyda, D. R., & Davidovics, S. Effects of induced muscle tension upon the visual evoked potential and motor potential. *Psychonomic Science*, 1970, **20**, 245–247.

Baginsky, R. G. Voluntary control of motor unit activity by visual and aural feedback. *Electroencephalography and Clinical Neurophysiology*, 1969, **27**, 724.

Basmajian, J. V. *Muscles alive: Their functions revealed by electromyography*. Baltimore: Williams & Wilkins, 1962.

Basmajian, J. V. Conscious control of single nerve cells. *New Scientist*, 1963, **20**, 662–664 (a).

Basmajian, J. V. Control and training of individual motor units. *Science*, 1963, **141**, 440–441 (b).

Basmajian, J. V. Electromyography comes of age. *Science*, 1972, **176**, 603–609.

Basmajian, J. R., Baeza, M., & Fabrigar, C. Conscious control and training of individual spinal motor neurons in normal human subjects. *The Journal of New Drugs*, 1965, **5**, 78–85.

Basmajian, J. V., & Simard, T. G. Effects of distracting movements on the control of trained motor units. *American Journal of Physical Medicine*, 1967, **46**, 1427–1449.

Belmaker, R., Proctor, E., & Feather, B. W. Muscle tension in human operant heart rate conditioning. *Conditional Reflex*, 1972, **7**, 97–106.

Birk, L., Crider, A., Shapiro, D., & Tursky, B. Operant electrodermal conditioning under partial curarization. *Journal of Comparative and Physiological Psychology*, 1966, **62**, 165–166.

Black, A. H. Cardiac conditioning in curarized dogs: The relationship between heart rate and skeletal behavior. In W. F. Prokasy (Ed.), *Classical conditioning*. New York: Appleton-Century-Crofts, 1965.

Black, A. H. Transfer following operant conditioning in the curarized dog. *Science*, 1967, **155**, 201–203.

Black, A. H. Autonomic aversive conditioning in infrahuman subjects. In R. Brush (Ed.), *Aversive conditioning and learning*. New York: Academic Press, 1971. Pp. 3–104.

Black, A. H., Carlson, N. J., & Solomon, R. L. Exploratory studies of the conditioning of autonomic responses in curarized dogs. *Psychology Monographs*, 1962, **76**, 1–31.

Black, A. H., & Dalton, A. J. The relationship between the avoidance response and subsequent changes in heart rate. In W. F. Prokasy (Ed.), *Classical conditioning.* New York: Appleton-Century-Crofts, 1965. P. 46.

Black, A. H., & Lang, W. M. Cardiac conditioning and skeletal responding in curarized dogs. *Psychological Review,* 1964, 71, 80–85.

Blumenthal, M. *Lingual myographic responses during directed thinking.* (Unpublished doctoral dissertation, University of Denver), 1959

Brinley, F. J., Jr., Kandel, E. R., & Marshall, W. H. The effect of intravenous d-tubocurarine on the electrical activity of the cat cerebral cortex. *Transactions of the American Neurological Association,* 1958, 83, 53–58.

Buchwald, J. S., Standish, M., Eldred, E., & Halas, E. S. Contribution of muscle spindle circuits to learning as suggested by training under Flaxedil. *Electroencephalography and Clinical Neurophysiology,* 1964, 16, 582–594.

Carlsöö, S. S., & Edfeldt, A. W. Attempts at muscle control with visual and auditory impulses as auxiliary stimuli. *Scandinavian Journal of Psychology,* 1963, 4, 231–235.

Cohen, M. J., & Johnson, H. J. Relationship between heart rate and muscular activity within a classical conditioning paradigm. *Journal of Experimental Psychology,* 1971, 90, 222–226.

Davis, R. C. Response patterns. *Transactions of the New York Academy of Sciences,* 1957, 19, 731–739.

Davis, R. C., Buchwald, A. M., & Frankmann, R. W. Autonomic and muscular responses, and their relation to simple stimuli. *Psychological Monographs,* 1955, 69 (20, Whole No. 405), 1–71.

Dewan, E. M. A demonstration of the effect of eye position and accommodation on the occipital alpha rhythm. *Electroencephalography and Clinical Neurophysiology,* 1968, 24, 188.

DiCara, L. V., & Miller, N. E. Changes in heart rate instrumentally learned by curarized rats as avoidance responses. *Journal of Comparative and Physiological Psychology,* 1968, 65, 8–12. (a)

DiCara, L. V., & Miller, N. E. Instrumental learning of peripheral vasomotor responses by the curarized rat. *Communications in Behavioral Biology,* Part A, 1968, 1, 209–212. (b)

DiCara, L. V., & Miller, N. E. Instrumental learning of systolic blood pressure responses by curarized rats: Dissociation of cardiac and vascular changes. *Psychosomatic Medicine,* 1968, 30, 489–494. (c)

DiCara, L. V., & Miller, N. E. Instrumental learning of vasomotor responses by rats: Learning to respond differentially in the two ears. *Science,* 1968, 159, 1485–1486. (d)

DiCara, L. V., & Miller, N. E. Long term retention of instrumentally learned heart-rate changes in the curarized rat. *Communications in Behavioral Biology,* 1968, 2, 19–23. (e)

DiCara, L. V., & Miller, N. E. Heart-rate learning in the noncurarized state, transfer to the curarized state, and subsequent retraining in the noncurarized state. *Physiology and Behavior,* 1969, 4, 621–624. (a)

DiCara, L. V., & Miller, N. E. Transfer of instrumentally learned heart-rate changes from curarized to noncurarized state: Implications for a mediational hypothesis. *Journal of Comparative and Physiological Psychology,* 1969, 68, 159–162. (b)

DiCara, L. V., & Stone, E. A. Effect of instrumental heart-rate training on rat cardiac and brain catecholamines. *Psychosomatic Medicine,* 1970, 32, 359–368.

DiCara, L. V., & Weiss, J. M. Effect of heart-rate learning under curare on subsequent noncurarized avoidance learning. *Journal of Comparative and Physiological Psychology,* 1969, 69, 368–374.

Dinges, D. F., & Klingaman, R. L. Effects of induced muscle tension upon the visual-evoked potential and motor potential: A replication. *Psychonomic Science,* 1972, 28, 303–305.

Doehring, D. G. Conditioning of muscle action potential responses resulting from passive hand movement. *Journal of Experimental Psychology,* 1957, 54(4), 292–296.

Douglas, W. W. Autocoids. In L. S. Goodman & A. Gillman (Eds.), *Pharmacological Basis of Therapeutics*. New York: McMillan, 1970. Pp. 620–662.

Duffy, E. *Activation and behavior*. New York: Wiley, 1962.

Eason, R. G., Aiken, L. R., White, C. T., & Lichtenstein, M. Activation and behavior: II. Visually evoked cortical potentials in man as indicants of activation level. *Perceptual and Motor Skills*, 1964, 19, 875–895.

Estable, C. Curare and synapse. In D. Bovet, F. Bovet-Nitti, & G. B. Marini-Bettolo (Eds.), *Curare and curare-like agents*. Amsterdam: Elsevier, 1959.

Faaborg-Andersen, K., & Edfeldt, A. W. Electromyography of intrinsic and extrinsic laryngeal muscles during silent speech: Correlation with reading activity. *Acta oto-laryngologica*, 1958, 49, 478–482.

Fenwick, P. B. C., & Walker, S. The effect of eye position on the alpha rhythm. In C. R. Evans & T. B. Mulholland (Eds.), *Attention in neurophysiology*. New York: Appleton-Century-Crofts, 1969.

Fields, C. Instrumental conditioning of the rat cardiac control system. *Proceedings of the National Academy of Sciences*, 1970, 65, 293–299.

Fink, J. B. Conditioning of muscle action potential increments accompanying an instructed movement. *Journal of Experimental Psychology*, 1954, 47, 61–68.

Fink, J. B., & Davis, R. C. Generalization of a muscle action potential response to tonal duration. *Journal of Experimental Psychology*, 1951, 42, 403–408.

Fruhling, M., Basmajian, J. V., & Simard, T. G. A note on the conscious controls of motor units by children under six. *Journal of Motor Behavior*, 1969, 1, 65–68.

Galindo, A. Curare and pancuronium compared: Effects on previously undepressed mammalian myoneural junctions. *Science*, 1972, 178, 753–755.

Germana, J. Psychophysiological correlates of conditioned response formation. *Psychological Bulletin*, 1968, 70, 105–114.

Goss, A. E. Early behaviorism and verbal mediating responses. *American Psychologist*, 1961, 16, 285–298.

Grob, D. Neuromuscular blocking drugs. In W. S. Root & F. G. Hoffman (Eds.), *Physiological pharmacology*. Vol. 3. *The nervous system: Part C, autonomic nervous system drugs*. New York: Academic Press, 1967. Pp. 389–460.

Hahn, W. W., & Slaughter, J. Heart rate responses in curarized rats. *Psychophysiology*, 1970, 7, 429–435.

Hardyck, C. D., & Petrinovich, L. F. Treatment of subvocal speech during reading. *Journal of Reading*, 1969, 12 361–368, 419–422.

Hardyck, C. D., Petrinovich, L. F., & Ellsworth, D. W. Feedback of speech muscle activity during silent reading: Rapid extinction. *Science*, 1966, 154, 1467–1468.

Harrison, V. F., & Mortensen, O. A. Identification and voluntary control of single motor unit activity in the tibialis anterior muscle. *Anatomical Record*, 1962, 144, 109–116.

Hefferline, R. F., & Keenan, B. Amplitude induction gradient of a small human operant in an escape-avoidance situation. *Journal of Experimental Analysis of Behavior*, 1961, 4, 41–43.

Hefferline, R. F., & Keenan, B. Amplitude-induction gradient of a small-scale (covert) operant. *Journal of Experimental Analysis of Behavior*, 1963, 6, 307–315.

Hefferline, R. F., Keenan, B., & Harford, R. A. Escape and avoidance conditioning in human subjects without their observation of the response. *Science*, 1959, 130, 1338–1339.

Hilden, A. H. An action current study of the conditioned hand withdrawal. *Psychological Monographs*, 1937, 49, 173–204.

Hodes, R. Electrocortical synchronization resulting from reduced proprioceptive drive caused by neuromuscular blocking agents. *Electroencephalography and Clinical Neurophysiology*, 1962, 14, 220–232.

Horridge, G. A. The electrophysiological approach to learning in isolatable ganglia. *Animal Behavior*, Supplement 1, 1965, 163–182.

Hothersall, D., & Brener, J. Operant conditioning of changes in heart rate in curarized rats. *Journal of Comparative and Physiological Psychology*, 1969, 68, 338–342.

Hudgins, C. V. Conditioning and voluntary control of the pupillary light reflex. *Journal of General Psychology*, 1933, 8, 3–51.

Hunter, W. S. Muscle potentials and conditioning in the rat. *Journal of Experimental Psychology*, 1937, 21, 611–624.

Ivanov-Smolensky, A. G. *Works of the institute of higher nervous activity: Patho-physiological series*. Vol. 2. Moscow, USSR: Academy of Science, 1956.

Jacobson, E. Electrophysiology of mental activities. *American Journal of Psychology*, 1932, 44, 677–694.

Johnson, L. C. Nonspecific galvanic skin response and respiration. *Psychological Reports*, 1961, 9, 516.

Kamiya, J. Conscious control of brain waves. *Psychology Today*, 1968, 1, 56–60.

Kimmel, H. D., & Davidov, W. Classical GSR conditioning with concomitant EMG measurement. *Journal of Experimental Psychology*, 1967, 74, 67–74.

Knott, J. R. Some effects of "mental set" upon the electrophysiological processes of the human cerebral cortex. *Journal of Experimental Psychology*, 1939, 24, 384–405.

Kodman, F., Jr. Validity of GSR conditioning. *Psychological Reports*, 1967, 21, 813–818.

Koelle, G. B. Neuromuscular blocking agents. In L. S. Goodman & A. Gillman (Eds.), *Pharmacological basis of therapeutics*. New York: McMillan, 1960. Pp. 601–619.

Leuba, C., Birch, L., & Appleton, J. Human problem solving during complete paralysis of the voluntary musculature. *Psychological Reports*, 1968, 22, 849–855.

Light, J. S., & Gantt, W. H. Essential part of reflex arc for establishment of conditioned reflex: Formation of conditioned reflex after exclusion of motor peripheral end. *Journal of Comparative Psychology*, 1936, 21, 19–36.

Lloyd, A. J., & Leibrecht, B. C. Conditioning of a single motor unit. *Journal of Experimental Psychology*, 1971, 88, 391–395.

Locke, J. L., & Fehr, F. S. Subvocal rehearsal as a form of speech. *Journal of Verbal Learning and Verbal Behavior*, 1970, 9, 495–498.

Maltzman, I. The orienting reflex and thinking as determiners of conditioning and generalization to words. In H. H. Kendler & J. T. Spence (Eds.), *Essays in neobehaviorism*. New York: Appleton-Century-Crofts, 1971.

McGuigan, F. J. *Thinking: Studies of covert language behavior*. New York: Appleton-Century-Crofts, 1966.

McGuigan, F. J. Feedback of speech muscle activity during silent reading. *Science*, 1967, 157, 579–580.

McGuigan, F. J. Covert oral behavior during the silent performance of language tasks. *Psychological Bulletin*, 1970, 74, 309–326.

McGuigan, F. J. External auditory feedback from covert oral behavior during silent reading. *Psychonomic Science*, 1971, 25, 212–214.

McGuigan, F. J. Electrical measurement of covert processes as an explication of "higher mental events." In F. J. McGuigan & R. A. Schoonover (Eds.), *The psychophysiology of thinking*. New York: Academic Press, 1973.

McGuigan, F. J., & Pavek, G. V. On the psychophysiological identification of covert nonoral language processes. *Journal of Experimental Psychology*, 1972, 92, 237–245.

McGuigan, F. J., & Rodier, W. I., III. Effects of auditory stimulation on covert oral behavior during silent reading. *Journal of Experimental Psychology*, 1968, 76, 649–655.

McIntyre, A. R., Bennett, A. L., & Hamilton, C. Recent advances in the pharmacology of curare. In A. R. McIntyre (Ed.), Curare and anticurare agents. *Annals of the New York Academy of Sciences*, 1951, 54, 297–530.

Miller, N. E., & Banuazizi, A. Instrumental learning by curarized rats of a specific visceral response, intestinal or cardiac. *Journal of Comparative and Physiological Psychology*, 1968, 65, 1–7.

Miller, N. E., & DiCara, L. V. Instrumental learning of heart rate changes in curarized rats: Shaping, and specificity to discriminative stimulus. *Journal of Comparative and Physiological Psychology,* 1967, **63**, 12–19.

Miller, N. E., & DiCara, L. V. Instrumental learning of urine formation by rats, changes in renal blood flow. *American Journal of Physiology,* 1968, **215**, 677–683.

Mulholland, T. The concept of attention and the electroencephalographic alpha rhythm. In C. R. Evans & T. B. Mulholland (Eds.), *Attention in neurophysiology.* New York: Appleton-Century-Crofts, 1969. Pp. 100–127.

Okuma, T., Fujmori, M., & Hayashi, A. The effect of environmental temperature on the electrocortical activity of cats immobilized by neuromuscular blocking agents. *Electroencephalography and Clinical Neurophysiology,* 1965, **18**, 392–400.

Pappas, B. A., DiCara, L. V., & Miller, N. E. Learning of blood pressure responses in the noncurarized rat: Transfer to the curarized state. *Physiology and Behavior,* 1970, **5**, 1029–1032.

Penfield, W. Some mechanisms of consciousness discovered during electrical stimulation of the brain. *Proceedings of the National Academy of Sciences,* 1958, **44**, 51–66.

Petajan, J. H., & Philip, B. A. Frequency control of motor unit action potentials. *Electroencephalography and Clinical Neurophysiology,* 1969, **27**, 66–72.

Prosser, C. L., & Hunter, W. S. The extinction of startle responses and spinal reflexes in the white rat. *American Journal of Physiology,* 1936, **117**, 609–618.

Ray, R. Classical conditioning of heart rate in restrained and curarized rats. Unpublished doctoral dissertation, University of Tennessee, 1969.

Roessler, R. L., & Brogden, W. J. Conditioned differentiation of vasoconstriction to subvocal stimuli. *American Journal of Psychology,* 1943, **56**, 78–86.

Sasmor, R. M. Operant conditioning of a small-scale muscle response. *Journal of the Experimental Analysis of Behavior,* 1966, **9**, 69–85.

Scully, H. E., & Basmajian, J. V. Effect of nerve stimulation on trained motor unit control. *Archives of Physical Medicine and Rehabilitation,* 1969, **50**, 32–33.

Simard, T. G. Fine sensorimotor control in healthy children: An electromyographic study. *Pediatrics,* 1969, **43**, 1035–1041.

Simard, T. G., & Basmajian, J. V. Methods in training the conscious control of motor units. *Archives of Physical Medicine and Rehabilitation,* 1967, **48**, 12–19.

Simard, T. G., & Ladd, W. L. Conscious control of motor units with thalidomide children: An electromyographic study. *Developmental Medicine and Child Neurology,* 1969, **11**, 743–748.

Simpson, H. M., & Climan, M. H. Pupillary and electromyographic changes during an imagery task. *Psychophysiology,* 1971, **8**, 483–490.

Skinner, B. F., & Delabarre, E. B. In B. F. Skinner (Ed.), *Behavior of organisms.* New York: Appleton-Century-Crofts, 1938.

Slaughter, J., Hahn, W. W., & Rinaldi, P. Instrumental conditioning of heart rate in the curarized rat with varied amounts of pretraining. *Journal of Comparative and Physiological Psychology,* 1970, **72**, 356–359.

Smith, K. Conditioning as an artifact. *Psychological Review,* 1954, **61**, 217–225.

Smith, S. M., Brown, H. O., Toman, J. E. P., & Goodman, L. S. The lack of cerebral effects of d-tubocurarine. *Anesthesiology,* 1947, **8**, 1–14.

Sokolov, A. N. Speech-motor afferentation and the problem of brain mechanisms of thought. *Soviet Psychology,* 1967, **6**(1), 3–15.

Sokolov, E. N. *Perception and the conditioned reflex.* New York: Macmillan, 1963.

Solberg, K. B., Tyre, T. E., & Stinson, G. M. Ivanov-Smolensky conditioning in adults and children using an electromyographic response measure. *Psychonomic Science,* 1970, **18**(b), 365–366.

Solomon, R. L., & Turner, L. H. Discriminative classical conditioning in dogs paralyzed by curare can later control discriminative avoidance responses in the normal state. *Psychological Review,* 1962, **69**, 202–219.

Sutton, D., & Kimm, J. Reaction time of motor units in biceps and triceps. *Experimental Neurology,* 1969, **23,** 503–515.

Taub, E., & Berman, A. J. Movement and learning in the absence of sensory feedback. In S. J. Freedman (Ed.), *The neurophysiology of spatially oriented behavior.* Homewood, Ill.: Dorsey Press, 1968.

Thysell, R. V. Reaction time of single motor units. *Psychophysiology,* 1969, 6, 174–185.

Trowill, J. A. Instrumental conditioning of the heart rate in the curarized rat. *Journal of Comparative and Physiological Psychology,* 1967, **63,** 7–19.

Unna, K. R., & Pelikan, E. W. Evaluation of curarizing drugs in man. VI. Critique of experiments on unanesthetized subjects. In A. R. McIntyre (Ed.), Curare and anti-curare agents. *Annals of the New York Academy of Sciences,* 1951, **54,** 297–530.

Van Liere, D. W. Characteristics of the muscle tension response to paired tones. *Journal of Experimental Psychology,* 1953, **46,** 319–324.

Westcott, M. R., & Huttenlocher, J. Cardiac conditioning: The effects and implications of controlled and uncontrolled respiration. *Journal of Experimental Psychology,* 1961, **61,** 353–359.

9

CLASSICAL CONDITIONING, AS IT CONTRIBUTES TO THE ANALYSES OF SOME BASIC PSYCHOLOGICAL PROCESSES[1]

Delos D. Wickens
The Ohio State University

The philosophy that directs this paper is the belief that there are certain mechanisms that underlie behavior in a variety of situations, and that, although there may be phenotypical differences, there are far fewer genotypical differences. Perhaps not all psychologists would agree with this position, and many might be inclined to hold that their own fields are something special, with laws unto their own, essentially isolated from other disciplinary areas. Given my predisposition, however, it is natural to believe that there are fundamental processes common to many behaviors, and that, like geological strata, they intrude in various locations and may be studied in the context of each location—better studied, perhaps, than in one location alone. Specifically, I believe that the context of the conditoning situation can serve as a most effective vehicle for the identification of the functional characteristics of processes that are not ordinarily considered a part of the classical conditioning paradigm.

I propose to discuss several subjects to which classical conditioning has contributed valuable empirical information about basic processes, and I shall concentrate primarily upon some experiments conducted at our laboratory at the Ohio State University. It is obvious that many researches besides those from our laboratory could be included in my general topic, but, unfortunately, the space and scope of this paper do not permit more than a passing mention of a few. Further, since I am primarily concerned with the extension of classical conditioning to the investigation of realms of behavior not ordinarily considered to be within its premises, I must omit the many contributions that classical

[1] The research presented in this paper was made possible by an NIMH grant, MH 08423.

213

conditioning has made to therapy in the clinical field—and I think these contributions are increasing each year; and I shall omit the recognizedly important applications of classical conditioning to behavior theory as represented, for example, by the works of Hull, of Spence, and of others.

STIMULUS SELECTION

My first topic deals with the field long designated as attention, or, in somewhat more objective terms, as stimulus selection. I prefer the latter terminology, since "attention" has, since the days of William James (1890), implied a conscious privacy that is not compatible with today's experimental psychology. During recent years, there has been a considerable revival of interest in this area, and this revival has evidenced itself not alone in work with humans, but also in studies with lower animals.

The usual conditioning situation is not one in which attention or stimulus selection presents much of a problem to the investigator. Typically, those who research in conditioning run their subjects in sound-deadened rooms with fairly homogeneous visual environments. They choose as conditioned stimuli sounds that are a goodly number of decibels above background noise level, and lights that are fairly bright. If their subjects are humans, they are inclined to inform them of the relevant stimuli before embarking upon their experimental procedures. True, they speak of orienting reflexes, but they go to great pains to be assured that the OR will be made to the stimuli of the experimenter's choice. It is really only when the subject dwells in an environment of complex stimulation that the stimulus selection process becomes a variable of potential importance. A possible exception to this general principle arises from a monotonous environment, but investigators try to beat this potential state by using variable intertrial intervals and relatively short sessions.

The beauty of the classical conditioning situation is that its experimenters have relatively precise control over the stimuli, and can introduce clearly identifiable levels of complexity. The typical approach to stimulus selection has been to use a compound stimulus of a light and a tone. Researchers take care to see that each one of these elements is an effective conditioned stimulus when it appears alone, and they can expect—or can demonstrate—each one to be an equally effective component of a compound. They can then introduce manipulations of one of the elements, and can discover how these manipulations influence the response strengths of either of the two elements, when presented alone. Thus, Kamin (1969) has shown that prior conditioning to one of the elements prevents the other element from acquiring response strength when the subject is subsequently given experience with the compound. A different approach has been taken in the researches of Rescorla and Wagner (1972). They give concurrent experience with one of the elements alone, interspersed among the training trials on a compound, either reinforcing an element or not reinforcing it. A number of most interesting findings have developed out of such techniques of measuring transfer effects to elements of a compound, as functions of different types of experiences with one of the elements in isolation. Looked at more generally, these and other researchers in stimulus selection clearly demonstrate the utility of the classical conditioning situation for throwing light upon processes that do not ordinarily seem to be part of the body of knowledge that we call the classical conditioning literature.

Several times during this paper, I shall refer to conditioning research that we are conducting at the Ohio State University, and it will save space if I describe our general experimental situation at this point. My research associates for all the studies that I shall describe in any detail are Carol Wickens and two graduate students, David Tuber and Anthony Nield. Our subjects are cats who are shaped to hang in a sling as shown in Figure 1. Almost any reasonably tame cat can be shaped to hang relatively quietly in the manner shown, for periods of 15 minutes to half an hour, and longer. The restraints upon the cats are minor ones, and the animals can move any paw without difficulty. Shall we say that the restraints are more psychological than physical? A shock electrode is attached to either of the two forepaws, and the shock serves as the UCS, the response being recorded through a strain gage connected to the paw and the table. The typical conditioned response is a paw flexion, and Figure 2 shows recordings of several conditioned paw responses, actually each given at a

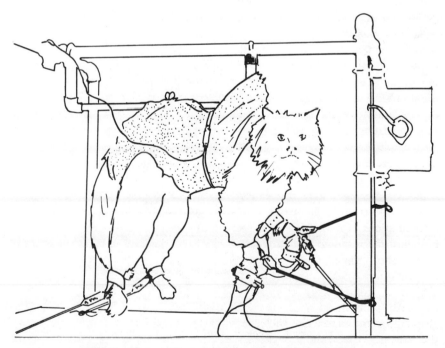

FIG. 1. The cat, Plum, hanging in the experimental sling.

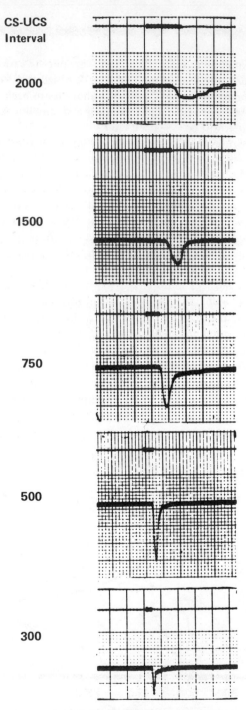

FIG. 2. Typical forms of the conditioned paw-movement response at different interstimulus intervals.

different interstimulus interval. We have, in our situation, two potential conditioned stimuli: the illumination of a bank of lights directly in front of the cat; and the sounding of a tone 20 decibels above room background level. Thus, we are in business for studying compounding and stimulus selection, as well as other businesses that will be described later.

Sometime back in the 1950s, after writing a chapter entitled "Stimulus Selection and Response Variability," I became convinced that, if we are to predict behavior by relating its occurrence to the stimulus environment, and if, as seems to be the case, organisms in a complex environment select certain stimuli as being relevant and disregard others, then we must be able to predict what stimulus will be selected. Of course we have long known that physical characteristics of the stimuli—their intensities, for example—are important, but we need also to know how learning experiences of one sort or another influence eventual stimulus selection.

As the vehicle for an investigation of the topic, I chose the classically conditioned GSR. The variable selected was based on the oft-tested CS-UCS interval function, an example of which, obtained in this instance from cat-paw conditioning, is shown in Figure 3. Suppose now that one conditions a subject to a compound stimulus whose elements differ from one another in their onset times with respect to the UCS. One of these—CS_2, the shorter in duration of the two elements of the compound—is chosen to occur 500 msec. before the UCS, and its length remains the same for all experimental groups. The longer of the two elements, CS_1, has a greater time period between onset and occurrence of UCS. The experimental groups are set up so that CS_1 is longer for each of the

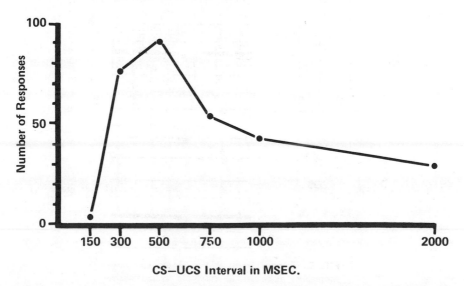

FIG. 3. Total number of conditioned paw responses to extinction criterion as a function of the interstimulus interval.

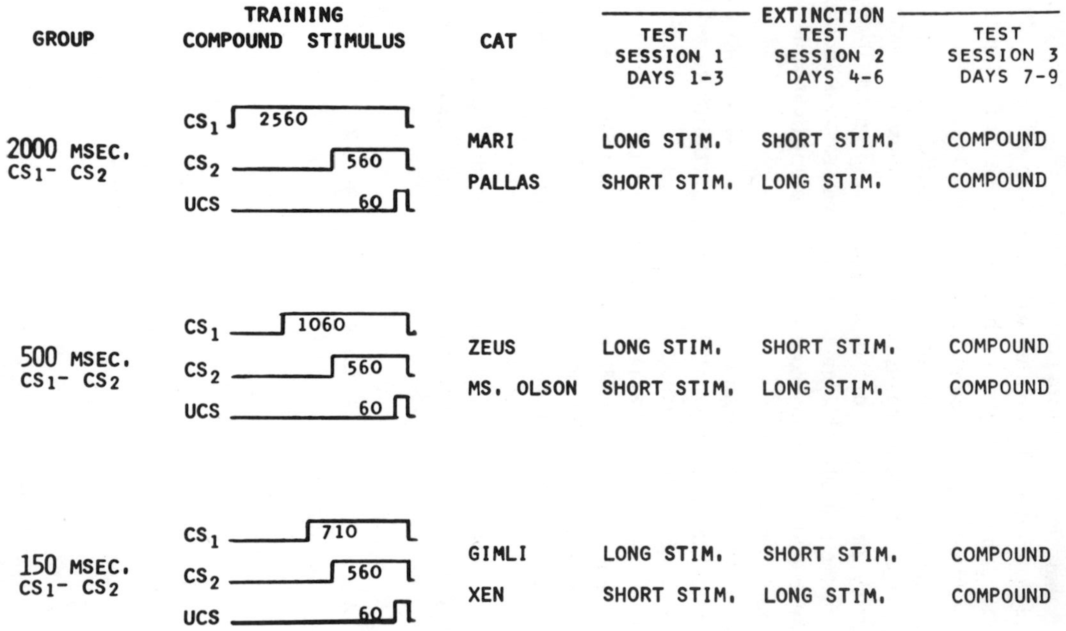

GROUP	TRAINING COMPOUND STIMULUS	CAT	EXTINCTION TEST SESSION 1 DAYS 1-3	TEST SESSION 2 DAYS 4-6	TEST SESSION 3 DAYS 7-9
2000 MSEC. CS$_1$– CS$_2$	CS$_1$ 2560 / CS$_2$ 560 / UCS 60	MARI	LONG STIM.	SHORT STIM.	COMPOUND
		PALLAS	SHORT STIM.	LONG STIM.	COMPOUND
500 MSEC. CS$_1$– CS$_2$	CS$_1$ 1060 / CS$_2$ 560 / UCS 60	ZEUS	LONG STIM.	SHORT STIM.	COMPOUND
		MS. OLSON	SHORT STIM.	LONG STIM.	COMPOUND
150 MSEC. CS$_1$– CS$_2$	CS$_1$ 710 / CS$_2$ 560 / UCS 60	GIMLI	LONG STIM.	SHORT STIM.	COMPOUND
		XEN	SHORT STIM.	LONG STIM.	COMPOUND

FIG. 4. The arrangement of stimuli and the testing sequence in the three groups, for a sample squad of six animals.

three groups to be run. In such a situation, would the shorter element control a constant response strength and the longer element an increasingly smaller response strength as its CS-UCS interval increased? The study was run, and it produced some interesting results, but I'll not describe it now. In that experiment, we were, as noted, using the GSR as the dependent variable, and this response is particularly sensitive to the changes in pattern of stimulation that must occur as one shifts from the compound to an element of said compound. Any associative connections formed could not be unambiguously differentiated from responding due to the orienting reflex.

The associative relationship can better be tested by using a response that cannot possibly be construed as an OR. For this reason, we have performed a conceptual replication of the first experiment. We have used the cat as the subject and the conditioned paw flexion as the dependent variable; the paw movement we use never appears as an OR to the stimuli we use. The strategy of the later experiment was the same as that of the first, i.e., to condition the subject to a compound whose elements have different onset times with respect to the UCS, then to test to each element alone.

Three major groups were formed. For all groups, the shorter stimulus, CS_2, commenced 500 msec. before the 60-msec. shock to the paw, and terminated with it. For one group, the longer stimulus, CS_1, began 150 msec. before the shorter one; for another, 500 msec. before CS_2; and, in a third group, 2,000 msec. before the shorter CS_2. Like the short CS_2, the longer CS_1 terminated with the offset of the 60-msec. UCS. After 42 days of training to the compound, with 12 paired trials a day, the cats were tested to one element or another, and, eventually, to the compound. Needless to say, the modality (light or tone) of the long and of the short stimulus was counterbalanced across the entire experiment.

There were 48 cats in the study, 16 in each CS_1 - CS_2 group. Typically, the animals were run in squads of six, two at each CS_1 - CS_2 interval, with the test sessions to the long and to the short elements counterbalanced. Figure 4 represents the design of a typical squad. The second column shows the training condition (the different CS_1 - CS_2 intervals), the next the pair of cats in each training condition. The following three columns indicate, for each cat of the squad, the nature of the first 3-day test session, the second 3-day test session, and the third test session for the compound. It can be noted that the order of testing to the elements, modalities of light and tone, were counterbalanced across the study.

Figure 5 shows the results for test session 1, as expressed by the percentage of paw withdrawal CRs in each CS_1 - CS_2 group for the long and for the short element. A similar presentation for test session 2 is displayed in Figure 6. It should be recalled that the cats who contributed to the short-stimulus data in test session 1, gave the long-stimulus data of test session 2. Nevertheless, the two sets of data are strikingly similar for the two sessions, and their highly similar statistical analyses run as follows: There were no main effects of modality or of interval, but a highly significant interaction between stimulus length and groups.

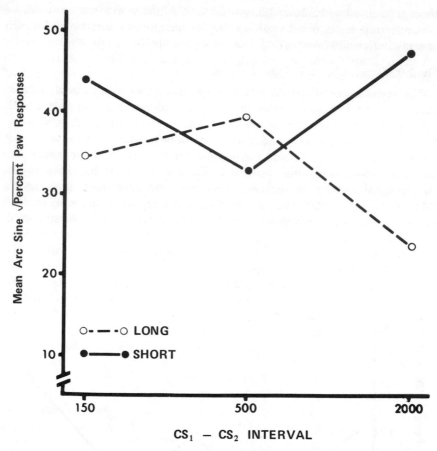

FIG. 5. Conditioned paw responsiveness to the long and short elements on the first test, as a function of the CS_1-CS_2 interval.

Furthermore, the quadratic trends for both the long and the short stimulus were significant and of opposite sign. The curves of Figures 5 and 6 may seem strange to the reader, but they were not strange to the experimenters, for the same type of result had been found in the two earlier studies that had used the GSR—one of these with human subjects and the other with cats. Figure 7 summarizes the findings of the entire paw experiment, showing the performance on each element on each test, together with the responding to the compound at the close of the experiment It will be noted that response strength for the compound is essentially constant across groups, and that it holds up surprisingly well, considering that the cats have had six days of some sort of "extinction."

It seems to us that no simple or single interpretation can be made of these data. Obviously, prediction from the stimulus-asynchronism curve (Hull, 1943) is inadequate. One needs only to point out that the effectiveness of the short stimulus varies as a function of the long stimulus. It is also obvious that a general concept such as redundancy (Egger & Miller, 1962) will not serve as an explanation. It is our belief that different interpretations are necessary for each interval, and we will briefly sketch out some possibilities.

The 2,000-msec. CS_1 - CS_2 Interval Group

The performance of the group that experienced a CS_1 - CS_2 interval of 2,000 msec. can rather easily be interpreted. One can assume that two independent CRs were being formed, one to the short stimulus and one to the long stimulus. Furthermore, the response strength to each can be assumed to be a function of the time between its onset and the onset of the shock UCS, without regard to the other stimulus. In the paw-conditioning situation, it has been shown (Wickens, Nield, Tuber, & Wickens, 1969) that optimal conditioning occurs at a CS-UCS interval of 500 msec., and that the efficiency of conditioning declines monotonically across longer intervals. Using the curve from the Wickens et al.

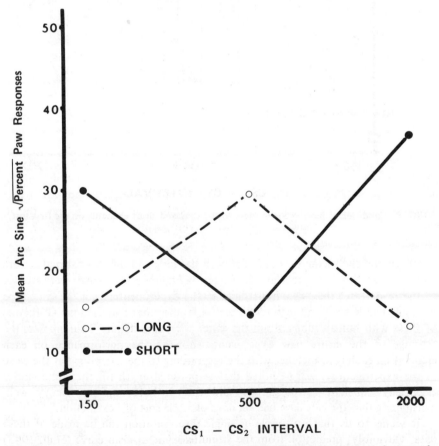

FIG. 6. Conditioned paw responsiveness to the long and short elements on the second test, as a function of the CS_1-CS_2 interval.

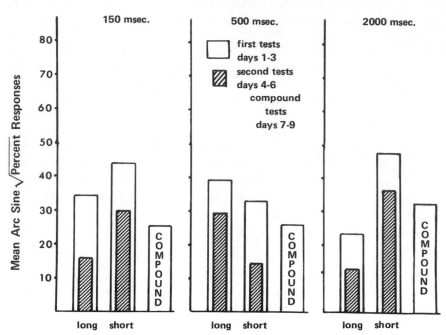

FIG. 7. Summary of paw responsiveness on the tests to the elements and to the compound.

experiment, the number of responses at the 500-msec. ISI was arbitrarily given a value of 100%, and, with this as a standard, the percentage of response for an ISI of 2,500 was determined. This proved to be 29%. A similar computation was made of the response percentages for the long and short stimuli in the present experiment (with the value for the short stimulus arbitrarily set at 100%). The values for the long stimulus were 28% for the first test session, and 33% for the second. It is apparent that the ISI function obtained with a single stimulus can be used to predict quite accurately the relationship of the response strengths of the 2,000-msec. CS_1 - CS_2 compound. Whether this is or is not the proper interpretation cannot be determined on the basis of the research presently available, but it is obviously the most parsimonious explanation, and it predicts extremely well.

The 500-msec. CS_1 - CS_2 Group

It is evident that the ISI function cannot be used to interpret the results of the 500-msec. group, since, for the cats of this group, the longer stimulus is the most effective. The interpretation presented here is the same one that was offered to account for similar results in an earlier study (Wickens, Born, & Wickens, 1963). It states that a form of sensory conditioning may occur between CS_1 and CS_2 because of a favorable temporal relationship between the two stimuli, there being some evidence that sensory preconditioning has a similar ISI function to that found with overt responding (Wickens & Cross, 1963). The interpretation assumes that, because of sensory conditioning, CS_1 is capable of redintegrating the sensory effect of the sequential stimuli, and therefore it acts much as does the compound itself, evoking a considerable response. The CS_2 cannot do so, for it has a backward relationship to CS_1, and, through stimulus generalization decrement, it is not capable of producing much responding. This explanation further implies that a true interactive compounding occurs between the elements at this temporal interval, an interpretation that one does not need to make for the 2,000-msec. group.

The 150-msec. CS_1 - CS_2 Group

From the point of view of the experimenters' reaction to the 150 msec. CS_1 - CS_2 compound, the results for this group are surprising. When the stimulation was given, the experimenters had great difficulty in discerning a temporal difference between the onset times of the two stimuli, although, with intense concentration, it was possible. Despite this fact, the onset differential appears to have a fairly large effect upon the cat's conditioning.

It is true that the long stimulus is less effective than is the short—as it should be according to the single-stimulus ISI function. When, as for the 2,000 msec. group, comparisons are based upon the relative performance at the 650- and the 500-msec. intervals in the Wickens et al. (1969) study, we find that performance at the 650-msec. ISI was 78% of that at the 500-msec. ISI. In the present study, the values for the 650-msec. ISI were, for the first and second tests respectively, 67% and 46% of the 500-msec. CS_2 values. It seems that a single-stimulus ISI function does not predict with high accuracy in this instance, and another interpretation might be sought.

It is possible that the difference in conditioning between the long and the short stimulus may be related to the general information-processing type of phenomenon such as is demonstrated in the refractory period studies (Herman & Kantowitz, 1970). More specifically stated, the occurrence of the second stimulus may interfere, to some extent, with the processing of the first stimulus. The second stimulus certainly does not prevent the human observer from experiencing the first stimulus, as in backward masking, but it may have some depressing effect upon the processing of it. In a study by Helson and Steger (1962), it was shown that the reaction time to a light was retarded, if a second light to which the subjects were instructed not to react, occurred within the range of 10 to 170 msec. subsequent to the onset of the first light. Perhaps something analogous occurs with short-interval compounds in conditioning. Whether one wishes to introduce another mechanism into the rather pluralistic constructs already considered to be necessary in accounting for other interval results, depends upon how seriously he takes the discrepancy in prediction between the single-stimulus ISI function and the data obtained with the 150-msec. group.

Other Interpretations of Stimulus Selection

In considering the discussions of the various interpretations for the different time-interval groups, it should be pointed out that there is a basic difference between this experiment and the many studies that approach the problem of stimulus selection by the CER or by discrimination boxes. In the CER studies in particular, the CS_1 - CS_2 intervals, as well as the CS_2 - UCS intervals that are employed, are typically longer than any that were used in this experiment. It seems to us that each kind of research may require quite a different interpretation. There is probably no conceptual conflict between the interpretations of stimulus selection offered for the situation of our study and those offered for others where time and techniques were very different. There may be no single mechanism that can predict the stimulus selection activity for all situations—a not unreasonable conclusion when one considers the complexity of life situations.

The Reciprocal Relationship of the Two CRs

A very marked characteristic of our data on stimulus selection is the essentially mirror-image relationship between curves for the long and the short stimulus. As one stimulus gains in effectiveness, the other seems to lose its control. These data fit very neatly into the Rule 2 of Sutherland and Mackintosh (1971). Rule 2 reads in part: "Analyzer strengths sum to a constant amount. . . .when an analyzer is strengthened, the total strength of other analyzers is weakened by the same amount [p. 39]." It will be recalled that the main effect of interval was not significant in the Anovas; this would seem to permit the conclusion that the analyzer strengths sum to a constant amount. In addition, Figure 7 shows that the response to the compound was essentially the same value for all groups, and an Anova on the compound revealed no "Groups" effect.

Conclusion

Our overall conclusion from this section is that the conditioning paradigm lends itself very well to the investigation of the problem, and that its use has contributed to the identification of stimulus selection principles that might not have been so easily recognized by the use of other methods.

CONDITIONING, MEMORY, AND VERBAL BEHAVIOR

There are several general areas in which conditioned response data can offer us insight into psychological processes that may be difficult to investigate by other, apparently more direct, methods. One of these is the nature of memory, a topic that is more often than not studied by means of verbal materials; another is the power of verbal encoding.

Memory for a Classically Conditioned
Response after Interpolated
Conditioning Mimicking
Verbal Learning Paradigms

Although in recent years there has been an increased interest in the memory of lower animals, and a book entitled *Animal Memory* (Honig & James, 1971) has appeared, the truly sophisticated approaches to the normal causes of our forgetting have stemmed from the verbal learning researches. It is true that there are many studies of forgetting in animals as a function of electroconvulsive shocks—but how normal or how unusual an event is an ECS, and how can one extrapolate from these studies to the fact that we forget telephone numbers, a grocery list, the names of experimenters, and procedures? Did someone shock us after the last article we read? Most improbable! Some investigators—Spear (1971) and also Gleitman (1971), for example—are doing animal research that meshes closely with the normal human memory situation, but the work with mazes and runways does not ordinarily approach the technical elegance of research with verbal materials.

Sometime in the late 1940's, workers in verbal learning began to shift from studying performance on serial lists to studying performance on paired-associate lists (Underwood, 1948) in a serious and more analytical fashion than had been done in an earlier period. I say "more analytical" because, when the researcher moves into the paired-associate procedure, he can clearly identify the stimulus as well as the response, whereas stimulus identification is most difficult in the serial learning situation (Young, 1968). The change in emphasis has produced increasingly precise approaches to the conditions leading to forgetting—to the detailed analysis, in short, of proactive and retroactive inhibition effects. The verbal learning researchers now speak with some exactness of kinds of similarities between the stimuli and the responses of the two situations, PI and RI.

As I am sure the reader perceives, the shift from an emphasis on serial learning to emphasis on paired-associate learning has also moved the researchers of the verbal learning field into a realm that becomes most compatible with the way those of us who have worked in classical conditioning have long thought. The investigators of classical conditioning have conceived of their experimental situation in terms of a highly controllable stimulus, and, if they go to the trouble, a precisely measurable response. Thus, at least at the theoretical level adumbrated above, the conceptualizations of classical conditioning and the efforts of many of the verbal learning researchers have moved closer together, although there is presently some movement away from the verbal learning–classical conditioning analogy in the recent emphasis on the concept of organization (Mandler, 1967).

Let us consider the analytical verbal learning approach and some of its formalized vocabulary. In a retroactive inhibition design, the initial and eventually-to-be-recalled list is referred to as the *A-B* list, where *A* designates the

TABLE 1

Examples of the Various Paradigms of Verbal Learning Research

Paradigm designation	Original learning (OL)		Interpolated Learning (IL)		Recall
	Stimulus	Response	Stimulus	Response	Test to Stimulus A
A-B; A-D	12	Book	12	Car	12 - ?
	41	Tree	41	Shirt	41 - ?
	(A)	(B)	(A)	(D)	(A) - ?
A-B; C-D	12	Book	108	Car	12 - ?
	41	Tree	193	Shirt	41 - ?
	(A)	(B)	(C)	(D)	(A) - ?
A-B; C-B	12	Book	108	Book	12 - ?
	41	Tree	193	Tree	41 - ?
	(A)	(B)	(C)	(B)	(A) - ?
A-B control	12	Book	Rest		12 - ?
	41	Tree			41 - ?
	(A)	(B)			(A) - ?

226

stimulus items of the list, and *B* the various associated or paired response terms. Given this initial terminology, many second-list symbolizations can be developed. An example is *A-D*, where the same stimulus terms are used in the first and second list, but they are paired with completely different responses, called *D* responses, in the second list; or one can have a *C-B* paradigm, indicating different stimuli but the same set of responses. Yet another group is *C-D*, where both stimuli and responses are changed. Examples of the typical verbal learning paradigms are given in Table 1, where the stimuli are numerical items and the responses are common nouns. Usually there are eight to twelve such pairs in a list, and the subject is asked to anticipate the appropriate noun when the number comes in view. Many studies have been conducted on retention of the *A-B* list over short- and long-time intervals, and they have yielded interesting and differing results, depending upon the paradigm used in the interpolated learning as well as upon other factors.

In the Ohio State University laboratory, we are now in the process of using these verbal learning paradigms in a classical conditioning situation. As in the experimental procedure described in the earlier section on stimulus selection, our subject is again a cat, hanging in a sling in such a position that both front legs are relatively free to move, and a shock electrode can be attached to either forepaw. This procedure supplies us with two UCRs, the response of the *right leg* and the response of the *left leg*; and we may use these responses as we wish. In the parlance of the verbal learning theorist, we have a *B* and a *D* response. Since either a light or a tone can be employed as the stimulus, the *A* and the *C* terms are also available to us. Thus it is that we can train cats in an *A-B* paradigm, as tone–right paw, and, after they have reached a criterion, shift them to another alphabetical arrangement, as *C-D*, where a light becomes the stimulus and the left leg the one that is shocked—conditioned, in other words. Training on the second response can be given for a set period of time, then a forgetting interval can be introduced, and finally, many weeks after the original *A-B* learning, the cat can be tested to the *A* (tone) stimulus. Will he remember—give—the originally learned response, and how do the different treatments influence this responding?

Our actual experiment mimicks most of the usual verbal learning paradigms. The cats are first trained to respond to a tone (or light, since the two modalities are counterbalanced throughout). When they meet a criterion of 10 out of 12 conditioned responses (as shown by two test trials given each day), this training, called *A-B*, is terminated. Depending upon the animal (and the cats do differ in proficiency), such training requires from 4 to 11 weeks, with 10 pairings a day. Then, according to quasi-random determination, the animals are divided into four groups. One of these is a control group, and its subjects will remain in their home quarters for 10 weeks before being given nonreinforced tests to the original conditioned stimulus, *A*. If one likes the concept, the scores of the control group can be considered a measure of forgetting through decay. There are three experimental groups, each of which receives 4 weeks of interpolated training on a new task. One group, called *A-D*, has the same conditioned stimulus but is now shocked on the other front paw. It is called *A-D* because the stimulus is the same but the response requirement is changed. Another group, called *C-D*, has both the stimulus and the response of the interpolated conditioning different from the first, or *A-B*, conditioning. Group *C-B* continues the same response as that of original learning, but is conditioned to give it to a different stimulus. At the conclusion of the interpolated session, the cats return to their living quarters for a period of 6 weeks, and, at the end of this "rest" time, they are brought back to the experimental room and given 3 days of nonreinforced tests to the original *A* stimulus (extinction procedure). These test days are immediately followed by relearning the *A-B* conditioned response of original learning to criterion, another extinction of the CR, and, finally, when appropriate, a testing to the stimulus used in the second (or interpolated) task.

At this writing, we have completed the running of three animals in each of the four groups. The results have been highly consistent, and I'll describe what the trends seem to be, beginning with the nature of the behavior during the interpolated conditioning.

The *C-B* group (same paw–different stimulus) is of interest because, since the same paw is being shocked, a rather complete generalization of the response to the changed stimulus might be expected. Such, however, is not the case. This conditioned response is acquired far more rapidly than are those of the other paradigms, but there is clearly a time during the early days of training on the interpolated task when anticipatory or conditioned responses are *not* given to the new stimulus. Something like pseudoconditioning or sensitization is not in evidence. This finding, it seems to us, says something about the precision and specificity of the conditioning process in our experimental procedure.

The *A-D* situation (same stimulus–different paw) is of interest in another way. Since the cats are hanging freely and are well supported in the sling, they might well continue to give the old response even though a new response is being acquired. Actually, a number of double-paw responses do occur during the acquisition of the *A-D* paradigm; but by at least the third week of training, the *B* response to the CS drops out, and only the *D* response is given. This fact also points to the preciseness of the CR; it is not maintained by the simple occurrence of noxious stimulus, but clearly the locus of that noxious stimulus is the determinant of the particular response to be given.

During the interpolated *C-D* (different stimulus-different response) learning, the performance for the first week showed a few responses of both paws; during the next week, conditioned responses of the new paw began to appear with some regularity, developing quite strongly during the subsequent 2 weeks, with the other response dropping out.

We now turn to the performance of the cats when they were tested to the *A* stimulus of original learning 6 weeks after the end of interpolated learning. Table 2 presents the results for the various phases of the experiment. It shows trials to reach the first "list" criterion, responses to the *A* stimulus following the

TABLE 2

Results for All Groups, as of July 1972, on Original Learning, and on the Tests
Given Subsequent to the Interpolated Learning

Condition	Cat	OL trials to learn A-B	Test responses to stimulus A			RL trials to relearn A-B	Savings $\frac{\text{OL-RL}}{\text{OL}} \times 100$
			B	or D	or B&D		
	Roger	204	6	0	1	24	88
A-B; A-D	Mephisto	468	12	2	3	60	87
	Maggie	456	13	1	0	36	92
		1128	33	3	4	120	89
	Tom	240	0	8	2	156	35
A-B; C-D	Rita	396	0	13	0	60	85
	Linda	528	0	9	4	72	86
		1164	0	30	6	288	75
	Marta	252	23	0	0	24	90
A-B; C-B	Stubs	480	13	0	0	24	95
	Diana	408	16	0	0	24	94
		1140	52	0	0	72	94
	Cindy	432	5	0	0	36	92
A-B; rest	Grace	324	10	0	0	24	93
	Wally	336	6	0	2	24	93
		1092	21	0	2	84	93

interpolated learning (this being broken down into the particular paw response
made), the trials for relearning A-B, and the savings score. The results of the
"retention" test are presented graphically in Figure 8.

The animals of the A-D group were consistent in their behavior. When tested
on the first day to the nonreinforced A stimulus—after the interpolated learning
and the 6 weeks waiting period—all three showed a strong tendency to give the
B, or first-learned, responses, and to give quite a number of them, as shown in
Table 2. Presumably this response had undergone spontaneous recovery during
the 6 weeks after the end of the interpolated learning. Actually, we had chosen
this time of waiting with a view to just this possibility. The finding is interesting
in that there is a fair amount of evidence in support of spontaneous recovery of
verbal lists in the A-D paradigm, although the time intervals are much shorter, of
course, than those we have used in this experiment (Kamman & Melton, 1967;
Postman, Stark, & Fraser, 1968; Silverstein, 1967).

The C-D cats (new stimulus and new response in the interpolated conditioning) showed somewhat surprising results. All three of the animals tested to date
clearly tended to give the second-learned response, D, to the A stimulus, and this

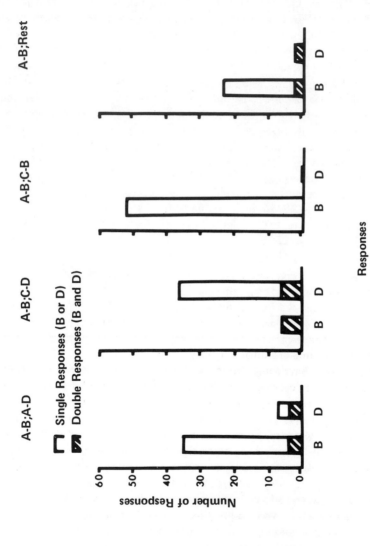

FIG. 8. Bar graph showing the response frequency of each paw to stimulus *A*, for each paradigm in the retention test.

response had never been associated (so far as a UCR is concerned) with that stimulus. This result stands in marked contrast to that for the *A-D* group, which showed a strong bias toward making the first-learned, or *B,* response. A simple failure of stimulus discrimination does not appear to be a very plausible explanation. Why should discrimination failure bias the responding in one particular direction? Why is discrimination poor in this instance, when there was no generalization (failure to discriminate) in the interpolated learning of the *C-B* group? The capacity of the *C-D* paradigm to interfere with *A-B* recall is a finding that would not be predicted by the verbal learning-conditioning analogy (Newton & Wickens, 1956), but, in recent years, such interference has been demonstrated to be a powerful factor in retroactive inhibition (Keppel, Henschel, & Zavortink, 1969). Indeed, this type of effect has been suggested to be the major cause of retroactive interference (Postman, Stark, & Henschel, 1969). And so, although the results for our *C-D* cats may seem odd, they are not without their parallels in other research.

The *C-B* cats (same paw but different stimulus for the interpolated learning) showed excellent retention of the *A-B* paradigm, and even surpassed the control-group animals in retention. We will need much more of several kinds of data before speculating on the whys of the behavior of this group.

It is apparent that the research I have been describing is costly of time, effort, and money. Insofar as verbal learning is concerned, the paradigms can be more cheaply investigated by having college students learn the various types of paired-associate lists, and I have done, and am still doing, a great deal of verbal learning research. What, then, is to be gained by employing the classical conditioning situation with cats, as a vehicle for probing into the processes that seem to be determinants of human memory?

First, I suppose I have long adhered to the doctrine that says that a science should bend every effort toward explaining as broad a range of phenomena as possible with the fewest of principles. It is an attitude that I acquired from my graduate advisor, Professor J. F. Dashiell, in the days of controversies about insight, trial-and-error learning, and conditioning. It has always pleased me to discover, in one type of situation, a principle that is also of predictive value in quite a different situation. Essentially, this is the justification for continuing basic research.

Another rationale for the research I have been describing lies in the fact that verbal learners have, for years, used classical conditioning terminology, and it seems to me that it is important to determine whether these extensions fit, or whether they are confusing insofar as general learning principles are concerned. In a 1948 paper, Underwood suggested "extinction" rather than "unlearning" as a proper term for Melton and Irwin's (1940) "factor X," and thereby introduced some of the advanced concepts of classical conditioning into the verbal learning area. From that time on, a great number of researches in verbal learning have been influenced by Underwood's suggestion, and it has served an important role in the generation of new research problems. In recent years, there has been a trend against the formulation of verbal learning problems in these terms, but even those supporting this trend cannot deny the fact that concepts derived from classical conditioning could predict the results of certain verbal learning experiments.

Work with humans has the problem (as well as the advantage) of what are now called control processes (Atkinson & Shiffrin, 1968) in the human subject. A college-student subject can, for example, decide to rehearse the first, or second, or both lists to himself during the retention interval, obviously producing a distortion of some undetermined sort in the data. Rehearsal of this sort is not possible in the conditioning situation, and freedom from contamination may expose the more fundamental processes of association. I am less sure of my next comment upon the role of control processes, since their absence may be both an advantage and a disadvantage in the research I have described. With humans, one can tell the subject that he should give the first (or second) list response when the appropriate stimulus is displayed, and indirectly, through between-group comparisons, one can determine the strength of either of these sets of associations. In our procedures, we simply infer response strength from the occurrence of one response or the other.

Finally, I firmly believe that there is a crying need for the study of memory in classical conditioning itself. No work of any high degree of sophistication seems to have been done on memory for the conditioned response, and most of the experimentation shows only that the CR is extremely well retained. In the typical laboratory conditioning experiment, the subject does not experience interpolated interference of the types that verbal learning research has shown to be important, but surely, in real life situations, our CRs must be exposed to many such interpolations. If we wish to speak authoritatively of the retention of the conditioned response, and to extrapolate to real life situations, we need to contrive, in the laboratory, various types of interfering, as well as noninterfering, procedures and then to compare their outcomes. Paranthetically, I must add that I believe that conditioned response principles play a heavy role in the development of our motivational states (vectors) and hence have a significant effect upon the nature of individual behavior. Verbal learning has given us some valuable and well-tried interference paradigms; it is time to use them in the important life-area of classical conditioning.

Verbal Stimuli in Differential Conditioning

There is another, quite different way in which the classical conditioning paradigm may throw light upon verbal processing. I refer to the research of David Grant (1972) and his students on the topic of verbal stimuli in differential conditioning. This work does much to throw light upon the power and obligatory nature of verbal encoding. It gives evidence for what might be called the tyranny of language. Although Dr. Grant has contributed a chapter to this volume, he does not present this aspect of his work in his contribution. The following, therefore, will give you my brief account of the basic character of the research and its significance for verbal behavior.

Grant uses two evocative verbal stimuli, the word BLINK, or the words DON'T BLINK. These words serve as conditioned stimuli in his differential eyelid-conditioning situation. The experiments can pair the words and objective reinforcement in such a way that word content and air-puff contingencies are compatible or are incompatible. Disregarding a conditioning typology (that I shall mention later), he finds that verbal conditioned stimuli have a powerful effect upon behavior, enhancing discrimination when the verbal contents and the objective contingencies are compatible, and diminishing, or nearly eliminating, discrimination when they are incompatible. If, however, stimuli that are nonevocative, such as JUMP and DON'T JUMP, are used, a similar discordance is not apparent. Clearly, the conditioned response behavior is telling us something about the power of words. It is something that, in my opinion, could not be readily achieved by known methodology in the strictly verbal behavior context, except, perhaps, in the Stroop (1935) test or its variants.

I mentioned conditioned typology just now. The phrase refers to the fact that the form of the conditioned response alone identifies two types of responders in Dr. Grant's experiments, the Vs and the Cs. I shall not go into details about the behavior differences between these two classes of subjects in conditioned discrimination. It suffices to say that they do differ in Grant's experiments. Perhaps modern conditioning approaches are beginning to move into the area of personality differences in a more incisive manner than did Pavlov—or whichever typologist you wish to name.

Conclusion

In this section, I have attempted to show that the conditioning paradigm may be elaborated in such a fashion that it can relate to the principles of verbal behavior in much the same way as, in the past, verbal learning research related to the concepts of classical conditioning. It is my belief that our own research promises to throw light not only on a kind of conditioning behavior—specifically, memory—but also upon the operation of more general mechanisms that may be important in many situations.

Professor Grant's work on semantic conditioning offers an insight into the power of language as a determinant of behavior. There is little research in the verbal area alone that speaks so convincingly of the control that verbal stimuli can have over our actions, and of the role that personality characteristics can play in the verbal processes.

CONFLICTING PROCESSES IN CLASSICAL CONDITIONING

This section of our paper will report some research that preceded the study of memory and interference in classical conditioning. In fact, the success of the experiments I am about to report gave rise to the idea of doing the experiment with the verbal learning paradigms. I believe that this research also can be extended to give insights into behavior outside the formal area of classical conditioning itself.

In earlier work, we had noted that differences in interstimulus interval produce, in a classically conditioned paw movement of the cat, marked and almost completely reliable differences in both form and latency. Figure 2, which appeared in the first section of this paper, demonstrates these differences very well. We became interested in determining whether the effects we had noted incidentally in the between-group designs of prior experiments would be the same in a within-group situation. This interest grew out of a consideration of the findings of Grice and Hunter (1964), which showed that the effects of CS intensity apparent in between-group experiments was exaggerated in a within-group design. Before we were through, we added a further objective. In all, there were three different experiments: (*a*) A *between-group* design, in which left-forepaw responses of cats conditioned at a 2,000-msec. interstimulus interval were compared with those of animals conditioned at a 500-msec. ISI. (*b*) A counterpart *within-group* design, in which, in each cat, the left-forepaw movement was *concurrently* conditioned with a 2,000-msec. ISI for one modality and a 500-msec. ISI for another modality. (*c*) Another within-group design, in which we used both forepaws in the same cat. One forepaw was conditioned at a 2,000-msec. ISI, using one modality, while *concurrently*, the other forepaw was conditioned at a 500-msec. ISI, using another modality.

The conditioning procedures were very similar to those that we described in Section 1. The cats were shaped to hang quietly and amicably before training commenced. The two modalities, light or tone, were always counterbalanced. Fixed shock electrodes were attached to one or another forepaw, or to both forepaws.

For the long interstimulus interval, the conditioned stimulus (tone or light) continued for 2,060 msec. Sixty msec. before termination, the unconditioned stimulus of shock to the paw occurred. For the short ISI, the conditoned stimulus also lasted for 2,060 msec., but, 500 msec. after onset, a 60-msec. shock was delivered; the conditioned stimulus continued on for the full 2,060-msec. duration. That is, the interstimulus intervals were short and long, but the conditioned stimuli were not, and the effect studied was specifically on ISI effect, and not that of long or short tones or lights.

Experiment 1 was relatively simple. We used four cats. Two of them were conditioned at a 2,000-msec. interstimulus interval, one to the tone modality and one to the light. Two were conditioned at a 500-msec. ISI, one to tone and one to light. Conditioning schedules consisted of 10 paired stimulations and two no-shock test trials per day. There were 48 days of such training.

Conditioning arrangements for *Experiment* 2, within-S, were much the same. In this research, however, *one* forepaw was concurrently conditioned at two different ISIs. Again we used four cats; all were conditioned at both the

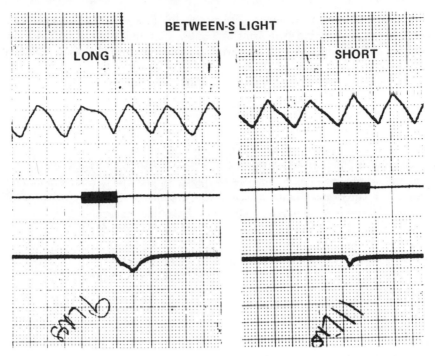

FIG. 9. Typical CRs of two animals toward the end of training. The CR in the *left panel* had developed from a *light* CS, with a long, 2,000-msec. ISI. *Right panel* response developed from a short, 500-msec. ISI light CS. The duration of the two stimuli is the same.

2,000-msec. ISI and the 500-msec. ISI. In all experiments, after the end of the 48 days of training, animals were tested to the separate modalities without shock, and also to a light and a tone presented simultaneously (a compound, if you will).

The results of Experiment 1, between-S, indicated that, as in previous studies, clear differences in form and latency that could be related to the ISI, developed in the conditioned response over time. Figure 9 shows the typical conditioned responses of two animals toward the end of training. One had had a conditioned stimulus of a light, with a long ISI; the other had had a conditioned stimulus of a light, with the short ISI. As one can see, the short-ISI stimulus produced a short-latency, sharply shaped, short-duration response. The long-ISI stimulus brought about a long-latency response and one which was longer in duration and more gradual in rise and fall. Figure 10 shows the responses of two other cats. In these cases, the modality was tone. Response characteristics were consistent for all animals. Table 3 compares the latencies of the last 10 responses for the 500-msec. ISI cats—an average of 460 msec.—and the last 10 for the 2,000-msec. ISI cats—an average of 1,710 msec. The difference was highly significant at $p < .005$.

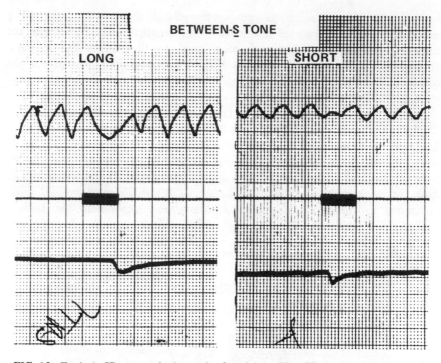

FIG. 10. Typical CRs toward the end of training. The CR in the *left panel* had developed from a *tone* CS, with a long, 2,000-msec. ISI. *Right panel* developed from a short, 500-msec. ISI tone CS. The duration of the two stimuli was the same.

TABLE 3

Response Latencies, in Milliseconds for the Between-S and the One-Paw and the Two-Paw Within-S Groups

Condition	500 ISI		2,000 ISI	
	First 10 CRs	Last 10 CRs	First 10 CRs	Last 10 CRs
Between-S	420	460	1150	1710
Within-S one paw	536	440	980	1368
Within-S two paws	516	496	910	1310

The results for Experiment 2, within-S (one paw conditioned concurrently at two different ISIs) are similar to the between-S results with respect to latency, but different when one considers the form of the responses. Although differentiation of form began to appear much as in other experiments, form changed in strange ways as the study progressed. All conditioned responses became larger, higher, and more vigorous. For all cats, the short ISI resulted in a single high spike, the long ISI in a series of high multiple spikes. Gradually, the responses became more like each other until, by the end of the 48 days, conditioned responses to both ISIs were remarkably alike. Except for the considerable height, both resembled the short ISI-type response far more than the long ISI form. Figure 11 shows responses of one cat on day 46. To the left is the conditioned response to the tone that has been conditioned at a long ISI; to the right is a conditioned response to a light that has been conditioned at a short ISI. Note that the forms are similar but the latencies are different. Figure 12 shows the responses of another cat on day 46; this time the light (at the left) has been conditioned at the long ISI, and the tone (on the right) at the short. Again note the appropriate latencies but the similar forms. Latency changes, then, continued to follow the course of the between-*S* experiment. As Table 3 indicates, the 500-msec. ISI, at the end of Experiment 2, produced conditioned

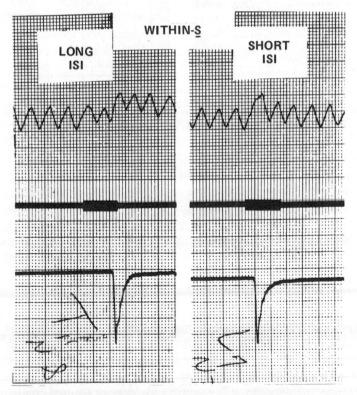

FIG. 11. Responses of the cat Abby on day 46. *Left panel* shows the CR to a tone which has been conditioned at a long, 2,000-msec. ISI. *Right panel* shows CR to a light conditioned at a short, 500-msec. ISI. Note that forms are similar but latencies are different. The duration of the two stimuli was the same.

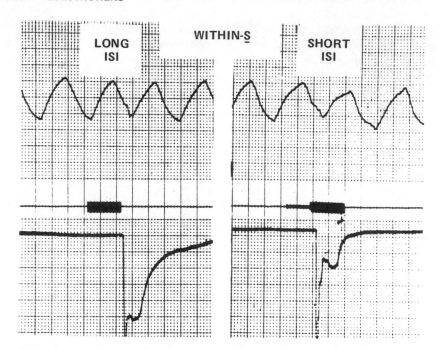

FIG. 12. Responses of cat Casey on day 46. *Left panel* shows CR to *light* which had been conditioned at the long ISI. *Right panel* shows CR to *tone* which had been conditioned at the short ISI. Note that forms are similar but latencies are different. Duration of the two stimuli was the same.

responses significantly different ($<$ .005) in latency from those produced by the 2,000-msec. ISI.

At this point, we began to speculate concerning what might happen if we were to observe the effect of different ISIs upon two different response systems in the same cat (i.e., two paws), rather than the effect of different ISIs on the same system (one paw). Experiment 3, the two-paw within-*S*, also used four cats. The procedure of the two-paw experiment was the same as that for the within-*S* one-paw study, except for the fact that the left paw was associated with one ISI, and the right with the other. Conditioning did occur, and there were several results worthy of mention.

1. The short, 500-msec. interstimulus interval was always a more potent conditioning interval than the 2,000-msec., ISI. It produced conditioning first, and the CRs, once they had appeared, were consistent as to presence, latency, and form.

2. The cats were capable of discriminating between the two different ISIs in the two-paw situation. In particular, they were able to discriminate by latency. Again, as in the other two groups, highly significant differences developed between the 500-msec. ISI CRs and those of the 2,000-msec. ISI group, by the last 10 days of training. These latency data are presented in Table 3. An

additional point of interest lies in the latency data for the first and the last CRs for the 2,000-msec. ISI group. In all three experiments, the latencies increased over the course of training. All differences between first and last responses are significant at $<$ .005. Of course, Pavlov told us this long ago.

The data of Experiment 3 also showed clear discriminations as to form, particularly in some cats. Complete discrimination could be demonstrated in three ways: by appropriate latency, which, as we have seen, became quite evident; by appropriate form (as judged by form data from the between-S experiment), and this too developed quite consistently in three out of the four cats; and third, by appropriate occurrence, i.e., by a conditioned response given by the appropriate paw only, the paw that had received pairing of the modality being tested. This discrimination also appeared increasingly in three of the four cats.

Figure 13, from one of the last days of the experiment, shows the no-shock responses of the cat, Lake, to three different stimuli in the same test session. The record of the left paw is to the left, of the right paw to the right. The left paw has always received a shock reinforcement to a 500-msec. ISI tone, and the upper panel shows the left paw responding with appropriate short form and short latency, to a tone stimulus. There is no response of the other paw. The right paw has always been reinforced to a 2,000-msec. ISI light, and the middle panel of the figure shows a CR to the no-shock light that is appropriate both in its long form and long latency. Note again that there is no response of the other paw. The lowest panel shows conditioned responses to a no-shock compound, the light and the tone (of the same duration) presented simultaneously for the first time. To this compound, the cat gave with the left paw (which had always been conditioned to a short ISI tone) a short-latency, short-form conditioned response. With the right paw (which had always been conditioned to a long ISI light) she gave, on that same trial, a long-latency, long-form response. Three of the cats showed this kind of discrimination by the last week of the experiment.

Interpretation and Discussion

By way of interpretation, at least at the molar level, there is not a great deal that can be said of these experiments, but there is a clear relationship to other research in the literature. Just about the time we were completing our third (two-paw) experiment, Kimble, Leonard, and Perlmuter (1968) published an experiment investigating ISI effects in a between-S and a within-S design, using the eyelid conditioned response in college students. They found that the two procedural situations were not equal in their behavioral effects, and we have found the same to be true, even though the details of our experimental differences are not the same as theirs. Their subjects showed a poor latency differentiation and ours did not, perhaps because of the much greater duration of our training. Nevertheless, our animals failed in form of response discrimination in our within-S one-paw experiment, despite extensive training. It would

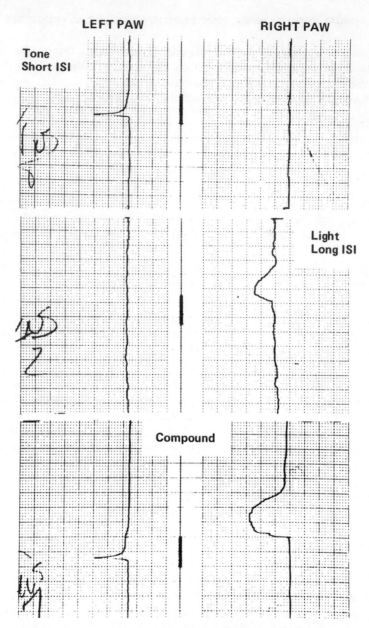

FIG. 13. Conditioned responses of the cat Lake in the two-paw situation on a day toward the end of training. Left paw record is at *left*; right paw record at the *right*. *Top panel* shows the CR of the left paw which has received a shock reinforcement to a 500-msec. ISI tone. *Middle panel* shows a response of the right paw which has always been conditioned to a light of 2,000-msec. ISI. *Lowest panel* shows conditioned responses of both paws when, with simultaneous onset, a compound of light and tone was presented.

seem that concurrent learning of two CRs produced by different ISIs, when in the same response system (one-paw), puts some kind of strain on the organism, a strain that introduces a kind of confusion.

In our third experiment, two response systems were used, and the confusion was neither so great nor so consistent as it had been with the one-response system. This suggests that the strain arises from the use of the same response system for the two ISI values, and implies that the nature or number of the response systems available influences the information processing system. Our three experiments, considered together with Kimble et al., suggest that the conditioned response is not the formation of a simple connection between S and R, but is a complex learning situation involving interactions between the organism's structure and the environmental demands that the particular conditioned response paradigm places upon it.

At another level, this research (and others) raises questions concerning the generality of conclusions drawn from investigations using either a between-subject design or a within-subject design. The issue is a complex one. As Grice and Hunter (1964) showed, the within-S design exaggerates the influence of CS intensity, but our second experiment and the Kimble et al. (1968) research find diminished differences between conditions in the within-subject design, when the ISI function is the variable under investigation. Yet the third experiment, using two response systems, restores the within-subject design to the norm of between-subject differentiation. Taken all together, these various conditioning experiments raise questions about the extent to which our general conclusions in psychology are bound to our particular methodology.

CONCLUSION

As the primary aim of my paper, I have chosen the goal of sampling some ways in which the classical conditioning paradigm contributes to an understanding of behavioral principles that do not seem to belong to the domain of conditioning. I think that I have presented a few valid examples, and I am sure that there are many more. My major theme is not only that the classical conditioning paradigm is well worth studying for its own sake (and there is much to be learned about it), but also that, because of the extremely controllable characteristics of its procedures, it has served us—and can continue to serve us—as a vehicle for probing into psychological problems and general methodology outside of the boundaries that are often considered its limits.

REFERENCES

Atkinson, R. C., & Shiffrin, R. M. Human memory: A proposed system and its control processes. In K. W. Spence & J. K. Spence (Eds.), *The psychology of learning and motivation.* Vol. 2. New York: Academic Press, 1968.

Egger, D. M., & Miller, N. E. Secondary reinforcement in rats as a function of information value and reliability of the stimulus. *Journal of Experimental Psychology,* 1962, **64,** 97–104.

Gleitman, H. Forgetting of long-term memories in animals. In W. K. Honig & P. H. R. James (Eds.), *Animal memory*. New York: Academic Press, 1971.

Grant, D. A. A preliminary model for processing information conveyed by verbal conditioned stimuli in classical conditioning. In A. H. Black & W. F. Prokasy (Eds.), *Classical conditioning II*. New York: Appleton-Century-Crofts, 1972.

Grice, G. R., & Hunter, J. J. Stimulus intensity effects depend upon the type of experimental design. *Psychological Review*, 1964, 71, 247–256.

Helson, H., & Steger, J. A. On the inhibitory effects of a second stimulus following the primary stimulus to react. *Journal of Experimental Psychology*, 1962, 64, 201–205.

Herman, L. M., & Kantowitz, B. H. The psychological refractory period effect: Only half the double-stimulation story. *Psychological Bulletin*, 1970, 73, 74–88.

Honig, W. K., & James, P. H. R. (Eds.), *Animal memory*. New York: Academic Press, 1971.

Hull, C. L. *Principles of behavior: An introduction to behavior theory*. New York: Appleton-Century, 1943.

James, W. *Principles of psychology*. New York: Henry Holt, 1890.

Kamin, L. J. Association and conditioning. In N. J. MacKintosh & W. K. Honig (Eds.), *Fundamental issues in associative learning*. Halifax: Dalhousie University Press, 1969. Pp. 42–64.

Kamman, R., & Melton, A. W. Absolute recovery of first-list responses from unlearning during 26 minutes filled with an easy or difficult information processing task. *Proceedings of the 75th Annual Convention of the American Psychological Association*, 1967, 63–64.

Keppel, G., Henschel, D. M., & Zavortink, B. Influence of nonspecific interference on response recall. *Journal of Experimental Psychology*, 1969, 81, 246–255.

Kimble, G. A., Leonard, T. B., & Perlmuter, L. C. Effects of interstimulus interval and discrimination learning in eyelid conditioning using between- and within-Ss designs. *Journal of Experimental Psychology*, 1968, 77, 652–660.

Mandler, G. Organization and memory. In K. W. Spence & J. T. Spence (Eds.), *The psychology of learning and motivation*. New York: Academic Press, 1967.

Melton, A. W., & Irwin, J. M. The influence of degree of interpolated learning on retroactive inhibition and the overt transfer of specific responses. *American Journal of Psychology*, 1940, 53, 173–203.

Newton, J. M., & Wickens, D. D. Retroactive inhibition as a function of the temporal position of the interpolated learning. *Journal of Experimental Psychology*, 1956, 51, 149–154.

Postman, L., Stark, K., & Fraser, J. Temporal changes in interference. *Journal of Verbal Learning and Verbal Behavior*, 1968, 7, 672–694.

Postman, L., Stark, K., & Henschel, D. Conditions of recovery after unlearning. *Journal of Experimental Psychology Monographs*, 1969, 82 (1, Part 2).

Rescorla, R. A., & Wagner, A. R. A theory of Pavlovian conditioning: Variations in the effectiveness of reinforcement and nonreinforcement. In A. H. Black & W. F. Prokasy (Eds.), *Classical Conditioning II*. New York: Appleton-Century-Crofts, 1972.

Silverstein, A. Unlearning, spontaneous recovery, and the partial-reinforcement effect in paired-associate learning. *Journal of Experimental Psychology*, 1967, 73, 15–21.

Spear, N. E. Forgetting as retrieval failure. In W. K. Honig & P. H. R. James (Eds.), *Animal memory*. New York: Academic Press, 1971.

Stroop, J. R. Studies of interference in serial verbal reactions. *Journal of Experimental Psychology*, 1935, 18, 643–661.

Sutherland, N. S., & Mackintosh, N. J. *Mechanisms of animal discrimination learning*. New York: Academic Press, 1971.

Underwood, B. J. Retroactive and proactive inhibition after five and forty-eight hours. *Journal of Experimental Psychology*, 1948, 38, 29–38.

Wickens, D. D., Born, D. G., & Wickens, C. D. Response strength to a compound conditioned stimulus and its elements as a function of element interstimulus interval. *Journal of Comparative and Physiological Psychology,* 1963, **56**, 727–731.

Wickens, D. D., & Cross, H. A. Resistance to extinction as a function of temporal relations during sensory preconditioning. *Journal of Experimental Psychology,* 1963, **65**, 206–211.

Wickens, D. D., Nield, A. F., Tuber, D. S., & Wickens, C. D. Strength, latency, and form of conditioned skeletal and autonomic responses as a function of CS-UCS intervals. *Journal of Experimental Psychology,* 1969, **80**, 165–170.

Young, R. K. Serial learning. In T. R. Dixon & D. L. Horton (Eds.), *Verbal behavior and general behavior theory.* Englewood Cliffs, N. J.: Prentice-Hall, 1968.

10
PSYCHOPHYSIOLOGY OF LEARNING AND CONDITIONING

Joseph Germana
Department of Psychology
Virginia Polytechnic Institute and State University

BRAIN/BEHAVIOR

One well-favored description of "brain/behavior" belongs to Roger W. Sperry (1952): "The principal function of the nervous system is the coordinated innervation of the musculature. Its fundamental anatomical plan and working principles are understandable only on these terms [p. 298]." Exceptional for its incisive character, this statement is nevertheless representative of a perspective that views nervous and behavioral functions as completely interrelating (cf. Germana, 1969a). The term "brain/behavior" stands for this conception and the fundamentally inextricable relation, itself.[1]

Brain/behavior has been suggested for organized neural tissue at all phylogenetic levels. Thus, C. Judson Herrick (1961) asserted that even the most primitive systems "form a network that serves to keep all parts of the body in communication and so facilitates orderly coordination of the bodily movements. In higher animals with more complicated structure and behavior special collections of nerve cells are set apart to provide more efficient coordination and integration [p. 255]."

At the same time, an objective study of the coordination and regulation of motor activities reveals the inherent complexity of behavior. The Russian physiologist Bernstein (1967), for example, has identified the essential problem of behavioral regulation in the following way: "The first clear biomechanical distinction between the motor apparatus in man and the higher animals and any

[1] The symbol "/" represents interventions to the complete system introduced by the particular methods of scientific and rational analysis. *Particular* interventions are both necessary and necessarily arbitrary.

245

artificial self-controlling devices . . . lies in the enormous number . . . of *degrees of freedom* which it can attain . . . [p. 125] ."

Analysis of some elementary behaviors reveals the anatomical, mechanical, and physiological sources of these degrees of freedom, the types of error with which they can be associated, and therefore the complexity of the spatiotemporal problems involved in the regulation of even such simple behaviors. On this basis, Bernstein has defined "coordination" as *"the process of mastery of redundant degrees of freedom* . . . [p. 127; italics in original] ."

However, the process of behavior "selection," the apparently specific increase or decrease in the probability of a behavior accomplished by conditioning, can also be regarded as a process of mastery of behavioral degrees of freedom. A psychophysiological analysis suggests that the foundations of behavior selection may rest in the peripheral coordinating activities of brain/behavior.[2]

PSYCHOPHYSIOLOGY

Previous definitions of psychophysiological research reflect certain technical limitations that need no longer exist. For example, "psychophysiology," as "any research in which the dependent variable is a physiological measure and the independent variable a 'behavioral' one [Stern, 1964, p. 90] ," unfortunately excludes the application of experimental techniques, such as systematic replication, which derive from the control of "private events" through feedback and operant conditioning (cf. Hefferline & Bruno, 1971).

More basically, previous definitions demonstrate conceptual limitations, which can, *in part,* be avoided by defining "psychophysiology" as the experimental investigation of covert responses—the observationally minor, peripheral activities of the organism—that stand within the relation of brain/behavior.[3]

---

[2] The inadequacy of our total descriptive technology and the consequent problems generated by categories of brain/behavior function, designed on the basis of one /, are revealed in such discussions. Additional limitations are introduced by the hierarchical, "one-way" scheme in which brain and peripheral events terminate in overt behavior (brain → behavior, stimulus → response). The converse relations are perhaps equally important.

Much of the present discussion follows the limits of brain/behavior "divotism." According to Lieber (1972), "the basic premise of divotism is this: At the point of contact with the ball, where the divot is actually dug up, the movement of the clubhead sums up and embodies all the ingredients that went into the entire swing . . . flaws will be expressed in the kind of divot the club carves out of the ground—its shape, its depth, and the trajectory it describes through the air . . . [p. 12] ."

[3] Psychophysiology involves an analysis based on a different /. The component systems of brain/behavior which develop from any intervention are, in large part, determined by the nature and "position" of the / introduced to the complete system. Thus, the analytic procedures of overt behavioral psychology produce systems of "conditioning," "motivation," "performance," etc., whereas a psychophysiological analysis produces two systems of brain/behavior.

The use of brain/behavior as conceptual reference for the analysis of covert responses implies that the functions of such covert responses may be treated as "behavioral" or "physiological." However, covert responses are not described as events of "behavior," just as they are not identified as events of "brain."

Restriction of the term "behavior" to overt behavior is not only dictated by the definition of covert responses, as events occurring *within* brain/behavior, but also by the fact that recent research has only provided demonstrations that some covert and overt events may generally be affected by the same operations. Psychophysiological observation reveals important, specific differences in the relationships which obtain between experimental operations and covert responses, on the one hand, and between the same operations and those events which more typically have direct "commerce with the outside world [Skinner, 1938, p. 6]."

THE SPECIFICATIONAL SYSTEM OF BRAIN/BEHAVIOR

A first system of brain/behavior represented in covert responses may be described as "specificational," in the sense that the essential function or effect of the system consists of the reduction of peripheral degrees of freedom.[4]

Covert responses of the specificational system may be regarded as: direct antecedents of overt behavior, immediate determiners of behavior, "specific" preparations for behavior, or prior members of covert response–overt behavior chains. The implications of these different characterizations have not been worked out.

There is also the question of whether both skeletal and autonomic events are to be included as covert responses of the specificational system. The small amount of experimental data concerning covert responses of this system is limited to skeletal activities. There are, however, some suggestions that a full appreciation of the behavioral role of autonomic functions has not yet been obtained.

The first suggestion concerns the central representation of autonomic functions. It is well known that a very clear discrimination can be made between the autonomic and somatic systems in their peripheral aspects, for example, on the basis of innervated effector mechanisms, etc. But, brain intervention reveals a quite different picture—one of extensive overlap in the representation of autonomic and somatic events. This integration was so salient to Hess (1954), in his brain stimulation studies of the diencephalon, that he discarded the

---

[4] von Bertalanffy's (1968) simple definition of a "system" as "a set of elements standing in interaction" is sufficient for the discussion of covert responses, if two positive implications can be acknowledged. First, the phrase "elements standing in interaction" is translatable into "elements producing a distinguishing, resultant effect" for all but random interactions. Second, the elements of one system participate in other interactions or systems. Both implications are relevant in the "systematization" of covert responses.

autonomic-somatic dichotomy and proposed, instead, systems of "ergotropic" and "trophotropic" response for those central areas and functions that involve the association of somatic-behavioral responses with sympathetic and parasympathetic responses, respectively. Later studies seem to reveal that many of these integrative structures belong to the "extrapyramidal" system, which has long been implicated in the control of "posture" or "readiness to respond."[5]

These data are more relevant to covert responses of a second system to be described, but they are noted here since they show that the central integration revealed by direct intervention into the central nervous system may not duplicate conceptions based on purely peripheral distinctions. This last conclusion may prove relevant in the operant conditioning of autonomic events.

One difficulty in the conception of operantly controllable, autonomic events was, and still is, that these responses typically do not have direct "commerce with the outside world." Miller (1969) has suggested "we will expect the animal to learn those glandular and visceral responses mediated by the central nervous system that promptly restore homeostasis after any considerable deviation [p. 443]." But, there are other possibilities, including the possibility that autonomic responses may form prior members of covert response–overt behavior chains and/or autonomic elements of "preparations" for behavior. Under "natural" conditions, they may be subject to operant control in this indirect manner.

The speculation is based on some independently significant data reviewed by Hefferline and Bruno (1971) which appear to show that operantly conditioned, skeletal electromyographic responses can form initial members of a covert response–overt behavior chain. An early demonstration in the series was provided by Hefferline and Perera (1963).

In a more recent study, Hefferline and Bruno (1971) provided a systematic replication of an experiment originally performed by R. C. Davis (1952). In the first stage of the more recent experiment, human subjects were trained to make abductive and adductive *covert* responses of the little finger to "red" and "green" discriminative stimuli. In a second stage, subjects were trained to make *overt,* micro-switch-closing, abductive and adductive responses of the same finger to 86- and 104-decibel tones, respectively, and these behaviors constituted judgments of "soft" and "loud."

Stimulus generalization functions to 11 test stimuli, ranging from 80 to 110 decibels, demonstrated a "response bias" in the "soft" and "loud" directions, dependent upon the presence of covert abductive and adductive responses, emitted in the presence of the appropriate discriminative stimuli. These results

[5] Gellhorn (1967) has reviewed evidence that ergotropic responses (which may appear as responses of "activation" or "arousal") are produced by stimulation of such regions as: motor and sensorimotor areas of the neocortex, areas of the limbic system, subcortical structures such as those comprising the basal ganglia, the medial thalamus, and the reticular formation.

Wang's (1964) list of excitatory and regulatory regions for electrodermal phenomena may serve as an example: sensorimotor cortex, anterior limbic and infralimbic cortex, anterior hypothalamus, a region of the dorsal thalamus, and the lateral reticular formation.

constitute an important demonstration of the "response-biasing" functions of covert responses attributed to the specificational system.

In another study, Perera (1969), employing the same experimental arrangement, first trained subjects to make *overt* abductive or adductive responses to avoid a 1/2-second burst of random noise at 110 decibels. The aversive stimulus, scheduled for presentation every 20 seconds, could be terminated and/or postponed by the overt avoidance response. Perera was able to identify "early pre-overt" and "late pre-overt" changes in muscle action potentials (MAPs) from both agonistic and antagonistic muscle groups. Figure 1 presents these data.

The *late* pre-overt responses of the agonistic group, beginning 1/2 to 1 1/2 seconds before the overt avoidance response, remained "very consistent throughout each experimental session ... [Perera, 1969, p. 4]." Figure 2, however, shows that the changes in the early pre-overt MAPs, which occur from operant level, through conditioning and extinction, are highly comparable for both the agonistic and antagonistic covert activities, suggesting that these MAP changes are relatively more general in nature. The specific course of these changes is a topic reserved for later discussion.

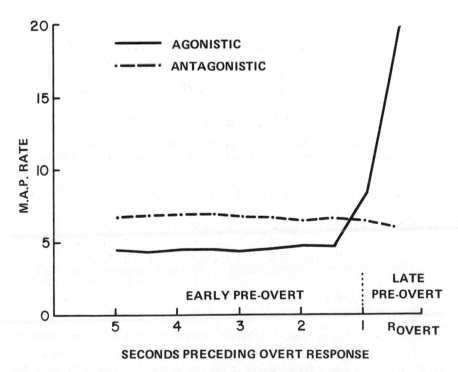

FIG. 1. Rate of muscle action potentials (MAP rate) for agonistic and antagonistic covert (pre-overt) responses as a function of time preceding the occurrence of an overt, behavioral response. (From Perera, 1969.)

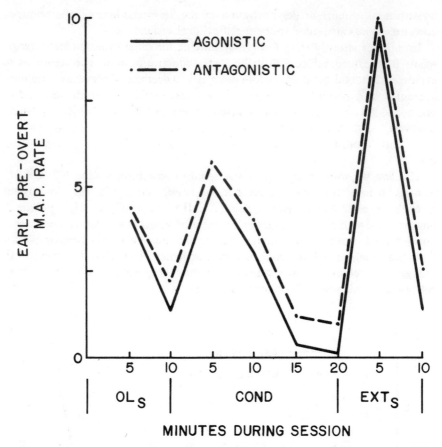

FIG. 2. MAP rate for agonistic and antagonistic, "early pre-overt" responses during sessions of operant level, conditioning, and extinction. (From Perera, 1969.)

Although there are other data which suggest the operation of a specificational system of covert responses, they are not presented here, either because the evidence they provide is not direct, or because the covert responses could more easily belong to a second system. There is, then, a very limited amount of information presently available on covert responses of the specificational system.

THE VARIATIONAL SYSTEM OF BRAIN/BEHAVIOR

Again employing a brain → behavior approach, it would seem that, if specificational functions are concerned with the selection-coordination of behavior through a process of reduction of degrees of freedom, then any substantial source of indeterminacy, occurring within the system, can produce "behavioral uncertainty." Uncertainty would precede and accompany the performance of behaviors that have not been transformed into adaptive sequences of highly coordinated, automatic events.

Uncertainty, basically derived from the inherent complexity of behavior, can be augmented by several conditions that produce additional sources of indeterminacy. These additional degrees of freedom may be generated: by increasing stimulus uncertainty, by modifying the conditional nature or complexity of behavior, or by changing the consequences of behavior. In all cases based on this "one-way" analysis, the additional uncertainty which results appears centered around the basic problem of producing adaptive behavior in an efficient manner.[6]

A second system of covert responses, introduced under conditions of behavioral uncertainty, consists of widely generalized somatic, autonomic, and central events. The covert responses of this system may be regarded as: nonspecific antecedents of behavior, immediate indeterminers of behavior, "general" preparations for behavior, or indicants of a state of "activation" or "arousal."

Since they apparently function to increase, rather than decrease, the number of degrees of freedom at the periphery, though more diffuse excitation, and may act to increase systematic behavioral variability, these covert responses may be described as representing a "variational" system of brain/behavior. A variational system is conceived as one which *actively* tends to produce changing values in the parameters of behavior topography and a greater "equalization" of the probabilities associated with a variety of behaviors.

Table 1 is a simple illustration of an intended, variational function, in crude values so as not to convey an empirically based sophistication which does not exist. Complex conditioning procedures are treated as producing an occlusive increase in the probability of Response 2. Without the intervention of extinction procedures, activation produces a temporary tendency (here complete) toward regression to a state of equal probabilities. All of the many qualifications which are necessary are not discussed here.

It has been shown that covert responses of this system can be produced by the following operations: (*a*) presenting a "novel" stimulus to the organism, evoking the orienting reflex; (*b*) *immediately* conferring signal significance to a stimulus or immediately changing signal significance, i.e., pairing a stimulus with an overt behavior or a different behavior, by instructions to human subjects, or by arranging for abrupt acquisition in both animal and human subjects: (*c*)

---

[6] The fact that uncertainty can apparently be produced by indeterminacy at any point of a complete "stimulus-response-consequence" cycle suggests that the term "behavioral uncertainty" may be the somewhat arbitrary result of a brain → behavior or S → R analysis.

It should be noted that even diagrams that include "consequences" or "feedback" to complete a single cycle or loop, and to serve as paradigm, do not represent the existence of many simultaneously active cycles, operating at different rates on different occasions. A cross-section of such a three-dimensional diagram, performed at any point in time, would reveal many cycles in different phases.

TABLE 1

Hypothetical Demonstration of "Specificational" and "Variational" Effects

Before conditioning	"Later" conditioning	"Later" conditioning + activation
Response probabilities		
R1 = .33	R1 = 0	R1 = .33
R2 = .33	R2 = 1.00	R2 = .33
R3 = .33	R3 = 0	R3 = .33
Values of R2		
Wide range of values in the latency, magnitude (force), duration, etc., of R2	Restricted range of R2 values (cf. Notterman & Mintz, 1965)	Temporary extension of R2 values, including demonstrations of "increased vigor"

applying classical or instrumental procedures which produce apparently graded, behavioral acquisition and extinction; and (*d*) employing other, more complex procedures which cannot easily be characterized in a general manner, e.g., making more parameters of behavior critical for appropriate or successful performance, or giving human subjects response choices.

Some of these operations for producing covert responses of the variational system have been demonstrated in some simple experiments performed in this laboratory. In one series of experiments, the subjects were human, the overt behaviors and manipulations of behavior were intentionally elementary, and the psychophysiological data were typically those obtained to stimuli, occurring in advance of the overt behavioral responses.

Figure 3 presents the results of a recent experiment (Germana, 1972) which analyzed the galvanic skin responses (GSRs) of three groups of subjects to repeated presentations of two stimuli. The stimuli consisted of slides, presenting the letter "R" or the letters "NR." Each slide was presented for 30 seconds, and each subject received five NR slides followed by ten R slides. Subjects were instructed to: attend to the stimuli (ATT), make an overt button-pressing response, *on command,* to the R slides (forced-response, FR), or to temporally bisect each period during which an R slide was being presented (BIS).

Figure 3 shows a second-by-second analysis of the GSRs to the stimuli on the first trial (NR1), on the first R trial (R1), and on the final trial (R10). GSRs occurring to the first, NR1 stimulus were comparable for all three groups, but the GSRs to R1 reveal that signal significance (FR), i.e., the association of a stimulus with an overt behavior, produces substantial changes in the magnitude and shape of the response. The addition of a critical temporal or timing

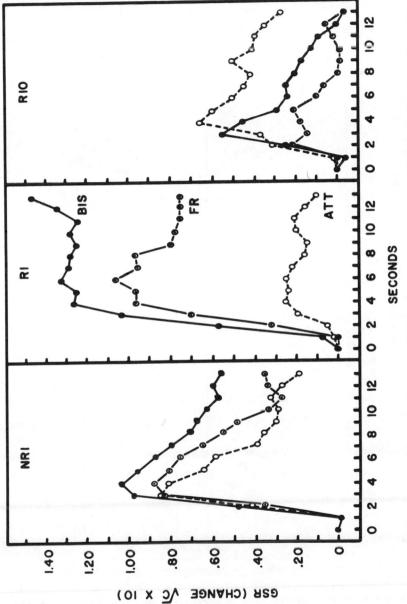

FIG. 3. Second-by-second analysis of galvanic skin responses (GSRs) to the first nonsignal (NR1), the first signal (R1), and the last signal (R10) stimuli. Subjects were instructed to attend (ATT) to the stimuli, to make an overt response, on command, to the R stimuli (FR), or to bisect the time-interval of R-stimulus presentation with an overt response (BIS). (From Germana, 1972.)

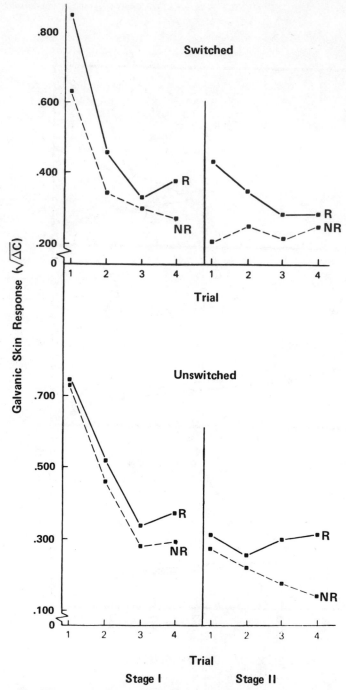

FIG. 4. GSRs to signal (R) and nonsignal (NR) stimuli across habituation trials. The Stage II, switched-unswitched differences are not discussed. (From Germana, 1968b.)

characteristic to the overt behavior (BIS) further augments and otherwise changes GSR. After the behavioral responses have been practiced (R10), GSR differences are reduced or abolished.

The fact that stimuli associated with overt behavior initially produce GSRs (and other covert responses) of larger magnitude than nonsignal stimuli has been well replicated, and may be demonstrated by the data from another experiment. In this experiment (Germana, 1968b), subjects were presented slides of single-digit odd and even numbers. One-half of the subjects were instructed to behaviorally respond by saying the even numbers, *after* they had been presented; the other half responded to the odd-number slides in a similar manner. Figure 4 shows that larger GSRs occurred to signal (R) than to nonsignal (NR) stimuli. (The Stage II data are not discussed here.)

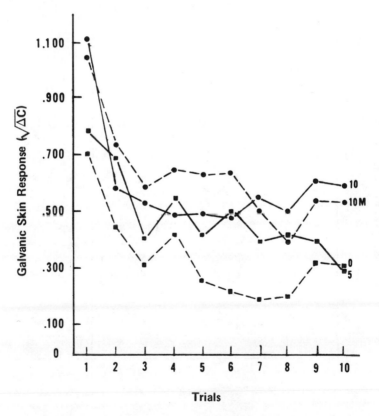

FIG. 5. GSRs to stimuli associated with no instructed behavioral response (*0*), 1 of 5 possible behavioral responses (*5*), 1 of 10 possible responses (*10*), or 1 of 10 possible, mixed-class responses (*10M*) on ten trials. (From Germana, 1968b.)

In a different experiment (Germana, 1968b), subjects were permitted various degrees of response choice to diffuse light stimuli. Four groups were employed: *0*—no overt behavior required; *5*—choice of saying any number from 1 to 5 (6 to 10 for balancing subjects), immediately after the period of presentation of the light stimulus; *10*—choice of saying any number from 1 to 10; *10M*—choice of saying any number from 1 to 5 (6 to 10) or the letters A to E. Figure 5 presents magnitude of GSR to the light stimulus on ten trials. Statistical analysis revealed significant differences between all but the 10 and 10M groups.

A final study in this series (Germana, 1968b) explored the effects of behavioral response *change* on the GSRs to a diffuse-light signal stimulus. In Stage I, one group of subjects was required to make one up-down finger

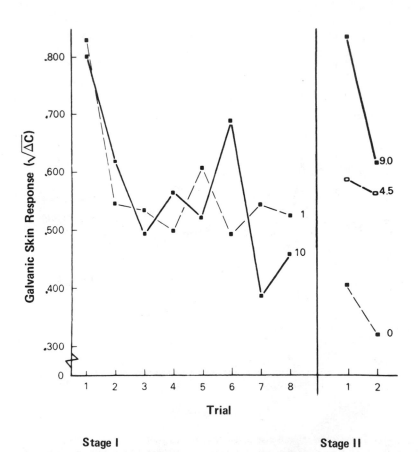

FIG. 6. GSRs to stimuli associated with either 1 or 10 finger movements, during habituation in Stage I, and with instructed response changes of 0, 4.5, or 9.0 movements in Stage II. (From Germana, 1968b.)

movement, immediately after the period of stimulus presentation, whereas a second group was required to make 10 movements to each stimulus. In Stage II, one-third of the subjects were told to continue the same response (1:1 and 10:10, for 0 change), one-third were instructed to produce 5 movements (1:5 and 10:5, for an average 4.5 change), and the remaining one-third experienced a 1:10 or 10:1 shift (9.0 change). The results, presented in Figure 6, indicate that the magnitude of GSR to the stimulus was directly related to degree of behavioral change.[7]

VARIATIONAL PROCESSES OF SENSITIZATION AND HABITUATION

Covert responses of the variational system are subject to two processes: sensitization and habituation. Both processes are demonstrated in the results of an experiment (Germana, 1969b) in which: the subjects were again human, the conditioning method was that of Ivanov-Smolenskii (an intended variety of Pavlovian conditioning), and the psychophysiological analysis was performed on GSR, heart rate (HR), and muscle action potential (MAP) responses and levels. The "conditional stimulus (CS)" was an asterisk slide, preceded by four blank periods of equal duration, and presented on nine trials. The "unconditional stimulus (UCS)" was the verbal command "press," delivered by the experimenter immediately after the period of "CS" presentation on the last six trials. The subjects had been instructed to press a button positioned in the left hand, on command.

The data of Figure 7 are integrated MAP, recorded from the brachioradialis region of the left forearm during four segments of the nine trials. Segment 5 is the period of "CS" presentation, the remainder are preceding blank intervals. Habituation occurred on the first four trials but was reversed by the application of the "UCS" at the end of Trial 4 and subsequent trials. Similar effects were demonstrated for GSR and HR responses and for level of skin conductance.

These data are congruent with those from Perera's (1969) experiment, in which it was shown that "early pre-overt" activities in both agonistic and antagonistic muscles habituated during operant level and demonstrated sensitization in the early stages of conditioning and extinction. On the basis of these considerations, Perera and Kelley (1970) replicated the experiment with

[7] According to the scheme developed by Sokolov (1963), degree of reemergence of the orienting reflex directly reflects the degree of mismatch between the "neuronal model of a stimulus," established on the basis of repeated exposure to the stimulus, and a "new" stimulus. On this basis, Sokolov has apparently demonstrated that various physical parameters of the repeated stimulus are denoted in the "model."

Using the same logic on the data of the last study, one might include "associated behavioral characteristics" of a stimulus into the "neuronal model." But, this is merely another demonstration that the orienting reflex consists of covert responses which most generally belong to the variational system.

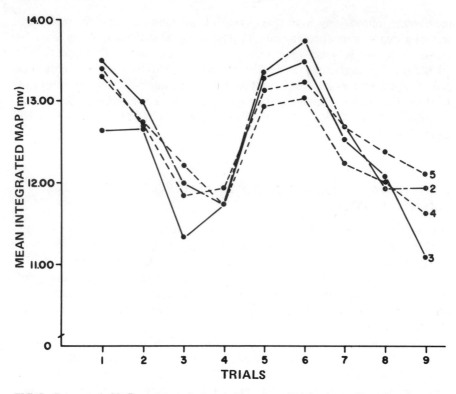

FIG. 7. Integrated MAP activity during habituation (Trials 1 to 3) and subsequent conditioning (Trials 4 to 9). Four segments of each trial are represented. (From Germana, 1969b.)

the addition of GSR and produced essentially the same effects in this measure.

The pattern of more gradual sensitization followed by habituation, which occurs within this system of covert responses during the "earlier" and "later" stages of conditioning or learning, respectively, has previously been termed "activational peaking" (Germana, 1968a).[8] In addition to the two studies reported above, and the earlier studies of sensitization apparently occurring within the conditional response measure (e.g., Prokasy & Ebel, 1967; Stewart, Stern, Winokur, & Fredman, 1961), the effect has been well replicated.

---

[8] The term "activational peaking" was employed to signify that the pattern is general in nature and may be demonstrated by many of the covert responses which represent this system. However, in addition to the fact that the term is unnecessary, it also has significant negative side effects: it indiscriminately groups the two processes of sensitization and habituation, it perceptually isolates their occurrence during conditioning from their occurrence during other operations (e.g., extinction), and it fails to include demonstrations of immediate dishabituation. As Groves and Thompson (1970) have noted, dishabituation should be considered a demonstration of sensitization.

For example, the gradual sensitization-habituation pattern of covert responses has been demonstrated: in classical aversive conditioning studies, for GSR in human subjects (Orlebeke & van Olst, 1968; Shmavonian, Miller, & Cohen, 1968; Schramm & Kimmel, 1970), for GSR in immobilized cats (Van Twyver & King, 1969), and for HR and respiration rate in rabbits (Manning, Schneiderman, & Lordahl, 1969; Yohlo, 1968). It has been shown for HR in rats during appetitive conditioning (Seward & Braude, 1969), and during positive reward training of GSR in human subjects (Schwartz & Johnson, 1969). In addition, the effect is evident in GSR during concept formation (Germana & Pavlik, 1964), rule induction (Elias, 1970), serial learning (Finesmith, 1959), paired-associates learning (Germana, 1968a), and for electroencephalographic (EEG) desynchronization in human subjects during serial learning (Thompson & Obrist, 1964) and in monkeys during classical conditioning (Morrell & Jasper, 1956). Additional data, resulting from other interventions are presented in the Appendix.

Habituation is, of course, a basic process of response decrement, and requires only references of general nature (cf. Graham, in press; Lynn, 1966; Sokolov, 1963; Thompson & Spencer, 1966; and van Olst, 1971). As a variational process, habituation occurs either when no explicit or implicit, behavioral contingency has been in effect (for some time and trials) or when a contingency has been well-established (for some time and trials). Habituation occurs during repetition of a nonsignal stimulus, during "later" conditioning, and during "later" extinction. In all such cases, habituation is associated with *decreasing* behavioral uncertainty.

On the other hand, abrupt (or dishabituational) and incremental sensitization is associated with *increasing* behavioral uncertainty. Sensitization occurs when a "novel" stimulus has recently been presented or when the behavioral significance of a stimulus or situation is in the process of change (with minimal positive transfer). Sensitization continues until behavioral limits (limitations) are established by specificational "mastery" and the apparent contingencies or noncontingencies of behavior. Thus, sensitization not only occurs to a "novel" stimulus, but also during the "earlier" stages of conditioning, and during the "earlier" stages of extinction.

Sensitization and habituation may prove to be general, process analogues of conditioning (learning) and extinction, but variational functions appear to be related to the specificational in this orthogonal manner.

CONCLUDING NOTE

The different interventions of a more complete science of brain/behavior may reveal many such relationships, since multiple, integrative comparisons may become established along any parameter of an experimental variable. A *comprehensive* psychophysiology would assume an inclusive system of observable physiological and behavioral responses as its conceptual reference, and would take as its subject matter the functional interrelations of these organismic responses.

Unfortunately, much of what is presently known about the more complete system is limited and biased, in conception and methodology, by a highly exclusive, brain → behavior orientation, in which "reflex arc" remains the implicit, conceptual unit. Mere acknowledgement of continuously completing "feedbacking" renders the system without "absolute zeros" and all semblance of nonarbitrary intervention.

APPENDIX

Since the classifications and experimental reconstructions of variables developed by an intervention depend on the nature of the intervention, itself, the results obtained by one approach should be related to the results of another as circumstantial evidence. This appendix traces the contours of some circumstantial evidence surrounding the major points of the paper through a series of statements typically from recent authoritative reviews of experimental data. All discussion and connective phrasing has been avoided.

Interventions into Interneurons

1. "In maintaining the comparability of habituation characteristics for responses of the spinal cord and the intact animal, we are forced to the prediction that the independence of habituation and sensitization will also hold for the intact animal [Thompson & Spencer, 1966, p. 28]."

2. "Results of the interneuron studies to date are strikingly (and unexpectedly) clear. Three categories of interneurons responding to cutaneous stimuli have been found with approximately equal frequency: a 'nonplastic' type showing no changes in response, and two types of 'plastic' interneurons, one showing habituation and one showing sensitization [Groves & Thompson, 1970, pp. 428–429]."

3. "We suggest that these two classes of interneurons subserve the processes of habituation and sensitization for the flexion reflex of the acute spinal cat and that similar classes of interneurons may exist in the brain to mediate habituation and sensitization in the intact organism [Groves & Thompson, 1970, p. 431]."

4. "It is of particular speculative interest in regard to anatomical and functional relations that the isodendritic core of the entire brain stem and spinal cord is remarkably uniform throughout its length ... [Groves & Thompson, 1970, p. 431]."

5. "All of these considerations suggest that generalized, isodendritic neurons are characteristic of cell regions not completely (or sufficiently) 'monopolized' by a particular specific afferent system [Ramón-Moliner & Nauta, 1966 p. 321]."

6. "In order to account for other physiological properties ascribed to the same neural apparatus, one could propose the term 'homeostasis' or

'maintenance of posture,' or suggest a mechanism controlling the general 'degree of responsiveness' of the organism [Ramón-Moliner & Nauta, 1966, p. 323]."

7. "It has been often noted that the phylogenetically 'primitive' reticular formation ... represents a continuation of the anatomical arrangements found in the spinal cord and includes many of the neuronal cell types found there ... [Groves & Lynch, 1972, p. 238]."

8. "Habituation and sensitization occur reliably in the cells of the reticular formation with a time course similar to these phenomena in the intact organism ... [Groves & Lynch, 1972, p. 241]."

Neurophysiological Interventions

1. "Because of procedural differences among the experiments described, detailed comparative evaluation is not possible. An EEG change in frequency-specific responses that builds up during early training and regresses when a high level of performance is reached seems to be the most commonly observed phenomenon [Thomas, 1962, p. 91]."

2. "Several conclusions regarding brain activity during learning can be drawn. During the initial phases of learning, the cortex is widely activated by the training stimuli. Later in training, cortical activity subsides to the primary sensory cortex associated with the stimuli and the motor cortex associated with the response. Such redistribution of cortical activity is usually preceded by activity increases in various brainstem 'nonspecific' systems. Brain activity changes usually start prior to the appearance of the overt response [Thompson, Patterson, & Teyler, 1972, p. 85]."

3. "In situations where the cerebral neocortex becomes 'desynchronized' or 'activated' ... the hippocampus shows 'synchronization,' and presents rhythmic sinusoidal waves of 4 to 7 per second, usually referred to as 'theta waves.' When the cortex shows synchronization the hyppocampal activity is desynchronized. The functional role of this reciprocal relationship is not clearly understood. It appears, however, that both structures are influenced from the reticular formation [Brodal, 1969, p. 528]."

4. "It has been proposed that the hippocampal theta waves which accompany operantly conditioned responses are related to arousal ..., motivation ..., orienting responses ..., low-intensity motivational processes involved in approach ..., motivated responding to a conditioned stimulus when the stimulus response connection is not well established ..., and the establishment of a connection between an S^D and an operantly conditioned response ... [Black, Young, & Batenchuk, 1970, p. 15]."

5. "All of these observations indicate that during voluntary movement there is more activity in the ascending nonspecific projections to the neocortex, as well as to the hippocampus, than is present during behavioral immobility or automatic types of movement. A possible interpretation of this is that the neocortex and hippocampus play an active role in voluntary behavior but are less

crucially involved in automatic behavior or the maintenance of an unchanging posture [Vanderwolf, 1971, p. 99]."

6. "As conditioning proceeds, RSA (rhythmical slow activity in the hippocampus) appears in association with prominent orienting movements ('vicarious trial and error' in American psychological writings) which occur early in acquisition .... After additional training, as the learned response becomes well established, RSA ceases to appear [Vanderwolf, 1971, p. 100]."

Interventions of Behavioral Psychology

1. "It appeared further ... that the VTEing began to appear just as (or just before) the rats began to learn. After the learning had become established, however, the VTEs began to go down [Tolman, 1948, p. 197]."

2. "The mean number of CPRs (cue producing responses) per trial increases rather rapidly during the acquisition phase, reaching a maximum somewhere in the neighborhood of criterion (90% correct). With over-training, the number of CPRs gradually diminished to its initial, low level [D'Amato, Etkin, & Fazzaro, 1968, p. 430]."

3. The increase in CPRs during reversal, extinction, and acquisition would be interpreted as a 'search' for information to resolve the uncertainty which non-reinforcement in the first two cases, and inconsistent (to the subject) reinforcement in the last, occasions (D'Amato, Etkin, & Fazzaro, 1968, p. 433]."

4. "The rise in observing responses made before any change in choice behavior and the subsequent fall as learning criterion was reached were characteristic of all the birds. The learning criterion was met rapidly, but by no means immediately, after the break in position preference [Hamlin, 1972, p. 18]."

REFERENCES

Bernstein, N. *The coordination and regulation of movements.* New York: Pergamon Press, 1967.

Black, A. H., Young, G. A., & Batenchuk, C. Avoidance training of hippocampal theta waves in flaxedilized dogs and its relation to skeletal movement. *Journal of Comparative and Physiological Psychology,* 1970, 70, 15–24.

Brodal, A. *Neurological anatomy.* New York: Oxford University Press, 1969.

D'Amato, M. R., Etkin, M., & Fazzaro, J. Cue-producing behavior in the Capuchin monkey during reversal, extinction, acquisition, and overtraining. *Journal of the Experimental Analysis of Behavior,* 1968, II, 425–433.

Davis, R. C. The stimulus trace in effectors and its relation to judgment responses. *Journal of Experimental Psychology,* 1952, 44, 377–390.

Elias, M. F. Heart rate, skin potential response, and latency of overt response, as indicators of problem recognition and solution. *Psychonomic Science,* 1970, 18, 337–339.

Finesmith, S. Systematic changes in GSR activity as a physiological correlate of paired-associate learning. Paper presented at the meeting of the Midwestern Psychological Association, Chicago, May 1959.

Gellhorn, E. *Principles of autonomic-somatic integrations.* Minneapolis: University of Minnesota Press, 1967.

Germana, J. Psychophysiological correlates of conditioned response formation. *Psychological Bulletin,* 1968, **70**, 105–114. (a)

Germana, J. Response characteristics and the orienting reflex. *Journal of Experimental Psychology,* 1968, **78**, 610–616. (b)

Germana, J. Central efferent processes and autonomic behavioral integration. *Psychophysiology,* 1969, **6**, 78–90. (a)

Germana, J. Patterns of autonomic and somatic activity during classical conditioning of a motor response. *Journal of Comparative and Physiological Psychology,* 1969, **69**, 173–178. (b)

Germana, J. Response uncertainty and autonomic-behavioral integration. *Annals of the New York Academy of Sciences,* 1972, **193**, 185–188.

Germana, J., & Pavlik, W. B. Autonomic correlates of acquisition and extinction. *Psychonomic Science,* 1964, **1**, 109–110.

Graham, F. K. Habituation and dishabituation of responses innervated by the autonomic nervous system. In H. V. S. Peeke & M. J. Herz (Eds.), *Habituation: Behavioral studies and physiological substrates.* New York: Academic Press, in press.

Groves, P. M., & Lynch, G. S. Mechanisms of habituation in the brain stem. *Psychological Review,* 1972, **79**, 237–244.

Groves, P. M., & Thompson, R. F. Habituation: A dual-process theory. *Psychological Review,* 1970, **77**, 419–450.

Hamlin, P. H. Observing responses as an index of attention in chickens. Unpublished doctoral dissertation, Rutgers University, 1972.

Hefferline, R. F., & Bruno, L. J. J. The psychophysiology of private events. In A. Jacobs & L. B. Sachs (Eds.), *The psychology of private events.* New York: Academic Press, 1971. Pp. 163–192.

Hefferline, R. F., & Perera, T. B. Proprioceptive discrimination of a covert operant without its observation by the subject. *Science,* 1963, **139**, 834–835.

Herrick, C. J. *The evolution of human nature.* New York: Harper & Row, 1961.

Hess, W. R. *Diencephalon: Autonomic and extrapyramidal functions.* New York: Grune & Stratton, 1954.

Lieber, L. Golf's secret formula. *Signature,* 1972, **7**, 12–14.

Lynn, R. *Attention, arousal and the orientation reaction.* New York: Pergamon Press, 1966.

Manning, A. A., Schneiderman, N., & Lordahl, D. S. Delay versus trace heart-rate classical discrimination conditioning in rabbits as a function of interstimulus interval. *Journal of Experimental Psychology,* 1969, **80**, 225–230.

Miller, N. E. Learning of visceral and glandular responses. *Science,* 1969, **163**, 434–445.

Morrell, F., & Jasper, H. H. Electrographic studies of the formation of temporary connections in the brain. *Electroencephalography and Clinical Neurophysiology,* 1956, **8**, 201–215.

Notterman, J. M., & Mintz, D. E. *Dynamics of response.* New York: Wiley, 1965.

Orlebeke, J. F., & van Olst, E. H. Learning and performance as a function of CS-intensity in a delayed GSR conditioning situation. *Journal of Experimental Psychology.* 1968, **77**, 483–487.

Perera, T. B. Agonistic and antagonistic pre-overt muscle responses during human escape-avoidance conditioning. Paper presented at the meeting of the Eastern Psychological Association, Philadelphia, April, 1969.

Perera, T. B., & Kelley, D. B. Galvanic skin response activity during human Sidman avoidance conditioning. Paper presented at the meeting of the Eastern Psychological Association, Atlantic City, April, 1970.

Prokasy, W. F., & Ebel, H. C. Three components of the classically conditioned GSR in human subjects. *Journal of Experimental Psychology,* 1967, **73**, 247–256.

Ramón-Moliner, E., & Nauta, W. J. H. The isodendritic core of the brain stem. *Journal of Comparative Neurology*, 1966, **126**, 311–336.

Schramm, C. F., & Kimmel, H. D. Resistance to extinction in GSR conditioning following different numbers of postpeak acquisition trials. *Journal of Experimental Psychology*, 1970, **84**, 239–243.

Schwartz, G. E., & Johnson, H. J. Affective visual stimuli as operant reinforcers of the GSR. *Journal of Experimental Psychology*, 1969, **80**, 28–32.

Seward, J. P., & Braude, R. M. Changes in heart rate during discriminative reward training and extinction in the cat. *Journal of Comparative and Physiological Psychology*, 1969, **66**, 396–401.

Shmavonian, B. M., Miller, L. H., & Cohen, S. I. Differences among age and sex groups in electrodermal conditioning. *Psychophysiology*, 1968, **5**, 119–131.

Skinner, B. F. *The behavior of organisms: An experimental analysis.* New York: Appleton-Century-Crofts, 1938.

Sokolov, E. N. *Perception and the conditioned reflex.* New York: Pergamon Press, 1963.

Sperry, R. W. Neurology and the mind-brain problem. *American Scientist*, 1952, **40**, 291–312.

Stern, J. A. Toward a definition of psychophysiology. *Psychophysiology*, 1964, **1**, 90–91.

Stewart, M. A., Stern, J. A., Winokur, G. S., & Fredman, S. An analysis of GSR conditioning. *Psychological Review*, 1961, **68**, 60–67.

Thomas, G. J. Neurophysiology of learning. *Annual Review of Psychology*, 1962, **13**, 71–106.

Thompson, L. W., & Obrist, W. D. EEG correlates of verbal learning and overlearning. *Electroencephalography and Clinical Neurophysiology*, 1964, **16**, 332–342.

Thompson, R. F., Patterson, M. M., & Teyler, T. J. The neurophysiology of learning. *Annual Review of Psychology*, 1972, **23**, 73–104.

Thompson, R. F., & Spencer, W. A. Habituation: A model phenomenon for the study of neuronal substrates of behavior. *Psychological Review*, 1966, **73**, 16–43.

Tolman, E. C. Cognitive maps in rats and men. *Psychological Review*, 1948, **55**, 189–208.

Vanderwolf, C. H. Limbic-diencephalic mechanisms of voluntary movement. *Psychological Review*, 1971, **78**, 83–113.

van Olst, E. H. *The orienting reflex.* Amsterdam: Mouton, 1971.

Van Twyver, H. B., & King, R. L. Classical conditioning of the galvanic skin response in immobilized cats. *Psychophysiology*, 1969, **5**, 530–535.

von Bertalanffy, L. *General system theory.* New York: Braziller, 1968.

Wang, G. H. *The neural control of sweating.* Madison: University of Wisconsin Press, 1964.

Yehle, A. L. Divergences among rabbit response systems during three-tone classical discrimination conditioning. *Journal of Experimental Psychology*, 1968, **77**, 468–473.

11
MEMORY AND CONDITIONING

W. K. Estes
Rockefeller University

In a recent review of several years' literature on learning (Estes, 1972b), I have noted that the two most effervescent areas of research have been, on the one hand, research on animal learning and conditioning involving electrophysiological techniques, and on the other, research on human memory within the framework of information-processing concepts. Both of these lines of research abound in new theoretical developments, but there appears to be a steady tendency toward divergence, the former leaning more toward neurophysiology, the latter toward theoretical ideas coming from the study of computers and automata. Thus it seems timely to consider whether we can find any positive measures that might tend to bring these two flourishing but divergent lines of theoretical development together within a common theoretical framework that might be advantageous for the direction of both research and application.

If the separation of theories of conditioning and memory resulted only from differences in the types of subjects characteristically used and in the complexity of experimental situations, the way to improve matters would be relatively clear. But I think the source lies much deeper.

There are two basic ways of conceiving a learning experiment. Always an organism is given a sequence of experiences either in a single situation or in a set of situations, and changes in performance over the sequence are bases for inferring learning. But both experimental designs and interpretations of the results may be either (*a*) response-oriented or (*b*) memory-oriented. In the response-oriented tradition, the organism's tendency to make some response is the theoretical dependent variable. Appropriate measures of this tendency are experimentally defined, and learning is traced via changes in these measures as a function of various independent variables operating over time or trials. Learning is learning of a response, an action, or a habit. It is recognized that what the investigator defines as the same response at different stages of learning may nonetheless vary greatly in form. However, these variations are treated in terms of transfer of learning or response generalization. In the memory-oriented tradition, one exposes the organism to some sequence of situations and then asks what has been learned. The result of learning is memory for the sequence of events that has been experienced, the memory being manifest in behavior in a variety of ways on later occasions.

Some major bodies of research and theoretical development have evolved almost entirely within one or the other of the two traditions. In the case of category (*a*), operant conditioning is the prime example. Much work on human memory would fall almost entirely in category (*b*). Latent learning straddles the two traditions and has never been fully absorbed into either type of theory.

Much of what we now think of as classical learning theory, and in particular the approaches of Hull (1943), Guthrie (1935), and Skinner (1938), developed almost entirely within the response-oriented tradition. It is doubtless no coincidence that the hegemony of response-oriented learning theory coincided so closely with the period in which operationism had its greatest impact and broadest sway in psychology. This orientation has all the advantages of parsimony, bypassing difficult questions of definition of subject matter. The cost of these advantages is the hazard of missing much of what goes on in a learning experiment and evolving theories too barren in structure to deal with the richness of learning phenomena.

From time to time over a long period, individual investigators have exhibited dissatisfaction with the narrowness of response-oriented theory, and in particular with the idea that one can arbitrarily select a particular response, for example, the unconditioned response in a classical conditioning experiment, trace the course of learning in terms of changes in measures of this response tendency, and validly assume that the response maintains its identity through various phases of an experiment. Even in the cases which have seemed most compatible with this assumption, salivary and eyelid conditioning, it is the rule rather than the exception that there are many differences in detailed topography between the unconditioned and the conditioned response (Kimble, 1961). In one of the few studies presenting detailed records of behavioral changes during salivary conditioning in dogs, Zener (1937) reported radical differences between the behavioral patterns aroused by the US and, following conditioning, by the CS. In a study which he aptly termed a "search for the conditioned response," Warner (1932) subjected rats to repeated presentations of stimulation by a buzzer or a light followed by shock. He found that no specific parts of the original response to the shock, except possibly autonomic reactions such as breathing rate, were regularly conditioned.

Thus by the end of the 1930's there was substantial reason to suspect that theoretical formulations of conditioning were being perhaps too strongly shaped by conventional and convenient experimental procedures. Rather than concentrating almost wholly upon questions concerning the circumstances under which an unconditioned stimulus becomes connected to a conditioned stimulus, one should perhaps be inquiring as to the memory state of the organism with respect to the relationship between CS and US.

The critical experimental question was how to measure changes in tendency to perform some particular reference response originally evoked by an unconditioned stimulus. At this point, Skinner and I hit on the idea of indexing changes in an organism's memory in terms of indirect effects on some ongoing behavior. We found that we could trace with considerable sensitivity changes in an animal's memory for a tone-shock sequence, for example, by measuring the disturbing effects of the tone upon otherwise stable ongoing operant behavior (Estes & Skinner, 1941). Though the technique is one of frankly indirect measurement, this property sets it apart from the more traditional conditioning procedures only from the standpoint of a response-oriented, or stimulus-substitution, theory. From a memory-oriented theoretical viewpoint, all conditioning experiments involve indirect measurement, and decisions among them can be based only on considerations of reliability and fruitfulness of the data obtainable. In these respects, as is well known, the technique of the "conditioned emotional response" (CER) proved to stand rather well as attested by a now substantial literature; in particular, the CER has been a technique of choice by a number of recent investigators whose novel and intriguing results on such phenomena as the blocking effect (Kamin, 1969) and the role of reinforcement contingencies (Rescorla, 1969) have done much to rejuvenate interest in the whole field of conditioning. Following a somewhat different approach, Brown, Kalish, and Farber (1951) showed that latency of a startle response to an extraneous stimulus could be utilized to trace changes in strength of a CER.

The technique of indexing memory for consequences of a stimulus by its effects on some baseline performance is not, of course, limited to traumatic consequences. By use of a paradigm analogous to that of the CER, it proved possible to trace changes in an organism's memory for a rewarding event which followed an originally neutral stimulus (Estes, 1943, 1948; Herrnstein & Morse, 1957; Trapold & Overmeier, 1972).

But theory tends to lag behind experimental developments, and even today we hear the result of a conditioning experiment almost universally described in terms of the conditioning of a response rather than in terms of the storage of information in memory. I am not unmindful of the viewpoint which has been dubbed the S-S conception of conditioning (Spence, 1951), and which has long maintained a small presence, though lacking representation in major theories except as one of many component processes in Tolman's (1932, 1949) system. A few years ago I suggested that in our present state of knowledge the S-S conception provides a rather more promising basis than the S-R conception for the development of conditioning theory (Estes, 1969a). But in trying to work out the theoretical program I sketched then, I have begun to feel that the S-S conception, though a step in the right direction, is too small a step to take us far toward a theory that might account for the many new findings emerging from current studies of conditioning. Neither S-S association nor S-R associations, nor any manageably simple way of chaining these together, seems to provide a promising basis for explaining the ways in which various factors combine to determine performance in even the simplest conditioning and learning situations. A basic difficulty appears to be that the accumulation of information concerning relations between events which results from an organism's experiences in a conditioning situation enters into a more complex organization than can be represented by linear chaining of associations.

Since the most notable advances in the treatment of human memory during the last few years have been precisely in the area of handling organization of information, it has occurred to me to try to reverse the usual procedure—that is, to draw upon new developments in theories of memory to aid in the formulation of more adequate models for basic conditioning and learning. In the remainder of this chapter I should like to review a few of these recent developments in theories of memory, in particular those having to do with memory for order of events, and to explore in a very preliminary way the possibilities of carrying over some of the specific concepts which appear fruitful in connection with memory organization to the interpretation of conditioning.

Salient among the issues and distinctions which require consideration are the following: (a) the distinction between short-term and long-term memory; (b) memory for attributes versus memory for events; (c) the hierarchical organization of information as distinguished from chain associations; (d) the distinction between storage and retrieval processes and the concept of retrieval cues. In a general way I shall be following current usage as represented, for example, in Norman (1970) or in Tulving and Donaldson (1972). In details I shall be following the approach represented in my own recent work (Estes, 1970, 1972a) and in that of Bower and his associates (Anderson & Bower, 1972; Bower, 1972). First I shall discuss in a general way the mode of application of concepts of memory in relation to conditioning; then I shall try to illustrate the approach in operation by analyzing several basic conditioning paradigms.

THE COORDINATION OF CONCEPTS OF MEMORY TO CONCEPTS OF CONDITIONING

A distinction between short- and long-term memory is widely accepted among current investigators, but the precise nature of each of these and the relationship between them are matters of some controversy. My own view (shared at least by Konorski, 1967) is that short-term memory is nonassociative and represents, rather, a persisting excitation or reexcitation of neural representations of a stimulus and the organism's response to it. This persisting activity of the stimulus and response units depends upon the context in which the stimulus-response events occurred remaining intact and normally runs its course within a few seconds, the decay owing to inevitable shifts in context with time. I would suggest that a model representing this process—for example, the one developed in Estes (1972a)—can apply directly to experiments on short-term memory in animals—for example, delayed-response experiments—or to the special studies of short-term retention of stimulus information reported by Medin (1972). However, nearly all of the phenomena of conditioning are to be interpreted in terms of long-term memory processes which are basically associative in character.

Long-term retention of a conditioning experience requires the storage of information regarding attributes of behavioral events and their interrelations. What are the relevant attributes? The broadest, and perhaps the most fundamental, classification pertains to the type of drive system—positive or negative (adient or abient)—to which the stimulus is related (Pfaffmann, 1969; Schneirla, 1965). I hasten to add that this classification is not to be thought of as having to do with an immutable property of the stimulus; rather, we should assume that the association which will be formed, and the attribute which will be stored in memory, is determined by the general character of the reaction evoked by the particular stimulus in a particular context.

Progressing from the attributes which convey least to those which convey most specific information about the stimulus, an intermediate group would include modality and general properties of a sensory event such as abruptness of onset or offset of a stimulus. Still more specific attributes would be represented in associations relating to the outputs of analyzers, or feature detectors, having to do with such properties as pitch, color, and form.

In the spirit of virtually all treatments of long-term memory, we should assume that associations involving the broader categories are stored first, are most readily accessed, and therefore represent information which is best retained. Also it should be emphasized that my conception of a representation of a stimulus in memory is not simply a cluster of attributes, but rather a cluster of associations of attributes with the context in which the stimulus occurred. Thus retrieval of information stored in memory concerning a stimulus must always begin with reinstatement of at least a portion of the context in which the stimulus event occurred. However well established in memory, a stimulus will not be recognized if the context in which it occurred is completely changed, and, more generally, the probability of recognition of a previously experienced stimulus is assumed to be directly related to the degree of communality between the context at the time of the original stimulus event and the context at the time of a later test. By *context* I refer both to the background stimulation from an experimental environment and to internally generated stimulation arising from postural adjustments or drive states.

Long-term memory for the constituent events of a conditioning trial comprises, therefore, an assemblage of associations representing relations among aspects of these events. In informational terms, the organism's task is to remember that a CS and a US each occurred in a particular context and in a

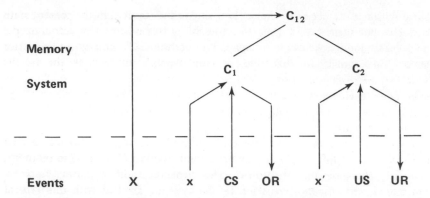

FIG. 1. Schema representing the memory structure resulting from an effective conditioning trial. Items *below* the dashed line denote input and output events, including background stimulation (X) and local context (x and x'). Items *above* the dashed line denote control elements of the memory system and bidirectional associative connections between them.

particular temporal relationship. A simplified schematization of the resulting memory structure is presented in Figure 1. The entries in the bottom row of the diagram denote observables, those in the upper rows representations in the memory system. The Cs with subscripts denote the relational elements (termed *control* elements—Estes, 1972a) of the memory system and replace the associations or connections of traditional association theory. The element C_1 denotes the representation in memory of the occurrence of a CS in a particular context x of background stimulation; C_2 denotes the representation of the US in a context x' which is largely, but not in general entirely, identical with that of the CS; C_{12} denotes the representation of the joint occurrence of the two behavioral events in relation to their common situational background X. The paths, denoted by arrows, between observables and control elements represent one-way communication, but all paths connecting control elements with one another represent two-way communication.

The basic rule for reactivation of control elements once they are established is temporal summation of inputs, any element being activated when it receives input simultaneously over any two paths connecting it with other control elements or with observables. Simultaneous stimulation from the CS and its local situational context activates C_1, and similarly simultaneous input from the US and its local context activates C_2. However, C_2 can also be activated in the absence of the US if simultaneous input from the background X and control element C_1 excites C_{12}, and then the output from C_{12} arrives at C_2 simultaneously with input from the local context x'.

When one is considering the implications of schemata such as that of Figure 1, it is natural to think in terms of transmission of nerve impulses from the receptors to the control elements and between the various control elements of the system. As a heuristic device this way of thinking may well be useful and is unlikely to lead to any confusion so long as one is clear that, in the present state of development of the model, the control elements are abstract concepts without any specific neurophysiological interpretation. To emphasize this latter point, I shall speak simply of transmission of information between the various elements of the system.

MEMORY AND PERFORMANCE

Given that the result of an effective conditioning experience is the establishment of associations between representations of CS and US in memory, how does the storage of information lead to a change in the organism's response on a subsequent presentation of the CS? In order to deal with this critical question, it is essential first of all to distinguish between direct and indirect connections of stimuli to responses. By direct connections I refer to the associative connections established during development of the organism which are assumed in virtually all theories of conditioning to be responsible for the reactions termed *original* or *unconditioned responses* to stimuli. On the more controversial question of the permanence of these direct connections, I shall assume that, once established, they are permanent and are not modified as a result of learning experiences. The considerations bearing on my decision at this choice point have been reviewed by Konorski (1967, p. 267). Further, it is necessary to assume that any stimulus which might serve as a US has multiple connections to reactive mechanisms at different levels of response specificity.

The higher, or nonspecific, level involves the connections of the stimulus with the neural mechanisms responsible for the generation of drive stimuli which deliver excitatory input to families of stimulus-response units. Examples of these families are consummatory behaviors in the case of stimuli associated with appetitive drives, defense or flight reactions in the case of stimuli associated with aversive drives. Excitatory input from the drive mechanisms (which I have elsewhere termed "stimulus amplifiers"—Estes, 1969a, 1969b) does not lead directly to overt responses. Its function is rather to produce a state of heightened excitability in a family of stimulus-response units. As a consequence of this heightened excitation, responses belonging to the given family are more likely to be evoked upon occurrence of the associated stimuli than responses to other competing stimuli in the situation which have not received the same facilitatory drive input.

The lower level of direct connections involves specific motor units. Only in special cases, including visceral reactions and some skeletal reflexes, do these direct connections evoke organized patterns of motor activity which occur relatively independently of context. In the majority of cases, including most skeletal behavior, the responses arising from direct stimulus-response connections are not fully determined in form by the innate organization; rather, the precise form of the response evoked depends also upon the current context of background stimulation.

In the latter cases it is to be assumed that the direct connections involve isolated motor units or subassemblies of them which must be combined with others evoked by concurrent stimuli to produce organized responses. Among the unconditioned responses commonly studied in conditioning experiments, the pupillary response and the GSR would fall in the category of those which are relatively context-free; unconditioned responses in eyelid or salivary conditioning experiments depend to some extent on context, and withdrawal from a shock stimulus would represent an instance of a response strongly dependent on context.

Indirect connections between stimuli and responses, which include all of those established by conditioning and learning, are mediated by associations between representations of stimulus events in memory. Evocation of a response via an indirect connection occurs when the stimulus presented on a given occasion is associated by way of a control element with another stimulus which is connected to the given response and which at the time of conditioning occurred in a context identical to or at least overlapping that of the evoking stimulus. The resultant form of the conditioned response depends upon the similarity of the two contexts and the degree of organization of the original stimulus-response connections. Context-free responses are carried over largely as units, whereas context-dependent responses change in form to fit the new situation.

In cases in which an unconditioned response is relatively context-free, its later evocation by a conditioned stimulus is a useful index of the extent to which the organism has stored an association between the two stimuli in memory. But when the unconditioned response is relatively context-dependent, it may be difficult to define any form of the unconditioned response which can be identified as a later response to the conditioned stimulus. However, we have noted that any unconditioned stimulus evokes activity of some drive mechanism in addition to any directly connected motor units. Since positive and negative drive mechanisms are mutually inhibitory (Estes, 1969a, 1969b), this circumstance provides a basis for the indirect measurement of memory of a stimulus referred to in the introduction to this chapter. If, for example, an unconditioned stimulus (say an electric shock) is associated with a negative drive mechanism, then activation of the representation of this stimulus in memory via an association with the conditioned stimulus may be indexed by the extent to which presentation of the CS results in interference with an ongoing response maintained by a positive drive, as in the case of the CER.

Two aspects of the model as already presented bear on the question of the precise point in time following CS onset at which the conditioned response should be expected to occur. Firstly, temporal attributes of stimuli are properties which can be represented in memory just as other aspects of a stimulus event. An important consequence of this assumption is that, once a representation of a CS has been formed in memory, this representation will not be fully activated on a later occasion until the original stimulus duration has been reproduced. Secondly, the local context, departures from which constitute effective stimuli, in general varies somewhat even within a single conditioning trial. In particular, continuing stimulation from a CS (under a delay procedure) constitutes part of the local context at US onset and distinguishes this local context from that of the time of CS onset.

As already indicated, probability of evocation of a response, in this instance the unconditioned response, via an indirect association varies directly with the degree to which the original local context of the US has been reproduced. On a test trial in a conditioning experiment, the point in time at which there is maximum reinstatement of local context falls at the point in time following CS onset at which the US previously occurred. Thus it is implied that under a classical conditioning procedure, CRs will tend to occur with a latency approaching the original CS-US interval.

INHIBITION AND INHIBITORY ASSOCIATIONS

We have seen that it is quite easy to find a natural translation from the idea of excitatory connections between stimulus and response events to that of storage of information in memory concerning relations between events. But we cannot go much further in the interpretation of conditioning phenomena until we are able to bring inhibitory processes also into the system. The task is rendered particularly difficult by the multiplicity of meanings of "inhibition." In its most universal, and perhaps most basic, application, the term *inhibition* refers to the reciprocally interfering effects of simultaneously excited control or response units which compete for common output pathways. I shall follow the lead of Guthrie (1935) and Konorski (1967) in limiting usage of the term inhibition to this type of reciprocal interaction. Numerous phenomena of conditioning are customarily interpreted in terms of additional concepts of internal and external inhibition (Pavlov, 1927), reactive inhibition (Hull, 1943), and so on. However, rather than multiplying basic concepts, I should like to investigate the possibility that these phenomena can be adequately interpreted in terms of the limited concept of inhibition together with the set of concepts we have drawn from more general theories of memory.

Inhibitory processes will be assumed to enter into the memory system in a manner entirely analogous to that of excitatory processes. Thus, just as I have defined positive, or excitatory, associations as representations in memory of excitatory interactions between elements of the memory system, I shall use the term *inhibitory association* to denote the representation in memory of the outcome of an inhibitory interaction. Two principal cases will be of basic importance in the interpretation of conditioning phenomena.

The first involves reciprocal inhibition among alternative responses to a single stimulus. In many instances the stimulus used as a US in a conditioning experiment is associated with a number of incompatible responses. This is typically the case with electric shock, for example. In such instances, onset of the US results in excitatory input to all of the associated responses; since only one can occur overtly at a time, the response most strongly excited inhibits its competitors. The assumption concerning this type of inhibition that I propose incorporating into the memory model is that the result of an inhibitory interaction among responses is represented in the memory system by inhibitory associations running from the prepotent to the inhibited response units. The significance of the inhibitory associations is that the response last evoked by a stimulus on a given occasion will have increased probability of being the first evoked on the next recurrence of the situation.

The second principal type of inhibitory association represents memory for an inhibitory interaction between the activations of two different stimulus representations in memory. The occasion for such an interaction arises when some stimulus, say S_1, has occurred in a context x, giving rise to a representation in memory, C_1, and subsequently a different stimulus, S_2, is presented in the same context x. The result of this sequence of events, as illustrated in Figure 2, is the establishment of a higher-level control element, C_{12}, associating the two stimuli with each other and the common context, but in addition an inhibitory association from C_2 to C_1. The result is that when on a later occasion the control element C_{12} is activated by virtue of its association with some other element then active in memory, excitatory input is transmitted to both C_1 and C_2, but the inhibitory association suppresses the former, and therefore only memory of S_2 is reactivated. An important application of this schema will occur in the interpretation of extinction, when US and no-US take on the roles of S_1 and S_2.

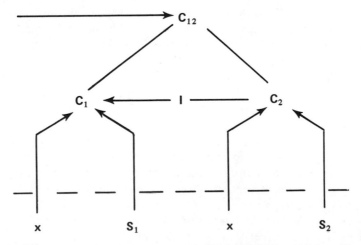

FIG. 2. Simplified schema showing the inhibitory association (I) between two control elements resulting from an inhibitory interaction between two stimuli which occurred successively in the same local context (x).

INTERPRETATIONS OF CONDITIONING SITUATIONS

With the basic machinery now in hand, it will be possible to elucidate the intended meaning and usage of the concepts of the memory model by considering the interpretation of a number of variants of standard conditioning situations.

Sensitization

Let us consider first of all the effect of a simple presentation of an unconditioned stimulus alone. The result will be storage of information in memory that the given stimulus occurred in that particular context. In terms of the model, a control element is established representing the association of the US with the given context. The behavioral result is that when the organism is returned to the given situation, reinstatement of the context will result in partial excitation of the representation of the US, thus increasing the probability that any other stimulus which shares attributes with the US will activate the US representation and lead to occurrence of a UR. This result would be termed "sensitization" or "pseudoconditioning."

Establishment of an Inhibitory Stimulus

The minimal experimental conditions for a stimulus S_I to become inhibitory are that this stimulus and some US involving direct connections to at least partially incompatible drive and response units be presented repeatedly in the same situation, but be negatively correlated so that the US never occurs during some critical interval following presentation of S_I but has a relatively high probability of occurring when there has been a longer interval following the last S_I occurrence. The result in terms of the model is that for the organism the experimental context will be differentiated into two local contexts, x which prevails immediately following S_I occurrences and x' which prevails at other times. Since the US occurs in context x', the elements of x' become associated with the representation C_u of the US in memory. The onset of stimulus S_I is always followed by $\overline{US}$—absence of the US. Therefore the representation of S_I in memory becomes associated with that of $\overline{US}$. When the organism enters context x', the level of excitation of C_u is raised, but if S_I then occurs, the representation of $\overline{US}$ is activated in memory and inhibits the facilitatory input from x' to C_u. The result is that presentation of the US either simultaneously with or just following S_I will yield a diminution of the UR.

Interaction of OR and UR during Conditioning

The general treatment of a simple conditioning experiment has been outlined in a previous section, but it is of interest to consider the way in which the original response OR to the conditioned stimulus interacts with the UR as a function of the CS-US interval. When a CS and US are presented in succession in a conditioning situation, representations of each in their local contexts and an association between them are established in memory. The result is a tendency for a presentation of the CS to lead to occurrence of the UR by way of an indirect connection. The CS together with its context activates the control element associating the two stimuli, and this in turn excites the representation of the US in memory, which in turn leads to evocation of the UR. If on a paired presentation the interval between the two stimuli is such that the US occurs before or during evocation of OR by the CS, then an inhibitory interaction between the two response tendencies occurs, the result under normal conditions of stimulus intensity relationships being that the OR is inhibited and the UR is evoked by the US. The result of this sequence is the establishment of an inhibitory association so that on subsequent occasions, activation of the US representation by the CS leads to suppression of the OR and evocation of the UR only. If the CS-US interval is lengthened just enough so that the inhibitory interaction does not occur on a conditioning trial, then no inhibitory association is formed, and the result to be expected on a later test is that presentation of the CS will lead first to the OR and then to the UR.

Experimental Extinction

The experimental operations giving rise to extinction are a paired presentation of a CS and US followed by repeated presentations of the CS alone. In informational terms, the organism first stores information that the CS and US occurred together in a given context, then information that the CS occurred in

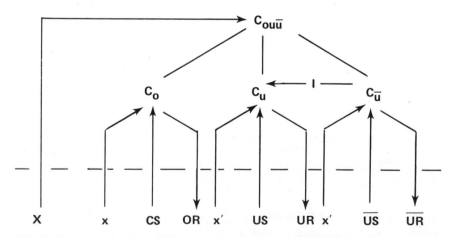

FIG. 3. Memory structure resulting from conditioning followed by extinction. During extinction, no-US ($\overline{US}$) occurred following the CS; consequently an inhibitory association was established between the representation of $\overline{US}$ and that of the US.

the same context without the US, and finally information as to the order in which these events occurred. The representation in terms of the memory model of the excitatory and inhibitory associations is illustrated in Figure 3. The crux of the interpretation is that the organism first forms a representation in memory of the occurrence of US in a particular local context x' and an association of this with the preceding CS, then is led to form a representation of an incompatible stimulus situation, no-US ($\overline{US}$ in the figure), in the same local context x'. Representations of two different stimulus patterns in the same context cannot be activated simultaneously; consequently there is an inhibitory interaction, and the representation of the US, which is undergoing activation by associations in memory, is inhibited by the representation of no-US, which is activated by incoming stimulation on the extinction trial. The result is establishment of an inhibitory association so that on later occasions presentation of the CS activates only the representation in memory of no-US. It should be noted further than since the original response OR to the CS ceases to occur during conditioning only because of inhibition from activation of the US in memory, this source of inhibition will be removed during extinction and the OR will again tend to be evoked by the CS since its direct connections remain intact.

Escape Conditioning

The present model offers a particularly simple interpretation of experiments involving escape contingencies. In a typical experimental routine, the organism is confined in the apparatus and an unconditioned stimulus, most often an electric shock, is administered, with stimulation continuing until some predesignated response occurs. We must assume that the shock has direct connections to a variety of responses ($R_1, R_2, \ldots, R_E$) of which only R_E will be effective in terminating the shock. The first consequence of a conditioning trial is that a representation of the US in its context will be established in the memory system. Then as each of the responses R_i occurs and fails to terminate the US, it will be supplanted by another, and the consequence of the inhibitory interaction will be the establishment of an inhibitory association between the two; and this process will continue until R_E occurs. Since only R_E can never be the recipient of an inhibitory association, it will tend to occur earlier on successive trials until it has supplanted all competing responses and occurs with minimal latency. The representation of the final state of affairs in the memory system will be as illustrated in Figure 4.

Rather direct evidence bearing on this interpretation is available in a series of studies of escape conditioning in rats by Woods and his associates (Woods & Holland, 1966; Woods, Markman, Lynch, & Stokely, in press). These investigators recorded detailed observations of both an escape response (swimming from an "alley" tank containing cold water into a "goal" tank containing warmer water) and various overt competing responses during both conditioning and extinction. They found that the systematic reduction in escape time during

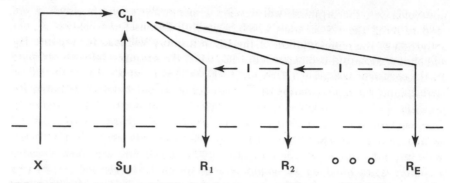

FIG. 4. Memory structure established during escape conditioning, with inhibitory associations from the escape response (R_E) to extraneous responses R_1, R_2, etc.

conditioning resulted from "the gradual elimination of competing responses, with the relevant response of swimming remaining essentially unchanged [Woods & Holland, 1966, p. 405]."

According to the present model, connections of the "eliminated" competing responses to the US and context are actually unchanged during conditioning, but these responses are suppressed by inhibitory associations from the escape response. Consequently, during extinction the source of inhibitory input will be removed, and the competing responses should be expected again to appear overtly. This implication of the model is in good accord with the observations of Woods et al. (in press) that during extinction, competing responses regularly reappear in virtually full strength.

The escape-conditioning paradigm is transformed into that of avoidance by the addition of a CS whose onset precedes that of the US and a contingency such that occurrence of response R_E during a critical interval following CS onset prevents the administration of the US. In terms of the memory model, the course of conditioning up to the point of the first successful avoidance response involves nothing new, being simply a combination of classical and escape conditioning. On early trials the latency of R_E to US onset progressively decreases, and in addition the organism establishes representations of the CS and US in memory such that CS onset comes to evoke recall of the US. Ultimately the escape response R_E occurs with sufficiently short latency following CS onset so that the US is avoided. How can we account for the fact that this short latency response may become stable rather than undergoing infinite cycles of conditioning and extinction?

The answer in terms of the present model is that the organism must distinguish the difference in local context following CS onset on occasions when it has initiated R_E in contrast to occasions when the immediate response to the CS is any behavior other than R_E; let us denote the two local contexts as $\bar{x}'$ and x'. During a sequence of trials involving a mixture of avoidances and nonavoidances, the organism will develop a memory structure in which it will tend to recall the US on trials which begin with CS onset and context x', but activation of the representation of the US in memory will lead to response R_E and thus a successful avoidance. On trials when the organism initiates response R_E immediately following CS onset, it will be in context $\bar{x}'$; the result will be activation of the representation of US (absence of shock), but since response R_E has already occurred, this also will be a successful avoidance trial. The prediction from the theory then is a final state of affairs in which nearly all trials are avoidances but in which the latency of the avoidance response fluctuates, increasing following avoidance responses and decreasing following nonavoidance responses. Data obtained in avoidance experiments with rats and guinea pigs have frequently been found to confirm this expectation (see, for example, Sheffield, 1948).

I hasten to add that I am well aware that other avoidance experiments, particularly those conducted with dogs as subjects and utilizing long CS-US intervals and intense shocks, lead to a more stable final state in which a short-latency avoidance response is maintained over long series of trials (see, for example, Solomon & Wynne, 1954; Wahlsten & Cole, 1972). I am inclined to believe that these cases can be interpreted within the memory model without any basically new assumptions; however, they require more detailed discussion of the interactions of negative and positive drive systems than can be undertaken in the present paper.

Higher-Order Conditioning

One speaks of higher-order conditioning if, following the conditioning of a CR to a CS, some new, originally neutral, stimulus CS_2 is paired with the first CS, and following such paired presentations CS_2 exhibits some tendency to evoke the CR. In terms either of classical conditioning theory or of the memory model, one would expect that higher-order conditioning might be generally difficult to achieve and unstable at best. The reason is that on the trials when CS_2 is paired with CS, no US is presented, and consequently these constitute extinction trials for the original conditioned response to the CS. Therefore during the paired presentation trials, extinction of the conditioned response to CS must be occurring concurrently with conditioning of the same response to CS_2. In terms of the memory model, the organism should be expected to acquire the information that CS_2 is followed by the CS but not by the US; therefore occurrences of CS_2 would evoke a representation in memory of CS only and thus would not lead to a conditioned response.

In Pavlov's original studies and in most of the relevant work reported since, higher-order conditioning has indeed been found a somewhat unstable and fragile phenomenon. Thus it is striking to find in the series of very carefully conducted studies reported in the present volume by Rescorla that the higher-order CR is not only readily and reliably obtained but is so robust that it can be subjected to many novel lines of analysis.

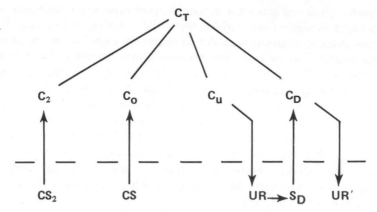

FIG. 5. Memory structure established during higher-order conditioning in which CS_2 is paired with a CS which has previously been paired with a US. Drive stimulus feedback from the UR is denoted S_D, and the response evoked by S_D is UR'.

I suspect that Rescorla's unusual success in obtaining robust higher-order conditioning is related to his use of the conditioned suppression technique with an unconditioned stimulus (electric shock) which evokes a broad spectrum of visceral and muscular reactions. Therefore the unconditioned response immediately gives rise to a massive barrage of interoceptive and proprioceptive stimulation which is associated with aversive drive mechanisms. In terms of the memory model, the result of an effective conditioning experience is that the CS comes to activate a representation in memory not only of the US but also of the stimulus complex S_D generated by the unconditioned response. Therefore on a higher-order conditioning trial, when CS_2 is paired with a CS which has preceded shock, even though the shock does not occur, there is opportunity for the representation of CS_2 to become associated in memory with representations of the CS and also the representation of S_D. The memory structure resulting from an effective higher-order conditioning trial would be as illustrated in Figure 5, the contextual terms being omitted for simplicity. It would be difficult to predict in advance the precise form of the response that would be evoked by CS_2 following such a higher-order conditioning experience, since the response pattern (UR') to S_D would in general not be entirely the same as the response pattern evoked by the shock itself. However, the drive components would be very similar, and it could be predicted with assurance that presentation of CS_2 would lead to interference with an ongoing response maintained by food reinforcement, as in Rescorla's conditioned suppression experiments.

This analysis enables us to account for an otherwise surprising phenomenon arising from one of Rescorla's ingenious variations on the higher-order conditioning paradigm. In one of his experiments (Rescorla, this volume), animals were given standard CER conditioning trials on which a CS was paired with shock, then higher-order conditioning trials on which CS_2 was paired with CS in the absence of shock. Now before testing for higher-order conditioning, Rescorla gave a series of extinction trials on which the CS occurred without shock. His intention was to test a type of memory hypothesis in which presentation of CS_2 following higher-order conditioning would lead to recall of the CS and this in turn to recall of the US. In the present experiment, in view of the interpolated extinction trials, one might expect that on a test with CS_2 there would be evoked memory for the CS but none for the US, and therefore that no CER would be observed. However, in terms of the analysis just given, we observe that even though the association between CS and shock may have been neutralized by an inhibitory association as a result of the extinction trials (the presentation of CS now leading to recall of no-US), nothing has occurred that would be expected to interfere with the association between CS_2 and the representation in memory of S_D which had been established on the higher-order conditioning trials. Thus we would predict the result which Rescorla observed, namely, that on the test trials in his experiment, CS_2 evoked the CER even though the original CS did not.

Sensory Preconditioning

Another variant of the classical conditioning paradigm which may be handled in an extremely natural way in terms of the memory model is sensory preconditioning. This procedure is rather closely related to that of higher-order conditioning, differing only in the sequence of operations. In the case of sensory preconditioning, paired presentations of CS_2 and CS would be given at the beginning of the experiment, then the CS would be paired with the US, and finally test trials would be given in order to determine whether CS_2 now evoked a conditioned response. In general positive results have been rather more consistently obtained in a variety of situations with the sensory preconditioning paradigm than with that of higher-order conditioning.

In terms of the memory model, the first stage of a sensory preconditioning experiment results in the establishment of a control element representing the association of the representation in memory of CS_2 with the representation in memory of CS. During the second stage of the experiment, the representation of the CS comes to evoke in turn a representation in memory of the US. The resulting memory structure would be as illustrated, in simplified form, in Figure 6. The prediction of the model is, of course, that on a final test, presentation of CS_2 should activate a representation of CS in memory, and that this in turn should activate a representation of US leading to occurrence of the response associated with the US; in this instance the result would be observation of a CER. Once again, Rescorla posed an additional problem for theory by introducing a variation in the experiment in which he gave animals sensory preconditioning (CS_2-CS) followed by conditioning (CS-US) trials, then gave a period of extinction on which the CS was presented without the US before a test

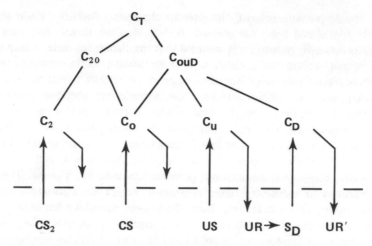

FIG. 6. Memory structure established during sensory preconditioning in which CS_2 is first paired with CS, then CS with US.

for sensory preconditioning. In this situation, unlike the case of higher-order conditioning discussed in the previous section, there is no opportunity for a representation of S_D in memory to become associated with CS_2 during the sensory preconditioning trials. Consequently when the link in memory between CS and US is rendered ineffective by extinction trials, the result on a final test should be that presentation of CS_2 will yield recall of the CS but no recall of the US and therefore no CER. This is the result reported by Rescorla.

DISCUSSION

The preceding sections may serve to illustrate in a provisional way some of the possibilities of interpreting conditioning phenomena in terms of a more general theory of memory. The model outlined for this purpose envisages conditioning as the establishment of a structure in memory which incorporates representations of stimuli in context and associations between these representations.

The model I have presented cannot be localized strictly within either the S-R or the S-S tradition in learning theory. The present theory recognizes no basic distinction between stimuli and responses—all behavioral events have both aspects. The stimulus as it comes to be represented in memory is the stimulus as reacted to by the organism; this conception is close to Lawrence's (1963) "stimulus as coded," but places more emphasis upon the relations between stimulus and context. A response always involves stimulus feedback, and the representation of this feedback in memory has the same properties as the representation of any other stimulus.

In one important respect the present theory is closer to those learning theories that have been categorized as S-S than to those that have been categorized as S-R. Namely, it is assumed that the change in mode of response to a CS which occurs as a result of a conditioning experience is mediated by the organism's memory for the sequence of stimuli it has been exposed to rather than a simple rerouting of connections between stimuli and responses. I see the greatest communality between my formulation and that of Wagner (1969), whose analyses of contingencies in conditioning derive from the concepts of "signal value" and "informativeness" of stimuli.

However, memory alone does not generate performance. The evocation of a CR is assumed to occur when a representation of the US is activated in memory simultaneously with actual input from the at least partially reinstated stimulus context in which the UR occurred. The response that results always reflects interaction of stimulus (or memory of a stimulus) and context. Only the drive components of unconditioned responses are assumed to be largely exempt from this restriction (that is, to be virtually context-free); thus it is these components that provide the most sensitive indices of memory for stimulus sequences.

The structure established in memory as a result of conditioning is assumed to be hierarchical in organization rather than a matter of serial chain associations. The representation of an association between two stimuli in the present model is not just a connection, or pathway, but rather a control unit (control element) which can in turn relate both constituents to other units in memory.

An important aspect of the hierarchical organization is the dominance of situational context. The entire hierarchical structure resulting from an effective conditioning experience is inactive unless the situational background of the conditioning trial is at least partially reinstated. However, background cues do not combine with stimulation from a CS or US in an additive fashion. Summation of inputs from background and a specific stimulus (or memory of a stimulus) is required, and in the absence of either component no overt response is evoked.

The hierarchical model with the summation principle appears to account in a rather simple and natural way for the dominance of situational context observed in many of the Russian studies of Pavlovian conditioning. In particular, it is an implication of the model that a CR established in one experimental situation will not be evoked if the CS is tested in an entirely different situation. The other side of the coin is that repeated conditioning trials, and in particular repeated trials with relatively wide temporal spacing, provide an opportunity for a CR to become imbedded in a wider range of situational contexts and thus increase the probability of evocation of the CR in a new test situation. Another obvious implication is that there should be no difficulty in establishing different CR's to the same CS in two different experimental situations. Intuitively I should expect this prediction to be confirmed, but I have not found relevant experiments in the classical conditioning literature.[1]

Inhibition enters into the present theory, not as a special process or state, but as memory of inhibitory interactions, represented by inhibitory associations which have the same properties with regard to learning as excitatory associations.

Even in the present preliminary stage of development, the memory model provides not merely another way of talking in general terms about conditioning, but rather a systematic and integrated interpretation of a variety of specific phenomena. These include: the interaction between the original responses to the CS and US during conditioning and extinction; the point of occurrence of the CR in the CS-US interval; relationships between classical, escape, and avoidance conditioning; the relationship between higher-order conditioning and sensory preconditioning, and in particular the way each of these is affected by extinction of the conditioned response to the primary CS before test of the secondary CS.

It seems that the model should be readily extendable also to instrumental and operant conditioning. Presumably the same concepts regarding memory would be employed, but with an important role for the drive feedback mechanism (Estes, 1969a, 1969b) in mediating the connection between memory and performance. However, detailed consideration of the instrumental and operant cases is beyond the scope of the present chapter.

I believe one of the principal results of the present investigation is to show that there need be no sharp dichotomy between treatments of conditioning in terms of memory and in terms of more traditional concepts of association. Analyses in terms of ideas of information processing lead to new ways of looking at some phenomena. However, the results of informational analyses can be incorporated in an associational model, though one richer in content and more complex in structure than those of more traditional conditioning and learning theory.

One of the advantages of continuing to maintain close correspondence between concepts of memory and concepts of association has to do with the ease of relating psychological to neurophysiological theory. The most ambitious and elaborate effort toward a neurophysiological model of conditioning that has appeared in the literature is that of Konorski (1967). As compared to Konorski's earlier (1948) formulation, the new theory shows a major shift from a response-oriented toward a memory-oriented framework, but without any sharp break from the associationist tradition. Konorski's distinction between perceptual and associative processes seems to correspond in a general way to my distinction between encoded representations of stimuli and control elements, Konorski's "gnosic units" representing a proposed neurophysiological mechanism with much the same function as the control elements in my theory.

---

[1] Note added in proofs: For confirmatory findings, see E. A. Asratian, Genesis and localization of conditioned inhibition. In R. A. Boakes and M. S. Halliday (Eds.), *Inhibition and Learning.* New York: Academic Press, 1972. Pp. 381–397.

Perhaps the most important similarity between Konorski's approach and mine, however, is our common interest in opening the traditionally rather compartmentalized area of conditioning to more fruitful interactions with other disciplines having to do with the broad problems of information storage and retrieval.

REFERENCES

Anderson, J. R., & Bower, G. H. Recognition and retrieval processes in free recall. *Psychological Review*, 1972, 79, 97–123.

Bower, G. H. Stimulus-sampling theory of encoding variability. In A. W. Melton & E. Martin (Eds.), *Coding processes in human memory*. Washington, D. C.: Winston, 1972.

Brown, J. S., Kalish, H. I., & Farber, I. E. Conditioned fear as revealed by magnitude of startle response to an auditory stimulus. *Journal of Experimental Psychology*, 1951, 41, 317–328.

Estes, W. K. Discriminative conditioning. I. A discriminative property of conditioned anticipation. *Journal of Experimental Psychology*, 1943, 32, 150–155.

Estes, W. K. Discriminative conditioning. II. Effects of a Pavlovian conditioned stimulus upon a subsequently established operant response. *Journal of Experimental Psychology*, 1948, 38, 173–177.

Estes, W. K. New perspectives on some old issues in association theory. In N. J. MacKintosh. & W. K. Honig (Eds.), *Fundamental issues in associative learning*. Halifax, N. S.: Dalhousie University Press, 1969. Pp. 162–189. (a)

Estes, W. K. Outline of a theory of punishment. In B. A. Campbell & R. M. Church (Eds.), *Punishment and aversive behavior*. New York: Appleton-Century-Crofts, 1969. Pp. 57–82. (b)

Estes, W. K. *Learning theory and mental development*. New York: Academic Press, 1970.

Estes, W. K. An associative basis for coding and organization in memory. In A. W. Melton & E. Martin (Eds.), *Coding processes in human memory*. Washington, D. C.: Winston, 1972. (a)

Estes, W. K. Learning. In P. C. Dodwell (Ed.), *New horizons in psychology, II*. London: Penguin Education, 1972. (b)

Estes, W. K., & Skinner, B. F. Some quantitative properties of anxiety. *Journal of Experimental Psychology*, 1941, 29, 390–400.

Guthrie, E. R. *The psychology of learning*. New York: Harper, 1935.

Herrnstein, R. J., & Morse, W. H. Some effects of response-independent positive reinforcement on maintained operant behavior. *Journal of Comparative and Physiological Psychology*, 1957, 50, 461–467.

Hull, C. L. *Principles of behavior*. New York: Appleton-Century-Crofts, 1943.

Kamin, L. J. Selective association and conditioning. In N. J. MacKintosh & W. K. Honig (Eds.), *Fundamental issues in associative learning*. Halifax, N. S.: Dalhousie University Press, 1969. Pp. 42–64.

Kimble, G. A. *Hilgard and Marquis' Conditioning and Learning*. New York: Appleton-Century-Crofts, 1961.

Konorski, J. *Conditioned reflexes and neuron organization*. Cambridge: Cambridge University Press, 1948.

Konorski, J. *Integrative activity of the brain*. Chicago: University of Chicago Press, 1967.

Lawrence, D. H. The nature of a stimulus: Some relationships between learning and perception. In S. Koch (Ed.), *Psychology: A study of a science*. Vol. 5. New York: McGraw-Hill, 1963. Pp. 179–212.

Medin, D. L. Evidence for short- and long-term memory in monkeys. *American Journal of Psychology*, 1972, 85, 117–120.

Norman, D. A. (Ed.), *Models of human memory*. New York: Academic Press, 1970.

Pavlov, I. P. *Conditioned reflexes*. Trans. by G. V. Anrep. London: Oxford University Press, 1927.

Pfaffmann, C. Taste preference and reinforcement. In J. Tapp (Ed.), *Reinforcement and behavior*. New York: Academic Press, 1969. Pp. 215–241.

Rescorla, R. A. Conditioned inhibition of fear. In N. J. MacKintosh & W. K. Honig (Eds.), *Fundamental issues in associative learning*. Halifax, N. S.: Dalhousie University Press, 1969. Pp. 65–89.

Schneirla, T. C. Aspects of stimulation and organization in approach/withdrawal processes underlying vertebrate behavioral development. *Advances in the Study of Behavior*, 1965, 1, 1–74.

Sheffield, F. D. Avoidance training and the contiguity principle. *Journal of Comparative and Physiological Psychology*, 1948, 41, 165–177.

Skinner, B. F. *The behavior of organisms*. New York: Appleton-Century-Crofts, 1938.

Solomon, R. L., & Wynne, L. C. Traumatic avoidance learning: The principles of anxiety conservation and partial irreversibility. *Psychological Review*, 1954, 61, 353–385.

Spence, K. W. Theoretical interpretations of learning. In S. S. Stevens (Ed.), *Handbook of experimental psychology*. New York: Wiley, 1951. Pp. 690–729.

Tolman, E. C. *Purposive behavior in animals and men*. New York: Appleton-Century-Crofts, 1932.

Tolman, E. C. There is more than one kind of learning. *Psychological Review*, 1949, 56, 144–155.

Trapold, M. A., & Overmeier, J. B. The second learning process in instrumental conditioning. In A. H. Black & W. F. Prokasy (Eds.), *Classical conditioning II*. New York: Appleton-Century-Crofts, 1972. Pp. 427–452.

Tulving, E., & Donaldson, W. *Organization of memory*. New York: Academic Press, 1972.

Wagner, A. R. Stimulus validity and stimulus selection in associative learning. In N. J. MacKintosh & W. K. Honig (Eds.), *Fundamental issues in associative learning*. Halifax, N. S.: Dalhousie University Press, 1969. Pp. 90–122.

Wahlsten, D. L., & Cole, M. Classical and avoidance training of leg flexions in the dog. In A. H. Black & W. F. Prokasy (Eds.), *Classical conditioning II*. New York: Appleton-Century-Crofts, 1972. Pp. 379–408.

Warner, L. H. An experimental search for the "conditioned response." *Journal of Genetic Psychology*, 1932, 41, 91–115.

Woods, P. J., & Holland, C. H. Instrumental escape conditioning in a water tank: Effects of constant reinforcement at different levels of drive stimulus intensity. *Journal of Comparative and Physiological Psychology*, 1966, 62, 403–408.

Woods, P. J., Markman, B. S., Lynch, W. C., & Stokely, S. N. Partial reinforcement effects in instrumental escape conditioning. *Learning and Motivation*, in press.

Zener, K. The significance of behavior accompanying conditioned salivary secretion for theories of the conditioned response. *American Journal of Psychology*, 1937, 50, 384–403.

12
COGNITIVE PRINCIPLES?[1]

David Premack[2]
University of California at Santa Barbara

In this chapter I will discuss four possible psychological mechanisms which, despite considerable laboratory maneuvering, I still cannot discuss as other than possibilities. These possibilities concern what we may call: (*a*) symbolization—a process whereby one item is represented by another item; (*b*) rule induction—a process whereby the subject induces or figures out the rule that can be used to generate the exemplars that he experienced; (*c*) transformations—mechanisms that can be used to solve problems; and (*d*) the structure of memory and its possible effect on what is learned.

Each of these possibilities concerns a mechanism which, for proper understanding, should be placed in the context of theory. Ideally, we should say, here is how information is acquired and used, and here is the place and role of the putative mechanism in that overall scheme. Nonetheless, I am going to shun this larger responsibility. It may not be premature, despite the paucity of data, to propose a theory of mental operations, but those I am familiar with do not seem to represent a significant advance on common sense; and I cannot do any better. So, rather than put simple maidens in fancy dresses—outfit common sense with technical language—I will be content to describe each possibility more or less in isolation of the other, without benefit of a theoretical frame, and concentrate on the operational analysis. What do we mean by the possibility? How can we test for it? And what guidance is given by available snippets of data?

[1] This research was supported by grant MH-15616 from the National Institutes of Health.
[2] I am indebted to Deborah Barone, Amy Samuels, and Michael McClure for their patience and ingenuity in collecting the present data.

EFFECT OF MEMORY STRUCTURE ON
WHAT IS LEARNED

Start with the most sweeping and necessarily least clear of the possibilities, which is compensated somewhat by the fact that we have more data in this case than in some others. This is the proposal that what a subject learns is affected by the memory structure. Even though no one has offered a fully persuasive model of memory, there is unanimity on this point: memory has some structure. Information is not stored in a random manner. Models appeal to hierarchical organizations of one kind or another (e.g., Kintsch, 1970); in addition, structuralists hold that the form or organization of memory is not learned but is a product of the hard wiring. For the sake of discussion, assume that something along these lines is roughly the case: the individual, given normal experience, will end up with his knowledge stored in a largely predetermined fashion. What consequences could this have for learning, more specifically for the course of learning?

Because memory has a structure, information will be acquired in a definite order. An elegant deductive approach to this hypothesis would consist in assuming a specific memory structure and then predicting from that structure either the order in which the subject will learn certain things, or the most efficient order in which to present the information to the subject. We will settle for a simpler approach, in keeping with the informal nature of the present hypothesis. After first describing the experimental situation in which the naive subject appears to learn nothing, I will show that, in fact, it learns several things; the things learned appear to follow a definite order, perhaps a necessary one, and this order can be understood by assuming that it is the product of a hierarchical memory structure.

The experimental situation is one in which we are trying to teach a simplified form of written language to young chimpanzees, and more recently to dogs. In the beginning the attempt could not be more frustrating. Despite hundreds of trials, the subject appears to learn nothing. Finally, however, it does learn. And then, equally mysterious, the same training procedure that earlier appeared to teach nothing, succeeds nicely.

Consider the situation. The chimp is presented with a piece of fruit and a piece of colored plastic. The plastic is backed with metal and, if placed on a magnetized vertical board alongside the chimp, will adhere lightly to the board. The chimp has been trained to put the plastic on the board, after which it is given the piece of fruit. After four or five such trials, a new piece of fruit is introduced, along with a new word, and the process is repeated. These errorless trials, in which only one would-be word is present, are followed by choice trials, in which the subject is presented with one piece of fruit and two words. The choice trials serve to show whether or not the subject learned anything on the errorless trials and, of course, can also serve as a source of learning; if the subject places the correct word on the board, it receives a piece of fruit; otherwise not.

We typically introduce several pairs of words concurrently, whether learning has taken place on the first pair or not. We start the subject with, say, the pair apple-banana, giving errorless trials on each as described, follow this with choice trials, and repeat the cycle, errorless trials–choice trials, until learning is shown. At the same time we start a second pair of fruits, say, raisin-apricot, with the same training, and often a third pair as well, say, grape-orange.

To adapt the procedure to the dogs, the trainer placed either one or two words (on errorless and choice trials, respectively) about 2 feet behind the animal and then sat down facing the dog. Food was shown the dog, after which it turned around, picked up a word in its mouth and brought it to the trainer. The trainer took the word, giving food on all errorless trials and on those choice trials when the dog was correct. Words were made of blocks of wood and varied in size, shape, and design. Most of the training was noncorrection, for both the chimp and dogs, though when subjects were upset by errors, they were allowed to correct.

We say the subject has learned nothing when, for example, it is offered the would-be words "apple" and "banana," in the presence of a piece of apple on some trials and a banana on others, and responds at chance level. By learning we have in mind an item-item relation. The relation between the word "apple" and the piece of apple, for example, or that between the word "banana" and the piece of banana.

But item-item relations are only one of several relations that are contained in this situation. For example, the sophisticated subject will almost immediately divide the stimuli into two classes, words or symbols on the one hand, and referents on the other. That he imposes this classification can be seen in the different operators he associates with each class. He eats members of one class and puts members of the other class on the board. Moreover, he does this before learning the item-item relations. At a time when the subject does not yet know what word goes with what fruit, he nonetheless does not attempt to eat the words nor to write with the fruits. This is true for the sophisticated subject, the normal child, for example.

To appreciate that not all subjects know the operator-class relations, you have only to watch the naive chimp when it is first transferred from the production to the comprehension mode. In comprehension, the experimenter puts two fruits before the subject and then places the name of one of them on the board. The chimp is to take the fruit that it thinks is correct (or in a later procedure, point to the correct one). So here is the chimp, all of its previous experience confined to production (in which it is to put a word on the board and then receive a fruit), now confronted with two fruits and the word already on the board. What did our star pupil, Peony, do in this situation? She picked up a piece of fruit, smeared it around on the board, and then attempted to eat it. An interesting compromise in a sense between what the experimenter wanted the subject to learn and what she, in fact, did learn.

The experimenter is trying to teach, among other things, that there are two classes, words and referents, that one writes with words and in that way gets referents. In addition, not any word will get any referent; there is a one-to-one relation between words and referents. But what the subject has learned, apparently, is that it must place something on the board before it can eat. The something available to it on comprehension trials consisted of two pieces of fruit. At this stage, the subject has apparently learned an association between an act and an outcome, not an association between the consequence of an act and an outcome. In a sense this conflicts with our theories about response classification.[3]

This training situation like all others encompasses a number of relations, not only the item-item relation in terms of which we restrictively define learning, nor even the word-referent classification and the operators associated with each class. The tests to be described represent an attempt to uncover several relations the subject acquires in this situation, and the order in which it acquires them. Why is initial learning so slow? The answer has been, because the subject must unlearn primitive hypotheses such as position habit and acquire efficient problem-solving strategies (Harlow, 1959; Restle, 1962). This is the truth, I suspect, but not the whole truth. First, long after the present subjects ceased to show position habit or the like, they continued to respond at chance on word-referent relations. Second, and more important, initial learning only appears to be slow. Having defined learning restrictively, we fail to consider the several relations which the subject apparently must acquire before it can go on to learn the one relation in terms of which we have chosen to define all learning.

Word Knowledge

At a time when the subject did not know what word went with what fruit, what did it know about the word class? In this language like the natural one, the word class has some fairly definite properties. All things that are words in this language are plastic, are backed with metal, adhere to the writing board, have certain dimensional characteristics, e.g., surface area, length, width, hardness, cannot be eaten, etc. No member of the referent class has this conjunction of properties, and the only point at which the two classes overlap at all is the dimensional one. Words and pieces of fruit are about the same size. Could the

[3] Typically, responses are classified not in terms of topography, but on the basis of their consequences. Thus we count bar presses or runway excursions, not the actions whereby these behavior products are accomplished. Interestingly, however, the chimp apparently put greater emphasis on the act than on the product of the act. What is the necessary condition for getting a piece of fruit in this situation: the behavior product, which is a word on the board, or the act of causing something to adhere to the board? Somewhat in contrast to prevailing theories about the criteria to be used for response classification, the chimp apparently favors the latter view. What counts is not the word on the board, but rather the act of placing something on the board. In any case, in the beginning the chimp essentially ignored the word placed on the board by the trainer, and instead tried to place something there itself even though, from our point of view, the something was highly inappropriate.

subject tell a word from a nonword? A potential word from a nonword? A potential word from a trained word? By trained word I mean merely a piece of plastic that has been used in the training as described; by potential word, a piece of plastic that has the properties of the word class but has not yet been used in training; and by a nonword, any item that may have a few or many of the word-class properties but does not have all of them. Thus, a nonword might or might not adhere to the board, but if it did it would be lacking in other features.

The subjects were three African-born chimps, two females and a male, ranging in age from about 2½ to 4 years; and four dogs, two mongrels and two poodles, ranging in age from 8 months to 2½ years. Each subject was trained on three pairs of words, a different amount of training per pair to see whether or not the relations the subjects acquired would be reflected in the amount of training. The word pairs were "apple-banana," "raisin-date," and "orange-apricot" in the case of the apes, and items more appropriate to carnivores, such as "tuna-weiner," in the case of the dogs. The absolute amount of training varied from subject to subject, ranging from as few as six errorless trials per pair of words, i.e., three trials per word, to as many as 90 trials per pair. In addition, to the errorless trials, subjects were given varying numbers of choice trials, ranging from as few as 30 per pair to as many as 200 (see Tables 1, 2, and 3).

Words Versus Nonwords

Consider the tests given Peony, a 2½-year-old female, which were representative in all major respects. During training, members of a pair were consistently presented only with each other—e.g., "banana" was the only would-be word presented with "apple"—and this arrangement was maintained throughout the present series. Since apple-banana was the pair on which she had received the most training, the first test was made with it. Despite 128 choice trials plus a total of 90 errorless trials, Peony still had formed no detectable association between the words and fruits. Could she nonetheless distinguish the would-be words "apple" or "banana" from nonwords? Six nonwords were introduced— magnet, ice-cream stick, car, box, eraser, paper clip—all approximately word size, and all either metallic or magnetized. She was given 20 trials consisting of a nonword paired with a word in the presence of either a piece of apple or a piece of banana; each nonword was presented at least three times with each word. When she responded correctly she received the fruit, otherwise not, as in the original training. Following the test on apple-banana, she received the same kind of test on rasin-date, and then on apricot-orange, pairs on which she had received an intermediate amount and the least amount of training, respectively. She made a total of three errors in 60 trials, two on the first problem, one on the second, and none on the third.[4] The ability to distinguish words from nonwords—at a

---

[4] Even the three errors were probably not true errors but attempts to see whether or not the new objects would stick to the board (they did since all nonwords were equipped with

(*Footnote continued on p. 292*)

TABLE 1

Production

Tests	Foods	Peony	Apes Elizabeth	Walnut
Base data	Apple (A)/banana (B)	61/128	36/64	30/70
	Rasin (R)/date (D)	64/153	10/20	63/137
	Orange (O)/apricot (A)	20/54	55/131	30/60
Word,	A/B	2/20	0/20	2/20
nonword	R/D	1/20	0/20	0/20
	O/A	0/20	1/20	5/10
New word,	Pinapple (P)/cherry (C)	1/20	2/20	0/20
nonword	Pear/fig	1/20	1/20	1/20
Word,	A/B blackberry	2/20	1/20	4/20
potential word	R/D peach	8/20	5/20	10/20
	O/A grapefruit	0/20	0/20	5/20
Word,	A/B, B	8/20	10/20	9/20
new word	R/D, P	11/20	9/20	9/16
	O/A, G	8/20	5/12	9/20

Note.—Numbers = $\dfrac{\text{incorrect}}{\text{total}}$

time when the subject had not learned a single word-referent association—was not confined to Peony. In many respects she was the star pupil, but as Table 1 shows the other two chimps and the four dogs gave largely comparable results.

New Word Versus Nonword

In the next test series, potential words (or new words) were substituted for words, and the subject was required to choose between new words—members of the word class on which no training had been given—and nonwords. Four new pieces of plastic were assigned as the names of pineapple, cherry, pear, and

---

magnets). In the chimpanzee, an error evidencing a mistake in judgment is typically accompanied by a visible sign of displeasure. The signs vary from a pout or merely the trembling of a lip to stomping and pounding heralded by piercing screams. Being unobscured by socialization, they are easily seen even in the weakest degree. These errors were not accompanied by such signs and therefore were probably explorations rather than mistakes.

TABLE 2

Production

Tests	Foods	Dogs			
		Lazlo	Remus	Lefty	Fordy
Base data	Hamburger (H)/chicken (C)	96/204	77/171	55/140	62/128
	Tuna (T)/liver (L)	31/60	25/60	21/60	20/60
	Salmon (S)/weiner (W)	10/20	8/20	4/20	5/20
Word,	H/C	4/20	0/20	2/20	2/20
nonword	T/L	4/20	2/20	2/20	0/20
	S/W	1/20	1/20	1/20	0/20
New word,	Thuringer/liverwurst	4/20	1/20	0/20	1/20
nonword	Smokies/ham	0/20	0/20	0/20	0/20
Word,	H/C Vienna sausage	4/20	7/20	6/20	1/20
potential word	T/L corned beef	4/20	0/20	3/20	6/20
	S/W turkey	9/20	9/20	9/20	8/20
Word,	H/C, V	10/20	8/20	5/20	6/20
new word	T/L, CB	8/20	8/20	6/20	10/20
	S/W, T	11/20	9/20	6/20	3/20

Note.—Numbers $= \dfrac{\text{incorrect}}{\text{total}}$

grape, respectively (for Elizabeth and Walnut, who were tested later, "fig" was substituted for "grape," since grapes were out of season). Peony was given 20 trials, 10 pairing "pineapple" with nonwords in the presence of pineapple, and 10 pairing "cherry" with nonwords in the presence of cherry. She was given comparable tests on "pear" and "grape," the two other new words. She made one error on each test, of a kind more indicative of exploration than of a mistake in judgment. The other subjects performed comparably.

Word Versus Potential Word

In the next series, words were substituted for nonwords, and the subject was required to choose between words (on which training had been given) and three potential words (different from those used in the previous test). Twenty trials were given on apple-banana, 10 in which the potential word "blackberry" was paired with "apple" in the presence of apple, and 10 in which it was paired with "banana" in the presence of banana, with trials intermixed. Comparable tests were given on raisin-date and on apricot-orange. The old word was always correct, there being no trials on which blackberry or the fruits corresponding to the other new words were presented. Peony made two, eight, and zero errors per 20 trials on the first, second, and third test of the series as shown in Table 1. Elizabeth was also correct on two of the three tests but, more reasonably, failed on words for which she had been given the least training; Peony failed on the pair given intermediate training. The other subjects were correspondingly poorer on this test. It is more difficult apparently to distinguish a word from a potential word, both of which fulfill the same physical properties, than to distinguish either from a nonword.

Word Versus New Word

A still more difficult test of word knowledge was made by requiring the subject to choose between old and new words, with new words correct as often as old ones. In the preceding series, none of the new fruits corresponding to the new words were presented, so that the new words were never correct. But now blackberry was present on some of the trials, as were the other new fruits. She was given 20 trials with the words: "blackberry" and "apple," half the time with apple, and half the time with blackberry; "blackberry" and "banana," half the time with banana, and half the time with blackberry; "apple" and "banana," half the time with banana, and half the time with apple. Thus old words were paired with both old and new words, and both were correct on occasion. Trials

TABLE 3

Comprehension

Tests	Foods	Peony	Apes Elizabeth	Walnut
Base data	A/B	16/20	6/12	2/10
	R/D	16/40	10/20	17/40
	O/A	14/31	9/20	29/56
Fruit,	A/B	22/80	1/20	4/20
nonfruit	R/D	5/20	2/20	10/20
	O/A	3/20	1/20	5/20
New fruit,	Cantaloupe/grape	0/17	2/20	1/20
not fruit	Watermelon/plum	2/20	1/20	
Fruit,	A/B prune	3/20	0/20	6/20
potential fruit	R/D cranberry	1/20	4/20	13/20
	O/A blueberry	2/20	0/20	0/20
Fruit,	A/B, P	11/20	10/20	4/40
new fruit	R/D, C	12/20	8/20	8/20
	O/A, B	11/20	9/20	

Note.—Numbers = $\frac{\text{incorrect}}{\text{total}}$

were mixed, and approximately equal numbers were given on the three pairs of words. Comparable tests were given combining the new word "peach" with the old words "raisin" and "date," and the new word "grapefruit" with the old words "apricot" and "orange."

Peony, and all other subjects, performed at chance on this most difficult test (see Table 1), though the error distributions of the two female chimps were different from those of the other subjects. Both female chimps showed an initial avoidance of the new word, followed by an increased tendency to use it. Notice how convenient we find it in discussing the results to divide words into "new" and "old." Suppose the chimps were to engage in a similar classification. They would be left with two response dispositions of quite different strengths. Members of the class "old" have a long history of about 50% reward, whereas members of the class "new" have a decidedly shorter reward history. If a subject chose a new word, for whatever reason, and was rewarded, this should increase its tendency to take new words, provided, that is, it coded the word as "new" in the first place. If, however, it did not classify words as "old" or "new" but relied exclusively on physical features, say, redness, then reward should have a different effect: it should increase the subject's tendency to take red words. The increase in the female chimps' tendency to use new words could be explained by assuming that they used the classification "old-new." We regard the position habit and stimulus preference as primitive hypotheses; perhaps the coding of items as "new" or "old" is a relatively primitive classification strategy.

Referent Knowledge

In the next series of tests, we shifted to the comprehension mode and raised the same question concerning referents that we raised previously concerning words. For example, could the subject tell a referent from a nonreferent? A potential referent from a nonreferent? A potential referent from a used or familiar referent? In the production mode to which training had been restricted to this point, the trainer placed two words before the subject along with one piece of fruit, and the subject was to place the correct word on the board. In shifting to comprehension mode, the trainer put one word on the board and two pieces of fruit before the subject. The subject was to examine the word on the board and then take the piece of fruit that was named by the word. Ultimately, the subject would learn both comprehension and production, so that ultimately it would be of interest to test transfer between them. At this stage, however, the subject could not even produce accurately and had had no training whatsoever on comprehension.

We have already commented on Peony's initial response to the comprehension situation, her attempt to first place the fruit on the board before eating it. Ultimately we taught her to choose merely by pointing rather than by taking the food she considered correct; this solved certain technical problems and allowed testing to proceed. She was given tests on knowledge of the referent class analogous to those given on the word class. Referents were contrasted with nonreferents, all of which were foodstuffs and some of which were fruits; potential referents (fruits not yet used in training) were contrasted with nonreferents (all foods, but no fruits); and finally, trained or actual referents were contrasted with potential referents. Her performance was generally comparable to that on the word class though the error level was higher, as may be seen in Table 1. Results for the other apes were generally comparable.

Keep in mind that the subject was at chance on comprehension of item-item relations no less than on their production. She made 145 errors in 325 trials on production, and 46 errors in 71 trials on comprehension—thus chance on item-item relations in both modes. Nevertheless, she could tell a referent from a nonreferent, a potential referent from a nonreferent, and a potential from an actual referent in all three cases. Foods used as nonreferents were all foods she had experienced, indeed relished, *outside* the training situation, and included cookies, snacks (potato chips and fritos), and several vegetables. The overall results could not be attributed to preference; in tests made outside the language-training situation, she showed a preference for most cookies over most fruits. Also, quite interestingly, in the test in which lime was pitted against cookie (potential referent versus nonreferent), she quit after only 17 trials rather than the 20 usually given, but for the last 14 trials, on each of which she chose lime, she did not eat the lime or even put it to her mouth. She chose lime as the "appropriate kind of thing to take in this situation," despite the fact that she did not eat it or make any attempt to take it with her after leaving the test situation.

Stimulus Generalization

Can the results be explained by either familiarity or stimulus generalization? Familiarity can be ruled out on the basis of similar tests run previously on Sarah, a chimpanzee involved in a long-term language project (Premack, 1971). At a time when she had not learned a single word-referent association, two old words were paired with either of two potential words, and she was given 240 trials of this kind. Though continuing to respond at chance level on the old words, she never chose the potential words. If novelty were the critical factor, her choice of potential words should have increased progressively; in 240 trials, familiarity of potential words must have approached that of old words.

Can we not say that the subject simply chose the object for which she had been rewarded most often, or the object most like the ones for which she had been rewarded? Words had been rewarded about 50% of the time, so the tendency to choose them should have been stronger than that for both potential words and nonwords, moreover, stimulus generalization would account for the tendency to take potential words rather than nonwords. We have no reason to doubt that choice was affected by reward, both direct and generalized. Nevertheless, stimulus generalization itself will not explain the main outcome. Subjects apparently learned to respond to rewarded items before learning to respond to item-item relations. That is, the data are: performance that exemplifies class relations precedes performance that exemplifies item-item relations. Stimulus generalization can be invoked to account for the class relations, but not for the order effect per se.

There is a further and more compelling basis for questioning the adequacy of stimulus generalization. Consider what appears to be an impressive instance of transfer by Sarah. As with so many other cases of chimp behavior, this too was not the product of an experiment but a chance observation.

The observations come from an extremely early point in training, before Sarah had learned a single word, indeed before the project was funded. One morning Dr. Arthur Schwartz and I were standing in the corridor before Sarah's cage, surveying the somewhat mottled scene and wondering how it would strike a site-visit team. We were sipping coffee, something we had not done previously in Sarah's presence, while staring balefully into the cage and paying less than the usual amount of attention to its occupant. Shortly we noticed Sarah reaching out from the cage, more or less waving her arm at us. She proved to have a monkey pellet in her hand, an object about the size of her plastic words and the only object in her cage of those dimensions available to her. To guess what she had in mind required putting together the two novelties in the situation. We had not drunk coffee in her presence before, and she had not waved a monkey pellet at us before. We accepted the pellet from her and then offered her a sip of coffee. She accepted the sip and returned almost immediately with another pellet. We took this one from her too and gave her another sip. After four or five such exchanges, we decided that the hypothesis was not one that could be proved further on that occasion. We gave her the rest of the coffee and left. We left filled with self-pity for the fact that Sarah had not reserved her display for the site visitors. Of course, Schwartz and I were agreed we would not mention it to the site visitors, except in the most casual way, and were also agreed that there was something wrong with our experimental program; all the interesting data came from chance observations.

Ordinarily we would treat the above case as an impressive example of transfer, and would explain it in terms of stimulus generalization. The generalization would appear to be of more than usual interest because it concerns both items in the relationship, i.e., both the wordlike monkey pellet and the food or referentlike coffee. (Only one stimulus is changed in most generalization tests, e.g., a bird trained on yellow is tested on orange. The present case is more interesting because it involves two stimuli, a conditional rather than simple discrimination.)

The monkey pellets could be considered wordlike on three grounds. (a) Dimensional properties: they were about the same size and weight as the plastic words. (b) Location: the sink top was the site of the language lessons at this stage; words were spread out there during the lesson even as monkey pellets were poured out there as a food supply during other times of the day. (c) Relative value: most important perhaps, coffee was preferred to the monkey pellets even as the food or prerogatives Sarah received for the plastic words were preferred to the words. Indeed, if they were not, she could not be expected to use the words as she did.

The coffee, or that which we were sipping from the plastic cups, would be considered food or referentlike on functional grounds—the fact of our behavior toward it combined with the assumption that the chimp (and other species) can identify human eating as readily as eating by conspecifics.[5]

In the light of these similarities between words and monkey pellets, on the one hand, and coffee and fruit items on the other, Sarah's apparent case of transfer may seem more inevitable than impressive. But there is a serious mistake in regarding this case as a standard example of transfer, explicable in terms of generalization. Sarah carried out this would-be case of transfer at a time when, so to speak, there was nothing for it to transfer from. That is, she had not yet formed a single association between a word and its referent; nonetheless she used monkey pellets in a wordlike way to obtain coffee.

Normally, we speak of transfer when a subject has been taught to make response A to stimulus B, and then shows a similar response A_1 to a similar but not an explicitly trained stimulus B_1. In the present case we have A_1-B_1 (pellets-coffee), an association between stimuli for which there was no explicit training, but we appear to lack A-B, an explicitly trained association between a word and a referent.

The lack of a parent or explicitly trained association from which to derive transfer can be solved by considering that before the subject learns item-item relations, it forms, indeed must form, an association between the two classes to which the items belong. That is, the first association to form may be that between the classes per se, e.g., any member of the word class can be used to obtain any member of the referent class. Only after this superordinate association has been formed can the subject go on to learn associations between specific members of the two classes. On this interpretation, Sarah's apparent use of monkey pellets to get coffee was not so much transfer, as an example of what she had learned in the first place.[6]

---

[5] When the chimpanzee observes man eat, it shows the same eagerness to have a bite as it does when it observes a chimp eat. I am confident that experiments in social facilitation of eating would show this conclusively; indeed, if facilitation were proportional to status of the model, the human exemplar might be more facilitating than that of the conspecific. But chimps are not alone in being able to identify eating on the basis of human exemplars. Dogs, monkeys, and, to my surprise, even perhaps pet mynah birds do this (though admittedly, my present tests are highly informal and lack vital controls for olfactory cues). Can we order species in terms of their ability to identify exemplars of their own behaviors in other species? For example, can the chimp or dog identify eating in the bird? Moreover, are behaviors orderable in terms of their identifiability? For example, both ingestion and aggression seem highly identifiable across species, more so perhaps than copulation, and the latter more so than friendly acts. We need a comparison of the conceptual structure of different species; answering simple questions of the above kind is one way to begin (Premack, in press).

[6] We cannot state the features in terms of which Sarah defined the two classes, and for all we know she may have relied more on value then on physical properties. Her behavior may have been an instance of the rule: give a less-valued thing for a more-valued thing. In this case, the dimensional overlap between pellets and plastic words, as well as the fact of their common location, would have been secondary or largely irrelevant.

Training Situations Exemplify Many Relations

In general, any training situation will exemplify indeterminately many relations of which the experimenter will be cognizant of only a few. The subject may not focus upon the relation in whose exclusive terms the experimenter reads the situation, but may learn a relation unforeseen by the experimenter. Worse still, the experimenter may never discover what the subject really learned, for luck may not conspire to lead him to those tests that will reveal something he was not prepared to see in the first place.

Consider two relations that are exemplified by the present training situation, one the subject should learn and one he should not. In the beginning and for some time thereafter, this highly simplified language is a one-to-one, rather than a many-to-many, mapping. Unlike natural language, words do not have multiple meanings; in addition, there are no synonyms. We thought pairing one word with one referent, and vice versa, to be the most efficient way of introducing the desired association between words and referents; also, we thought that starting in this way would not interfere with subsequently giving the language a polysemous character, as well as teaching synonyms. It remains to be seen whether this guess is sound.

In addition to the one-to-one word-referent *mapping*, the training situation also exemplifies a one-to-one word-referent *exchange*. That is, one word was always exchanged for one piece of fruit. However, this is not a relation which we want the subject to learn for, in fact, language, simplified or natural, does not have this character. This will become clear as the subject advances; it will no longer receive one piece of fruit per word but will be required to produce sentences (involving a number of words) in order to receive one piece of fruit. Moreover, the quantifiers, such as were taught Sarah (Premack, 1971), will permit the subject to modulate the amount of material it receives in a way that completely violates the one-to-one character of the exchange found in early training. "One," "some," "none," and "all" are all single words, yet they will result in quite different magnitudes of the object which they are used to modify. The one-to-one character of the exchange is strictly an incidental property of early training. Nevertheless, it is definitely contained in the training procedure; therefore there is some likelihood that the subject will learn it, and even that it will impair the acquisition of other relations.

Of the two relations, the mapping and the exchange, which is more forcefully exemplified by the training situation? Forcefulness of the exemplification could be judged in terms of three factors: (*a*) simplicity of the relation, (*b*) frequency with which the relation is instanced, and (*c*) number of different examples of the relation contained in the training. Presumably a simple rule instanced frequently by many (though perhaps not too many) different examples is what the subject will learn most readily.

Only the last criterion suggests a difference between the two cases. In mapping, many different examples are presented, each word-referent pair representing a different example; whereas in exchange, only one example is presented. That is, one word is traded for one piece of fruit, but there are no cases in which two words are exchanged for two pieces of fruit, three words for three pieces, etc.

What bearing does this analysis have on the possibility that subjects learn superordinate or class-class relations before they learn item-item relations? The superordinate relation could be seen as the equivalent of the word-referent exchange (give a wordlike object for a referentlike object, or in motivational terms, a less-valued object for a more-valued object). By the same token, the item-item relations could be seen as equivalent to the word-referent mapping, to specific word-referent associations. We have seen that class-class relations appear to form first. But this order effect could be meaningful only if we can assume that in training, the two relations are exemplified with equal force. This is a reasonable assumption in light of the above analysis, for it suggests that if there is an advantage, it favors item-item associations, the relation that develops later.[7]

Is the apparent order effect a logically necessary outcome of the way in which we arrange the stimulus material and in this sense an artifact? Consider a hypothetical test which generates a highly disconfirmable prediction, and thus shows that the order effect is not logically necessary. Suppose we were to divide words and referents into subclasses on some simple functional basis in a way that would permit a systematic relation to develop between the two subclasses. For example, we might give all dried fruits names that were colored red. The relation *dried fruit—red name* would inhere in the language; but it could be concealed or highlighted at any time simply by biasing the training sample to include few or many examples of the relation. In order to maximize learning of the relation, at what point in training should examples of the relation be introduced? Should they be introduced before or after the subject has learned class-class relations? Before or after it has learned item-item relations? According to the present hypothesis, subclass relations will not be learned (or will be learned inefficiently) if introduced either before class-class relations are formed or after item-item relations are formed. The premature introduction of subclass relations would simply delay their learning and would be inefficient; but introducing them after the subject had already formed item-item relations might permanently impair their acquisition. For a subject operating at the level of item-item relations would have to reverse the hypothesized order of learning in order to acquire subclass relations, and reversals of this kind might take place inefficiently, only under special conditions, or not at all.

In summary, at a time when a subject did not know what word goes with what referent, it nonetheless classified some items as words or nonwords, and others as referents or nonreferents. It was also able to distinguish between

---

[7] On the other hand, since every instance of an item-item relation is necessarily an instance of the class-class relation, we might predict earlier learning of the latter on the basis of frequency alone (criterion 2). See the hypothetical experiment on subclass relations in the next section for a control on this point.

members of both classes on which it had and had not received training. This classification may be a prerequisite for the formation of associations. In addition, the first association to form may be that between the classes per se, e.g., any member of the word class can be used to obtain any member of the referent class. Only after this superordinate association has formed may the subject go on to learn associations between specific members of the two classes. This is one way in which to understand the apparent slowness of the initial learning. If a structure of the above kind must first develop before specific associations can be formed, we can understand the initial training as contributing to the development of the structure, and the speed or efficiency of subsequent learning as exploiting a structure that was already formed.[8]

SYMBOLIZATION

Symbolization, the use of one item to represent another, may be a more primitive disposition than we have supposed. We appear to have evidence of it in the chimpanzee. After Sarah had extensive experience with the plastic words and sentences formed with the words (using the sentences both to obtain desired items—[e.g., "Mary give Sarah apple"]—and to describe situations arranged by the trainer—[e.g., "red is on green"]) we raised the question, when is a piece of plastic a word? On the basis of what evidence do we identify an item as a word? The standard answer has been, when it is used as a word, i.e., used in grammatically appropriate positions in sentences on semantically appropriate occasions. We added to this, when the properties ascribed to the referent can also be ascribed to the word in the absence of the referent (and we might add the opposite case: when the physical properties of the word can be elicited by the referent in the absence of the word).

To determine whether this condition obtained, we resorted to our old friend match-to-sample. On each trial Sarah was given an actual apple as the sample and a pair of alternatives to choose between. The alternatives included: red versus green, round versus square, square with a stemlike protuberance versus a plain square, and square with stemlike protuberance versus round. In this test and others like it, Sarah consistently chose the alternatives that accord with the human analysis of the properties of apple. For example, in the alternatives above she chose red, round, and square with a stemlike protuberance (versus plain square) 100% of the time, and round over square with stemlike protuberance about 65% of the time. These results show that the chimpanzee is capable of analyzing a complex object into its component features and is of interest as such. Nevertheless they are not evidence for, but merely a prerequisite for a test of, symbolization.

---

[8] If the subject learns essentially different things in early and late stages, structure in one case and associations located in structure in the other, perhaps the training methods should be adjusted to this difference. Methods optimal for the formation of associations may not be optimal for the development of structures; we have speculated on that topic elsewhere (Premack, in press).

The test is completed in the next step by removing the actual apple and substituting for it the word "apple," which in this language is a small blue triangle. Now the subject is required to make the same judgment for the blue triangle that it previously made for the red apple. Sarah assigned the same features to the word "apple" that she previously assigned to the object, including consistent choice of all features except for round over square with a stemlike protuberance where she repeated the inconsistency shown with respect to the actual apple (especially when one positive feature is pitted against another, the point cannot be that one assignment of features is more correct than another; the point is rather the *agreement* between the assignment in the case of the word and the referent). Sarah showed the same kind of evidence for four other cases; in some tests the word was presented before the referent, and in some the alternatives were words naming the properties (e.g., "red" and "green"), and not, as in the present case, objects (e.g., red and green plaques) instancing the properties.

We have also carried out a few tests in which the subject was required to proceed in the opposite direction, i.e., to assign the features of the word to its referent in the absence of the word. For example, we gave Sarah an actual apple as the sample and required her to choose between blue and green, triangular and square, etc., properties of the word "apple." She was generally successful on this test though, unfortunately, we have carried out too few tests of this kind to be confident of her ability to process in this direction. The tests from "apple" to the properties of apple suggest that the presence of apple is not a necessary condition for her to think apple, to generate an internal representation, and that the word "apple" may be a sufficient condition for the internal representation. This is compatible with other pieces of evidence (Ploog & Melnechek, 1971; Premack, in press) that support her ability to do what linguists call "displacement" (Hockett, 1960)—talk about objects that are not present. The test from apple to the properties of "apple" suggests that a word need not be present in order for her to think of the word; instead, in merely looking at an object she may be able to think of the name of the object; but the evidence for this case is slight.

In these tests of symbolization, we have made the evidence depend heavily on how the subject analyzes, or represents objects to itself in the first place. We have said, in effect, let us determine how the subject represents objects to itself, and then see whether it can assign the same representation to names of the object. The test suffers from the fact that we cannot do justice to the first question, How do animals represent objects to themselves? Having difficulty with that question, we have difficulty with the next question, Do they assign the same representation to objects that stand for other objects?

Positive outcomes with this test are informative, but negative ones are not. For instance, if Sarah were unable to decompose, say, apple into the features we choose, this need not mean that she was incapable of symbolization or even that she could not analyze an object in terms of features. With other features, she might pass the test; or her system of internal representation, for whatever reason, might make it difficult for her to do a features analysis of any kind.

Are there tests of symbolization that would escape these difficulties? Certainly there are alternative ways to study the relation between words and referents. For instance, objects could be shown tachistoscopically, and the subject required to choose not the object but the name of the object from a set of words, and vice versa. The duration of the recognition process from object to word could be compared with that from object to object, and that from word to object with that from word to word. These tests are worth doing, though I fear they may lead us into a morass of inferences rather than teaching us anything direct about how the subject represents things to itself.

Is the symbolization shown by Sarah a special product of the methods used to teach her language, or is it instead a primitive disposition likely to show itself in any case of learning? To put it bluntly, is it possible that what we call discriminative stimuli may in fact be symbols—which we fail to recognize as such because we do not make the proper tests?

What form would symbolization take in a lower organism such as a pigeon? Consider a multiple schedule in which a vertical line is associated with the opportunity to eat corn and a horizontal line with the opportunity to eat wheat. Wheat and corn differ in terms of color, shape, and size, and the test would start out by requiring the bird to do a features analysis on each food. That is, using wheat as a sample, the bird would be offered as alternatives, two colors, two shapes, two sizes, and various combinations thereof. The same thing would then be done for corn. Then we would associate the vertical line with wheat, and the horizontal line with corn, perhaps in the context of a simple multiple schedule. We would finish off by returning to the match-to-sample format, now, however, replacing the wheat with the vertical line and the corn with the horzontal line. Could the bird ascribe to the vertical line the same features that it ascribed to wheat, and to the horizontal line the same features that it ascribed to corn?

We cannot answer those questions at this time, though I may assure you it is not for lack of trying. The main thing we have learned to date is that the pigeon may be incapable of match-to-sample on color—and perhaps on any dimension. It can peck the red rather than green alternative when the sample is red, the green one when the sample is green, and do this for four other color pairs; but when a new color is introduced, its performance drops to chance. The pigeon's failure is the more striking since we know that it is capable of distinguishing, for example, man from nonman, water from nonwater, even perhaps person X from other persons, and body of water X (photographed variously) from other bodies of water (Herrnstein & Loveland, 1964; Siegel & Honig, 1970). It is premature, however, to link the pigeon's success in one case and failure in the other to differences in the kind of concept, since procedural differences divide the two cases also. For example, match-to-sample requires the subject to reverse its choices—to pick red when the sample is red but not when it is green. Evidence for the other concepts does not require reversals but only that the subject respond correctly to ever-new instances of man, water, etc. We are now applying the latter type of procedure to color judgments to see whether procedure alone will account for the differences or whether a conceptual explanation may be necessary. If we can pinpoint the pigeon's failure, it may be as instructive as the chimpanzee's success.

These failures do not prove that what we call discriminative stimuli are not symbols, even in the pigeon. They may prove rather that the proposed operational definition of symbol cannot be applied to a pigeon, and we will need a different test, one which does not require that the subject be able to decompose a complex object into its features.

However, for the moment we changed the species rather than the test. We tried essentially the same thing with dogs—two poodles and two mongrels. We taught them match-to-sample, first with the correct alternative identical to the sample, and then with the correct alternative merely more similar to the sample than the incorrect alternative. After they were proficient on match-to-sample, we required them to do features analyses on both a Frisbee and a tennis ball, objects they enjoyed playing with. The analyses attempted to get at shape, size, texture, and smell. With the tennis ball we used the following alternatives:

ball-size tin can	vs.	non-tennis ball	shape
block of wood	vs.	non-tennis ball	shape
box	vs.	box with tennis ball smell	smell
block	vs.	block covered with coarse felt	texture
ball 1″ in diameter	vs.	ball 3″ in diameter	size
ball 6″ in diameter	vs.	ball 3″ in diameter	size
block of wood	vs.	sponge	texture

The alternatives for the Frisbee were:

box	vs.	box with Frisbee smell	smell
block	vs.	block covered with hard plastic	texture
block	vs.	small plate	shape
ball	vs.	small plate	shape

Preferences were controlled by mixing the alternatives from Frisbee and ball, so that what was positive for one would be negative for the other. For example, plate rather than round object was positive for Frisbee, while the reverse held for ball. Likewise, block covered with plastic rather than with felt was positive for Frisbee but negative for ball.

Two of the four dogs performed above chance on the first and subsequent tests, the mature female poodle doing best, followed by one of the mongrels. The poodle made one error in 12 trials on the first test on ball, and three errors out of 12 trials on the first test on Frisbee. Her performance on the first two tests was 2/32 errors on ball and 3/16 on Frisbee.

The ability to analyze an object into features is merely a prerequisite for a test of symbolization, not evidence for it, and we have been unable to take the next step since we have not yet succeeded in teaching words to the dogs. There is some reason to believe, however, that this type of learning may be within their competence. First, Sir John Lubbock, noted British naturalist, reported (1888) teaching his dog to use arbitrary objects in wordlike ways, i.e., to obtain such things as food, water, and the prerogative of going out. Our procedures are remarkably like his, and from the report he gives, Lubbock's experiment appears to have been well controlled. Secondly, the number of trials given the dogs is not yet so great as to bespeak failure; we have found chimps to require more trials to learn the first word. In the event the dogs succeed in learning words, we can take the next step: determine whether or not the features they assign to Frisbees and balls can also be assigned to arbitrary objects that can be used in wordlike ways to get Frisbees and balls. At the present we cannot say whether symbolization is a primitive mechanism, an integral part of all learning, or a mechanism more or less restricted to higher primates.

RULE INDUCTION

In the 1920s Esper (1925) studied language processes by offering human subjects what he called miniature linguistic systems, actually matrices in which, say, four colors were systematically combined with four shapes, giving 16 cells each of which could contain a color-shape combination. One technique was to offer the subject only a part of the matrix and see whether or not he could fill in the rest of it. Forty years later, Kirk Smith (1966) and others modified Esper's procedures in an interesting way, using them as the basis of free recall. Matrices that had one list of letters on the vertical and a second list on the horizontal were used to generate lists of letter-letter pairs. All pairs laying along the diagonal of the matrix were discarded; the rest of the content of the matrix was combined in a random list and read to the subjects, who were subsequently asked to recall as many of the letter pairs as they could. The most interesting error, which occurred significantly more often than any other error, was the so-called grammatical intrusion—letter pairs which belong to the matrix but which were never read the subject. One of the ways in which to explain the subject's performance is to assume that he induces the structure underlying the list, memorizes the content of the vertical and horizontal lists, and generates his output on the basis of the grammer $S \rightarrow V + H$, i.e., any member of the vertical can go with any member of the horizontal.

Structuralists favor this proposal. Indeed they consider the attempt to induce the structure of any set of exemplars to be an essentially automatic property of mind. The fact that aborigines such as the bushmen have a systematic knowledge of the regional flora and fauna, one apparently much in excess of the relatively few plants and animals that are actually eaten, has been cited as circumstantial evidence of this disposition to organize experience in a systematic manner.

Is the disposition to induce an underlying structure confined to man, or would the chimpanzee show rule induction, i.e., grammatical intrusions, if it were exposed to the partial content of matrices? To answer this question, we shifted from the recall used with human subjects to recognition, and from letters to simple objects, which is not necessarily a loss since there is no reason to believe that rule induction is confined to language even in man. We needed to present the chimps with a list of objects, representing the partial content of a matrix, remove the objects, present a set of alternatives, and examine the errors the chimps made in identifying the objects they were shown. The test amounts to delayed match-to-sample, different from the usual test of this kind only in that the sample must consist of many items rather than the traditional one item. Fortunately, even young chimps proved to be capable of delayed match-to-sample with a highly multiple sample.

Starting with one-item samples, two-item alternatives, and no delay, we moved by degrees to 12-item samples, 20-item alternatives, and up to 30 seconds delay. This does not represent a limit on chimpanzee capacity so much as a ceiling on experimenter frustration tolerance. The test is unwieldy, requiring the experimenter to bring separate boxes of samples and alternatives to the test room. He throws the sample out before the subject, to assure a "random" arrangement, and then records the order in which the subject hands back the objects (for purposes of studying semantic clustering and subjective organization).[9] The sample is collected, restored in its box, and after a predetermined interval ranging from 3 to 10 seconds, the alternatives are thrown out. Again the experimenter records not only what items the subject chooses but the order in which they are chosen.

Two of the matrices we have used consisted of bottles and lids (cultural artifact), and bottles and trinkets (de novo combination). In the first case, three different bottles were combined systematically with three different lids making nine different bottle-lid combinations. The three that lay along the diagonal were eliminated, and the remaining six were presented to the subject in the manner described. The six items were then removed and subsequently presented in a set of 18 alternatives consisting of the six items shown, the three which belonged to the matrix but which were not shown, three pairs of bottles stuck together, and three pairs of lids stuck together. Only one of the young chimps (Elizabeth) made more, though not reliably more, grammatical than nongrammatical errors; surprisingly, the other two chose pairs of bottles as well as pairs of lids about as often as they chose bottle-lid combinations (the bottle-lid combination was not a cultural artifact for any of the young animals). Sarah, on the other hand, made only one error of intrusion, otherwise choosing only bottle-lid combinations, and chose those that had not been shown almost as often as those that had been shown.

The next matrix consisted of combinations of three different bottles and three different trinkets—paper clip, tiddlywink, bell—the trinkets being put

---

[9] Sarah showed clustering on the categories fruit, candy, and clothes, more clearly on simply handing back the sample but also on the subsequent recognition test.

inside the bottles. The three objects from the diagonal were then removed, and the test was performed in the manner described. The alternatives presented to the subjects consisted of the six bottle-trinket combinations shown, the three which belonged to the matrix but were not shown, three empty bottles, and three bottles each with two of the trinkets in it. Again, the young chimps made as many errors of intrusion as grammatical ones. Sarah, however, made significantly more grammatical than intrusive errors, choosing over twice as many bottles with one trinket in them as bottles with either zero or two items in them. She chose as many one-trinket bottles that were not shown her (content of diagonal) as one-trinket bottles that were shown her, and as few empty bottles as bottles with two trinkets in them. In not distinguishing between bottles with, so to speak, too little and too much in them, she differed from some of the 3- to 5-year-old children we have tested on the same procedure. The latter distinguished not between a bottle with one thing in it and all other bottles but rather between filled and empty bottles. Containers with a movable object in them were not an entirely new object in Sarah's experience but were decidedly more so than a bottle with a lid on it.

TRANSFORMATION

In 1937 Heinreich Klüver published a remarkable monograph describing the retesting of a mature female Cebus monkey on a series of problems it had encountered 3 years earlier. In the interval, the animal had been retired from experimental duties and had simply lived, tethered to an iron post, in the small room in which it was tested.

In some of the problems given the monkey, food was suspended from the ceiling, and in others it was at one end of the room, in both cases out of the tethered animal's reach. A number of objects stood between the animal and the food: sticks, rake, box, a gunnysack, and a table. In a third and fourth kind of problem, not only the food but also the only object that could procure the food was out of reach. Moreover, the food and the "tools" were in some cases out of reach on the same axis, e.g., both on the horizontal, and in other cases on different axes, e.g., tool on top of a table and food out of reach on the horizontal.

Some of the materials given the monkey, such as the stick, retained their shape throughout all their uses. By being handled differently, rigid objects can nonetheless serve multiple purposes, as a stick can be used as a club, fishing pole, something to make a hole with, something to poke into a hole, etc. Other objects given the monkey were nonrigid and underwent notable transformations in the course of their use. For instance, the gunnysack, in being used by the animal as both a horizontal and a vertical extension, took two quite different shapes. Some of the time it was whipped out by a rapid extension of the arm and used as a horizontal extension. But other times it was crumpled up, compacted in some fashion by the animal, and then stood upon and used as a vertical extension. There appear to be two classes of objects that can be used as tools. One can be used because of their shape and a rigidity that enables them to preserve shape throughout all their uses. But another can be used because they can assume numerous shapes, provided the subject knows how to make the changes.

Cases of the latter kind suggest that one kind of problem-solving mechanism could be described as a set of transformations, each one defined by three terms: an initial state, a terminal state, and the behavior needed to get from the initial to the terminal state. A mastery of a transformation would be shown by the subject's ability to get to the terminal state from a variety of initial states. For instance, a gunnysack could start out rolled up in a cylinder, stretched out like a doormat, crumpled like a handkerchief, folded into a square, even cut to pieces. An animal capable of producing the same terminal state, e.g., vertical extension, from all these initial states would be a master of the transformation. In practice, needless to say, we would anticipate varying degrees of competence, some terminal states being reached more slowly or less frequently from some initial states than from others.

Ultimately, in trailing the monkey through its 120 problems, the reader begins to sink into detail: "...food suspended beyond reach above floor; cardboard box (41 x 23 x 28 cm.) 200 cm. off center, standing between goal and wall BC...food beyond reach on floor, T-stick within reach and near floor; food suspended...etc." Unfortunately, I have no data to report at this time, only the recommendation that if, while working through the problems, you ask, What are the transformations? What of the materials present could instance them? you will be restored to the surface by the potential economy of the formulation.

SUMMARY

Four mechanisms were recommended as possibilities. *First,* I raised the question whether the hierarchical structure of memory may not itself impose an order on what is learned. At a time when the subject does not know what word goes with what referent, it nonetheless can tell a word from a nonword, a referent from a nonreferent, both potential words and referents from familiar ones. Classification sets the stage for a superordinate association between the two classes, after which associations between specific members of the two classes become possible. *Second,* is it possible that what we call discriminative stimuli are actually symbols, and would prove to be such if we made the proper tests? *Third,* is it possible that organisms store a bounded set of experiences by seeking the rule or structure that will generate the experiences? This is suggested by the tendency for grammatical errors to exceed errors of intrusion. *Fourth,* can problem-solving ability be summarized as a set of transformations on the one hand, and a knowledge of materials that will instance the transformation on the other?

REFERENCES

Esper, A. E. A technique for the experimental investigation of associated interference in artificial linguistic material. *Language Monographs*, 1925, No. 1.

Harlow, H. Learning set and error factor theory. In S. Koch (Ed.), *Psychology: A study of a science* New York: McGraw-Hill, 1959

Herrnstein, R. J., & Loveland, D. H. Complex visual concept in the pigeon. *Science*, 1964, **146**, 549–551.

Hockett, C. F. Logical considerations in the study of animal communications. In W. E. Lanyon & W. N. Tavolga (Eds.), *Animal sounds and communication*. Washington, D. C.: American Institute of Biological Science, 1960. Pp. 392–430.

Kintsch, W. *Learning, memory and conceptual processes*. New York: Wiley, 1970.

Klüver, H. Re-examination of implement-using behavior in a Cebus monkey after an interval of three years. *Acta Psychologica*, 1937, **2**(3).

Lubbock, J. *On the sense, instincts, and intelligence of animals*. New York: Appleton, 1888.

Ploog, D., & Melnechek, T. Are apes capable of language? *Neurosciences Research Program Bulletin*, 1971, **9**(5), 688–692.

Premack, D. Language in chimpanzee? *Science*, 1971, **172**, 808–822.

Premack, D. *Language and cognition in ape and man*. New York: Holt, Rhinehart & Winston, in press.

Restle, F. The selection of strategies in cue learning. *Psychological Review*, 1962, **69**, 320–343.

Siegel, R. K., & Honig, W. K. Pigeon concept formation: Successive and simultaneous acquisition. *Journal of Experimental Analyses Behavior*, 1970, **13**, 385–390.

Smith, K. Grammatical intrusions in the recall of structured letter pairs: Mediated transfer or position learning? *Journal of Experimental Psychology*, 1966, **72**, 580–588.

AUTHOR INDEX

Numbers in italics refer to the pages on which the complete references are listed.

A

Aiken, L. R., 178, *208*
Allen, C. K., 29, *47*
Amassian, V. E., 183, *206*
Amsel, A., 35, *45*
Anderson, D. C., 130, 142, *148, 149*
Anderson, J. R., 268, *285*
Anderson, N. H., 100, *106, 107*
Andreassi, J. L., 178, *206*
Anger, D., 71, *106*
Annau, Z., 79, 80, 82, *106*
Annett, M., 42, *45*
Appleton, J., 180, *209*
Asdourian, D., 36, 38, *46*
Asratian, E. A., *284*
Atkinson, R. C., 232, *241*

B

Baeza, M., 188, *206*
Baginsky, R. G., 188, *206*
Banuazizi, A., 182, *209*
Basmajian, J. V., 185, 188, *206, 208, 210*
Batenchuk, C., 261, *262*
Baum, M., 77, 85, 86, 87, 93, 95, 99, *106*
Beecroft, R. S., 92, *106*
Belmaker, R., 179, 181, *206*

Bennett, A. L., 180, 183, *209*
Berman, A. J., 73, *109,* 185, *211*
Bernard, C., 118, *125*
Bernstein, N., 245, *262*
Bersh, P. J., 75, *106*
Beyda, D. R., 178, *206*
Birch, L., 180, *209*
Birk, L., 182, *206*
Birney, R. C., 51, *66*
Black, A. H., 75, 77, 79, 80, 85, 87, 89,
    95, 96, *106, 107,* 180, 181, 182, 183,
    206, 207, 261, *262*
Blaustein, J., 155, 159, *172*
Blumenthal, M., 204, *207*
Bolles, R. C., 70, 74, 79, 84, 95, 100, *106*
Born, D. G., 29, *47,* 222, *242*
Bower, G. H., 41, *45,* 268, *285*
Braude, R. M., 259, *264*
Brener, J., 182, *209*
Brimer, C. J., 75, 80, 87, 95, 96, *107*
Brinley, F. J., Jr., 183, *207*
Brodal, A., 261, *262*
Brogden, W. J., 189, *210*
Brown, H. O., 180, 183, *210*
Brown, J. S., 88, 93, *106,* 267, *285*
Brownstein, A. J., 34, *46*
Bruno, L. J. J., 246, 248, *263*
Brush, E. S., 70, 77, 82, 93, 97, *107, 109*

311

L

M

N

SUBJECT INDEX